Honour and Violence

To the memory of my father,
Albert Rudolph Blok (1906–1994), sailor

Honour and Violence

Anton Blok

Polity

The right of Anton Blok to be identified as author of this work has been asserted in accordance with the Copyright, Designs and Patents Act 1988.

First published in 2001 by Polity Press in association with Blackwell Publishers Ltd

Editorial office:
Polity Press
65 Bridge Street
Cambridge CB2 1UR, UK

Marketing and production:
Blackwell Publishers Ltd
108 Cowley Road
Oxford OX4 1JF, UK

Published in the USA by
Blackwell Publishers Inc.
350 Main Street
Malden, MA 02148, USA

Library of Congress Cataloging-in-Publication Data
Blok, Anton.
    Honour and Violence / Anton Blok.
        p.   cm.
    Includes bibliographical references and index.
    ISBN 0-7456-0449-8
    1. Mafia – Italy – Sicily – History.   2. Brigands and robbers – Netherlands – History.   3. Crime – Europe – History.   4. Violence – Europe – History.   I. Title.

HV6453.I82 S61225 2000
364.1′06′09458 – dc21

                                                                            00-036717

A catalogue record for this book is available from the British Library.

Typeset in 10 on 12 pt Sabon
by Best-set Typesetter Ltd., Hong Kong
Printed in Great Britain by TJ International, Padstow, Cornwall

This book is printed on acid-free paper.

Contents

Illustrations

Plates

Table

Figures

Preface

The title – honour and violence – seeks to capture what became and has remained my main intellectual interest since I went to Sicily in 1961 as an undergraduate student of anthropology. I wanted to understand what happens to people when central control over the means of violence is weak or absent.

I learned then and noticed later that it is hard for people to survive physically and socially when they are not in some way 'respected'. Violence underwrites reputation – either directly, as in Sicily's western interior (and in many other places following the disintegration of modern empires), or indirectly, when the state holds an effective monopoly over the means of violence and can thus protect its citizens.

Rituals of transition – baptism, marriage and funeral – mark the main stages of the human life cycle. This is what anthropology is often about. Less well understood are the various ways in which concerns of honour and violence affect human lives, in particular when the state falls short of its quintessential task. Most of the essays collected here seek to chart these still largely unknown territories. This should be taken quite literally. As the term 'essay' suggests, my explorations are tentative, like the earlier monographs on nineteenth- and twentieth-century Sicily and the eighteenth-century Dutch frontier. One problem in studying these questions lies in the present state of the social sciences, where the emphasis has long been on system, structure and stability, rather than on process, motion, flow, and the movement of people and of culture. In the conceptualization of society, the bounded, integrated and pacified nation-state has long been a major paragon. Now the 'historic turn' is gathering strength, anthropologists are once more in a position to break new ground.

The original publications on which these essays are based acknowledge help and support from many people, including friends, colleagues and students. The revised versions benefited from the comments of Rod Aya and Peter Burke, who both read the whole collection, and from the remarks and suggestions of Leena Avionus, Matthijs van den Bosch, Léon Buskens, Remco Ensel, Longina Jakubowska and Eric Venbrux, who read single essays, or provided references. I am most grateful to them for their help. I thank Léon Buskens for his unfailing interest in my work on animal symbolism. I owe a special debt to Rod Aya for his substantial commentary and editorial work. A special word of thanks is in order for Ingrid Grimes who skilfully edited the manuscript for Polity Press and who suggested numerous textual improvements. For secretarial assistance in the last stages of writing I remain indebted to Ada Tieman, who showed great patience and understanding.

Two institutions provided ideal conditions for rewriting some of the essays collected in this volume. I am most grateful to the Netherlands Institute for Advanced Studies (NIAS) at Wassenaar and the Program for Agrarian Studies at Yale University, in particular its director James C. Scott, for the research fellowships they generously granted in the autumn of 1987 and the spring of 1993.

Acknowledgements

The author and publishers wish to thank the publishers of the following for permission to use copyright material:

'Social Banditry Reconsidered', in *Comparative Studies in Society and History* (1972), 14, 495–504 (including a rejoinder of E. J. Hobsbawm). Reprinted by permission of Cambridge University Press.

'Bandits and boundaries: robber bands and secret societies on the Dutch frontier (1730–1778)'. Reprinted by permission of the University of Minnesota Press, from *Challenging Authority: the historical study of contentious politics*, edited by Michael P. Hanaghan, Leslie Page Moch and Wayne Te Brake (Minneapolis: University of Minnesota Press, 1998), 91–106. A French version was published in 'Survivre: Réflexions sur l'action en situation de chaos', edited by Gilles Bataillon, in *Cultures et conflits* (1996–97), 24/5, 11–34.

'Infamous occupations', a translation from the Italian version ('Mestieri infami') published in *Ricerche Storiche* (1996), 26, 59–96. An earlier, Dutch version appeared in *Symposion* (1981), 3, 104–28.

'Why chimney-sweeps bring luck', in *Dutch Dilemmas: anthropologists look at the Netherlands*, edited by Jeremy Boissevain and Jojada Verrips (Assen: Van Gorcum, 1989), 164–84. Reprinted by permission of Van Gorcum & Co. An Italian version appeared in *Quaderni Storici* (1986), 62 (XXI), 537–60.

'Mafia and blood symbolism'. An earlier version of this chapter was presented at the conference 'Risky transactions, kinship, and ethnicity', organized by the Max Planck Institute for Human Ethology, 23–5 September 1996, at the Reimers Foundation in Bad Homburg, Germany.

'The meaning of senseless violence'. Dutch versions of this chapter appeared in *Amsterdams Sociologisch Tijdschrift* (1991), 18, 189–207 and in Henk Driessen and Huub de Jonge (eds), *In de Ban van Betekenis. Proeven van symbolische antropologie* (Nijmegen: SUN, 1994), 27–45. The present version is based on a paper presented at the 5th Biennial EASA Conference held in Frankfurt, 4–7 September 1998, in the section 'Worldviews and Violence'. Reprinted by permission of SUN.

'The narcissism of minor differences', in *European Journal of Social Theory* (1998), 1, 33–56. Reprinted by permission of Sage Publications Ltd, London.

'Explaining agro-towns', in *Comparative Studies in Society and History* (1969), 11, 121–35. Reprinted by permission of Cambridge University Press. The revised postscript, prompted by two brief visits to western Sicily in 1982 and 1983, originally appeared in *Urban Cultures in Italy and the Netherlands*, edited by Heidi de Mare and Anna Vos (Assen: Van Gorcum, 1993), 51–7. Reprinted by permission of Van Gorcum & Co.

'Nicknames', in *Focaal* (1996), 26, 77–94. Reprinted by permission of the editors.

'Mediterranean totemism', in *Man* N.S. (1981), 16, 427–40. Reprinted with permission of the editors and the Royal Anthropological Institute of Great Britain and Ireland. An Italian version appeared in *Quaderni di Semantica* (1980), 1, 347–72, including a rejoinder of Mario Alinei.

'Female rulers and their consorts', in *Transactions: essays in honour of Jeremy Boissevain* (1994), edited by Jojada Verrips (Amsterdam: Het Spinhuis), 5–33. Reprinted with permission of Het Spinhuis.

'Rediscovering *ars moriendi*'. A Dutch version appeared in *Medische Antropologie* (1996), 8, 251–77. Reprinted by permission of Het Spinhuis.

Introduction

One underlying assumption of the essays collected here is that social action is inherently paradoxical, ironic and tragic. Despite persistent claims to the contrary, human interaction is shaped by forces that elude the control and comprehension of those who take part in it.

Although people create society, culture and history – and thus attest to 'agency' – they are also the creatures and products of their own time. What makes them both agent and product are the unintended conditions and consequences of intended interactions. People make choices, follow strategies and scenarios by trial and error. At best they resemble *bricoleurs*, who combine what they find at hand (as the etymology of the verb 'discover' suggests). They therefore rarely anticipate, let alone control – specifically in the long term – the outcome of their plans and decisions. In the end, they have to make sense of these unanticipated results.

Unintended conditions and unintended consequences of intended human interaction render social reality opaque, mysterious, enigmatic. The enormous discrepancy between design and outcome – which implies a fundamental lack of understanding of social worlds on the part of their very members – creates space for playwrights and students of human society; that is, a place for people who are willing to stand back, observe and listen dispassionately, and reflect, and who succeed, by their very detachment and by questioning the obvious, in making familiar things strange. Insight comes with distance, with *dépaysement*. This holds for science no less than for the humanities. Both Darwin and Mendel made their discoveries from positions of great obscurity.

1

Obvious examples of these unplanned yet structured processes include demographic movements and bureaucratization. As Weber argues, Protestant asceticism created the very wealth it rejected. Technical progress entailed pollution; the Great Leap Forward produced the greatest famine the world ever witnessed. Less apparent, but no less compelling, examples include state formation and civilizing processes. As Tilly (1990) demonstrates, states made wars, but wars also made states. The problem of unintended consequences of social action has been most clearly set out by Elias:

> Out of the interweaving of innumerable individual interests and intentions – be they compatible, or opposed and inimical – something eventually emerges that, as it turns out, has neither been planned nor intended by any single individual. And yet it has been brought about by the intentions and actions of many individuals. And this is actually the whole secret of social interweaving – of its compellingness, its regularity, its structure, its processual nature, and its development; this is the secret of sociogenesis and social dynamics. (1969a. [1939] II: 221)

In a later publication, he summarizes this approach in a memorable phrase, 'Underlying all intended interactions of human beings is their *unintended interdependence*' (1969b: 143, my italics). An early attempt to conceptualize this insight can be found in Marx's famous statement in the opening of *The Eighteenth Brumaire*: 'Men make their own history, but they do not make it just as they please [*nicht aus freien Stücken*], they do not make it under circumstances chosen by themselves, but under circumstances directly encountered, given, and transmitted from the past' (1973, II: 226).[1] Whereas Marx emphasizes the unintended conditions of social action, later social theorists (most notably Merton in his article on the unanticipated consequences of social action and his essay on manifest and latent functions) point to the more obvious unintended consequences of intended social practices. Referring to Merton's classic text, Boudon recognizes that unintended consequences (which he calls 'perverse effects') are present everywhere in social life, but they have hardly been studied: perverse effects are as rare in modern social analysis as they are common in social life (1982: 1–3). Curiously, however, the issue of the unintended consequences of social action remains unsolved in social theory.

In her well-known review of recent theory in anthropology, Sherry B. Ortner does not arrive at a different conclusion from her mainstream forerunners. She points out several defects of practice theory, including its insistence on the intentionality of action, its essential individualism, its neglect of collective action, its disregard for the larger historical con-

texts of social action, and its undervaluation of the powerfully con-
straining forces of culture (1994: 388–402). Ortner mentions, though,
that Bourdieu, who made so much of practice theory, recognizes the
central role of highly patterned and routinized behaviour (1994: 394)
and cannot, therefore, be charged with voluntarism. Yet Ortner still
nurses hope for the practice model (and for a synthesis between 'agency'
and 'structure') on the very point where she might thoroughly have
revised it, pushing the argument a decisive step further. She writes (obviously without realizing the fundamental theoretical implications of her
criticism):

> The irony is this: that although actors' intentions are accorded central place
> in the [practice] model, yet major social change does not for the most part
> come about as an *intended* consequence of action. Change is largely a by-
> product, an *un*intended consequence of action, however rational action
> may have been. . . . To say that society and history are products of human
> action is true, but only in a certain ironic sense. They are rarely the pro-
> ducts the actors themselves set out to make. (1994: 401)

In a footnote Ortner underscores this viewpoint in a reference to
Foucault, who summarizes it as follows: 'People know what they
do; they frequently know why they do what they do; but what they
don't know is what they do does'.[2] As an attack on the practice
model's most elementary assumption (intentionality), this view comes
close to what Kuhn calls a 'switch of gestalt' (1970: 85). If 'practice'
is anything people do (Ortner 1994: 393), practice theory is certainly
not concerned with the unintended conditions and unintended consequences of what people do. It suffers from ahistorical assumptions and
remains caught in the ancient and false polarity between individual
and society, or its fashionable variant, the dichotomy between agency
and structure. Practice theory seems a far cry from what Mills envisioned
forty years ago as a programme for the social sciences: to explore
the intersections of biography and history within society (1959: 6–7,
143ff).

We thus stand in need of a revised theory of social action in which
practice is demystified – that is, historicized – and divested of its essential individualism, stripped of its voluntaristic aura. There are no direct
connections between intentionality and the outcome of pragmatic choice,
decision-making, active calculating and strategizing of individual actors.
This is so because, first, plans and intentions are drawn up in specific
historical contexts and cultural settings (which reduces the presumed
autonomy of individual actors to zero). Second, plans and intentions,
efforts and implementations are mediated, refracted, thwarted, distorted,

transformed by powerful cultural forces, human interdependencies, contingencies, imponderabilia, and chance.[3]

A few examples from the essays collected here may illustrate these complexities and thus reveal how paradox, irony and tragedy pervade social action.

Insecurity drove the rural population in southern Italy to live in huge agglomerations, the so-called agro-towns, which separated the peasants from the land. The quest for security resulted in an empty countryside, but a vast landscape without permanent habitation could only aggravate conditions of public insecurity. Banditry sprang, among other things, from tensions between landlords and peasants. It remained endemic and constrained those who had property to buy protection. But far from becoming 'champions of the poor' (Hobsbawm's 'social bandits') from whose ranks they were usually recruited, bandits – if they survived – ended up as retainers of landlords and political bosses who used them for their own ends: that is, against the peasants.

The post-war peasant movement in Sicily included occupations of *latifondi*, the extensively cultivated cereal-pasture holdings that were leased on short-term contracts. Supported by left-wing political parties, the movement forced the government to issue an agrarian reform law that aimed at expropriation of the estates of absentee landowners and allocation of land and adjacent farms to peasants, encouraging them to settle permanently in scattered hamlets. The outcome was quite different. The reform did much to kill the peasant movement, and powerful vested interests sabotaged its implementation: high-quality estates were divided among kinsmen of the owners; other *latifondi*, often part of huge patrimonies, were sold on a *mafia*-controlled market. Instead of moving to outlying and poorly equipped farms peasants eventually moved north, producing a massive exodus of rural labour to industrial centres in northern Italy, Switzerland and Germany.

As for paradox and irony, a comparative survey of so-called infamous occupations reveals that the most despised professions were also the most indispensable ones. Providing vital services for the community, skinners, healers, cleaners, entertainers and members of other dishonourable occupations found themselves excluded from normal social life and forced to live in separate locations at the margin of society because of their alleged pollution and the magical power ascribed to them. Ironically, legalizing prostitution or making the oldest profession 'honourable' would jeopardize a monopoly and thus eventually destroy the prostitute's 'profits of shame'. Tellingly, prostitutes themselves rarely advocate such reforms because the success of their trade remains predicated on the very dishonour attached to it.

For a long time, the Dutch and Austrian authorities in the eighteenth-century Meuse valley believed, as do local historians up to the present, that the plundering of churches and farms was the work of roaming vagabonds and disbanded soldiers. Far from being strangers and outsiders, however, the bandits, without exception, turned out to be local people who were born and grew up and lived normal lives among their victims, whom they robbed (and sometimes killed) during their nightly ventures.

We often believe that conflicts are most likely to rise between people who are divided by great cultural or social differences. But an outline of a general theory of power and violence cannot ignore the fact that the fiercest struggles often take place between individuals, groups and communities that differ very little – or between whom differences have greatly diminished. This was recognized by Freud and, more recently, by Girard, who argues that 'it is not the differences but the lack of them that gives rise to violence and chaos' – as can be attested by a series of contemporary and ruthless civil wars.[4]

Paradox and irony also beset the female ruler. Contrary to what is widely believed, female leaders rarely promote or even sympathize with women's emancipation. Regardless of the setting, they are social males and have a vested interest in patriarchal arrangements.

Where medical care is highly developed, dying takes longer. As Buñuel comments on dying in modern society: 'A death that's kept at bay by the miracles of modern medicine, a death that never ends. In the name of Hippocrates, doctors have invented the most exquisite form of torture ever known to man: survival' (1982: 256).

It is obvious that social action can no longer be explained in terms of the will of powerful anthropomorphic gods. But neither can we understand it in terms of law-like generalizations. Nor can it be explained only in terms of rules, norms or 'systems' either. Just as little can we infer it from the plans and intentions of (autonomous) actors. Yet, as the current vogue of practice theory shows, there always remains the temptation to slide back into a form of individualism – whether functionalist, transactionalist or otherwise – and explain social action in terms of intentions and designs of presumably autonomous individuals, who 'can choose', 'have options', etc. An entire vocabulary, both inside and outside the human sciences, attests to this belief: from 'state-making', 'nation-building' and 'social engineering' to things that are ambiguously described as 'man-made'.[5] The immensely popular western notion of 'agency' conveys the mystifying image of an autonomous individual separated from everything that went into his making: culture, society and history.[6]

Freud once remarked that in the course of the centuries science inflicted three major wounds upon the naïve self-love of mankind. First, Copernicus taught that the earth on which we live does not form the centre of the universe but only a tiny fragment of a cosmic system of scarcely imaginable vastness. Second, Darwin's biological research destroyed man's supposedly privileged place in creation and proved his descent from the animal kingdom and his ineradicably animal nature. Third, human megalomania suffered its most wounding blow from psychoanalytic research which argues that we are not master in our own house but must content ourselves with scanty information about what is going on in our unconscious mind (Freud 1991d: 326). To these injuries, remarks Goudsblom, the human sciences can add a fourth: the societies which people form together and the cultures they have created are the outcome of social processes that have evolved to a large extent blindly and unplanned. The nations into which humanity is divided, the languages that we speak, the relations between the various classes of our society: no preconceived plans underlie these fundamental social facts; they have not been previously devised and designed to be implemented afterwards. They have just 'become' (Goudsblom 1974: 178).

A correction and a corollary are in order here. The blow Darwin delivered to the self-love of man was even more damaging than Freud imagined. As Kuhn argues at the end of his essay on the structure of scientific revolutions, what bothered people was neither the notion of species change nor man's descent from apes. Evolutionists before Darwin had taken evolution to be a goal-directed process. But *The Origin of Species* 'recognized no goal set either by God or nature. . . . The belief that natural selection, resulting from mere competition between organisms for survival, could have produced man together with the higher animals and plants was the most difficult and disturbing aspect of Darwin's theory' (Kuhn 1970: 171–2).[7] Kuhn uses this example as an important analogy to underscore his own alternative view of scientific advance. The development he describes in his essay is not a goal-directed process either. It is a process of evolution *from* primitive beginnings but *toward* no goal: 'a process whose successive stages are characterized by an increasingly detailed and refined understanding of nature' (1970: 170).

Action theory, including practice theory, should deal with the fundamental and paradoxical aspect of social worlds: brought about by the intentions, designs and actions of numerous interdependent people, none of whom can possibly control or even fully understand them, social processes run their course blindly. They have a momentum and structure of their own, but they have no goals.

One is immediately reminded of the structure of classical drama, epic and fairy-tale. The course of action in these genres also displays a relative autonomy with respect to the intentions, plans and goals of the *dramatis personae* – a discrepancy that produces paradox, irony and drama, all of which underlie the human condition. Although unplanned, the sequence of events in these narratives reveals a distinct pattern: one move follows the other in such a way that the latter could only have come from the former – a pattern of contingencies only to be identified in retrospect. The course of events has not been desired, intended or foreseen – let alone controlled – by any of the participants. Nor do they have more than the faintest understanding of it. Yet they themselves contribute to the unfolding of events in their every move because of their interdependencies, because of the constraints they unintendedly put on one another (cf. Propp 1968: 64; and Blok 1974: 704–5).

All these elements – an unplanned yet structured course of events that eludes the control and comprehension of the participants who none the less bring it about – are perhaps best illustrated in Sophocles' *King Oedipus*. His self-blinding at the end has been interpreted in many different ways, but we may also recognize in it a reference to the metaphorical blindness that helped structure the course of the narrated events – a structure that we can only fully grasp retrospectively.[8]

Elias's paradigm thus finds confirmation in the structure of classical tales, a structure that in turn can help to clarify social action. But it can also be attested by the course of ethnographic and historical research, in all the stages of my own work, for example.

The essays in this collection originally appeared between 1969 and 1998. Except for the final essay on female rulers, they are by-products of two related research projects – one on Sicilian *mafia* and the other on rural banditry in the eighteenth-century Dutch Republic. Why this longstanding fascination with the theme of honour and violence?

The first project goes back many years when I explored the larger context (and genesis) of the rural *mafia* in a small, rural town in the Corleonese district of western Sicily, the area of vast cereal and pasture holdings in the hinterland of Palermo. This project took up most of the 1960s and early 1970s including thirty months of fieldwork in the same agro-town. The second project was an attempt to make sense of rural banditry along the south-eastern borders of the Dutch Republic in the second and third quarters of the eighteenth century. Tracing the lives of about 600 convicts, intermittent work on court records in Dutch, German and Belgian archives occupied a large part of the 1970s and 1980s. My choice of these subjects and areas was largely accidental – like my turning to anthropology at the University of Amsterdam in the late 1950s. It was fortuitous meetings with professors, colleagues and informants, rather than preconceived research plans, that led me in a particular direction that I could only afterwards identify.

After I embarked on research in Sicily in the summer of 1961, further chance encounters guided my moves toward local issues and preoccupations, including settlement patterns, attitudes toward work on the land, large estates, absenteeism, agrarian reform and public security. The focus of my research in Sicily only became clear to me gradually as I proceeded by trial and error. What clinched my decision to study *mafia* at the local level, in a rural town about whose history and social structure I already knew a great deal, were excellent informants, repeated statements denying its existence, and the absence in wider discussion on the subject of an approach that combined fieldwork, oral history, archival research and published sources.

The study of banditry in the eighteenth-century Dutch Republic also resulted from a chance encounter. During a conference of the Dutch Anthropological Association in September 1970 my review (partly based on the Sicilian experience) of Hobsbawm's ideas on 'social banditry' prompted a response from an Africanist, who had studied the Mau Mau movement in Kenya (Buijtenhuijs 1971). He suggested I should look into the case of the eighteenth-century *Bokkeryders*, the robbers and bandits who operated in the Meuse valley and who were supposedly less dependent on elite support. The secondary sources were limited but, because they suggested that artisans played a pivotal role in the bands, they made me curious about what remained of the trial records in the Maastricht archives. Who were these people, what was their background, what were they accused of, how could banditry persist in the hinterland of the garrison town of Maastricht for well over thirty years, and why had professional historians (as opposed to local folklorists and antiquarians) completely neglected it? My interest in the occupational background of the robbers and its relationship to banditry – problems I had addressed before in my Sicilian research – eventually led to comparative work on infamous occupations.[9]

Thus my research projects were governed by the field itself, theoretical issues and chance. In his reminiscences and reflections on fieldwork Evans-Pritchard writes:

> The anthropologist must follow what he finds in the society he has selected for study: the social organization of its people, their values and sentiments and so forth. I illustrate this fact from what happened in my own case. I had no interest in witchcraft when I went to Zandeland, but the Azande had; so I had to let myself be guided by them. I had no particular interest in cows when I went to Nuerland, but the Nuer had, so willy-nilly I had to become cattle-minded too. (1976: 242)

My choice of, and sustained interest in, the themes of honour and violence was also predicated on what struck and still strikes me as another puzzling lacuna: the paucity of studies on violence and its relationship to status and reputation. There is a tendency in western thought to avoid serious and systematic exploration of popular violence. This is not the place to discuss why the social sciences have always been more interested in social order than in its collapse; but one cannot help but notice the relevance of the historical setting in which the social sciences developed: the pacified nation-states and colonial empires of the West.[10]

What may also have motivated me to explore the dark side of social life was the belief that if birth, copulation and death are identified as the 'inevitable facts' of human experience (Myerhoff 1982: 109), one should include some consideration of honour and violence. Critical to both physical and social survival, they are no less basic to human life than birth, sexuality and death. People need protection against physical threats, and protection often takes the form of counterviolence. But they also need to fashion an identity and require some measure of recognition and repute, lest they die a social death. Over the ages, too, denial of proper burial has been considered one of the most humiliating inflictions. Honour and status are implicit in violence. The use of physical force, even in its most brutal and enigmatic forms, is rarely 'meaningless' or 'senseless'. On the contrary, it is often honorific – especially under conditions of political insecurity when people 'have to make themselves respected'. The expression 'senseless violence' has lately become fashionable. But it is a misnomer, produced by divorcing violence from its context: by under-reporting cases of violence and ignoring telling details of its circumstantiality, most notably aspects regarding meaning, reputation and status. Violence always makes sense from at least one perspective (that is, from the perpetrators' point of view), and, given the anthropologist's interest and expertise in culture and the minutiae of social life, he has a special licence to explore these meanings and their anchoring in local settings. A recent example of such an enterprise, including numerous sketches of popular violence, is a study of lynching in Georgia and Virginia between 1880 and 1930. Brundage writes in his Introduction: 'Few topics seem more appropriate to the application of some of the techniques of social anthropology than lynching. Because the richest details about incidents of mob violence usually relate directly to the act of execution by a mob, the significance and variations in the ritual of mob violence properly merit attention' (1993: 16). Rather than dismiss unlicensed and popular violence as 'senseless', and thus give up research at the very point where it should start, the anthropologist should examine form, context and meaning. In line with the earlier monographs on *mafia* and banditry, and bearing in mind that the Modernist ethos 'insists on confronting the ugly, the sordid, and the terrible, for that is where the most important lessons are to be found' (Singal 1997: 12), this is what the essays in this collection attempt to do.

Contrary to what is often assumed, the role of chance does not imply that there is no pattern, no structure – it simply means that the course of events and the results cannot be understood in terms of preconceived plans or scenarios alone. As mentioned above, the idea of a largely unplanned yet structured course of events is not new but has never met with general enthusiasm.[11] It goes against powerful convictions about meaning, social engineering and order. Above all, it goes against a strong sense of 'agency' that looms large in the minds of secularized people in the modern world. It also conflicts with the ideals and stereotypes of the development of scientific research, and ignores the fact that this development is far from a cumulative process. Important discoveries were made when people were looking for something else. Rather than a rational advance along a straight, ascending line, the progress of science describes a zigzag course and resembles the perambulation of sleep-walkers (Koestler 1964: 11; Kuhn 1970: 84). There is something serendipitous about ethnographic research too, the making of discoveries by accident, of finding things we are not always looking for.

If reality is opaque, writes Ginzburg, there are privileged zones – signs, clues – which allow us to penetrate it (1989: 123). Exploring the roots of an evidential (conjectural or semiotic) paradigm, Ginzburg perceives what may be one of the most ancient forms of research and discovery in the intellectual history of the human race: the (palaeolithic) hunter squatting on the ground, studying the tracks of his quarry (1989: 105). 'The hunter might have been the first "to tell a story" because he alone was able to read, in the silent, nearly imperceptible tracks left by his prey, a coherent sequence of events' (1989: 103). In the course of the nineteenth century various 'disciplines', most notably medicine, palaeontology, history, geology, archaeology and psychoanalysis, adopted the conjectural paradigm of semiotics and adopted what became known as 'Zadig's method' (Ginzburg 1989: 116–17, 123–4).[12]

In his study of civilizing processes and state formation in early modern Europe, Elias examines changing rules of etiquette as indications (that is, tell-tale signs) of the structure and direction of these larger transformations. The anthropologist who studies a little community may find himself in a similar position. 'One may make use of a community', writes Redfield, 'as a convenient place in which to study a special problem of general scientific interest. One may study a little community, not to find out all about it, but with reference only to a limited problem stated in advance' (1955: 155). Discussing the methodological problem which the microscopic nature of ethnography presents, Geertz agrees: 'The locus of study is not the object of study. Anthropologists don't study villages (tribes, towns, neighborhoods . . .); they study *in* villages. You can study different things in different places, and some things . . . you can best study in confined localities' (1973a: 22). Geertz concludes that social actions are comments on more than themselves: 'small facts speak to large issues . . . because they are made to' (1973a: 23). A similar 'worm's eye' view informs the work of French and Italian microhistorians who rely on human minutiae to bring the past to life. Discussing his book on class tensions in the small French town of Romans that led to a massacre during carnival celebrations in 1580, Le Roy Ladurie notes that he looked for communities and events which could illustrate an epoch. Such endeavours 'can succeed on condition that you point your instrument in the right direction – just as Galileo succeeded by pointing his telescope in the right direction'.

This method is what Peirce calls 'abduction', and describes as 'the only logical operation which introduces a new idea':

> Abduction makes its start from the facts, without, at the outset, having any particular theory in view, though it is motivated by the feeling that a theory is needed to explain the surprising facts. Induction makes its start from a hypothesis which seems to recommend itself, without at the outset having any particular facts in view, though it feels the need for facts to support the theory. Abduction seeks a theory. Induction seeks for facts. In abduction the consideration of the facts suggests the hypothesis. (1998: 106)[13]

Finally, the essays in this volume are comparative or have comparative implications. While recognizing cultural differences, I have gone beyond local case studies in an attempt to identify family resemblances between cases and to detect cross-cultural similarities and cultural universals.[14] This may allow us to reach some measure of transcultural understanding in a discipline that increasingly indulges in exoticizing others, in underscoring differences and the specificity of other cultures, in finding out more and more about less and less. Transcultural understanding is perhaps anthropology's most ambitious objective, but it has been overshadowed by the quest for cultural specificity and the display of cultural differences that have become ends in themselves. The idea of cultural relativism, which dominated much of anthropology in the twentieth century, may have outlived its usefulness. We have reached a point, writes a critic of the ethnographic genre, where the presentation of other cultures retains canonical status within the discipline at the expense of neglecting the relationship between theoretical interests, disciplinary procedures and case material (N. Thomas 1991: 308, 313).[15]

There are obvious reasons for this dominant orientation. Since Boas and Malinowski it has been the quintessential task of anthropological field-workers to discover and interpret the 'native's point of view'. They have vested interests in finding and recording differences between cultures. Native informants have similar interests in underscoring and even magnifying their differences from other (especially neighbouring) groups, if only because in difference lies identity. The essay on the narcissism of minor differences shows how easily these constructions can develop into collective fantasies that spark off ethnic wars.

Anthropologists and their informants unwittingly conspire to overplay difference and create 'alterity'. Taking the native's point of view too literally, at face value, and uncritically, while ignoring that natives have vested interests in insisting on their uniqueness and cultural specificity, thereby exaggerating differences between themselves and others, anthropologists fall victim to what may be called the 'ethnographic fallacy' – that is, a falling short in transcultural understanding, an error most succinctly expressed in the firm and time-honoured credo, 'the informant is always right'.[16] Note, for example, what Portuguese writers and aficionados who 'went native' say about '*saudade*'. Having no comparative framework and ignoring the Brazilian version of *saudade*, they insist that this sentiment not only defies translation but also can be fully comprehended only by the Portuguese themselves (Schoonen 1998; cf. Leal 1999). 'The native point of view', writes Brightman, 'may be inadequate for many purposes' (1995: 519).

If we want to move beyond localizing the human condition and avoid being caught in 'the multiplicity of isolated tongues' (N. Thomas 1991: 317), and to establish a connection between theoretical interests and case material, we cannot do without comparative research that is sensitive both to differences and similarities, a kind of comparative work in which the cases selected for study can comment on each other. Next to 'sensitizing concepts' (Blumer 1969: 147–52), we should look for 'sensitizing' or paradigmatic cases that present telling details and suggest links with larger patterns in other case material. Note, for example, the pastoral background of bandits in Mediterranean countries, and the leadership of shoemakers in nineteenth- and twentieth-century popular movements (Hobsbawm and Scott 1980). Bear in mind, too, the pivotal role of peasants with tactical power in six twentieth-century revolutions (E. Wolf 1969). The essay on female rulers attempts to de-exoticize the figure of the 'female husband', which was prominent in various Bantu societies. Her position may help us to understand the role of female rulers in more complex societies, including modern nation-states. I used a similar comparative strategy in making sense of the heterogeneous company of people with dishonourable professions. Rather than stressing differences between cultures and confining myself to empirically isolated cases, I looked for transcultural similarities and cultural universals in order to understand why members of widely different occupational groups in widely different contexts were set apart from the common run of people.

Interested in the minutiae of social life and in telling details, the anthropologist cannot but follow hunches and the strategy of a conjectural paradigm, or 'Zadig's method'.[17] If we are not prepared to embark on this kind of comparative research, the cultures we study and try to understand will each remain enclosed in its own signifying system, and we shall miss opportunities to understand other civilizations, past and present (Burkert 1996: 3). By overplaying differences between cultures and localizing our questions, we shall also miss the opportunity of raising more general issues and of experimenting with other kinds of writing (N. Thomas 1991: 312–17).

This introduction touches upon two paradigms. One concerns social action; it is theoretical. The other concerns clues, signs or indications; it is methodological. The former recognizes chance and addresses the nature of social reality: social interaction is shaped by forces that elude the control and comprehension of people who take part in it. The latter favours abduction and tells us how to study social reality: by making imaginative guesses (which can be stimulated by comparative research). Underlying both paradigms is the belief that social reality is opaque and that social action is inherently paradoxical.

1

Social Banditry Reconsidered

Dans un voyage de Minghetti à Camporeale en Sicile, à l'époque où il était ministre, le curé se présente à lui:
Curé: Je viens vous recommander un pauvre jeune homme, qui a besoin de votre protection.
Minghetti: Et pourquoi? Que veut-il?
Curé: Rien, seulement il lui est arrivé un malheur, il a tué un homme.
Quoted in Marco Alongi, *L'Abigeato in Sicilia*[1]

In the late 1950s, Hobsbawm presented an interesting argument on a then markedly little known subject for which he coined the term 'social banditry' (1959: 1–29). He claimed that social banditry is a universal and virtually unchanging phenomenon which embodies a rather primitive form of organized social protest of peasants against oppression. Social bandits are robbers of a special kind, for they are not considered by public opinion as simple criminals: they are persons whom the state regards as outlaws, but who remain within the bounds of the moral order of the peasant community. Peasants see them as heroes, as champions, and as avengers, since they right wrongs when they defy the landlords or the representatives of the state. Yet their programme, if indeed social bandits have any, does not go beyond the restoration of the traditional order, which leaves exploitation of the poor and oppression of the weak within certain limits. Social bandits are thus reformers rather than revolutionaries, though they may prove a valuable asset for those who seek to overthrow an established regime. By themselves, social bandits lack organizational capacity, and modern forms of political mobilization tend to render them obsolete. The phenomenon belongs largely to the past, if only to the very recent past. The golden age of brigandage coincided with the advent of capitalism, when the impact of the market dislocated large sectors of the peasantry.

In *Bandits* (1969) Hobsbawm elaborates some of the main themes he surveyed in *Primitive Rebels* (1959). Like its predecessor, this study is an essay on the uniformities of social banditry. The author maintains that these uniformities should not be seen as a consequence of cultural diffusion, but as reflections of similar situations within peasant societies: 'Social banditry is universally found, wherever societies are based on agriculture (including pastoral economies), and consist largely of peasants and landless labourers ruled, oppressed, and exploited by someone else – lords, towns, governments. lawyers, or even banks' (1969: 15). Hobsbawm starts out from generalizations and then proceeds to provide evidence for them from various parts of the world. For example, in discussing the recruitment of bandits, he enumerates the categories that are likely to supply outlaws, indicates the causal nexus, and closes with examples. According to Hobsbawm:

> The characteristic bandit unit in a highland area is likely to consist of young herdsmen, landless labourers and ex-soldiers and unlikely to contain married men with children or artisans. Such formulae do not exhaust the question, but they do cover a surprisingly large part of the field. For instance, of the south Italian band leaders in the 1860s, those for whom we have occupational descriptions include twenty-eight 'shepherds', 'cowherds', 'ex-servicemen', 'landless labourers', and 'field guards' (or combinations of these occupations) and only five others. (1969: 28)

In this way the author deals with several aspects of social banditry and distinguishes three main types of bandits: the noble robber, the primitive resistance fighter, and the terror-bringing avenger. Whatever the differences between them, they have in common the fact that they voice popular discontent.

This approach leaves little room for a more comprehensive analysis over time of particular bandits or bands – accounts which are badly needed, as I hope presently to demonstrate. Where Hobsbawm embarks upon an extended case, the result cannot be other than sketchy (1969: 96–108). We should therefore read this study as directed by the author in his Preface: as a postscript in essay form to *Primitive Rebels*. In this realm, *Bandits* seems an appreciable book, well written and elegantly edited, furnished with 62 illustrations. The reader is offered a necessarily selective overview of no fewer than ninety separate bandits, who comprise the raw material used to illustrate the author's ideas on brigandage at large.

Yet it is precisely because the interpretations do not extend far beyond those already contained in *Primitive Rebels* that the reader who is already familiar with the subject will be slightly disappointed. Anxious to find additional evidence for his hypotheses, the author avoids discussing the many cases contradicting them. If, as Popper said, theories are nets cast to catch what we call 'the world' – to rationalize, to explain and to master it – Hobsbawm does not seem particularly concerned to make the mesh ever finer. It could hardly be otherwise, for he tells us that he entertains the hope that the new data will not conflict with his original model as sketched out in *Primitive Rebels*. And he adds: 'Still, the wider the generalization, the more likely it is that individual peculiarities are neglected' (1969: 11). One might wonder about the type of generalization that permits the neglect of particular cases, the more so since there were several questions in the first book which required thorough reconsideration.

It is my contention that there is much more to brigandage than just the fact that it may voice popular protest. Though Hobsbawm mentions several other aspects of banditry, his model fails to account for these complexities, and even obscures them, because he insists on the interpretation of new data in terms of his original model.

This essay attempts to explore the model of social banditry as a particular type of peasant protest and rebellion. I shall argue that the element of class conflict as embodied in certain forms of banditry has received undue emphasis. Rather than acting as champions of the poor and the weak, bandits quite often terrorized those from whose very ranks they managed to rise, and thus helped to suppress them. The often ambiguous position of bandits may be understood when we appreciate the significance of the various links that tie the peasant community to the larger society. Likewise, the distinction between direct and constructed reference groups may help to explain why peasants and romanticists (including some of us) indulge in an idealized picture of the rural bandit as an avenger of social injustice, in spite of the obvious evidence to the contrary. The present discussion may contribute to a fuller understanding of peasant mobilization and peasant movements. If we agree that political mobilization is a process through which people seek to acquire more control over the social conditions that shape their lives, it may be argued that bandits do not seem the appropriate agents to transform any organizational capacity among peasants into a politically effective force. Rather than promoting the articulation of peasant interests within a national context, bandits tend to obstruct or to deviate concerted peasant action. They may do so directly, by means of physical violence and intimidation. In fact, we know that bandits have fulfilled pivotal roles in the demobilization of peasants. Indirectly, brigandage may impede large-scale peasant mobilization, since it provides channels to move up the social hierarchy, and thus tends to weaken class solidarity. In this essay, therefore, I shall focus on the interdependencies between lords, peasants and bandits. The vignettes are mainly based on Sicilian material since my field-work experience has been restricted to this area.

To appreciate the importance and ubiquity of the social bandit, we should recognize which categories Hobsbawm excludes from this type: all urban robbers, the urban equivalent of the peasant bandit as much as members of the so-called 'underworld'; rural desperadoes who are not peasants – for example, the bandit gentry; raiders who form a community of their own, such as the bedouin; *mafia*-like gangs; the landlord's bandits; and the classic blood-vengeance bandits (1969: 13–14). This narrows to a considerable extent the universe of social banditry.[2] There are even further provisos, since not all categories are necessarily mutually exclusive. Particular bandits may, either simultaneously or in the course of their careers, express popular discontent as well as exemplifying the power of the landlord or the state (1959: 13). Furthermore, we know of outlaws and bandits who were glorified, or at least accepted, in their native districts while feared as raiders far outside these areas. For example, the nineteenth-century Indian *Thuggee* (thugs), also called *dacoits*, who specialized in ritually strangling and robbing travellers, lived as ordinary peasants in their native areas, where they were protected by local rulers with whom they shared the booty, but operated well over a hundred miles from their homes (MacKenzie 1967: 64–6). As Barrington Moore has aptly said with respect to nineteenth-century China: 'It is necessary to be aware of romanticizing the robber as a friend of the poor, just as much as of accepting the official image. Characteristically the local inhabitants would bargain with the bandits in order to be left in peace. Quite often local gentry leaders were on cordial terms with bandits' (1968: 214).[3]

Hobsbawm is aware of these varieties and complexities, but he does not attempt to account for them. His prime interest is social protest: 'Though in practice social banditry cannot always be clearly separated from other kinds of banditry, this does not affect the fundamental analysis of the social bandit as a special type of peasant protest and rebellion' (1969: 33). However, when it is recognized that 'the crucial fact about the bandit's position is its ambiguity ... the more successful he is as a bandit, the more he is *both* a representative and champion of the poor *and* a part of the system of the rich' (1969: 76), we may question the heuristic value of his model of the social bandit with respect to brigandage at large. As Hobsbawm admits elsewhere, few bandits lived up to the role of popular hero. Yet, 'such is the need for heroes and champions, that if there are no real ones, unsuitable candidates are pressed into service. In real life most Robin Hoods were far from noble' (1969: 34). For instance, Schinderhannes, a famous bandit chief who operated in the Rhineland in the late 1790s, 'was in no sense a social bandit, [but] found it advantageous for his public relations to advertise that he robbed only Jews' (1959: 20).

The point I want to make is not that 'social banditry' cannot be a useful sociological concept. It certainly can, though in a very different sense from that suggested by Hobsbawm. In a sense, all bandits are 'social' in so far as they, like all human beings, are linked to other people by various ties – of protection, support and collaboration. We cannot understand the practices of bandits without reference to other groups, classes or networks with which bandits form specific configurations of interdependent individuals. What seems wrong with Hobsbawm's perception of brigandage is that it pays too much attention to the peasants and the bandits themselves. Before looking at them, it is necessary to look at the larger society within which peasant communities are contained. Without taking into account the higher levels, which include the landed gentry and the formal authorities, brigandage cannot be fully understood as, indeed, many particular characteristics of peasant communities are dependent upon, or a reflex of, the impact of the outside world. Given the specific conditions of outlawry, bandits have to rely very strongly on other people. It is important to appreciate that all outlaws and robbers require protection in order to operate as bandits and to survive at all. If they lack protection, they remain lone wolves to be quickly dispatched, and those who hunt them down may be either the landlord's retainers, the police, or the peasants. Our task is therefore first to discover the people on whom the bandit relies. In Hobsbawm's model of the 'social bandit' this dimension of banditry is systematically underplayed, if not totally ignored.

Protectors of bandits may range from a close though narrow circle of kinsmen and affiliated friends to powerful politicians, including those who hold formal office as well as grass-roots politicians. Protection thus involves the presence of a power domain. Of all categories, the peasants are weakest. In fact, this is the main reason why they are peasants.[4] It may hence be argued that unless bandits find political protection, their reign will be short. This yields the following hypothesis, which may be tested against data bearing on all kinds of robbery: *The more successful a man is as a bandit, the more extensive the protection granted him.* The first variable can be expressed in terms of the period of action: less than three years, like Schinderhannes in the Rhineland and Corrientes in Andalusia; or more, like the Sicilians Capraro (1868–75), Grisafi

(1904–17) and Giuliano (1943–50). The second variable may be difficult to quantify, though mere numbers and social positions of protectors
may prove helpful beginnings. Another measure of success involves the
bandit's actions and the extent to which they are organized. Rinaldi,
Rocco and Capraro, who controlled large areas of western and central
Sicily in the early 1870s, provide an example. Their mounted and well-
armed bands synchronized their actions and fought regular battles with
the police and the army.[5] Grisafi's domain was a mountainous corner in
south-western Sicily

> over which he ruled absolutely, interfering in every kind of affair, even the
> most intimate, making his will felt in every field, including the electoral
> field, and levying tolls and taxes, blackmailing and committing crimes of
> bloodshed without stint. Some 30 murders were put down to him, besides
> an unending series of crimes. . . . Grisafi relied on a network of assistance
> that had grown wide, thick and strong in the course of time . . . [involv-
> ing] 357 persons in all, of whom 90 were in his hometown alone. (Mori
> 1933: 130–4)

The more banditry is politically oriented and evolves into what
Italian scholars have called *brigantaggio politico*,[6] the more likely it is
that it will assume 'antisocial' features in the sense understood by
Hobsbawm: that is, anti-peasant. A surprisingly large number of the
bandits mentioned by Hobsbawm were anti-peasant during most of their
careers, which they typically initiated by righting *personal* wrongs.
Sooner or later they were either killed or drawn into, and constrained
by, the power domains of the established regional elites. Bandits, especially those whose reign was long, thus represented the other side of a
barely suppressed class war. Giuliano, who shot down peaceful Communist demonstrators upon orders of high-ranking politicians, is mentioned in passing by Hobsbawm as an example of a bandit whose long
career was due to 'a very great deal of political protection' (1969: 46n.).
Pantaleone, who is more explicit on this incident, observes:

> This was the most sensational of Giuliano's crimes, but of course not the
> only one. In the months between the Portella shooting [1 May 1947] and
> the April elections the following year, his gang concentrated its attacks on
> party members, trade unions and left-wing party headquarters, completely
> terrorizing the villagers in the provinces of Palermo and Trapani which
> were the usual setting for his activities. (1966: 133)[7]

A similar orientation holds good for Giuliano's contemporary, Luciano
Leggio. The zone of terror which he established in the island region

during the aftermath of the Second World War was primarily aimed at the demobilization of the peasants who had just begun to organize themselves in order to attain agrarian reform.[8]

Marxists have consistently argued that peasants require outside leadership in order to change their conditions.[9] Bandits are not instrumental in turning peasant anarchy and rebellion (e.g. *jacqueries*) into sustained and concerted action on a wider scale. As Hobsbawm (1959: 5, 26) maintains, this is not because their ambitions are modest and because they lack organization and ideology; but rather, because their first loyalty is *not* to the peasants. When bandits assume retainership (either part-time or full-time) they serve to prevent and suppress peasant mobilization in at least two ways: first, by putting down collective peasant action through terror; second, by carving out avenues of upward mobility which, like many other vertical bonds in peasant societies, tend to weaken class tensions. Though bandits are thus essentially conservative, politically speaking, there are none the less specific circumstances under which they may become effective in destroying an established regime. This is most likely to happen when they can rely on a promising rival power which questions the existing power structure. The armed bands who had helped Garibaldi to unsettle Bourbon government in Sicily in 1860 are an example of the strategic role which bandits may fulfil in major upheavals. Even then, however, bandits may provide embarrassments since they may simply dissolve, change their allegiance according to the occasion, or fail to understand the situation in a wider context.[10]

Though Hobsbawm describes the myths and legends about bandits, his two studies fail to penetrate them – or to distinguish them from the social reality of brigandage. Even when we admit that it is the urban middle class rather than the ordinary peasantry who idealize the bandit, we may well ask to whom or what the peasants refer when they glorify the bandit. Here we may follow Elizabeth Bott, who draws on a distinction between direct and constructed reference groups. The former are groups in which the referent is an actual group: either membership or non-membership groups whose norms have been internalized by the individual. The latter concern groups in which the referent is a concept or social category rather than an actual group: 'The amount of construction and projection of norms into constructed reference groups is relatively high' (1964: 167–8).

The 'social bandit' as conceptualized and described by Hobsbawm is such a construct, stereotype or figment of human imagination. Though such constructs may not correspond to actual conditions, they are real since they represent fundamental aspirations of real people, in this case of the peasants. Successful bandits stand out as men who have evolved from poverty to relative wealth, and who have acquired power. To use a standard Sicilian expression, they are men who have *made themselves respected*. The notion of honour as expressed in a person's successful control over resources by means of physical force is characteristic of medieval Europe, contemporary Mediterranean societies and other agrarian societies, including large parts of Latin America. This concern with personal honour and the specific meanings attached to it are related to the relatively low level of state formation in these societies. In the absence of stable central control over the means of violence, people could not rely for protection on state institutions. With respect to sheer physical survival, they were largely dependent on themselves, or on the protection of more powerful persons.[11] Successful bandits inspire fear and respect. Hence the fascination they radiate, especially for those who are themselves in no way respected – the peasants, from whose ranks they usually emerge.

The element of social protest is expressed in the myth which thus builds up around the bandit. This process, or at least part of, is illustrated very skilfully and with great subtlety in Francesco Rosi's film *Salvatore Giuliano* (1962), in which we see surprisingly little of the bandit himself. Indeed, the very physical absence of outlaws from ordinary, day-to-day life facilitates the formation of myths and legends in which the bandit appears as a man fighting the rich to succour the poor. We idealize all the more readily those things and people with whom we are least acquainted, or whom we rarely actually see, and we tend to ignore information that is detrimental to a cherished image.[12] Actual bandit life is often unpleasant and grim. It involves prolonged residence in humid caves and long, toilsome marches, as well as frequent and brutal action against numerous poor and helpless victims.[13] Physical discomfort might be one reason why bandits seek to come to terms with their protectors in a more definite way: that is, when they assume the role of retainer. Many notorious delinquents and bandit leaders, like Di Miceli and Scordato in mid-nineteenth-century Palermo, were given special responsibility for public security.[14] In Sicily this and similar avenues to 'respectability' are institutionalized in the *mafia*, on which brigandage largely depends. We must expect to find similar mechanisms in Sardinia, Spain, Mexico and the Philippines.[15] Like the bandit's real life, these conversions in which bandits turn into retainers and help reinforce oppression of the peasantry do not provide attractive ingredients for myths and ballads.

Actual brigandage expresses a man's pursuit of honour and power. This holds true for the bandit as much as for his protector, who manipulates him in order to extend his power domains. The myth of the bandit (Hobsbawm's 'social bandit') represents a craving for a different society, a more human world in which people are justly dealt with and in which there is no suffering. These myths require our attention. It has been argued that they are the institutionalized expression of a dormant protest element which, under certain conditions, may 'gather force and break through the culturally accepted patterns which kept it within its institutionalized bounds' (Wertheim 1964: 32). Hobsbawm's comparative treatment of banditry overemphasizes the element of social protest while at the same time obscuring the significance of the links which bandits maintain with established power-holders. In future research on the subject, the relative importance of both elements must be accounted for.

Reviewing the literature on banditry that appeared over the last twenty-five years or so, three things stand out. First, it is to Hobsbawm's credit that he has stimulated research on an important but long-neglected subject that was, according to Fernand Braudel, an 'agile, cruel, every-day war, a war hardly noticed by traditional historians, who have left what they consider a secondary topic to essayists and novelists' (Braudel 1973: 745). Over the years, the critical literature on banditry has grown considerably and is indeed hard to catch up on.

Second, this corpus of excellent historical studies endorses the core arguments of my early critical commentary (including the acceptance of the concept of 'political banditry') and rejects Hobsbawm's portrayal of social banditry. Research on banditry in Europe, the Mediterranean area and Latin America revealed that bandit–elite ties played a key role in the dynamics of rural society and were far more important than bandit–peasant connections. On the whole, bandits have shown little consideration for, let alone solidarity with, peasants. What united people behind banditry were kinship, friendship and patronage – not class.[16] What animated banditry was the quest for honour and respect. What often motivated it was revenge – bandits invariably started their careers to avenge personal wrongs. Social causes were attributed to them by others, if they did not deliberately promote them themselves. The late Colombian drugs baron Pablo Escobar is a recent case in point.

The third point that strikes us in the discussion of comparative banditry is Hobsbawm's insistence on the concept of social banditry. In spite of the overwhelming evidence to the contrary, which demonstrates that social banditry refers to myths and legends rather than to the reality of banditry, he still holds on to the 'special relationship' between bandits and peasants, to the idea of banditry as a form of social protest.[17] As one critic aptly puts it:

The Corsican example also lends weight to the view elaborated by a number of writers in criticism of Hobsbawm, that, where banditry had a political dimension, it was less as a protest against the rich and the powerful in pursuit of liberty and justice and more as a component of intensified competition among local élites in the circumstances of incorporation into a modern state. (S. Wilson 1988: 335)

To which was added the following note:

It should be noted that Hobsbawm frequently acknowledges those aspects of banditry highlighted by his critics but gives them little emphasis in his general interpretation. (1988: 507n.)

This response to his critics, which also surfaces in later editions of his book *Bandits*, has done little to stop the widespread vulgarization of Hobsbawm's model of social banditry that tends to see virtually all brigandage as a manifestation of peasant protest. Ironically, the main victim of this popularization is Hobsbawm himself, a Marxist scholar whom one can blame for mixing up reality and myth – a myth, moreover, that urban intellectuals fashioned to fit urban bourgeois taste.

In his brief discussion of brigandage in the mountainous regions of the Mediterranean, McNeill points at the blurring of lines between brigandage, herding, and soldiering in frontier regions and other areas of weak central control. He distinguishes between successful and less successful bandits. Success depended on protection from local landlords, in which capacity bandits were in a position to exploit the local peasantry (1992: 118). The author recalls el-Raisuli of Jbala who operated at the turn of the century in the Rif and who 'acquired hundreds of followers and became rich, fat, and finally governor of Jbala'. But for every successful el-Raisuli there were scores of poor and desperate bandits – in the Rif as much as in the Taurus, the Pindus, the Sierra Nevada and southern Italy. In all these areas, writes McNeill, brigands worked routinely for large estate owners:

More successful brigands suffered little harassment from the state because they in effect became the retainers of the local authorities and magnates. In return for occasional illegal chores, brigands were permitted to batten on the local peasantry. The most successful *klephts* in the Pindus became *armatoles*, rural gendarmes permitted wide latitude by Ottoman authorities in exchange for pursuit of less successful brigands and protection of state interests. In the Taurus, too, the Ottomans set brigands to catch brigands. Consequently brigands competed among themselves to become so dangerous to the public and the state that the authorities would be moved to hire them to keep the peace. *This arrangement, far more common than the 'social banditry' that robbed from the rich and gave to the poor, suited all parties except the peasants.* (1992: 118–19, my italics)

Bandits in nineteenth-century Greece, writes Koliopoulos, were mostly young mountaineers, between twenty and thirty years old and often migratory shepherds. For these people,

> banditry was a transitory stage in their lives or ended, along with their lives, not long after they took to it. For many of them, banditry, like sheep-stealing, was not even an extraordinary venture but almost an unavoid-able practice: they took to robbery as they did to shepherding – they were born into it. (1987: 239)

Yet many of them hoped for a way out of banditry, a return to legality by obtaining an amnesty or pardon, joining the national guards, or through enlistment in irregular military bands. The majority of their victims were vulnerable people: shepherds, peasants, seasonal workers, artisans and travellers. Theft from elite families was exceptional because they were mostly out of the bandit's reach. The popular image of the bandit, or the concept of the 'social' bandit, writes Koliopoulos, is related to the bandits of this region and period in the way myth is to reality:

> The tendency to emphasize a certain sympathy towards bandits as reflected in popular ballads, and to see in that sympathy an affinity of interests between peasants and the bandits described as 'social' is distorting and contributes little to a sound analysis of banditry. (1987: 277)

The author recognizes that references to bandits considered noble and champions of the poor are not lacking, but it is only after their death that they are celebrated – in ballads and elsewhere. While alive, they were more feared than admired. It is one thing to study these popular mis-conceptions about bandits, but quite another to confuse them with the reality of banditry. The Greek experience confirms my earlier point that the bandit is sufficiently far removed from daily routines to facilitate the formation of myths and legends. The fascination with bandits is also predicated on their survival skills, most notably the successful use of vio-lence, and their upward mobility in a world that offers few chances to the poor and desperate rural masses. This reading of the myths and legends about bandits brings us closer to the reality of banditry and the dynamics of rural life than an insistence on seeing in banditry archaic or primitive forms of social protest. Nineteenth-century rural Greece shows little evidence of Hobsbawm's social bandits. In any case, bandits in that area had a low opinion of the weak and helpless peasantry. Far from being champions of the common people, writes Koliopoulos, they terrorized them more than they had the chance to terrorize the elite (1987: 280).

The discussion on Latin American banditry points in the same direction. In his long review of the recent literature on the subject, Joseph emphasizes three main objections that the 'revisionists' (who represent the 'new social history') raised against Hobsbawm's conception of social banditry. First, his portrayal of banditry rests almost exclusively on folkloric and literary materials, leaving police and judicial archives unexplored. Second, bandits have shown little solidarity with peasants: for Latin America this 'special relationship' is largely absent, exaggerated or mythical. Instead, they frequently forged links with families of the landed elite and other established power-holders. Third, there is no evidence that bandits represented any form of protest, whether 'primitive', 'pre-political' or 'social'. Referring to Slatta's important collection, Joseph notes:

> Slatta reports that he and his posse of social scientists 'have galloped in hot pursuit of bandits across several Latin American countries and through two centuries' and that the bandits they have unmasked in the criminal archives 'carry visages different from the ideal type postulated by Hobsbawm'. (1990: 11)

Joseph also emphasizes that in Hobsbawm's accounts, the 'popular' sources 'have not been balanced by painstaking research in the "official" police and judicial records that have become an important weapon in the social historian's arsenal since *Bandits* originally appeared in 1969' (1990: 8). Many of the heroic folktales and ballads that Hobsbawm relied on may reflect the poor's idealized aspirations rather than historical reality. Moreover, as suggested by several historians who worked in Argentina, Brazil and Cuba, such literary sources frequently reflect the views of romantic, ideological or commercially motivated *urban* writers rather than peasant folk tradition.[18] In Slatta's summary, as a group,

> bandits did not engage in the Robin Hood-style redistribution of wealth from the rich to the poor. If they robbed the rich more often, it was because the rich had more to take. But bandits also despoiled and pillaged the poor, seemingly with few qualms. Bandits were economically self-interested and forward-looking – more concerned with getting ahead than with looking backward toward the re-establishment of fading peasant values. . . . Banditry provided one of the many survival tactics used by the rural masses

in their attempts to cope with threatening social–political dislocations. It was not a *reaction against*, but an *adaptation to*, [Latin American] politics and society. (p. 198)

Banditry in twentieth-century China followed similar patterns. Rather than becoming the co-ordinators of peasant wrath, concludes Billingsley, bandits turned to the very oppressors of the peasants to sustain their existence:

> The greater their need to confirm their elite ties, the looser bandits' peasant connections became. The role of bandits in warlord China by and large confirms Blok's observation on the negative correlation between banditry and peasant mobilization. Not only were bandits effective in putting down by terror a growing tide of collective action; their own success as paid underlings of the rich (however temporary) also confirmed the possibility of upward social mobility under existing conditions, tending to drain off from the peasant movement many people who might have provided it with strong, charismatic leadership. (1988: 282)

In revolutionary France, social bandits were likewise conspicuously absent. Consider the members of the *bande d'Orgères* who operated in the area around Chartres in the 1790s. Tied together by links of kinship, friendship, region, and mobile occupations, the *bande* included women and children, and relied on a network of local accomplices. They robbed and killed travelling merchants as readily as defenceless farmers and their families on isolated homesteads in the middle of the night. In his sober style, Cobb reports that

> they went where there would be people with money to kill. . . . On the whole, they were local people, who operated locally against local people known to them by name and by sight. Their elaborate chain of complicity was likewise local. The *bande d'Orgères* belonged primarily to the Beauce; and it operated, for at least ten years, in the full sight of a large section of the rural community, either terrorized into silence, or sympathetic, or admirative. (1972: 185, 189)

Although the *bande d'Orgères* represented, to some extent, the banditry of the very poor, there was (writes Cobb) in the activities of its members no form of social protest. They 'were as likely to steal the only sheet of a poor widow, hanging on the line, as the whole wardrobe of a rich farmer's wife' (1972: 197, 204–5). Cobb is also sensitive to the cultural dimensions of banditry. He notes that the members of this band, like most bandits, 'prided themselves both on their cruelty and on their physical prowess' (1972: 200). Moreover, 'need was not the only incentive; the members of the *bande* were seeking to prove themselves. They belonged to a society which carried its own signs of recognition, its own language, and its own shared assumptions' (1972: 202).

Detailed studies of banditry in the Low Countries at the end of the eighteenth century and in various areas of Germany in the same period and later likewise show little evidence of social banditry. Highly mobile and tied together by links of kinship, ethnicity and occupation, the members of the *bande juive*, or *Grote Nederlandse Bende*, represented only themselves and pursued their own interests.[19] The German bands were also closely tied to mobile occupations, including tinkering, peddling, entertaining and begging. They lacked any edge of social protest. As the editor of a volume on German banditry summarizes this point of the collection:

> In all the cases a myth is left behind – the myth of the noble bandit. This product was distinctly marked, first by literature and later in painting. Schiller, Hauff, Vulpius or Zschokke have essentially, although in different ways, contributed to the image of the bandit as 'Verbrecher aus verlorener Ehre' (offender because of lost honour), the bandit as a romantic rebel, as a social revolutionary. It was the image of a bandit of a beginning bourgeois period, but it had little to do with historical reality. (Siebenmorgen 1995: 9)

Finally, there is the case of the so-called *Bokkeryders*, who robbed farms and churches in the Lower Meuse from the 1730s until the early 1770s.[20] The first bands coalesced around a regional and endogamous network of skinners living in the politically fragmented area north-east of Maastricht. Skinners were socially marginalized because of their trade, which was considered polluting. Later, members of other occupational groups, mostly artisans, local merchants and farmhands, reinforced these bands. What many of them had in common was a mobile profession and a strongly developed sense of place. Banditry in the Lower Meuse was sparked off by post-war unemployment that hit skinners and iron-workers in particular.

Ties with members of local elites were prominent among the leadership of the bands. Their influence on the political agenda of the bands could be inferred from increasingly military leanings and large-scale outings. The theme of social protest found expression in recruitment rituals and in millenarian prospects, including the expectation of an imminent 'Brotherhood of Happiness'. Yet the *Bokkeryders*, like other bandits, robbed and killed vulnerable people, including widows and other single women, as readily as prosperous farmers, innkeepers and priests.

Once more, the banditry experience forces us to distinguish between practices and beliefs, between the reality of banditry and its ideological, discursive and symbolic dimensions. Both are expressions of deep social divisions and conflicts. One can, therefore, agree with one of Hobsbawm's sharpest critics, who writes: 'Even if the social bandit did not exist in Latin America, the conditions to make him a believable and significant symbol to the rural masses did.'[21]

These complexities of banditry and the wider context in which the phenomenon took shape can perhaps be best illustrated by a recent and well-known case. The Indian 'Bandit Queen' Phoolan Devi was the daughter of a poor and illiterate, lower-caste fisherman from the badlands in Uttar Pradesh. Humiliated and abused by a much older husband whom she was forced to marry, she joined a *dacoit* band and took part in the killing of twenty members of the land-owning upper-caste Thakurs in Behmai, whom she accused of rape and of having murdered her lover. The massacre took place in February 1981. Two years later, Devi surrendered together with her fellow band-members. The surrender was artfully stage-managed. By the time she was released from prison, after eleven years without trial, she had achieved legendary status and had become a symbol of the revolt against lower-caste misery.[22]

The fascination Devi inspires lies not in her relationship with poverty but in the dramatic and miraculous way she overcame it. Her immense popularity lies in her iconic biography. She evolved from humble origins to celebrity by an extraordinary turn of fate that included ruthless violence and stage-managed martyrdom. Once poor, humiliated and abused, she later came to inspire fear and respect. Devi's curriculum vitae, like that of other successful bandits before her, includes the quintessential materials of which myths are made.

2

Bandits and Boundaries: Robber Bands and Secret Societies on the Dutch Frontier (1730–1778)

> The strength of collective biography is not in supplying alternative ex-
> planations, but in specifying what is to be explained. Historians who
> have specified what is to be explained via collective biography often find
> themselves turning to explanations stressing the immediate setting and
> organization of everyday life, or relying on something vaguely called
> 'culture'. That moves them back to anthropology.
>
> Charles Tilly: Anthropology, history and the *Annales*

Banditry has been identified as the easiest form of rebellion because it is
the most difficult for states to counteract, especially in mountainous frontier zones where central authority is weak (cf. Wallerstein 1974: 141–2;
Braudel 1973: 745–6). A case in point is the so-called *Bokkeryders*, who
in three successive episodes between 1730 and 1774 operated in the
hinterland of Maastricht – the border area between the Dutch Republic,
the Duchy of Gulik, and the Austrian Netherlands. It took the local
authorities in these fragmented territories well over forty years to come
to terms with a form of banditry that easily survived the first two
attempts in the 1740s to repress it.[1]

The raids of the bands fell into three distinct periods, each of which
came to an end with mass arrests, trials, and executions in the home
towns of the convicts. The first period (1730–42) saw more than sixty
such forays, most of which were directed against churches, though ten
raids involved massive attacks on farms, inns and rectories. The second
phase (1749–50) included just two operations and was for the most part
a short-lived revival of the remnants of the earlier bands. In the third
phase (1751–74) the ranks of the robbers swelled considerably. Assorted

local bands participated in several large-scale attacks against a dozen farms, two rectories, a hermitage, a monastery and a church. As had happened in the early 1740s, a haphazard theft not authorized by the leaders and carried out toward the end of 1770 led to the discovery and subsequent demise of the robber bands in the Lower Meuse.

In the early stages of Lower Meuse banditry, most of the robbers came from the easternmost enclaves of the Austrian Netherlands and the adjoining areas of the Duchy of Gulik. The Dutch territories were only modestly represented at that time, by the towns of Nieuwstadt and Heerlen. Later, large groups of people from neighbouring Dutch districts joined in the raids, while some Austrian territories and the Duchy of Gulik ceased to be important areas of recruitment. All attacks took place late in the evening or in the early morning. During these nocturnal ventures the robbers looked for money, jewellery, clothing, food, and other valuable goods. Victims were often maltreated (to make them talk first and to keep them quiet later), and some of them lost their lives. But not all operations involved the same level of violence, nor were they all equally successful. Several large-scale raids failed – some because the victims or their neighbours managed to raise the alarm; others because the robbers found only items of little value. It is significant that on a number of occasions, most notably during the large-scale operations in 1770, the victims were conspicuously spared – if they woke up at all.

How many people actually participated in the operations of these bands is impossible to tell. What we do know is that about 600 people were tried for being members of the 'notorious band' and that many others fled and successfully avoided prosecution. In the early 1740s, about 170 people appeared before local courts. The defendants included well over twenty women; most of them were linked to band members through kinship, marriage or concubinage. About ten years later, some thirty people were tried, including five men who had also been active during the first period. Throughout the trials of the 1770s, almost 400 people, including six women, were convicted. In all, I was able to trace more than 500 guilty verdicts, sentences for all of which were carried out, most of these through death by hanging, burning or breaking on the wheel.

This chapter seeks to trace the development of two forms of collective violence: banditry and its repression. It has been argued that no simple distinction between instrumental and symbolic practice makes sense anywhere: instrumental action is always simultaneously semantic (Comaroff 1985: 125; cf. Leach 1966: 403–4 and 1976: 9). Directed against property and people (expropriation and elimination), both forms of violence include a powerful cultural import affecting the reputation and social status of all protagonists.

We notice, first, that the occupational backgrounds of the robbers, their kinship structure and their place of origin strongly favoured the development of banditry in the Lower Meuse and, of course, also militated against stopping or controlling it. Second, we shall see that the military and political history of the area is a crucial factor in understanding the rise and fall of the *Bokkeryders*. The bands emerged some time after 1730 in a peripheral area characterized by a high degree of territorial fragmentation resulting from a long period of wars. This raises a third issue: the means the local authorities could deploy to control the bands. Fourth, in studies of popular collective violence, the issue of 'claims' usually looms large. Claims may be obvious when we deal with tax revolts, conscription riots, and similar examples of popular politics. But in cases of organized banditry, claims are less clear, or at least difficult to pinpoint, since motives, goals and agendas vary among participants and also change over time. This may be one reason why banditry, itself often elusive, diffuse and intermittent, does not take up a prominent place in studies of collective action.[2] Writing about banditry in sixteenth-century Mediterranean countries, Braudel characterized it as a 'cruel, everyday war hardly noticed by traditional historians, who have left what they consider a secondary topic to essayists and novelists' (1973: 745). Before returning to the issue of claims, we look at the context within which the bands took shape.

I

The *Bokkeryders* operated in the Lower Meuse, in the rural area enclosed by the towns of Maastricht, Aix-la-Chapelle, Gulik and Roermond. From the sixteenth to the early nineteenth centuries, this was part of a larger military frontier zone, with Maastricht as a strong fortress and garrison town and Liège as an important centre of the arms industry. It was in the Lower Meuse, at the crossroads of major east–west and north–south thoroughfares, that the spheres of influence of the great European powers touched and often collided. France, Spain, the Dutch Republic, Austria and, later, Prussia disputed sovereignty over this part of Europe. Up to the early eighteenth century, the area had suffered from frequent military incursions and subsequent territorial fragmentation, most notably the division of the so-called *Landen van Overmaas* between the Dutch Republic and Spain in 1662. Including Dutch and Spanish (after 1713, Austrian) territories, together with sections of the Duchy of Gulik and various semi-autonomous seigneuries, it was, in several respects, a border area *par excellence*.[3]

Apart from the political frontiers there were many different legal jurisdictions, and the boundary dividing Protestants from Roman Catholics – the result of the Protestantization that the Dutch (largely unsuccessfully) tried to impose on their territories – ran right across the area. The transitional character of the entire region was reinforced by its location on commercial and military crossroads. Situated in a major European interaction zone, the Lower Meuse connected Flanders with the Rhineland and the Dutch Republic with the southern Netherlands and France. Furthermore, the Dutch and Austrian territories of the Lower Meuse were extremely peripheral in relation to their political centres: The Hague and Brussels. Disconnected from the other parts of the Dutch Republic and the Austrian Netherlands, respectively, these fragmented territories constituted true enclaves.

At a time when there were no barracks, this part of the Lower Meuse – a fertile region of mixed farming where large, often fortified tenant farms prevailed among patches of veld, wood and heather – was much sought after as winter quarters for armies. As a deep hinterland of Maastricht, part of the area also functioned as a granary for the city and its garrison. But these resources also invited the scourge of disbanded soldiers, of which many villages in the locality had received their share. There were several industries in the area, not only in the towns but also in the villages, which produced textiles, metal and leather-work. The entire region formed an offshoot of the important industrial concentration around Liège (Thurlings and Van Drunen 1960). Apart from agriculture, therefore, people lived off rural domestic manufactories and commerce.

These arrangements reflected a highly stratified, 'seigneurial' social formation, which included a landed gentry and clergy who lived comfortably in splendid country houses (including the famous Rolduc monastery), and controlled most of the land; a group of landowning farmers who also managed the tenant farms; and a larger, more diversified group of artisans, labourers and retail merchants with little or no property. The local courts and other public offices were staffed by gentry and farmers. The power of landlords, clerics and farmers was also vested in the images of authority and subordination – in the architecture of the courtroom and the gallows, the country houses and castles, the monastery, and the scattered, walled-in tenant farms – and should therefore also be understood in terms of cultural hegemony. Together with the lifestyle, dress and gestures of the gentry, these houses and spaces were part of the orchestration of aristocratic power.[4]

II

From about 1730 until 1774 numerous Roman Catholic churches and farms in this part of the eastern Meuse valley were plundered in nocturnal forays by the *Bokkeryders*. The collective biography of the *Bokkeryders*, which I composed on the basis of court records, reveals that these people were not bandits, that is, 'outlaws', in the strict sense of the term. On the contrary, virtually all of them led ordinary lives in their home towns. Most of them were married with children and had a fixed abode. In fact, many were born and had grown up in the same area in which they carried out their raids – the politically fragmented territories north of Maastricht and Aix-la-Chapelle. Some of them lived in the same village as their victims, and a few were even their close neighbours.

Familiarity with the victims may explain the various forms of disguise that the robbers adopted. They operated by night; hence their nickname, *nachtdieven* (night thieves). We know that female participants dressed as men, while the men often wore military attire and used military expressions to mislead their victims. Others blackened their faces and put on visors, wigs, false beards, caps and other outlandish headgear 'in order not to be recognized', as one of the accused explained in court. It should not surprise us, then, that the robbers fled when the victims succeeded in raising the alarm and mobilizing their neighbours, as happened on various occasions. As local people, the *Bokkeryders* had good reason to fear recognition; they were part-time robbers, organized into secret societies of sorts, with dual identities, whose secret part they concealed behind their public personae as ordinary villagers and workmen.[5]

Looking at the occupational background of the robbers (which I was able to trace for two-thirds of them), one finds artisans (skinners, saddlers, shoemakers, iron-workers, spinners, weavers) and retail merchants (pedlars, carters, cattle dealers) strongly represented. Together they made up about 60 per cent of the participants in all three stages of band operations, while farmers and day labourers accounted for scarcely 20 per cent. In a distinctly rural area, people of agrarian background remained notably underrepresented in the bands (see Table 1).

Rural artisans, most notably skinners, played pivotal roles in the bands. In fact, the first bands coalesced around a widely extended network of skinners from no fewer than ten different locations. It was the skinners' job to kill sick animals, to dispose of dead cattle, to flay horses, and to remove other organic remnants from public areas. Skinners also assisted the executioner in the sessions of judicial torture and helped with his work on the scaffold; they were charged with the transport of dead bodies of convicts from the prison to the gallows (invariably located at the periphery of the jurisdiction), where they had to hang them in chains or bury their remains. The public perception of their ritual uncleanliness resulted from their handling of 'matter out of place' and forced them to live on the outskirts of the villages and towns, prevented them from marrying outside their occupational group, and made it difficult for them to find other work. As a consequence, the skinners constituted a wide-

Table 1   Occupational background of *Bukkeryders*

	Phase I	*Phase II*	*Phase III*	*Total*
Skinners	17	–	5	
Ironworkers	17	5	18	
Saddlers	1	–	6	
Shoemakers	5	7	20	
Spinners and weavers	14	2	49	
Other	8	1	44	
Artisans (total)	62	15	142	219
Commerce and transport	21	5	33	59
Agriculture	10	5	73	88
Authorities	3	3	11	17
Miscellaneous	27	2	29	58
Total	123	30	288	441

spread, regional and endogamous network.[6] Some of the women who participated in the raids showed a capacity for great cruelty. Among them we find wives, sisters and daughters of skinners, which reflects the close-knit character of the first bands (Blok 1995: 57–88, 435–6). When in the later bands the number of skinners decreased, the participation of women also dwindled.

Faced with economic hardship in the post-war years and virtually barred from other work because of their 'pollution', the skinners had been able to draw on their far-flung occupational network and the cultural capital entailed by their profession to organize themselves in bands across the borders of the Lower Meuse. Thus the skinners not only dominated the first bands in terms of numbers; they also had an important part in the preparation and organization of the raids, and the division of the booty and the sale of stolen goods (through Jewish receivers in the bigger towns) were mostly in their hands. To understand their prominence (which they maintained in the later bands even though their numerical dominance had drastically decreased), the implications of their profession deserve close scrutiny.

The skinners shared their low social status, their peripheral location and their mobility with other occupational groups – pedlars, part-time beggars, musicians, jugglers, carters, retail merchants, innkeepers and ex-soldiers – that were strongly represented in the bands. Although all these people had a fixed abode (and thus certainly did not belong to the *fahrende Leute*), they moved freely between the villages and towns. Most notably, innkeepers went back and forth between their rural inn and the towns for provisions and had sidelines as merchants. Like shoemakers, their workplaces served as centres for sociability.[7] As well as associating with these more or less itinerent folk (including spinners and weavers, who were strongly represented in the later bands), the skinners also maintained relations with other professional killers, like butchers and other craftsmen involved in leather-work – saddlers, shoemakers and cobblers.

The bands were thus united by occupational links, kinship and marriage (which were by now certainly not restricted to the group of skinners). But local bonds were also important. It is striking that the vast majority of the *Bokkeryders* were settled in smaller neighbourhoods and hamlets near the bigger villages and on the outskirts. Some of these settlements, like Heerlerheide and Chèvremont, were built on poor soils (heath), and developed a distinct subculture. Given their mobility and peripheral location, the *Bokkeryders* could not easily be subjected to tight forms of social control. These conditions held particularly true for the skinners, who could organize themselves over considerable distances. For a long time, they did so far more successfully than did the judicial authorities, who were bound to small jurisdictions. In a way, therefore, the regional, endogamous network of the skinners provided the infrastructure of the first bands. Many forays in those years had, indeed, the character of family affairs.

Other implications of the skinning trade were no less important for understanding the organization of the *Bokkeryders* bands and the collective violence they deployed. Even more than other itinerant people, the skinners had an excuse to hang around at unlikely times and places, which enabled them to acquire an intimate knowledge of the area in which they worked. Their spatial sense must have been formidable, for they could find their way in the middle of the night around a large area, going to the rendezvous and target and returning home before dawn, every step of which required precise timing. As they were the emergency butchers, their presence at uncommon times and places did not raise suspicion, nor did their transport of heavy packs and bundles. The cultural capital of the skinning trade also included skills in the use of violence and inflicting pain; it also entailed a familiarity with death. From descriptions of the raids on farms and rectories given by both victims and offenders, we learn that the skinners did not hesitate to use the same means on their victims that they employed in their work with animals and in their role of executioner's assistant.

The circumstances bearing on the social and spatial organization of the skinners and their allies cannot, of course, explain why these people organized themselves into robber bands and secret societies, breaking into churches and farmhouses, maiming and sometimes killing the habitants. These circumstances only tell us how the skinners and their accomplices were able to operate. They throw light on their power chances *vis-à-vis* the authorities, who were tied to jurisdictions of limited size. At this point, we should consider the cultural aspects of collective violence and the way in which notions of identity, pride and meaning were implied in banditry and its repression. We take our clues from the more 'expressive' aspects of the raids, from what these forays had to 'say'.

III

It is obvious that the skinners and various of their associates provided the community with indispensable services. Yet the established rural population of farmers (from whom the local authorities were largely recruited) excluded them from their ranks. It should not surprise us, therefore, that the *Bokkeryders* – from their first sorties in the early 1730s to their very last at the end of 1774 – directed their operations against the principal symbols of the rural community: churches and farms. Even if the stigmatization to which the skinners and their associates were subjected may have provided them with a cause, we are still left with the question of why the bands formed around 1730 and not before.

It is very likely that the skinners in the Lower Meuse enjoyed a certain measure of prosperity in the decades around 1700. The military operations that afflicted the area until the early eighteenth century and the cattle plagues that struck various regions of western Europe between 1713 and 1719 may both have favoured the skinning trade as much as they must have taken a toll on the farmers. By about 1720 these afflictions came to a temporary halt, but this meant that prosperous times for the skinners were over. As mentioned earlier, wars and other military operations, including a continuing military presence, provided work not only for those taking part in them but also for people whose services were required to sustain military activities. Among these, we find skinners, butchers, tanners, saddlers, shoemakers, blacksmiths, locksmiths and other iron-workers – occupations that were all strongly represented in the bands.[8] There are various indications of a marked decrease in employment for skinners, in particular, in the 1720s and 1730s. Some of them had to insist on their local monopoly; others were continually on the move in search of work; still others removed their business to other locations. As skinners they had few chances of finding employment outside their trade.

Although artisans remained prominent, the later bands also included people from different backgrounds and with different aims. In the 1750s and 1760s the bands came under the control of a local *chirurgijn* (surgeon) who had been an officer in the Austrian army and who could rely on pre-existing networks of the robbers as well as on the services of a string of innkeepers and various shoemakers – professions that had also been salient in the first bands.[9] In this way, the bands which had been and continued to be a segmented assortment of secret societies were cast in a military mould. Recruitment became a serious business, more important than the raids themselves, which, apart from five large-scale forays into the Duchy of Gulik in a single year (1770), took place less frequently and were hardly profitable. The operations of the *Bokkery-ders* in this stage looked very much like those of a *Freikorps* or militia in the making.[10] Whatever ulterior political aims the leaders may have had (and one cannot exclude the possibility of a secessionist movement), their project proved abortive when the authorities started the massive round-ups of *Bokkeryders* in early 1771 after one particular raid, not authorized by the leaders, led to the discovery of the bands.

The raids on churches, especially frequent in the early years when the bands were dominated by the skinners, involved more than the theft of goods and money – and not only because the goods included sacred objects. By itself, breaking into a church was already an act with strong symbolic overtones. Since the church, as a centre of sociability, formed the core of the community and was the 'House of God', such intrusions were defined as major violations and, if followed by theft, were considered sacrilege and were punished 'with fire', a sanction that evokes images of pollution and purification of both the church and the community of believers.[11] As Firth reminds us, this community of believers forms a body – the Body of Christ, its members being in mystical union with Him: the elect are knit together 'in one communion and fellowship, in the mystical body of thy Son Christ our Lord', as the Book of Common Prayer phrases it.[12] The attacks on churches assumed the features of what E. P. Thompson called the 'countertheatre' of the poor.[13] On several occasions, the operations included parodies of the Mass, during which one of the leaders acted as a 'priest' and distributed the Host among his followers. These performances involved the violation of another body: the eucharistic Body of Christ, the consecrated bread (and wine) that is received in Holy Communion.

'Every religious ceremony creates the possibility of a black mass', wrote Goffman (1967: 86). Through parody and contrast, the skinners imitated and at the same time distorted and violated the Holy Communion. The profanations with the *Corpus Christi* in an inverted mass foreshadowed the initiation rituals, the first of which may have taken place as early as 1737. With the expansion of the bands the counter-theatre of the *Bokkeryders* received further elaboration in secret cere-monies that marked incorporation into the bands, serving as an offensive and subversive frame within which to recruit new members. On these occasions the initiates were encouraged to affront holy bodies: images, icons, and effigies of the Virgin, the saints and Christ. New members had to swear an oath of allegiance in wayside chapels and other liminal loca-tions. The ceremonies took the form of an inverted Roman Catholic liturgy and were performed in front of an improvised altar with burning candles, holy statuettes and images of saints. The neophytes had to spit on a crucifix, throw it on the floor and step on it while renouncing God and the Holy Mother and swearing allegiance to the Devil, promising secrecy and commitment to theft. On some occasions the initiation cer-emonies took place around a burning candle put into a dead man's hand cut off from the corpse of an executed criminal to which the skinners, because of their profession, had easy access. Credited with magical power, the so-called *Diebshand* or *Diebslicht* was believed to facilitate burglaries: it would open locks, put the victims to sleep, prevent them from waking up, or, if awake, keep them from speaking, moving, and so on.[14]

The simple symbolic act of stepping and spitting on a crucifix also included references to that other Body of Christ – the community of believers. In this way the sacrileges helped the initiates to separate them-selves from mainstream society and become members of a countersoci-ety of sorts. For the skinners and several of their associates, this separation also involved an 'imitation' – the working of the mimetic faculty – since they had already been excluded from ordinary social life because of their occupation, their social exclusion being symbolized by their spatial segregation.

As in rites of passage elsewhere, the secret meetings of the *Bokkery-ders* must have enhanced the social cohesion of the robbers' network and underscored the difference between them and ordinary people (La Fontaine 1985: 58, 72–3). The initiation rituals (from which women were virtually excluded) may also have reinforced the *Bokkeryders'* daring. They made their appearance at the time when the bands were starting to grow rapidly and could not be bound together solely by links of kinship, marriage, friendship, occupation and other local bonds. But these ties continued to play a significant role – both in terms of struc-ture and in terms of sentiment. The robbers emphasized 'equality' and, during the third and last phase, the imminent foundation – by violent means – of a 'New Kingdom' and a 'Brotherhood of Happiness' (Blok 1995: 113–52).

It must have been the news about the initiation ceremonies as well as the remarkable mobility of the bands that earned the robbers the epithet of '*Bokkeryders*' (German: *Bockreiter*): that is, 'goat riders', a popular name bestowed on them only in the early 1770s when the last trials were in full swing and by which they have been known ever since. One does not find this denomination in the court records, which speak of 'bandits', 'night thieves', 'extortioners', 'members of the famous band', and the like, although the judges acknowledged the existence of a sworn confederacy. Rooted in an ancient and widespread folk belief that associates the billy-goat with evil and the Devil and his work, the use of the name '*Bokkeryders*' suggests that the speaker regarded the robbers as antisocial and attributed to them supernatural power – the ability to make magical, nocturnal flights on animals to far-off places, to steal and make their rendezvous.[15] But we do not know, of course, for whom – and for how many contemporaries – the name may have had ironic connotations.[16]

Having sketched the main features of the context in which collective violence from the lower echelons of society took shape, it is tempting to reflect briefly on the subversive bent of the swearing of the formulaic oath, the 'sacrilegious oath', as the judicial authorities phrased it, because it shows how closely popular and elite traditions, and both forms of collective violence, were related. Always the focal point of initiation rituals of secret societies, among the *Bokkeryders* the oath-taking took up most of the ceremony. It included references to (and suggested similarities with) proofs of allegiance and incorporation into four major social institutions: Holy Communion, enrolment in the army, recruitment for the local *schutten* (civil guard), and installation of new members of the local court. These inaugurations were imitated and at the same time, together with the institutions, parodied and subverted. Tellingly, the main locations for the oathtaking ceremonies during the 1750s and 1760s, when membership was soaring, were wayside chapels. One of them, the Saint Leonardus chapel, was situated on a hill of the same name, not far from the Rolduc monastery. During the repression of the bands in the early 1770s, the authorities required an additional place for the gallows; they demolished this profaned chapel and raised the new gallows on the place of the former sanctuary. These displacements and substitutions involved a twofold mimesis of attacks on bodies and provide an example of the dialogue or 'circulation' between popular culture and elite culture.[17] This brings us to the second form of collective violence: the means the authorities had at their disposal to repress banditry in the fragmented territories of the Lower Meuse.

IV

For a long time the local courts charged with the prosecution of criminals in their relatively small jurisdictions were ignorant of the real authors of the plundering of churches and farms. The magistrates believed that groups of vagrants were responsible for these crimes. All they could do in the absence of a regional police force was to enforce the *plakkaten* (decrees) against these people and insist on the vigilance of the local civic guard. In each of the three great operations against the *Bokkeryders*, local courts started their co-operation (exchanging information, handing over prisoners) only after the first members of the bands had been arrested. It is also significant that local prosecutors depended on the 'mistakes' made by those members of the band who went on haphazard and unauthorized forays or were recognized by their victims, as happened in 1741, 1750, 1770, 1773 and 1774.

As noted above, magistrates of several local courts were related by ties of kinship and marriage, which facilitated their co-operation. Yet without a regular police force and houses of correction, the courts did not have the means to repress the bands other than by theatrical violence, terror and defamation – as explicitly specified in the motive for capital sentences, 'tot afschrik en exempel' ('to inspire fear and set an example'), and in the additional stipulation that the body of the convict should be denied a Christian burial. For these reasons alone, it would be wrong to consider the hangings – between 1741 and 1778 in these territories there were more than 300 of them – only in instrumental or pragmatic terms: that is, as simple eliminations. Such an approach to collective violence from above would indeed miss the main point of criminal law under the *ancien régime*: the refusal of burial added infamy to death (cf. Linebaugh 1975; Spierenburg 1984; Rupp 1992).

In all recorded cases of hangings, the body of the condemned was left to hang in chains for birds to feed on until its total decomposition and decay. In their denial of a burial in consecrated earth and their spectacular displacement of the convict from centre (church) to periphery (veld, heath, moors), the punishments represented major cultural inversions. As extreme, public assaults on the body, they represented the ultimate outrage on a person's honour and status and on the reputation of his family and descendants as well. Thus the imagery of the violated body of convicts assumed great importance during the repression of the bands. Leaving aside the phases of arrest, detention and the rituals of judicial torture – which constituted serious infringements on a person's honour and status mediated by his physical body – we will examine briefly the ritual and symbolic aspects of the sentences and their execution.

The magical realism of the repression was most noticeable when the accused was a fugitive and was tried *in absentia*. In most cases these persons were banished, *voor eeuwig* (for ever), from the Dutch or Austrian territories, with the specification that they would be subjected to capital punishment if they returned. This written sentence was read in public and then nailed to the gallows. But we know of at least fourteen such cases (in which the accused had ignored the court's citations and remained at large) where the absent convict was hanged in effigy. An ordinary banishment did not suffice, and the convicted person – by means of an effigy, a dummy, an imitation of his body – had to be symbolically removed from the community. Like produces like, and like acts upon like (cf. Mauss 1975: 64ff; Tambiah 1985b: 64–72).

Attacks on the social identity of the convicts were also evident in three recorded cases in which the court ordered that the convicts' houses be destroyed, with the stipulation that their locations were not to be built on for a period of 100 years 'because of the horrible crimes committed by the owner and because it has served as shelter and rendezvous for thieves and *schelmen* (rogues)' (Blok 1995a: 158, 415). The attack on one's house or home – a quintessential *lieu de mémoire* – making the convict posthumously homeless, provides us with another instance of ritual cleansing, of an attempt to remove a polluted person magically from the community and from social memory as well.

The punishment directed against the house of the convict aptly illustrates the interplay between elite culture and popular culture, the dialogue between authority and subversion. Some of the operations of the bands, most notably some of the attacks on farms that were also inns, involved wilful destruction of furniture, doors, windows, closets, barrels and the like. This apparently retaliatory violence against property bears some resemblance to the more violent forms of *charivari* or 'rough music', forms of popular justice that in the German areas were called *Wüstung* or destruction and were intended to drive the residents out of the community as undesirable persons (Meuli 1975a: 457–75).

An important aspect of the collective violence inflicted on the *Bokkeryders* concerns its topography: the space of violence and death. Situated at the limits of the jurisdictions, the place of execution was a clearly demarcated location, usually an elevation or hill. The condemned had to be escorted from that other space of violence, the place of detention, usually located in the basement of one of the castles or country houses, all the way down to the outskirts of his home town. These processions were very much part of the choreography of punishment since they reinforced humiliation and disgrace. Each punishment also conveyed something of the crime that had been committed. Ordinary thieves were whipped and banished; those who had committed theft and robberies combined with violence against persons and material damage were hanged; murderers and bandit leaders were broken on the wheel; and arson and sacrilege (for example, church robberies) were punished by various forms of burning. In some cases, elements of the crime were literally reproduced in the punishment. Such re-enactments happened at the execution of some of the condemned who had blackened their faces when breaking into farms and had sworn allegiance to the Devil (cf. Foucault 1977: 43–5). As Radbruch notes in his commentary on the *Carolina* (1532): 'Wer mit dem Feuer gesündet hat, der Brandstifter, der Münzfälscher, soll durch das *Feuer* sterben' (Who has sinned with fire – the arsonist, the counterfeiter – should die by *fire*)' (1960: 10; see also Langbein 1974: 167). In short, the collective violence the authorities deployed to repress banditry revolved around terror and infamy. Hence the major elements of the punishments included the disintegration of the corpse and the denial of funeral rites.

The popular sensibilities regarding the integrity of the body and *post-mortem* care are obvious from attempts to intervene in the judicial process. We know of attempts to remove the bodily remains of kinsmen from the gallows at night and to provide for a decent burial. If discovered, such ventures were defined as theft and punished. For those who had died in detention, the authorities had, in most cases, no less dishonourable punishments in store. A sentence was passed on the corpse, which the skinner had to drag on a sledge to the gallows to be buried there or to be hanged to rot, depending on the condition of the remains. We know of a widow whose husband had died in detention without a confession and been buried under the gallows. She wrote a request to the States General in The Hague in which she asked for a revision of the dishonorable sentence, explicitly referring to the role of the skinner, and for a Christian burial for her husband. Her request was denied. Before it had passed sentence on the corpse the court had (according to a standard procedure) asked advice from a lawyer in Maastricht. This impartial legal expert had suggested that the body should be returned to the next of kin and be 'buried *de noctu*, without homage, but also without any offence against it from the department of executioner and skinner' (Blok 1995a: 168–71, 417).

The image of the decaying body is of considerable interest, and not only in the context of the repression of robber bands accused of theft and sacrilege. The decomposed, corrupt body enshrines a powerful metaphor. As Bruce Lincoln has pointed out in another but very similar context – the notorious exhumation and public display of the long-buried corpses of priests, nuns and saints in several towns and cities in Spain during the Civil War – the image of bodily decomposition provides a metaphor of moral corruption: 'Like its near-synonyms *rottenness* and *decadence*, corruption is most concretely and emphatically manifest in the state of bodily decomposition' (1985: 257). From a theological point of view, bodily corruption is a moral process as much as a natural one, for decay is the final physical result of a sinful – that is to say, corrupt – life. And what is more, the bodies of those who are purified of sin through the sacraments of the Church and the practice of a saintly life do not decay, but partake of eternity, freedom from decomposition being one of the foremost proofs of sanctity. (Lincoln 1985: 257)

V

Considering the extent to which elite culture and popular culture in the Lower Meuse formed models of and for one another, it would certainly not be an exaggeration to say that they developed in a mutually constitutive relationship. There was indeed a great deal of 'reflection' – imitation, mimicry, parody – on the part of subaltern groups, while the violence of the punishments reflected something of the scale, volume, form and meaning of the crimes, real and imagined. The massive violence that both groups inflicted upon the other (unprecedented in the history of the Dutch Republic and strangely neglected in official Dutch historiography) and its explicit magical realism cannot be understood without reference to the main features of these territories: their political fragmentation, their peripheral location and their seigneurial structure, which juxtaposed aristocratic splendour with plebeian misery. It is obvious that these conditions provided considerable space for dissident groups.

But these circumstances also prompted and shaped the repression. Confronted with massive and sustained forms of subversion, members of the ruling class, loosely tied together in a regional network of kinship and marriage, restored their domination through the theatre of law, drowning the voices of insubordination in the process. In this assertion of cultural hegemony, the courtroom, the place of detention, the street and the place of execution provided the setting for the emphasis on, and dramatization of, the distinction between the integral body, on the one hand, and the violated, dishonoured and decaying body, on the other – a distinction that served the restoration magically as a *pars pro toto*.

3

Infamous Occupations

I

Various trades and professions – some of which are now more or less respectable – have long been looked down upon, stigmatized, and proscribed, by law or by custom, in many different countries. Late medieval and early modern Germans called them *unehrliche* and *verfemte Berufe*, or dishonourable and proscribed occupations. In France they were known as *métiers vils* and *métiers illicites*, low and illicit trades. In other countries they were defined as 'floating' occupations.[1]

We are dealing with a large number of different professions, all of them involving indispensable work to which varying measures of opprobrium were attached. Not only executioners, skinners, prostitutes and beggars were considered dishonourable and treated with contempt, but also diviners, healers, barbers, bath attendants, collectors of night soil, scavengers, sweepers, town criers, jailors, tooth-pullers, linen weavers, grave-diggers, undertakers, caretakers of tombs, millers, blacksmiths, musicians, dancers, actors, jugglers, animal trainers, tanners, shepherds, pedlars and various itinerant artisans and entertainers all suffered stigmatization and social exclusion.

Contempt for these people surfaced at different times and in different parts of the world. Since low repute seems to be a common denominator of these professions, they became generally known as 'infamous' or 'dishonourable' occupations. Tellingly, the term 'infamous occupations' figures in dictionaries as a gloss on 'infamous'.[2] It does not follow, of course, that people whose professions were the object of such discrimination always accepted or agreed with it. We have reasons to believe that, in most cases, they did not.[3] But this essay explores the point of view of the host population: the people among whom these despised craftsmen lived. It poses the question: what made the majority of populations in different places and at different times stigmatize certain people who provided indispensable services, and exclude them from ordinary social life?

Some scholars recognize that the grounds for classifying such diverse occupations together are far from clear, and suggest that 'there need not be any common characteristic uniting the occupation of the butcher with that of the barber'.[4] Although, strictly speaking, barbers and butchers share important features that serve as tell-tale signs, the general point is well taken. Looking at the subject from a comparative perspective, we shall discover that infamous occupations show 'overlaps' and 'criss-crosses' rather than a fixed set of common characteristics; the problem I want then to explore concerns the 'family resemblances' of these different occupations and their remarkably large geographical distribution.[5]

We often find the same set of occupations defined as disreputable, polluting and frightful – not only in ancient Rome and medieval and early modern Europe, but also in Africa, the Middle East, the South Asian subcontinent, China and Japan. This 'universality' implies that we cannot explain the stigma of infamy branded on these professions in terms of local contexts only.

Members of these occupational groups were despised, treated with contempt and set apart from ordinary social life. Yet providing indispensable services, they were also very much part of the community that stigmatized them and excluded them from its ranks. In his fine study of marginal people of late medieval Paris, Geremek recognizes that not all of them were *inutile au monde*, or 'of no use to anyone':

> The studies of Oscar Lewis on 'the anthropology of poverty' in Latin American societies, or those of Danilo Dolci on the world of poverty in Palermo present a striking similar picture to the one which emerges from our documents for late medieval Paris. The obvious particularity of the marginal people of the Middle Ages, as compared with those studied by Lewis and Dolci, lies in the component elements which were branded by the seal of infamy, whilst remaining in close contact with the organised structures of society: the prostitutes, the lepers and the beggars. These three categories fulfilled a well-defined role in medieval society and were in some measure institutionalised. (1987: 302)

Most of the despised craftmen were indeed placed outside or at the margin of society, and many of them also lived separately, in clearly marked houses or in segregated areas and communities, usually on the outskirts of the towns and villages – if they had a fixed abode at all.

People avoided all normal contact with them. If they had access to public locations, like churches and inns, elaborate etiquette regulated these contacts. They had separate places and had to use a special door for entering and leaving these buildings. Their burial places, too, were often segregated from those of the mainstream population.

Some of the dishonourable occupational groups, like the skinners and executioners in pre-industrial German cities and the leather-workers and entertainers in different phases of Japan's history, had to be recognized by specific outfits, unusual headgear or had to wear bells to announce their arrival.[6] A Prussian decree of 1733 prescribed that skinners wear dark grey coats, with buttons of the same colour, and red, pointed hats, 'damit nicht unschuldige, ehrliche Leute aus Unwissenheit und unversehens an sie geraten' (that innocent and honourable people do not, from ignorance or by accident, get in touch with them).[7] All these prescriptions involved ritualization and thus served to regulate and formalize contact between the ordinary and the extraordinary aspects of life. The arrangements also symbolized and helped to enforce the separateness (and, unintentionally, the cohesion and solidarity) of these occupational groups. It follows that most of them were endogamous and had limited civil rights. For example, they were not allowed to bear arms and to give evidence in court.

II

One way to understand the diversity of infamous occupations and their remarkable recurrence in different cultural and historical settings is to distinguish three main aspects.

First, members of these occupational groups were often lumped together with criminals, illegitimate children, and members of subaltern ethnic and religious groups. As the thirteenth-century *Sachsenspiegel* (a 'mirror' or 'reflection' of customary law in Saxonia) phrased it: 'Prize fighters, children of prostitutes, criminals, and entertainers, they are all *rechtelös*' (deprived of civil rights).[8]

These groups often overlapped, since foreigners and outsiders have always been charged with work on which the majority look down. Jews and Gypsies specialized and sometimes held monopolies in erstwhile despised professions, like entertainment, banking, (horse-)trading and butchering. Chimney-sweeps working in western European cities mostly came from the Alps and were called 'Italians' and 'Savoyards'. In St Petersburg, chimney sweeping was in the hands of Finns. Itinerant artisans and entertainers in Pakistan belong to subaltern ethnic groups, like the Qalandar and Kanjar, who specialize, among other things, in animal training, the fabrication of toys, dancing, prostitution and begging.[9] As is well known, smiths in many African and Asian societies often belonged to distinct ethnic and endogamous groups and tended to be treated with a mixture of esteem and contempt.[10] Like iron-workers elsewhere, Cameroon smiths combine their profession with several liminal specializations, including funerary services and music, and hold pivotal roles in other rites of passage. Although they are not particularly esteemed, they do not seem to be ethnically distinct from the Kapsiki, who are dominant. But they are considered untouchable and form, as elsewhere in Africa, an endogamous occupational group.[11]

That outsiders, members of other ethnic groups, foreigners, criminals and (sometimes) former slaves or serfs often specialized in and controlled despised professions cannot, of course, explain why these occupations were considered dishonourable, for it does not answer the question of why these people were charged with these tasks in the first place (rather than with others).[12] However, we know of the degrading of otherwise neutral professions after they had come as sidelines into the hands of members of despised occupational groups.[13] The association with crime and (condemned) criminals is significant, since it draws attention to infamy, pollution and proscription. In his overview of outcasts in East Asia, Price notes:

> The outcasts of Tibet are known as the Ragyappa and number over a thousand. They live in a segregated part of the southern outskirts of the holy inner circle, known as the Lingkor, in the capital city of Lhasa. They are paid to do their required tasks of disposing of corpses and clearing the carcasses of dead animals from the streets and public places. They have special rights for begging, they may be called on to search for escaped criminals, and criminals and vagabonds are often put in their charge and are made to live in their communities. (1972: 9)[14]

Second, many of these professions were not only proscribed and despised, but also considered (ritually) unclean, as were the people practising them. It has been suggested that these conditions are closely related. Writing on ancient Rome, Richlin notes that both pimps and gladiators were *infames*, that is, 'they not only had limited civil rights but were "untouchable", each condition feeding off the other'.[15] Even if ordinary people so desired, they were by law or custom not allowed to find employment in these ventures; hence the designations 'verfemt', 'illicite', or proscribed. These professions had, therefore, quite unintentionally become monopolies in the hands of those who were barred from finding other work – which, together with other regulations imposed on them, implied restrictions of their civil rights.

We often find various infamous tasks carried out by the same group, 'practised by one and the same person'. This may be obvious given the impurity attributed to these professions. But it further attests to their affinity and may also help understand their close proximity to illegality and crime.

Third, and following from the previous qualifications, it was widely believed that members of these occupational groups had magical power. Though one would avoid ordinary contact with them for fear of pollution, several of them could, in a different context and when approached in an appropriate manner, also bring luck and prosperity, or restore health. Members of several despised occupations also worked as diviners and healers. As is well known, to encounter or touch a chimney-sweep (or, as a woman, to be kissed by him) is still today considered auspicious in several parts of Germany and Austria, where images of these craftsmen and their appurtenances also figure prominently in the iconography of New Year celebrations.[16] We are dealing with the lower-class counterparts of kings, to whom people in England and France have attributed miraculous healing powers for several centuries.[17] Like their more humble counterparts, kings were set apart from the common run of mortals, and it was their high, taboo status that made them untouchable and provided them with the healing power that has become known as the 'royal touch'.[18]

Considering these aspects of our subject, it seems over-optimistic to expect to understand the place and reputation of these professions and their representatives without recourse to the concepts of pollution, taboo, magic and ritual. Even so, ignoring an early statement of Mauss and subsequent discussions on (symbolic) classification in cultural anthropology, this is what some contemporary scholars who have occupied themselves with the issue have done.[19] A theoretical perspective that addresses and tries to understand symbolic activities is all the more expedient since we are concerned with occupations which were not only despised but also indispensable. No society could do without them. There were no 'practical reasons' for proscribing these occupations. Rather than in utilitarian terms, their outlaw and taboo status should be understood in terms of culture – in the context of dominant classification systems.

III

Recent studies of pollution and 'dirt' confirm that taboos mark the boundaries between a society's fundamental categories.[20] Taboos, as Van Gennep long ago recognized, 'are acts rather than negations of acts' (1960 [1909]: 8). Dirt is relative; it is matter 'out of place'. As a confusion of cherished categories, it implies both disorder and order: shoes on the table, food on the floor, cannibalism, incest, and so on. As Mary Douglas memorably phrased it, what is unclear is also unclean.

Both taboo and pollution behaviour focus on things and creatures which are ambiguous or anomalous in terms of accepted categories. By defining the boundaries between them, by delimiting and differentiating cultural categories, taboos help to endorse them, shape them, give them substance. This is why boundaries, margins, edges and peripheries are often populated by unusual, anomalous creatures, such as Cerberus from ancient mythology, the three-headed dog guarding the gates of the Underworld. In Christian Europe the Holy Virgin marks the boundaries between this world and the next. These examples suggest that anomalies – whether animals, humans or other creatures – can be credited with the magical means to mediate between major social categories. When harnessed in a proper ritual context, their magical power can prove beneficent.

In certain parts of nineteenth-century rural Sweden, prostitutes were believed to have the ability to evoke the children's disease rickets, for which reason they were kept away from married, pregnant women. Together with other marginal people in this peasant society, the prostitute acted as a barrier between groups. But as an agent in marking and reinforcing boundaries, she was also believed to bring luck:

> A whore was regarded as a lucky meeting for men, whereas decent women brought misfortune. When she was out on the road, she was in the male sphere. Here, men, animals of male sex or animals associated with men were considered to be fortunate meetings, whereas the opposite was the case for what belonged to the female sphere. The differences in male and female in this context may be regarded as a way of maintaining order in the cultural categories. (Frykman 1977: 222)

It seems less correct when Frykman writes that 'the whore brought luck because she was not an anomaly when she appeared alone in the public sphere' (1977: 222–3). The point is not whether or not she was an anomaly – she definitely was an anomaly in this rural society for the reasons Frykman specifies. Depending on context, the prostitute could be both inauspicious among pregnant women (associated with the home) and auspicious in the public (male) domain. These distinctions are important, but they have not always been sufficiently recognized.[21]

The literature on symbolic classifications suggests that there are various ways to deal with anomalies. They can be ignored or they can be suppressed or eradicated. But they can also be acknowledged and regarded as unclean or sacred, which means that, in order to avoid pollution and danger and harness their power, behaviour towards them has to be ritualized, or through formalized performances 'displaced' from the normal round of social activity.[22]

This is immediately relevant for a better understanding of the position of members of proscribed occupations. As mentioned earlier, they were too important – indeed indispensable – to be either ignored or suppressed. They provided salient services, in particular, but not exclusively, the removal of bodily dirt, for which reason they have, in some places, been described as specialists in impurity, as people who 'spared others the inevitable problems of dealing with pollution'.[23]

IV

It may be useful to distinguish between various forms of anomalies. Animals and humans may be considered anomalous because of their (1) morphology, (2) behaviour or practices, and (3) habitat.[24] Whether anomalies relate to just one or all three of them, we are invariably concerned with a confusion of main social categories. For example, in some societies twins are considered anomalies, because they blur major distinctions, including the boundaries between humans (characterized by single births) and animals (characterized by multiple births) or, more simply, by posing a problem of classification because two individuals appear where only one had been expected.[25] In other cases much more than morphology is involved. The celebrated pangolin, found among the Lele in Zaire, is considered an anomaly on several scores. This creature, a scaly ant-eater, occupies an intermediate position because of its morphology (a mammal with a scaly skin), its behaviour (it does not shun humans and reproduces like them) and its habitat (it lives in the forest instead of the river). Its symbolic connection with water may account for its association with fertility.[26] A similar case can be made for the stork in western Europe, which also has characteristics found in more than one category, involving both behaviour and habitat. The stork is a wild creature, but shares several features with human beings, like walking on two legs, having a family and a fixed abode to which it returns every spring with the same partner. What makes this bird even more anomalous, and hence an appropriate mediator and bringer of luck, is its close proximity to the human domestic domain, for it builds its nest on or near the roof or chimney of a human dwelling – only one of many possible houses, which underscores the stork's luck-bringing power. The stork lives both on land and near the water (preferably in the betwixt-and-between area of marshes or 'wet lands'), catching fish and frogs. Like humans, storks are monogamous and produce only one or two offspring at a time. No wonder, then, that these birds have long been objects of ritualization to harness their magical power. They were and still are widely regarded as luck-bringers (fertility) in western and central Europe.

What the pangolin and the stork have in common and may explain their being luck-bringers, is that they are wild creatures, that their encounters and visitations are rare enough (that is, depending on 'chance', 'fortuity') to invite ritualization, and that they share important features with humans, in particular features related to reproduction: domesticity, fixed abode, monogamy, and single births.

The ritual attitudes toward the chimney-sweep and the prostitute follow a similar pattern and result from similar categorizations. An encounter with a chimney-sweep on the public road is regarded as particularly auspicious for women, and even more so if they are brides (who are also liminal figures), especially if it is the first encounter in the morning (emphasis on rarity/chance). To see him, to touch his coat, soot, and so on, to be kissed by him – all these cultural practices present an ascending progression of auspiciousness.

But why the emphasis on women? The chimney-sweep is a symbolic mediator since his work makes him cross various boundaries. He is a cleaner and removes soot (dirt) from the chimney (mediating between inside and outside). Moreover, the chimney-sweep is itinerant, coming in the fall and leaving in the spring. He also crosses back and forth between public and private domains, coming into the house and working on its most central and most feminine location: the hearth, where he cleans the chimney.[27] The presence of a strange man in the domestic domain and the rarity of his visits match the chance encounter in public between him and a woman (who belongs to the home). A similar cultural logic works for males in what were regarded as auspicious encounters with a prostitute (in rural Sweden), since these meetings were also predicated on rarity, proximity, affinity, strong differentiation of gender, and analogous polarization of public and private domains. There are, then, family resemblances between chimney-sweeps and prostitutes, each case illuminating the other.

V

All reported cases of infamous occupations involve a confusion of dominant social categories. Perceived as potentially dangerous, all contacts with them had to be ritualized. A large group of these professions was formed by *healers* and *cleaners*, whose work centred on disposing of and removing bodily dirt, specifically that of humans, but also that of animals. This organic material, which includes corpses and virtually all (used) bodily products, is universally considered polluting.[28] Referring to Louis Dumont's famous study, Mary Douglas indulges in a plausible generalization by observing that 'wherever the organic erupts into the social, there is impurity; birth, death, sex, eating and defecation incur impurity and so are hedged with rituals' (1975: 214). But these statements are also problematic, for they ignore history and leave us with the question of the *variation* of notions of dirt and *changing* controls over bodily functions.[29]

For a long time, healing and cleaning were closely associated, since healing consisted mainly in cleaning, as in the removal of bodily products, including blood, urine, and impurities from festering wounds and sores. In the pre-industrial world this work was in the hands of various practitioners, 'empirics', who remained separated from medical specialists trained at universities. The latter restricted themselves to theoretical work and looked down on medical practice. Sjoberg, in his book on pre-industrial cities, writes:

> One kind of medicine, that practised by the priests or other literati, has taken the high road; the other has been plied by the generally illiterate diviners, herbalists, midwives, bonesetters, and 'surgeons', many of the last doubling as barbers, who engage in blood-letting, cupping, pulling teeth, and the like. These lower-class and outcast practitioners lack a standardized body of knowledge and a scholarly orientation. Contrariwise, the literate medical men evince these latter but eschew dissection, surgery – anything that involves contact with 'blood and guts', a source of ritual or physical 'defilement' . . . (1960: 313)[30]

Bodily waste also included parts of the human body that had been pulled out, like teeth, or cut off, like hair, nails, foreskin, and other protruding parts and limbs. The occupational category that had specialized in this field included barbers, bath attendants, quacks, surgeons, midwives, cuppers, tooth-pullers, grave-diggers, gelders, skinners, executioners, shepherds, prostitutes, and sometimes also butchers (of all animals or only of 'taboo' animals, like horses), tanners, and other leather-workers, like saddlers and shoemakers.[31]

Skinners were charged with cleaning, for they had to remove the carcasses of dead animals from the streets and other public places. They also acted as assistants to the executioner in the sessions of judicial torture and in the work on the scaffold. Skinners also removed the remains of convicts who had died in detention. The bodies had to be transported from the prison to the gallows, where they were disposed of in some fashion (burial or hanging, according to the sentence, which in turn depended on the condition of the corpse).[32]

The skinning trade dovetailed with that of executioners and shepherds in so far as their work involved the removal of dead bodies of humans or animals. Moreover, members of all three occupational groups were also sought after for medicine and medical treatment, mostly but not exclusively of a magical nature. Because of his anatomical knowledge, the executioner could set bones but he also had a reputation for healing people for whom ordinary physicians did not have any cure. In the German-speaking territories, for example, epileptics would ask him for the blood of executed persons and women would turn to him for advice when faced with impotent husbands.[33] The reasons why the executioner was avoided were, therefore, the same as those for which people approached him for medical treatment. Because of his work, he had access to bodily products and thus disposed of the means to which magical power was attributed. Apart from blood, he made much of a finger or thumb that had been cut off from the bodies of executed convicts. The executioner has been rightly recognized as a magician, and the ritual avoidance regarding him is also attested by the many different names by which his profession was known.[34] In some areas, executioners were also charged with the supervision of brothels and the collection and removal of urban refuse.[35] These sidelines should perhaps not surprise us, for they link up with eruptions of the organic and thus contain the metaphorical material to represent death. In discussing images of prostitution in nineteenth-century France, Alain Corbin has argued that they converged on bad smells, putrefaction, corpses, syphilis ('the only malady one dare not deny the power of contagion'), sewers and refuse dumps.[36] The etymology of the word 'brothel' – from the Anglo-Saxon verb *brothan*, to waste away, go to ruin – likewise suggests a close association between the images of prostitution and death.

Another representation of prostitution in nineteenth-century France discussed by Corbin is also of immediate interest to us, since it 'integrates the prostitute with that chain of resigned female bodies, originating in the lower classes and bound to the instinctive physical needs of upper-class males – an image that, today, has started to come undone' (1986a: 212–13). We should think here of the 'submissive bodies' of the nurse, the nursery maid, the servant with two – different – faces ('whose body serves as an object of obsession in the master's house'), and the old female attendant, who as nurse and layer-out concludes this series of women whose bodies serve the upper class ('the bourgeois body') and into which the prostitute fitted perfectly. 'Entrusted with all that is organic, the management of the body's needs', as Corbin phrases it, all these women (to whom one might add the wet nurse and the midwife) came close to what has earlier been called 'specialists in impurity', who spared others the inevitable problems of dealing with and removing bodily dirt: that is, pollution.[37]

VI

These examples suggest in what sense members in the healing and cleaning professions were considered anomalous. It is because of their practices, their work. They were charged with the removal of quintessential matter out of place: bodily dirt, involving corpses, bodily exudations (excrements, urine, mucus, blood, milk, spittle, sperm, nails, hairs, etc.), and bodily parts, like hands, fingers, heads, and other limbs and parts that have been cut off – either in sessions of healing or at the occasion of public executions. It is important to note that we are concerned not just with dirt, or the handling of dirt, but with the *removal* of dirt from public and other social spaces where its components were considered to be 'out of place' as powerful synecdoches of human decay and death.

What can one say in this respect about morphology and habitat? Only the latter seems to matter, since most members of these occupations did not differ physiologically from other humans, at least if we disregard the significance attached to differences in habitus because of ethnic origins, physical deformations and attributions of animality.[38] In some cases, members of infamous occupations have been represented as less than human, as animals, like the Eta in Japan, who have been referred to with the number four, meaning 'four legs' (of an animal), as in raising four fingers to them in derision.[39]

But habitat, or social space, is a most important criterion, since the members of many of these occupational groups lived separately from ordinary people, at the margins, peripheries, outskirts or altogether outside the towns and villages in which they worked. In his remarks on the magical qualities of members of certain occupations (doctors, barbers, blacksmiths, shepherds, actors and grave-diggers), Mauss unfolds a compelling perspective: 'It is their profession which places these people apart from the common run of mortals, and it is this separateness which endows them with magical power' (1975 [1903]: 29). This view prefigures the essays of Mary Douglas on pollution with its bottom line that dirt is matter out of place.[40] Still more important, Mauss's perspective suggests an intimate connection between the protagonists of proscribed occupations and the world of the dead.

The habitat of these occupational groups straddles main categories of social space (inside/outside, town/countryside). The landlocked German home towns, where people made so much of *Ehre* (honour), were turned inwards in an almost obsessive fashion. In defining them, Walker begins by observing that 'each lived apart from the others' (1971: 1). At a time when peace and security were restricted to towns protected and bounded by formidable walls, while urban space still included substantial rural sectors,[41] these sets of differences were homologous to those of order and chaos, culture and nature, life and death.

It is perhaps no coincidence that the notion of *Unehrlichkeit* (dishonour) developed with the revival of urban life in these landlocked

German towns and cities in the late Middle Ages, and was considerably less pronounced, if not entirely absent, in the commercial, outward-turned coastal towns of northern Germany and the Low Countries. The former have been appropriately called 'home towns', each living apart from the other. We are dealing with a code of honour originating in an area enclosed by city walls, which already suggests against whom one sought to defend oneself. As a minority, the free burghers of the towns lived in pacified enclaves, surrounded by still largely insecure rural areas, where the majority of the population had lived for centuries. The *Bürger* were organized into guilds or corporations, which provided them with their 'master status'.[42] Everything concerning the countryside – the people living there, the *fahrende Leute*, or travelling folk, the animals and the wilderness – posed a constant threat to the settled townsmen and frightened them. Hence the importance of city walls, about which Pirenne wrote in his book on the revival of commerce and urban life:

> The most pressing was the need for defence. The merchants and their merchandise were, indeed, such a tempting prey that it was essential to protect them from pillage by a strong wall. The construction of ramparts was thus the first public work undertaken by the towns and one which, down to the end of the Middle Ages, was their heaviest financial burden.[43]

This polarized structure provided the context for the displacement of craftsmen believed to be dishonourable, and greatly helped to reinforce their stigmatization and social segregation. Paradoxically, as Mauss recognized, mainstream life did much to create the conditions of anomaly, by drawing boundaries, by displacing these occupational groups and separating them from itself. Something of the betwixt-and-between habitat of some of these professions is still maintained in contemporary terminology, in words like *bordello*, *bordeel*, and so on, which derive etymologically from *bord*, border, margin. In the city of Amsterdam, for example, the red-light district is identified with and still mainly concentrated in and around the eponymous *wallen*, the streets where houses were built in or near the former city walls.[44]

VII
Anomalies in terms of social space bring us to a second large category of infamous trades: the *itinerant* or *peripatetic* groups, members of 'floating' and 'transient' occupations, people who, because of their craft, trade or work, had to travel. For entertainers in early modern Europe it was, in the words of Peter Burke, 'easier to change their audience than their repertoire, and to change their audience they had to travel from town to

town, from fair to fair, stopping at such villages as might be on the way'
(1978: 97). Similar reasons existed for several categories of nomadic
artisans in other parts of the world, including the Middle East, the
South Asian subcontinent and Japan.[45]

In various episodes of Japan's history, two main categories of despised
and untouchable occupational groups have been distinguished: the Eta
(later called 'Burakumin') and the Hinin. The former were more sedentarized, and they specialized in butchering, skinning, tanning and leather-
work. They also worked as cormorant fishermen, falconers, undertakers,
caretakers of tombs and executioners, and were charged with the trade
in night-soil fertilizer. The association of their work with death and the
border zone between life and death is obvious. The Hinin were more
mobile and worked as itinerant artisans and entertainers, moving back
and forth between the villages at regular times. Their ranks included
diviners, healers, beggars, prostitutes, various animal trainers, jugglers,
acrobats, and shooting-gallery keepers.[46]
   Although there were not always hard and fast demarcation lines
between the Eta and Hinin, and the latter were not completely closed off
from the ranks of the majority population, the distinction between the
two categories is instructive. On the one hand, there are the specialists
in (organic) impurity – who, in (Buddhist) Japanese society, also included
the occupations dealing with animals and their products, most notably
meat, leather and fur. On the other hand, we have the peripatetic artisans and entertainers, who, apart from prostitutes and healers, were not
professionally involved in the handling or removal of bodily dirt. The
question we have to address, then, is why these itinerant occupational
groups, in Japan as much as elsewhere, were lumped together with
people charged with the removal of bodily refuse.

VIII
The answer to this question must be sought both in their habitat and
their practices – that is, the nature of their work. Moving around in predominantly agrarian societies without an obvious permanent residence,
members of these 'floating' professions blurred distinctions between
animal and human forms. By travelling from one city to the next, they
confounded, and thus defied, major spatial categories. Moving back and
forth between these pacified enclaves, they had to cross large tracts of
wilderness. It has been argued that, until the late eighteenth century, very
few people travelled on the European continent. Apart from the ubiqui-
tous traders, there were two main social groups on the road. Next to the
privileged mobility of members of the dominant classes and their agents,
one finds the deprivileged, who, for whatever reasons, could or would

not stay home.[47] The latter included members of itinerant professions, but also soldiers, beggars, pilgrims, scholars, students and outlaws. One considered them with mistrust, an attitude that had its roots in the predominantly agrarian, small-scale character of these societies. People without a clearly defined relationship to the land, because they lacked property and a permanent residence (what the Germans call *Heimat*), raised suspicion, partly because their behaviour could not be monitored and controlled, and partly because they could not be held accountable in cases where they incurred debts, as they were elusive and did not have any property that could be claimed or seized. In this sense, too, they were anomalous. Locally engaged and, however briefly and marginally, included in local social life during high days, their itinerancy put them at odds with the local networks of reciprocity predicated on links of kinship, marriage and neighbourhood. In fact, they accepted money for their services, which was, by itself, perceived as a major infraction and inversion, because it ignored social relationships built on reciprocity. Moreover, not having a fixed abode (and, one may add, not having any property) came close to be defined as a crime in several parts of early modern Europe.[48]

The association with crime is important. Loss of residence was implied in banishment, the most common punishment for first offenders in societies that could not afford prisons.[49] This may help to explain why members of itinerant occupational groups were often associated with criminals. Both lacked a permanent residence, which, in cities and rural towns, provided the basis of the main focus for a person's identity and legal status. Even more than their sedentarized counterparts, members of itinerant groups were 'out of place'. More than just failing to fit the categories of the settled population, they often flouted, mocked and subverted them.

This was especially true for the entertainers, a heterogeneous group including musicians, singers, actors, magicians, acrobats, and animal trainers. In Europe generally known as *jongleurs* and *Spielleute* (a term also used to denote musicians), they were socially and morally rejected, since they took 'goods above honour' by accepting money for their playing (*Gut für Ehre nehmen*). Entertainers were not eligible for military service, not permitted to take an oath, they could not be witnesses nor claim idemnification, and they were also denied the right to carry arms.[50] In some areas they were lumped together with prostitutes for their alleged indulgence in presenting false identities and for 'selling their bodies for the lowest price'.[51] In other contexts, entertainers have even been lumped together with the dead: 'Spilleut . . . sind nicht Leut wie andere Menschen, denn sie nur ein Schein der Menschheit haben, und fast den Todten zu vergleichen sind' (Entertainers are not like other people, since they only have the appearance of humanity, and virtually resemble the dead).[52] The explicit symbolic equivalence with death is significant, since infamy represents social death – the loss of one's identity as a respectable (honourable) member of the community.[53]

Yet in spite of such strong condemnations, entertainers were indispensable and formed an integral part of medieval and early modern life. Tellingly, they were especially important at times of transition. With their instrumental music, song, dance, story-telling, acting and clowning, they assisted in the rites of passage that marked – and helped bring about – the main transitions in the life of the community as well as that of each individual member. In the words of Walter Salmen: 'The total population could be counted as their audience, for they were a part of festivals as well as the daily routines from birth to death' (1983: 21). But Salmen also recognizes that the itinerant musician was a homeless and independent individual who, through a 'mimetic taboo', removed himself as far as possible from social pressure:

> Although the musician is economically dependent on the ruling society, he is nevertheless not completely subservient; he often comments upon society or abandons it according to his whim. To be a *Spielmann* meant to lead a restless existence. Such a natural, uncontrollable 'Mimesis' was felt to represent an offensive relapse into a disorderly, heathen-like existence.[54]

In many respects, then, itinerant entertainers turned dominant classifications upside down – which is what generally happens when boundaries are ritually marked and crossed.[55] They took money (goods) for honour, substituted work for entertainment, reversed production and non-production, replaced exploitation of natural resources with exploitation of human resources, inverted self and other, animal and human. In sum, entertainers, however briefly, substituted 'play' for 'ordinary' life, subverting dominant structures and convictions during what has been aptly called the *intermezzi* and interludes in everyday life, which at the same time remind us of the role of entertainers as agents in marking boundaries.[56]

The itinerants' deployment of human rather than natural resources has been analysed in masterly fashion by Joseph Berland in his work on the peripatetic Qalandar and Kanjar, with whom he lived and travelled thousands of miles in North-West Pakistan in the 1970s. Through their extraordinary social skills and their 'structural flexibility' and 'social fluidity', these nomadic artisans and entertainers relied exclusively on human social resources. Unlike sedentary agriculturalists and pastoral nomads, who exploit natural resources, these 'other nomads' are not food producers. Berland writes:

Peripatetic groups, sparsely scattered through larger socioeconomic systems, offer a wide range of services and products which are frequently socially and economically inappropriate in more sedentary communities. In Pakistan, a single small town or village may not be able to support a full-time metalsmith or a group of entertainers, whereas a network of these sedentary communities can support such specialized activities. These networks of human production and personal needs, such as entertainment, I have called the *peripatetic niche*. (1982: 57)

The Qalandar and Kanjar, like itinerant entertainers elsewhere, also upset prevailing notions of ('productive') work by emphasizing social skills, exploiting human resources and turning entertainment into work; by their professional impersonations they confound the distinction between self and other, male and female. Implied in their social flexibility and fluidity are various forms of gender inversion. Men and women switch roles as men take care of infants at home, while women work outside as beggars, dancers, musicians and professional prostitutes. Sometimes as pimps and procurers for their wives, these peripatetics indulge in the symbolic reversal of fundamental social categories.[57] As the very embodiment of these inversions, they too mark and fortify cultural boundaries.

Following Durkheim, it may be argued that members of infamous occupations, like other outsiders, marginals and 'inverted beings', provide negative role models and thus help in the definition, construction and reinforcement of 'self' versus 'other', social order versus chaos. We have already referred to the prostitute in nineteenth-century rural Sweden who acted as a catalyst in marking differences – between inside and outside, society and chaos, health and illness, men and women, and, in particular, between male and female domains. A study of clerics and entertainers in medieval France shows the working of a similar logic. In their writings, clerics insisted on the most negative representation of the entertainers: as *ministri Satanae*, servants of the Devil, they were in every respect the opposite of the man of the church. Without mentioning him always, the *jongleur* served as a code of an elaborate system of differences:

Sans être toujours nommé, le jongleur est le terme permanent d'une comparaison implicite sur laquelle s'élabore la réglementation minutieuse jusqu'à l'obsession de la vie des clercs. Plus il est turpis, obscène, diabolique, plus le clerc, en contrepoint, s'affirme digne, honnête, saint.[58]

(Without always being mentioned, the juggler is the permanent term of implicit comparison on which one elaborates the detailed regulation of the life of the cleric, in an almost obsessive way. The more shameful, obscene and diabolical he is, the more the cleric, in contrast, shows himself to be dignified, honest and saintly.)

The image of the entertainer as *turpis histrio*, infamous actor, was somewhat attenuated with the appearance of the beggar orders. In his role as Dominican or Franciscan preacher, the man of the church had himself become a man of the road, sharing time and space with entertainers and other itinerants. The *jongleur* was gradually accepted as a man who (also) worked to make a living. But his earnings, although perhaps no longer considered illicit, remained, like that of the prostitute, *turpe lucrum*, infamous profit.[59]

In brief, apart from the more direct services they rendered, entertainers were indispensable in the symbolic construction of rural and urban life. Their visits to the towns and villages were often structured by seasonal fairs and festivals as well as by weddings and other major transitions in the individual lives of people and the annual cycle of their community.[60] Indispensable in these liminal stages in the lives of both the individual and the community as a whole, the peripatetic became associated with symbolic death and the other world.

Writing about itinerant occupational groups in Japanese history, Ohnuki has pointed out that these travelling entertainers, artisans, healers, diviners and priests – as stranger-outsiders – served as cultural brokers,

> providing entertainment and thereby breaking the monotonous cycle of farming life. Diviners, healers, and itinerant priests were in charge of the fate of the people; they cured illnesses and became mediators between humans and deities. While they had the power to act on behalf of the agrarian population, they could also turn off that power; by doing so, they could bring calamities upon the population. (1984: 288–9)

A mediating role of entertainers has also been recorded for medieval and early modern Europe. Their mobility, writes Salmen, increased

> the musicians' sphere of influence, something the performer with a fixed position did not enjoy. Thus the itinerant musician was the journalist of his day, the international transmitter of styles, melodies, standards, and values. . . . [They] were often used as messengers and even as spies during wars. In tight situations, musicians were often successful mediators between warring parties. (1983: 22, 24)

IX

Itinerant occupational groups included several professions which dealt with the body and its products, both human bodies and those of animals.

Among them we find the gelder or animal castrator, who also sometimes specialized in sterilizing sows. As Claudine Fabre-Vassas has pointed out in her work on the *châtreur* in France, the castration of pigs is a decisive action, since it makes possible their domestication: that is, the acceptance of these animals in the house, in order to raise and fatten them (1983: 5). The *châtreur* was thus instrumental in the process of domestication, which involves his mediation in the transition of animals from outside to inside (*ordre domestique*) – another permutation of the transition from nature to culture. To mark his unusual status, he was dressed in red, *la veste rouge, des bas rouges*.[61] He announced his arrival, which was in step with seasonal rhythms, by playing on a Pan flute – thus appropriately setting the stage for an unusual performance. The man performed his operation on the village square near the fountain, where he was admired by women and children for his 'dexterity and secret art to dominate the sex of the most unseizable animal'. Women regarded the *châtreur* as a healer-magician, because of his anatomical knowledge of female animals and his disposal of the ovaries of the sows on which he had operated and which were believed to have magical power and stimulate fertility.[62]

We know less about his social reputation in the villages he visited along his fixed and regular itineraries, which could reach all the way down to Andalusia. The craft passed from father to son and produced, in some areas, a certain wealth and a respectable social position. Like the chimney-sweeps, *châtreurs* came from the higher valleys of mountainous zones, including the Pyrenees and the Cevennes, and in some areas they visited, they were identified with their homeland, for instance, 'Béarnais' meaning 'châtreur'.[63] That his place of origin, his homeland, was known, may have made the *châtreur* less anomalous, less out of place, and may help account for what seems to have been the favourable attitudes of his hosts. In this respect, too, he resembled the other itinerant cleaner of domestic space – the chimney-sweep.[64]

The crossing and confounding of public and private space is also characteristic of the overlapping professions of barbers and musicians in eastern Afghanistan, where the (pejorative) term *dalak* refers to bath attendants, barbers, musicians, actors, dancers, prostitutes, procurers and actors.[65] The despised Dalak are considered an endogamous occupational group of outsiders. Managing most of the infamous crafts – barbers shave heads and whiskers, pull teeth, practise phlebotomy, carry out little operations, make a variety of organic medicines for curing diseases, act as professional circumcisers and also work as veterinarians, while their women practise blood-letting – they have their own segregated quarters and bury their dead outside the village cemetery walls. Although all barber groups do not necessarily include musicians and all musician groups do not necessarily include barbers, the *sorna* and *dohl* players are barbers themselves or related to them. The exclusion of these musicians may also be due to the alleged polluting quality of their instruments: 'the double reed of the *sorna* is placed entirely within the mouth of the player; thus, the reed, and by extension, the whole instrument is contaminated by the player's own spittle' (Sakata 1983: 79).

The Dalak share their low social position with the barbers in Swat, northern Pakistan, as described by Barth in his essay on social stratification.[66] Together with two other groups, including musicians, dancers, prostitutes, and thong and sieve-makers, the barbers occupy the lowest stratum of society, actually polluted castes. According to Barth, the reason for their low social status is related to the nature of the services they render. All rites of passage in Swat – birth, circumcision, betrothal, marriage and death – are marked by large-scale public celebrations. In performing them, people form neighbourhood associations, each of which is administered by a barber, who, in return for yearly payments and gifts, holds service contracts with each individual household in the association. These services include haircutting (of men by the barber, of women by his wife) and shaving. But barbers are also charged with the organization of celebrations and the announcement of the event to appropriate outsiders. Barth concludes: 'The "low", "taboo" status of the barber stems from this special role. Because it involves intimate contact with the domestic life of each family, in breach of the usual barriers of prudery and seclusion, the barber's status needs to be clearly segregated from that of other persons in the community' (1960: 123–4).

Regarding the Dalak musicians in Afghanistan, Sakata emphasizes that their services parallel those of the barbers in Swat, and suggests another reason why *sorna* and *dohl* players are so closely associated with them: 'the announcement of important events to outsiders is made by the playing of [these instruments], thus breaching the same barriers of privacy that the professions themselves breach' (1983: 81). But there is more to playing music that is of interest here. Art historians point out that the presence of musical instruments on early modern European still-life paintings, because of the transience of their sound – the fading of notes – are well-known *vanitas* symbols, which refer to the transience of human life.[67]

X

The infamy of millers is also related to habitat. Their bad reputation in some parts of Europe has often been noted, and their greed, dishonesty and drunkenness were almost proverbial, but their *Unehrlichkeit* still remains enigmatic.[68]

In some of the German territories millers were, up to the seventeenth century, charged with assistance at public executions by furnishing the gallows ladder, which must have reflected and reinforced their association with crime and criminals.[69] In his discussion of the stereotypes of millers in western Europe at Chaucer's time, Jones suggests that the infamy of millers may have been related to their location. He notes that 'millers were too scattered to form guilds, they could not protect their rights or their reputations as well as the better organized professions' (1955: 9). Moreover, millers were also outsiders of sorts, because their mills were not only scattered, but also built in isolated places, near streams and rivers, usually at some distance from villages and towns. The life of the miller and his family could, therefore, not be monitored and scrutinized as easily as those of people who lived in the villages and towns. In his study of a sixteenth-century miller in Friuli, Italy, Ginzburg points at the connection between openness to unorthodox ideas and the location of mills: 'Their working conditions made millers – like innkeepers, tavern keepers, and itinerant artisans – an occupational group especially receptive to new ideas and inclined to propagate them. Moreover, mills, generally located on the peripheries of settled areas and far from prying eyes, were well suited to shelter clandestine gatherings' (1980: 120). Because of their isolated location, millers were believed to be licentious and lawless. As Danckert phrases it: 'In popular imagination, lonely located mills were preferably chosen as the scenes for acts of robbery and murder. . . . The lonely mill is a beloved stage for peppered pornographic tales' (1963: 129, 131). He quotes an eighteenth-century popular song in which mills and adultery form narrowly related themes, as the first stanza testifies:

> Ich weiss mir eine Müllerin,
> Ein wunderschönes Weib,
> Wollt Gott ich sollt (bei) ihr mahlen,
> Mein Körnlein zu ihr tragen,
> Das wär der Wille mein.

> (I know a miller's wife
> A very beautiful woman,
> God grant I shall grind (with) her,
> To carry my seed to her,
> This is what I want.)

These representations of what happened in and around mills in the German territories, along with the stereotypes of millers already current at the time when the *Canterbury Tales* were composed, must have reinforced the idea of assigning them (and the linen weavers who had in large numbers come from the countryside to the towns in the fifteenth century) services associated with the preparation of the gallows. Whereas the linen weavers had to assist in the building of the scaffold, the millers had, as mentioned above, to provide the ladder. In some areas the stigmatization of millers persisted into the nineteenth century.[70] It seems that we must understand their bad reputation in terms of habitat (isolated location) and presumed practices (promiscuity, adultery, theft). They were themselves 'out of place' and involved with matter out of place. A recent study of mills and millers in Lozère, France, ascribes the bad reputation of millers to their isolated location, which kept them outside the local network of reciprocity, and open to suspicion of theft: '*Meunier voleur, meunier sorcier, l'habitant du moulin porte les stigmates d'une profession*' (Miller thief, miller witch, the occupant of the mill bears the stigmas of a profession).[71]

But millers did not have a bad reputation everywhere. The stereotypes mentioned before cannot, for example, be attested for the Dutch Republic. This may be due to the different location of mills and perhaps also to the urbanization and commercialization of these areas. In the Low Countries (where windmills prevailed and served many purposes), millers usually had their mills in or near towns: that is, near the centres of consumption, rather than scattered in the countryside. This spatial arrangement of mills in the vicinity of population centres must have made millers more 'sociable' and enabled them to form guilds or corporations – which may help to explain why millers in the Low Countries did not seem to have suffered from social opprobrium.[72] In Sicily's western interior, water mills were located along streams near the centres of production, the large estates or *latifondi*, and far away from the centres of habitation, the so-called agro-towns. But these isolated country mills never served as a permanent residence for families. Like the big farmhouse or *masseria*, mills were essentially work places: both the miller and his clientele, the *contadini*, who brought their grain on mules to the mills, had their permanent residence in the agro-town.[73]

Social isolation may also have played a part in the ambivalence towards iron-workers in several African and Asian societies. Unlike forging, which is a public event, smelting usually takes place outside built-up areas – hence the analogy between smelting and parturition: 'both take place in private or in the seclusion of the bush'.[74] In various parts of Africa smelters performed all the smelting operations entirely naked. As Eugenia Herbert explains the implications: 'Nakedness, special clothing of barkcloth, or animal skin may link the smelter more closely with nature, corresponding to his isolation in the bush during smelting and his mediating role between the wild and the civilized' (1993: 93–4,

160). Iron-workers are often organized in endogamous occupational groups, a fact that underwrites their displacement, their distance from the rest of the population. Significantly, they combine iron-working – itself a quintessentially 'transformative' craft – with other liminal professions, most notably everything that has to do with birth, initiation (circumcision), death, burial, healing and entertainment. Both valued and damned, both civilized heroes and outcasts, Mande blacksmiths are deeply involved in the articulation of social and cultural space: their ambiguous position predisposes them to numerous mediating roles (McNaughton 1988: 40). The Dom in northern India and Pakistan are known as iron-workers, but they also figure as musicians, bards, sweepers, grave-diggers, and tanners.[75] Despised and feared, and considered unclean, smiths in East Africa were ritually close to sacred kings, whom they served as bodyguards, messengers and executioners.[76] The symbolic equivalence between smiths (executioners) and kings makes sense since the mastery of fire was associated with both: 'fire was often identified with the force of life itself and with prosperity'. Indeed, the hammer/anvil constituted a quintessential emblem of royal power throughout Central Africa.[77] We notice that all three figures – smith, executioner and king – were set apart from ordinary mortal beings and straddled the boundaries between life and death, this world and the next.

If, as Burkert suggests, there are 'basic similarities in all forms of human culture, inasmuch as everywhere people eat drink, and defecate, work and sleep, enjoy sex and procreate, get sick and die',[78] the so-called infamous occupations are definitely a case in point. Closely tied up with the rituals that mark the passages of an individual through the life-cycle, they are set in the interplay of biology and culture, which has been called 'the subtext of all rites of passage'.[79] The inevitable facts of human experience – birth, copulation and death – create the space for ritual specialists who stand guard over these transitions and help bring them about. Like these ceremonies, infamous occupations are culturally and historically bounded but cannot be explained in isolation, in purely local terms. To paraphrase Van Gennep, beneath a multiplicity of forms, either consciously expressed or merely implied, a typical pattern always recurs: the pattern of the infamous occupations whose practitioners mediate major transitions.

What emerges from the study of these professions is a picture of a paradoxical craft: liminal and out of place, defiling and credited with magical power, marginalized and yet part of the community, despised and indispensable. About such 'universals' Burkert notes that they 'always appear integrated into specific cultures and take various shapes accordingly, but their unmistakable similarity makes them a general class transcending single cultural systems'.[80]

XI

In six different historical and geographical contexts – ancient Rome, medieval and early modern Europe, the Middle East, African societies, the South Asian subcontinent, and various episodes of Japanese history – we find largely the same set of occupations stigmatized and proscribed, and the members of these professions considered 'untouchable' and hence ritually segregated from the majority population. As Mauss has suggested, the spacial segregation of these professional groups was of fundamental importance in understanding their low, taboo status and the magical power attributed to several of them. But more was involved in the displacement of these craftsmen. As we have seen, they also set themselves apart from the major social categories of mainstream life, the boundaries of which they could then cross and break as often as bridge and mediate. Members of these occupational groups belonged to the community and yet were excluded from it.

Reviewing briefly the *tableau de la troupe* and the argument followed so far, there are, first, the specialists in impurity who moved bodily dirt from public domains to enclosed spaces, pushing 'organic eruptions' and matter 'out of place', including various bodily functions, '*hinter Kulissen*', or behind the scenes, as Norbert Elias has summed up the drift of these operations in the context of the civilizing process that transformed western European societies between about 1200 and 1800. The nature of the material they dealt with and removed (bodily waste, organic offal and decay) directly evoked images of death. Second, we have the peripatetic entertainers and artisans, whose ambiguity resided in their itinerancy – in their being 'out of place', and in their 'play', which involved the inversion of numerous categories. Entertainers were closely associated with all main rites of passage, both calendrical rites and life-crisis rites. Their liminal stages, as Van Gennep demonstrated long ago, represent symbolic death and involve symbolic funerals. In one way or another, members of the proscribed occupations maintained through their work a relationship with death, either *de facto* like the skinner, the executioner and the grave-digger, or symbolically like the entertainers: both groups were the main choreographers in the iconography of all major transitions in the lives of people and their communities. The similarities or 'family resemblances' we have been looking for between members of infamous occupations reside, then, in their association, directly or symbolically, with transitions – of which death in particular stands out.

It follows that one would have expected an attenuation of their infamy and pollution, and an improvement of their social status, when members of these occupations gave up their itinerancy, sedentarized, organized themselves into corporations, and moved their work from public domains to more enclosed settings. Along with the presumed disenchantment of the world and the impact of the civilizing process, this is indeed what happened with several erstwhile despised professions in early modern Europe. Consider, for example, the musicians. Their rehabilitation took a long time, but their way to respectability is instructive. A growing number of them became sedentary and put themselves under the patronage of secular lords and the church, changing their repertoire and restricting it to more 'civilized' genres, like the *chansons de geste* and the *vies de saints*. Among them we find famous minstrels and troubadours, who made their reputations as poets, story-tellers, *Minnesänger*, or musicians at the courts. Others organized themselves into guilds and fraternities, abandoning their itinerant life and finding protection and legitimation from the church and other powerful patrons.[81]

Apart from individual and social efforts in terms of organization, education and professionalization (which, together with the withdrawal of their practices from public domains to more enclosed spaces, hospitals in particular, strongly favoured the medical professions),[82] more impersonal forces also worked in favour of the *infames* – if history's invisible hand did not simply remove them, render them obsolete or redundant.[83] In many areas of Europe, these inward-looking communities became part of larger-scale and more differentiated social formations. Through this process of developing interdependencies they lost much of their local colour and their mechanical solidarity. Membership of such home towns no longer provided an exclusive focus for identification, while mobility had lost its uncommon quality. Moreover, with the pacification of the countryside in the nineteenth century, specific urban codes of honour, predicated on strong contrasts between town and country, lost their significance. As main symbols of this transformation, town walls disappeared and the open countryside, wild scenery, 'nature', rather than inspiring fear and confusion, became an object of idealization, even 'cultivation', for a growing number of people.[84] This was particularly the case in western Europe, where lonely figures, who spent part of the year in a now peaceful countryside – like the Austrian *Sennerin*, who herded cattle and made cheese on the *Alm* during the summer – could even become the focus of honour, pride and veneration.[85]

But in the southern reaches of Europe, the countryside remained for many people what it had been for centuries for virtually everyone on the continent: insecure, wild, uninviting. We are dealing with conceptions as well as realities. Until far into the nineteenth century, urban Frenchmen regarded large parts of their countryside and its population as lacking in civilization, and did not hesitate to define them as 'poor, backward, ignorant, savage, barbarous, wild, living like beasts with their beasts'.[86] Cities in Italy and Spain are still perceived as exclusive centres of *civiltà* and *cultura*. One looks down on peasants and pastoralists for their alleged lack of 'civility', because of their work and life on the land and their proximity to animals with which they sometimes have to share accommodation.[87] In their turn, peasants in isolated villages entertain negative opinions about herdsmen and other mobile people. About one of these places, in central Spain, a contemporary anthropological study reports: 'The more itinerant the outsider is, the greater is the contempt in which he is held. Thus next to Gypsies, the most despised groups are migrant herders and itinerant tradesmen or farm hands, for they are assumed to live outside the context of sedentary – and thus "civilized" – society.'[88] These perceptions alert us to what has been widely attributed to members of dishonourable occupations: their implied qualities of 'nature'. This is why they had to be ritually contained and controlled; hence their geographical and social segregation and numerous other restrictions attending their relations with members of 'civilized' society.

The persistence of certain infamous occupations into the present – and their concurrent proscription – is perhaps best epitomized by a well-known 'survival' within contemporary urban life: the prostitute. Representing the 'oldest profession', she also embodies the quintessence of the occupations which are the subject of this essay: infamy. Yet the success of her trade, more than any other, remains predicated on the very dishonour attached to it. Prostitution provides another example of 'deviance as success'. Its practitioners thrive on what one may call 'the wages of dishonour'.[89] Which leaves us with a paradox: if Mrs Warren's profession were ever to become honourable and legalized, it would mean the end of her trade.

4

Why Chimney-Sweeps
Bring Luck

Following on the discussion of infamous occupations in the previous chapter, this essay takes a closer look at the position of chimney-sweeps in early modern Europe and the prevailing attitudes towards them. Did they also belong to the ranks of disreputable occupational groups, and, if so, for what reasons, and what can this tell us about the notion of 'infamy' itself?

It is striking that the sweeps are always missing from studies of guilds. We do not find them in surveys and lists, in the iconography, or in the more comprehensive accounts of corporations. This already suggests that the trade was unusual and had perhaps not always been regarded as a craft at all. Nor do we learn much about chimney-sweeps from the literature on infamous occupations in which they are at best mentioned in passing. On the basis of fragmentary evidence about the social history of chimney-sweeps in western Europe, I shall argue that these people, because of their work and not unlike those who practised less honourable professions, occupied an unusual place in society and that therein lies the main reason why people commonly attributed them with luck-bringing power.

I

From the early sixteenth century, when we hear for the first time of chimney-sweeping as a regular occupation, until the nineteenth century, the trade was dominated, indeed virtually monopolized, by people from the areas of marginal farming in the higher Alpine valleys, the Pyrenees and the Massif Central. Together with other (seasonal) emigrants, such as mercenaries, stonemasons, brick-makers, barometer vendors, chocolate makers, cooks, domestics, chestnut roasters, tinkers, tinsmiths, coppersmiths, knife grinders and umbrella repairers, chimney-sweeps formed part of a substantial surplus population, which was regularly pushed out of the higher valleys of central Europe. Each valley had developed its own specialization and artisanal skills. The higher valleys in the Ticino (that is, the area just west and north of Lake Maggiore) were known for their chimney-sweeps. It seems that people with little or no professional training – especially those from the more isolated valleys – had few alternatives to chimney-sweeping, a trade they had consequently monopolized. All over Europe, from London to Vienna and from Amsterdam to Palermo, chimney-sweeping was left to these outsiders from the Alps. In this way, sweeps remained ethnically distinct from the local population.[1]

Chimney-sweeps who settled in Dutch towns, the German territories, Austria, Bohemia and parts of Hungary and Poland mostly came from the southern flanks of the Alps, from the Swiss–Italian border area – in particular from the poor valleys west of Locarno and Bellinzona, such as the Val Vigezzo in Italy, the adjacent Centovalli, the Onsernone and the Valle Maggia in the canton of Ticino, and the Valle Calanca and the Misox in the southernmost corner of the canton of Graubünden. They were generally called 'Italians', since they all belonged to the Italian-speaking population in this part of the Alps. The extent to which this border area had specialized in chimney-sweeping is attested (among other things) by the nickname of one of its valleys: already in the mid-sixteenth century, the Vigezzo, then part of the Duchy of Milan, was known as the *Kaminfegertal*.[2] Most of the sweeps who lived and worked in France, Belgium and England came from the poor mountain districts in the western Alps, especially from Savoy. They were, therefore, generally known as 'Savoyards', and in some areas this term became synonymous with 'chimney-sweep'.[3]

Although most sweeps seem to have settled permanently in urban centres, they often married women from their home communities. They also returned at set times to the Alpine region to recruit young apprentices – predominantly children in their early teens. Moreover, they took an interest in local affairs: for example, by providing for shrines and chapels in their home villages. Finally, older sweeps spent their last years in Alpine retirement.[4] Emigration from the Val Verzasca, located in the Ticino, was temporary. After the harvest, sweeps set out on foot for the bigger towns and cities in Piemont and Lombardy. In spring they returned to their valley, where they resumed agricultural work.[5]

This pattern of both permanent and seasonal emigration ensured that chimney-sweeps, already marginal in their home communities, also remained marginal with respect to the host population. For more than

300 years, they controlled an occupation in which ordinary people had little interest. Their monopoly over chimney-sweeping is no less significant than the general unwillingness to engage in it. Referring to Vienna and Lower Austria, Spiesberger writes: 'The chimney sweep's trade was not an indigenous profession. People from 'Welschland' had introduced the trade and developed it until it had become virtually inalienable. . . . Generally speaking, the Italians managed to keep the trade in their hands. The few masters with German surnames had at least relatives in the South' (1974: 14–15). A very similar form of 'Italian' control over chimney-sweeping has been noted in relation to the Netherlands and to the Dutch town of Groningen in particular.[6] It therefore seems that, on the whole, ordinary people shunned chimney-sweeping, which indicates the low esteem in which the trade and its practitioners were held. It is highly characteristic of many disreputable occupations to be associated, in one way or another, with cleaning, with the removal of refuse and dirt. It is no less striking that foreigners assumed or were charged with these tasks.

The question as to why certain valleys specialized in chimney-sweeping while others were known for less dishonourable activities has never received a satisfactory answer.[7] As noted above, this regional division of labour can perhaps best be understood in connection with ecological and political constraints. We have seen that valleys where chimney-sweeps originated from were areas of marginal farming, where people were unable to build up sufficient resources for the winter. Moreover, people from poor mountain valleys had no opportunity for more skilled employment, not only because they lacked the qualifications, but also because skilled trades were monopolized by the surplus population from lower and less poor valleys. Similar patterns of competition and monopolization were replicated by the sweeps themselves. For this interpretation, I draw upon some remarks of Niederer, in particular his observation: 'Those who did not have any professional training – above all those from the most isolated valleys in the Ticino – engaged themselves as chimney-sweeps as far as the Netherlands' (1980: 82).

II

That chimney-sweeping was generally looked down upon is further attested to by its association with various trades and activities that had an unfavourable reputation. Sweeps were often identified with itinerant people, who have always been widely suspect and held in low regard by their host population.[8] Apart from the roaming activity itself, the main reason why itinerant folk were considered disreputable was, of course, that they had no fixed abode (or were supposed not to have one) and were hence less subject to social control. In the German-speaking countries, sweeps were sometimes recruited from the ranks of the *fahrende Leute*, with whom they remained closely associated because of their work, which was itinerant even when the sweeps themselves had a fixed residence.[9] The seasonal sweeps from the Val Verzasca, who swarmed over the north Italian plain during the winter months, were highly mobile, moving back and forth between city and countryside. This brought them within the orbit of the itinerant population, with whom they also shared a distinct *argot*.[10] Writing about the seasonal chimney-sweeps in northern Italy, Bühler observes:

> As long as there was enough employment in the urban centres of the sweeps' territory, the sweeps stayed at night in rented rooms. Then, masters and apprentices went to the countryside in search of employment in villages and isolated farms. Often they set out on Sunday evening or Monday morning to reach the periphery of their districts. By the end of the week they were returning again to their headquarters. During the week or when they had not rented any lodgings, they slept in barns, in abandoned buildings, or just where they happened to be, in the cold, rain, or snow. (1984: 173)[11]

Regarding the itinerant and seasonal character of chimney-sweeping in nineteenth-century London, Meyhew reports:

> The sweepers, as a class, in almost all their habits, bear a strong resemblance to the costermongers. The habit of going about in search of their employment has, of itself, implanted in many of them the wandering propensities peculiar to street people. . . . The busy season in the chimney sweepers' trade commences at the beginning of November, and continues up to the month of May; during the remainder of the year the trade is 'slack'. When the slack season has set in nearly one hundred men are thrown out of employment. These, as well as many of the single-handed masters, resort to other kinds of employment. Some turn costermongers, other tinkers, knife-grinders, etc. (1968, II: 364, 375)

In the Scandinavian countries, chimney-sweeping was even more closely associated with other disreputable occupations and activities. In Denmark and Sweden, for instance, the despised *rakkerfolk* or *nadmansfolk* combined chimney-sweeping with other forms of cleaning and refuse collecting, including skinning and the related killing and butchering of horses. In fact, the word 'rakker' or 'racker' derives from the Lower German *raken*, that is, to remove refuse and dirt, while the word *nadman* or *nattman* denotes nightman or cesspool cleaner.[12] Discussing rural life in nineteenth-century Denmark, Rockwell writes that the *rakkerfolk* 'were a separate group in the population, attached to the peasant society but not part of it'. She continues:

> Their outcast status was partly due to their wandering life, for most of them travelled like gypsies. . . . But some of them lived permanently in huts outside and rather isolated from the village: they must have been despised for their occupational role, which was that of doing necessary but essentially dishonourable work. The chief of these jobs were: helping the hangman; killing horses, calves, dogs, and cats; flaying these animals and also cattle which had died of disease, gelding horses and castrating dogs and cats; sweeping chimneys, and cleaning latrines. (1974: 452ff)[13]

Very similar combinations of employment have been highlighted in a case study of an eighteenth-century *nattman* in southern Sweden. His name was Bollvig, and he combined chimney-sweeping with gelding and butchering horses, skinning, and assisting the hangman. As the author emphasizes: all these activities were considered infamous, and Bollvig lived at the margin of society, also literally, at the outskirts of town not far from the place of execution, in sight of the gallows (Balint 1980). Sweeps from the Alps also bought up human hair[14] and worked as entertainers. In France, the Low Countries and England, for example, young sweeps went from door to door during the off-season with marmots, which they brought from the Alps to show and make do tricks for money. They also played the hurdy-gurdy or *vieille*, a hand organ, which they accompanied with a nasal voice.[15] Thus the Savoyards, observes Mayhew, were once the 'general showmen and sweeps of Europe' (1968, II: 346).

For present purposes, it is also important to note that chimney-sweeps had to shout: not only through chimneys and from roof-tops, but also in the streets to announce their arrival. In this way they resembled the disreputable town criers, costermongers, knife-grinders, and other pedlars and hawkers, with whom they were indeed usually associated and identified. In fact, chimney-sweeps loom large in collections depicting and describing how (urban) people made their living on the street, hawking their goods and services.[16] What sweeps had also in common with hawkers, carters, drivers and coachmen was short apprenticeship and a bad reputation.[17]

Sweeps are often represented as shouting in seventeenth- and eighteenth-century engravings, whose captions describe shouting and wandering as hallmarks of the trade. A late seventeenth-century engraving by Francesco Curti, based on a drawing by Giuseppe Maria Mitelli (see Plate 1), is captioned as follows:

Plate 1   Lo spazzacamino. Chimney-sweep. Late seventeenth-century engraving by Francesco Curti based on a drawing by Giuseppe Mitelli. Photo by courtesy of Dr Fernando Bonetti, Archivio Cantonale di Bellinzona, Switzerland

Arabo al volto, al risuonar Caronte
girando le contrade, et ogni loco
Gridando va l'affumicato Bronte
Per trovar la sua sfera, il fumo e l'fuoco.

(Arab in countenance, reminiscent of Charon
Wandering through the country, and in every locale
Shouting goes the smoke-stained Thunder
To find his domain: smoke and fire.)

We shall come back to the image of Charon (the mythological figure who ferried the dead across the River Styx). The wandering and shouting of sweeps are also emphasized in another seventeenth-century portrait, by Jean-Baptist Bonnart. The caption of this engraving runs as follows:

Ce visage à geule beante
Dans les rües crie pour trante,
Ramones cy, ramones la,la la la,
La cheminée du haut en bas.

(That face with a shouting muzzle
Through the streets he cries for thirty
Sweep here, sweep there
The chimney from top to bottom.)[18]

A standard Italian phrase, *urlare come uno spazzacamino* (to shout like a chimney-sweep), still evokes a similar picture. Going from door to door helped fix the sweeps' image as itinerant folk. In some cities, including London and Vienna, wives of chimney-sweeps worked as street musicians and pedlars, again reinforcing the impression of itinerancy.[19]

It should be mentioned that soot, which sweeps collected and sold to farmers (who poured it on their meadows and wheat fields to destroy slugs and other pests), served as folk medicine.[20] The sweeps' identification with healers and quacks may also have been more direct. In fact, the expression 'chimney-sweep without a ladder', which appears in the Low Countries around the sixteenth century, refers to street vendors selling purgatives. The phrase also seems to denote (not only in Dutch, but also in French and English) a man looking for sexual adventures, a connotation one also finds in other sayings, like the Dutch expression 'to have her chimney swept', which refers to sexual intercourse.[21] The relationship between sweeping chimneys and sexual intercourse is made explicit in an Italian *canzone popolare*, entitled 'Lo Spazzacamino':

Su a giù per le contrade
di qua e di là si sente
la voce allegramente dello spazzacamin.
S'affaccia alla finestra
'na bella signorina,
con voce graziosina chiama lo spazzacamin.
Prima lo fa entrare
e poi lo fa sedere
gli dà da mangiare e bere allo spazzacamin.
E dopo aver mangiato
mangiato e ben bevuto
gli fa vedere il buco, il buco del camin.
Oh come mi dispiace
che il mio camin l'è stretto,
povero giovinetto, come farà a salir.
Non dubiti signora
son vecchio del mestiere,
so fare il mio dovere, su e giù per il camin.
E dopo quattro mesi
la luna va crescendo
la gente va dicendo 'l'è sta el spazzacamin'.
E dopo nove mesi
è nato un bel bambino
che somigliava tutto allo spazzacamin.[22]

(Up and down the country roads
from here and from there one hears
the cheerful voice of the chimney-sweep.
Coming to the window
is a beautiful girl
who calls the sweep with a gracious voice.
First she lets him in
And then she lets him sit down.
She gives the sweep to eat and to drink.
And after having eaten,
Eaten and having drunk well,
she lets him see the hole, the hole of the chimney.
Oh how sorry I am
that my chimney is so narrow,
poor youth, how will he manage to climb.
Don't worry, madam,
I am experienced in the craft
I know how to go about it, up and down in the chimney
And after four months
the moon is rising.
People say: 'The chimney-sweep has been there'.
And after nine months

A beautiful baby is born
who closely resembles the chimney-sweep.)

III

Chimney-sweeps formed a separate category of people. They were considered an unusual lot, and they also saw themselves as distinct from the people in whose midst they lived and worked. This is most clearly attested to by their common ethnic origin. But no less significant was the strong tendency toward endogamous marriages and the use of their Italian or French as well as the use of a special *argot*, the 'tarom', which further set the sweeps apart from their hosts.[23] Moreover, chimney-sweeps often lived in particular neighbourhoods or streets, which were sometimes named after them, like the 'Schoorsteenvegerssteeg' (chimney-sweeps' alley) in Amsterdam.[24] In Vienna and in other parts of Austria, chimney-sweeping was considered a *radiziertes Gewerbe*, that is, an occupation or trade that could be exercised in combination with the ownership of a specific house; hence a chimney-sweeping practice could only be acquired (through purchase or inheritance) along with the house.[25] This intimate link between occupation and location betrays both a tendency toward monopoly formation on the part of the sweeps and an attempt by the authorities to regulate the trade and to keep it in its place. Such arrangements, which helped to set the sweeps apart, again indicate the extent to which this occupation was considered unusual, as something out of the ordinary. Indeed, the residential pattern of sweeps may be viewed as a symbolic expression of their marginal status.

Rural folk from Europe's higher mountain valleys were able to practise chimney-sweeping because other people looked down upon it. At the same time, however, these marginal mountain peasants tried to monopolize the trade. Concerning sweeps from the Ticino, we know that masters, and often even entire families, had their own districts and territories, which were clearly demarcated and into which incursions were not tolerated.[26] This double bind – general avoidance and monopoly formation – is highly characteristic of infamous occupations, especially lucrative trades like prostitution and the work of the hangman. We should not forget that the word 'prostitution' had, and still has, a wider meaning, namely to relinquish one's honour for money.[27]

There are various indications that chimney-sweeping was profitable – precisely because it was both indispensable and widely shunned. In early nineteenth-century London, for example, some masters were very 'comfortable' and some were, 'comparatively speaking', rich.[28] A similar situation prevailed in Austria, where substantial profits from chimney-sweeping helped keep the trade in the hands of a relatively small, endogamous group of outsiders. Spiesberger observes: 'Generally speaking, the Italians managed to keep the trade in their hands. . . . The trade was considered profitable, and they tried to stabilize their resources through advantageous marriages. . . . In general, one can say that the chimney-sweeps had a relatively high standard of living' (1974: 15–16). Discussing the population growth during the first half of the nineteenth century in the hinterland of Locarno (comprising the Centovalli, the Val Verzasca and the Onsernone), Bühler notes that part of the surplus population joined the ranks of the sweeps:

> How should this population be nourished, where could one discover new opportunities to earn money? The economic prospects offered by agriculture were already exhausted given the agricultural techniques of that time. Only in connection with widely different sidelines and mainly through periodic emigration could one keep poverty under control. It is not surprising that in this period the crowd of apprentices still grow. The earnings from chimney sweeping also played a decisive role. Contemporary observers agree that the earnings of the emigrants were considerable. Already in 1869 the district-officer of Locarno estimated the seasonal earnings of masters at about 300 francs, those of apprentices over 14 at 60 to 80 francs, and those of the boys at 30 to 40 francs. A comparison with the wages paid in the Glarner textile industry tells us something about purchasing power: in the textile industry a skilled worker earned in 1869 an average of 40 to 50 francs a month. (1984: 175)

In the literature on chimney-sweeping, the relationship between ethnicity and occupation is widely recognized, as is the connection between monopolization of the trade and its profitability. But the dark side of this monopoly formation has received lesser attention. Profits derived from chimney-sweeping also greatly depended on public contempt for the trade as a dishonourable profession. Its low esteem put most people off chimney-sweeping, but it also facilitated monopolization and helped raise profits. Thus the dishonour of chimney-sweeping conspired to maintain its relatively high remuneration. When chimney-sweeping began to lose some of its stigma (perhaps owing to the introduction of a new technology), as in London around the middle of the nineteenth century, new people invaded the trade, and profits consequently decreased.[29] There seems to be no other way to explain the apparent contradiction implied in high profits from work that ordinary people shunned and left to outsiders.

IV

The unusual position of sweeps in (early) modern European society is also emphasized by their dress and the general way in which they were represented. As is well known, clothes are particularly suited to mark and stress social status and changes of social status. Taken out of context, Leach writes,

> items of clothing have no 'meaning'; they can be stacked away in a drawer like the individual letters which a typographer uses to make up his type-face but, when put together in sets to form a uniform, they form distinc-tive markers of specified social roles in specified social contexts. Male and female, infant, child, and adult, master and servant, bride and widow, soldier, policeman, high court judge, are all immediately recognizable by the clothing they wear. (1976: 55)

Since the early nineteenth century, sweeps have dressed either in black or white. Black was more common, and only in Holland did they sometimes dress in white.[30] Either way, these colours set chimney-sweeps apart from ordinary people, who never dressed entirely in black or white, except of course when they, too, became unusual, like widows or brides. Moreover, like people working in other infamous occupa-tions, sweeps wore unusual headgear (universally a standard status-marker). Their black top-hat was aptly called 'stove-pipe'. Though it had been in vogue in the mid-nineteenth century, sweeps were the only people who continued to wear this particular kind of hat – together with representatives of other unusual trades, including undertakers and magicians.[31]

For obvious reasons, members of infamous occupations had to be directly recognizable. Of course, the reverse also holds good: that sweeps could be easily recognized (their top-hat being a metonymic sign of their trade) suggests that they occupied a special and unusual place in society. In some German-speaking areas, the clothes sweeps wore were made partly of mole-skins.[32] Here we are dealing with another meaningful symbol, with an obvious structural analogy: moles, too, are anomalous – they have to find their way blindly through dark and narrow passage-ways. Such clothes and headgear have assumed the character of a stigma, marking sweeps as not quite human and placing them outside the moral community.[33]

The iconography of chimney-sweeps has much to teach us about the way sweeps were regarded and treated by ordinary people. A par-ticularly rich source on the imagery of sweeps is found in picture post-cards, mostly dating from the late nineteenth and early twentieth centuries.[34] In these documents several things are relevant. Virtually all of them are New Year's well-wishing cards, postcards one sends and receives during an important period of calendrical transition, to wish luck. Here we touch upon the quintessence of the unusual character attributed to sweeps, namely their intermediary role and their magical power. The sweep brings luck – in particular to brides – precisely because he is himself unusual. Therefore, he is associated with things which are likewise uncommon, abnormal, extraordinary. Since the chimney-sweep does not fit normal social categories, is betwixt-and-between, he can act as a mediator. He is liminal (from *limen*, boundary, threshold), and, like all liminal, things, events, situations and relationships, he is both taboo and an object of ritual value – and hence a source of danger and power.[35]

The liminality of chimney-sweeps is abundantly illustrated by these picture postcards. The earliest series, which dates from the late nineteenth century, shows the chimney-sweep as a gnomelike figure who, in a grotesque way, presents a gift (a bouquet, a calendar) to a young woman, whose status is ambiguous: she is neither a child nor married.[36] In a later series of New Year well-wishing cards, the chimney-sweep is romanticized and represented as a prim and proper boy. Many of these picture postcards show the chimney-sweep's boy in the company of a young girl, with whom he seems to be maintaining an amorous relationship. On a postcard of 1906 the boy stands behind her on a roof near a chimney, putting his hand into her muff. On another, also from the turn of the century, we see the boy sweep, dressed in black with a black top-hat, sitting on the snow-covered roof of a house. Next to him sits a young girl dressed in a Pierrot costume. They are close together, each with an arm over the other's shoulder. They raise their glasses and look at each other in a friendly way. In the background a church clock indicates midnight. Yet another postcard, of 1909, shows an adult chimney-sweep at the door of a house, smiling at a young woman dressed in white who stands on the threshold and returns his ambiguous glance.[37] The erotic overtones of these representations (chimney-sweeps are often depicted with women who are single) correspond to the folk belief that to see, touch or kiss a chimney-sweep brings luck, in particular to brides, who are, of course, also liminal figures: women neither married nor unmarried, but betwixt-and-between these social categories.[38]

The belief in the supernatural power of these encounters is so strong that when sweeps are not available, they are simply constructed, as Honigmann witnessed on the occasion of the *Almabtrieb* in Austria:

> The man who drove down the pigs [they went more slowly and needed separate attention] blackened himself like a chimney sweep. To see him brought good luck, just as it is still auspicious to encounter a chimney sweep on his rounds. For fun the man rubbed a bit of his color on the faces of the girls whom he pretended he wanted to kiss. (1964: 281)

Everything that surrounds the sweeps on these postcards is ambiguous. Apart from adolescents, brides and girls in Pierrot costumes, we see four-leaved clovers, sucking pigs, discarded shoes, fly-fungi, ladybirds, mistletoe, chimneys, thresholds and open doors. These materials are difficult to classify. They do not fit conventional categories, and thus form suitable symbols for persons who are unclear and abnormal themselves. Since, as mentioned earlier, almost everywhere people ascribe magical power to marginal and liminal things, especially dirt and refuse, we can now understand why all these objects are supposed to bring luck. They are mediators: each link seems to generate the next, facilitating the transition from one social category or clear-cut state to another.[39] Soot and ashes, apart from being refuse, are intermediary between hearth and roof, between earth and sky-vault just as chimneys, doors and thresholds mediate between inside and outside, as chimney-sweeps between male and female, unmarried and married, inside and outside, dirty and clean, old and new (New Year), as mistletoe is intermediary between deciduous trees and evergreen trees, and between summer and winter, as piglets between human and animal, as ladybirds between tame and wild, as brides between unmarried and married, as adolescents between children and adults.[40] These postcards thus reveal a significant pattern: the imagery conveys the idea of transition – the passage from one status state or category to another.

We should not assume, however, that mediators always bring luck. As is well known, some of them are highly inauspicious – as, for example, the executioner and, of course, various (anomalous) animals. Why then do some mediators bring luck, while others are believed to bring misfortune? It seems that this very much depends on their habitat and the kind of relation they maintain with ordinary people.[41] A chance encounter with an executioner must have been considered intrusive, since the man was outside his proper domain: that is, his house, the prison and the place of execution. Meeting him by chance meant being placed on a par with convicts and condemned prisoners. Such an encounter with the executioner thus established an unwanted contact and was therefore believed to be inauspicious. Chimney-sweeps, by contrast, were never intruders because their work required them to walk the streets and to enter the private domain of their customers. Moreover, their visits were welcome, for cleaning chimneys prevented fires that would destroy the house. Tellingly, St Florian, the sweeps' patron saint, is sometimes depicted with a bucket full of water (see Plate 2). Hence meeting them by chance in the street or touching them was considered auspicious. Finally, it should be clear that these encounters, both favourable and unfavourable, derived their magical power also from their relatively rare

Plate 2 Saint Florian, patron saint of chimney-sweeps. About 1850.
Oberammergau/Heimatmuseum, photo AKG London

occurrence: all were exceptional meetings. And both luck and misfortune have been and still are regarded as extraordinary.

V

It is no coincidence that chimney-sweeps were prominent in the collective representation of weddings. Together with funerals, weddings are the most important rites of passage in the human life cycle.[42] Further evidence of the unusual and liminal position of sweeps is the mediating role they played in important calendrical transitions. Sweeps not only appear on New Year's well-wishing cards; they actually assisted at banquets of the well-to-do between Christmas and New Year. The autobiography of a sweep from the Ticino indicates that belief in the power of sweeps to bring luck during major periods of transition was still widespread among the upper classes in the early twentieth century:

> At Christmas, as at New Year, we did not eat *polenta*. We were invited, as usual, by a count or rich landowner. We were not allowed to wash our faces. We all had to serve as messengers of good luck, and to sit at the table with a white tablecloth, on which was set out everything one could wish. Yet, we were forbidden to refer, even with a single word, to our misery. The rich people thus wanted to obtain all happiness for themselves and who knows what else. . . . During Christmas and New Year we visited the houses of the rich to wish good luck. We received a coin from almost everyone.[43]

A similar, mediating role, also in calendrical rites, was played by chimney-sweeps in England. Between approximately 1750 and 1850, sweeps dominated the popular May Day festivals in London and elsewhere. These celebrations took place during a period of transition: at the end of the busy season and at the beginning of the slack period – that is, during the passage from plenty to scarcity, an interval which coincided with the passage from winter to summer. Disguised in various ways, the sweeps paraded the streets for three days with garlands, collecting money at strategic places. They were fantastically dressed, with massive wigs, fine coats and huge crowns. Some sweeps were dressed in women's clothes, others danced and made noise – a sort of 'rough music', beating time with their shovels and brushes.[44]

It has been argued that such rituals of reversal express the liminality of the permanently structural inferior (Turner 1969: 168). Indeed, May Day was not only called 'Sweeps' Day', but also known as 'Chimney-Sweeps' Carnival'.[45] That the structurally weak were most prominent at this festival is also attested to by Mayhew's observation: 'It is but seldom that any of the large masters go out on May-Day; this custom is generally confined to the little masters and their men' (1968, II: 371). The feast-day of Saint Florian has traditionally been celebrated on 4 May, 'ever since the first professional chimney-sweeps began to leave Italy in the Middle Ages to seek work in neighbouring countries' (Phillips 1963: 382). Finally, we should remember that status reversals were also implied in wearing a top-hat, which had been both an upper-class fashion and a symbol of leisure.

We can now understand why – of all workers – chimney-sweeps in particular were so prominent at weddings and at certain festivals and in general loomed so large in the imagination of pre-industrial Europeans. As strangers whose indispensable work brought them to the heart of the domestic domain, sweeps bridged a number of powerful oppositions. They marked and helped bring about transitions in the annual cycle and the life cycle of individuals, clarifying major cultural categories in the process. In the life-crisis rites (such as the ceremony of marriage) the sweeps assisted in status elevation, and symbolized the transition to adulthood. We have seen that the chimney-sweep was identified with Charon, the mythological ferryman charged with the transport of the dead. This reference further underscores the sweep's mediating powers, with which he was credited. In the seasonal rites (Christmas, New Year, May Day), the sweeps attended and marked the transition of the entire society from one state to another through various rites of status reversal. As Turner notes: 'Life-crisis rites and rituals of induction into office are almost always rites of status elevation; calendrical rites and rites of group crises may sometimes be rites of status reversal' (1969: 168–9).

VI

These observations on chimney-sweeps may also throw some light on the issue of the so-called infamous occupations and on the notion of infamy itself.

There can be little doubt about the unusual and marginal place sweeps occupied in early modern European societies. Their peculiarities and low social status have often been noted, especially by urban observers such as Mayhew, who in his work on nineteenth-century London identified them as 'a class of public cleaners', and who wrote, referring to a passage from Shakespeare, that 'their employment was regarded as one of the meanest, a repute it bears to the present day' (1968, II: 339). Yet the marginality of the sweeps has never been further probed. Sweeps are usually described as part of the urban lower classes, at best as members of marginal groups. But the implications of 'marginality' are never spelled out: the ritual value of sweeps is either misjudged or ignored, and the rich folklore that developed around these people is seen as a collection of curiosities rather than as so many indications of their liminality.[46]

We have seen that chimney-sweeps tended to form endogamous groups, lived in separate locations and houses, had their own language and *argot*, and wore special clothes. All these collective marks contributed greatly to setting them apart from ordinary people, who only dealt with them in distinctly ritualized ways. In several countries, we are told, the chimney-sweep could not simply enter the house of his customer: the occupant (in most cases a woman) had first to break a twig off his brush.[47] This custom was believed to bring good luck, and we can understand it, like the ritual kissing and touching of the chimney-sweep (especially touching the soot on his brush or clothes), as a magical operation, as an attempt to ward off evil and to share in the good powers which one associated with this symbolic mediator. The belief in the luck-bringing power of sweeps and soot derived from the liminal quality of both. What may have reinforced the mediating capacities of the chimney-sweep and enhanced his ambiguity – thus increasing his ritual value – was that he entered the house of his customers as a stranger. As such, he worked on the most central and intimate location of the house, namely the hearth, which also happened to be the pivot of the female domain.[48] This may help us to understand why sweeps were often depicted and associated with women, why they were prominent at weddings, why they were sometimes represented as androgynous beings, and why some of them indulged in transvestism during certain festivals.

From other parts of the world we know that professionals whose work involves intimate contact with the domestic life of other people are also ritually segregated from the rest of the community. In chapter three, we have already mentioned the role of the barber in Swat, North Pakistan. Barth points out that the low, taboo status of the barber stems from his role in haircutting, circumcision, and the organization of celebrations required for the rites of passage of every individual: 'Because [his special role] involves intimate contact with the domestic life of each family, in breach of the usual barriers of prudery and seclusion, the barber's status needs to be clearly separated from that of other persons in the community' (1960: 123–4).[49] The custom of breaking a twig off the sweep's brush, together with the other forms of ritualization to which he was subjected, can also be understood as marking his special status before letting him cross the boundaries between outside and inside, between public and private.

The case of the chimney sweeps may then throw some light on people working in other dishonourable occupations and on the notion of infamy itself. Virtually all of them operated as cleaners or healers – and healing was long regarded as a form of cleaning. Surgeons, barbers, skinners, executioners, prostitutes, linen weavers, chimney-sweeps – they all handled offal, dirt and refuse.[50] A particular case in point was the executioner or hangman, who, in certain regions, combined his work with skinning, the supervision of brothels, curing the sick, and undertaking the cleaning of cesspools.[51] Like the sweep, whose work he sometimes assumed as well, he was an important mediator. The executioner had access to magical means (bodily remains) and bridged a whole series of oppositions, mediating such basic, clear-cut categories as ill and healthy, dirty and clean, life and death, inside and outside, this world and the next. Therefore, hangmen and chimney-sweeps invited the most elaborate ritualization in their dealings with ordinary people.[52] Only when ordinary people became abnormal themselves (ill, dirty, convicted), found themselves in another state of transition (marrying), or when something was wrong with their house or cattle (dirty, ill, dead), did they or their kinsmen turn – in highly ritualized ways – to members of these disreputable professions.

I have tried to explain why the relations with chimney-sweeps were strongly ritualized and why these craftsmen were credited with luck-bringing power. The example of the sweeps may then also illuminate the notion of infamy itself. Ambiguity, liminality, marginality and mediating capacities were the hallmarks of members of disreputable professions. The concept of infamy or, as the Germans called it, *Unehrlichkeit*, disguised the supernatural powers ascribed to chimney-sweeps and other workers in despised trades. We have seen how these capacities derived from the nature of their indispensable services and from the marginal position these people were granted in early modern European societies. When almost a century ago Mauss wrote his book on magic, he was on the right track when discussing the magical powers of members of certain occupational groups (including healers, barbers, executioners, grave-diggers and blacksmiths) he wrote: 'It is their profession which places these people apart from the common run of mortals, and it is this separateness which endows them with magical power' (1975: 29).

5

The Blood Symbolism
of *Mafia*

I

This essay considers the nature of social ties between people who conduct risky transactions. As the example of Sicilian *mafia* suggests, socially defined kinship and other institutions that draw on the metaphor of blood help to structure salient coalitions that are involved in extra-legal practices called 'organized crime'. Since members of these sodalities cannot – for obvious reasons – turn for protection to institutions of the State, trust and retaliation have to be generated within their own ranks – a point already recognized by Simmel in his treatise on secret societies.[1]

We shall see that the relationships through which *mafiosi* in Sicily operate evoke blood imagery, and that blood metaphors are used to mark and foster reciprocity. These relationships include agnatic kinship (consanguinity), affinal kinship, ritual kinship (godparenthood, co-parenthood) and ritual friendship (blood brotherhood). Moreover, violence and death mark sanctions and retaliation (vendetta). This essay explores how these relationships are socially and culturally defined, how loyalty and trust are built up, betrayed and sanctioned, and how organizational flexibility and structural fluidity are quintessential to extra-legal coalitions in modern nation-states.[2] From this perspective, I hope to shed some light on the question of why blood as a symbolic device dominates the discourse and practices of *mafiosi*.

II

At the local level, bonds of kinship and friendship make up coalitions of *mafiosi* called 'families' or *famiglie* (singular: *famiglia*). The idiom of kinship and blood is significant because not all members are authentic kinsmen.

Each family controls its own territory – a rural village or town, an urban street or neighbourhood. Incursions are considered slights and invite a violent response. The territory is closely identified with the family as seen from the prevailing naming practices and sensitivity to even minor forms of trespassing. Overwhelming evidence suggests that the power base of *mafiosi* is always local.[3]

The size of these local groups ranges between half-a-dozen and well over fifty members. Families include a boss or *capo*, an underboss or *sottocapo*, one or more *consiglieri* or counsellors, and other 'men of honour'. They all have a reputation for violence and are able to 'mind their own business': that is, keep secrets and cultivate *omertà*. At higher levels of integration, these local groups were represented in the so-called *Commissione* or *Cupola*, which makes rules and serves as a co-ordinating board. Since the early 1980s, following the confessions of several *mafiosi* who started co-operating with the authorities, much has been made of the alleged hierarchical and unified structure of the Sicilian *mafia* or Cosa Nostra. As the two notorious *mafia* wars of the early 1960s and the early 1980s demonstrate, however, centralizing tendencies have always been offset by segmentation. From the very moment the *Commissione* (meant to control internal fights) was set up in the late 1950s, local groups and their allies tried to control it and use it for their own ends.[4] The best-known example is the rise of the *Corleonesi*, originally a local group of *mafiosi* from Corleone (a rural town of about 14,000 inhabitants in Sicily's western interior) and their allies who carefully planned and established their hegemony after the cruel civil war of 1981–2 in which more than a thousand *mafiosi* lost their lives.[5]

As is well known, *mafia* enterprise involves control over the local economy (including real estate, building contracts and markets), canvassing votes for politician-protectors and (since the 1970s) international drug-trafficking. There were well over a hundred of these families in Sicily as a whole and about twenty-five in Palermo alone. In total there were several thousand *mafiosi*.[6] What is known about the composition and structure of these families?

First, they include agnatic kinsmen – that is, blood relatives who are exclusively related through males or, differently phrased, related on the father's side. Often, the core of these families consists of a father and his sons, a set of brothers, sometimes including one or more agnatic uncles and cousins.[7] In particular, sets of brothers have always been very common in *mafia* families, both in the city and in the countryside.

All these people are related by blood: that is, both biologically and culturally. Here applies what David M. Schneider wrote about American kinship: 'The facts of biological relatedness and sexual relations play a fundamental role, for they are symbols, culturally formulated symbols in terms of which a system of social relationships is defined and differentiated' (1977: 66).[8] Given its pre-eminence in *mafia* coalitions, agnatic kinship in Sicily, as in other Indo-European kinship systems, provides for relationships of 'diffuse, enduring solidarity' (ibid.).[9] If in the absence of effective state control trust can be found anywhere, it is primarily in the bonds between agnatic kinsmen.

Succession to positions of leadership usually follows the same agnatic lines. The oldest son often takes the place of his father, or, sometimes, his father's brother or, less commonly, his mother's brother. For example, in San Giuseppe Jato, Giovanni Brusca succeeded his father, Bernardo; in Palermo, Stefano Bontate succeeded his father, Paolino; in Alcamo, Filippo Rimi succeeded his father, Vincenzo; and in Riesi, Giuseppe Di Cristina also succeeded his father.

III

Bonds within and between *mafia* families are reinforced by intermarriage. Along with agnatic kinsmen, therefore, these families include in-laws, or affines. Also defined as kinsmen (*parenti*), they are relatives by marriage and as a rule not people to whom one is related by blood, although marriage between cousins does occur. Bonds with in-laws figure prominently in coalitions of *mafiosi*. Next to sets of agnatic kinsmen, one often finds sets of brothers-in-law as the core of these local groups of *mafia* families.

Among the famous *Corleonesi*,[10] for instance, Salvatore ('Toto') Riina maintained strong bonds with his brother-in-law Leoluca Bagarella, a brother of his wife. Riina was also on intimate terms with Giuseppe Marchese, whose sister married Leoluca Bagarella (see Figure 1). Moreover, in order to illustrate the organizational flexibility and structural fluidity of the Sicilian *mafia*, matrilineal relations are also used to build powerful alliances. Of particular importance are the bonds between a mother's brother and sister's son since the position of leadership may also be transferred matrilineally. This happened when Salvatore Inzerillo was chosen to head the intercontinental superclan by his retiring mother's brother, Rosario Di Maggio.[11]

The composition of these families, who were all involved in the international heroin trade, is instructive for our purposes because it illustrates the structural principles operating in groups that conduct risky transactions: kinship, marriage and ethnicity, each of which animates global networks as much as local groups.

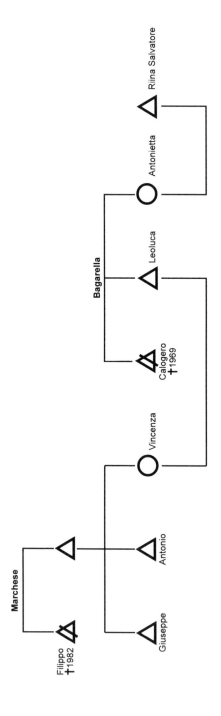

Figure 1 Kinship ties between *mafiosi*: brothers-in-law

In his discussion of the entrepreneurial *mafia* and the heroin economy, Arlacchi (1987: 196–200) quotes from a 1982 indictment of the Palermo Public Prosecutor's Office, which provides further details on these *mafiosi* related through marriage, including intermarriage with American *mafia* families (see Figure 2):

> that the Gambino brothers are cousins of the Spatola brothers Rosario, Vincenzo and Antonio, their father, Salvatore, being brother to the Gambino's mother; that Giuseppe Inzerillo married Giuseppa Di Maggio – sister of Calogero, Giuseppe and Salvatore Di Maggio – while Calogero Di Maggio married Domenica Spatola, thus strengthening the kinship links between these families. (1987: 200)

Although Arlacchi recognizes the implications of these alliances for the internal cohesion of these groups, he strangely but not untypically categorizes intermarriage, adoption and sponsorship as 'apparently irrational practices', and dismisses them as 'artificial' (1987: 199).

Drawing on the same report from the Palermo Public Prosecutor, Sterling (1990: 199–200) is more specific about these alliances and also more sensitive to their importance:

> The Spatolas were found to be one of the four Mafia Families forming a transatlantic colossus. The Cherry Hill Gambinos were another. The Inzerillos, closest of all clans to Stefano Bontate, were a third. The fourth, related to the other three by blood and marriage, were the Di Maggios of Palermo and southern New Jersey. Their intercontinental family ties resembled the Hapsburgs' or Hohenzollerns', the marriages arranged to strengthen dynasties and preserve the blood royal. There were six Spatolas involved, five Gambinos (three brothers and two cousins), four Di Maggios, and fifteen Inzerillos. The Gambinos' mother's brother was a Spatola. The Inzerillos' father has married a Di Maggio, whose brother had married a Spatola.
>
> Salvatore Inzerillo, the biggest heroin broker of all, had been chosen to head the Family's clan by his retiring uncle, Rosario Di Maggio. . . . Inzerillo was married to a Spatola. His sister was married to a Spatola. His uncle in New Jersey was married to a Gambino. His cousin and namesake in New Jersey was married to a Gambino. His cousin Tommaso was a brother-in-law of John Gambino, who was married to a different Gambino. His cousin Maria Concetta was the wife of John Gambino's younger brother, Giuseppe. All the American-side members of these families were made Men of Honor from Sicily; and all had homes in or around Cherry Hill.

As Sterling's source, the Sicilian Prosecutor Sciacchitano, concludes:

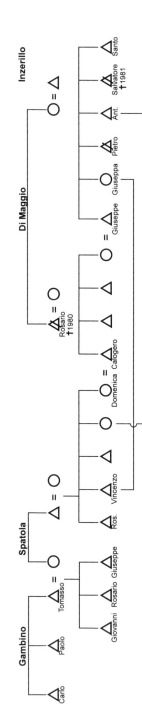

Figure 2 Kinship ties between four *mafia* families in the USA and Sicily

Sources: Sciaccitano (1982); Arlacchi (1987: 193–202); Sterling (1990: 107, 199–202); Stille (1995: 31–2, 36–7, 269–72)

These four families, living partly in Sicily and partly in New York, form a single clan unlike anything in Italy or the United States – the most potent Family in Cosa Nostra. John Gambino is the converging point in the United States for all of the group's activities in Italy, and the final destination for its drug shipments. Salvatore Inzerillo has emerged as the Gambino brothers' principal interlocutor, the central personage in Sicily, with myriad interests and heavy capital investments.

Like most of their fellow *mafiosi* in America, writes Sterling, the Gambino brothers were sending their heroin money back to Sicily. It was going to Inzerillo and Spatola, to be invested in legitimate business like the construction industry and real estate. By 1982, the Gambino–Inzerillo–Spatola holdings in Palermo alone were found to be worth about one billion dollars.[12]

Next to agnatic bonds, affinal ties, especially relations between brothers-in-law, are salient options for *mafiosi*. These relations help build and strengthen the basic units of the Sicilian *mafia*, both within and between local groups or families. Before Rosario Di Maggio retired (and died), he had left the leadership of these interrelated families to Salvatore Inzerillo, who was his sister's son (Sterling 1990: 200).

The once-powerful Rimi – father and son Vincenzo and Filippo – of Alcamo, in the province of Trapani, solidified their ties through intermarriage with Gaetano Badalamenti, the boss of Cinisi who controlled Palermo airport in Punta Ráisi: Filippo and Gaetano were brothers-in-law.[13]

Discussing the relations between *mafiosi* from both sides of the Atlantic who were involved in the drug trade, Gambetta (on the basis of a 1985 report from the Italian Parliament) touches on the structural principle of ethnicity underlying transnational *mafia* networks:

> Mafiosi were attractive intermediaries because of their strong connections with the Sicilian Americans running the market in the United States. These ties allowed greater flexibility and safety.
> In the relationships between mafioso organizers and the Italo-American gangs receiving the merchandise, where there is mutual trust over time, it is possible for one courier to arrive from America with the money while the merchandise itself is entrusted to another courier. Since no such privileged bonds existed between Sicilians and Middle Eastern suppliers, importing was a more cumbersome operation. (1993: 236)

Three organizations are capable of handling drugs on a wholesale, intercontinental scale: the Chinese Triads for heroin, the Colombian cartels for cocaine and the Sicilian *mafia* for both (Sterling 1990: 311). It would be rewarding to explore how these transnational operations are masterminded and orchestrated in remote hinterlands (precisely the kind of places anthropologists used to select for their field-work); to investigate how these operations hinge on kinship, marriage and ethnicity (precisely the kind of subjects anthropologists used to study in such remote places), and how they sustain a form of globalization that no government can stop or control: the transport of unlicensed cultural goods from the world's peripheries and the transformation of its metropolitan centres in North America and Europe.

IV
Although in-laws are related by marriage rather than blood, the concept of blood is not entirely lacking from the bonds between affines. First, affinity involves relationships with people who are related by blood among themselves. Second, in Sicily, as elsewhere in the Mediterranean, people place a strong emphasis on virginity and female chastity.[14] Ideally (at least in the Christian tradition) brides should come from outside the agnatic group and should be virgins.[15] The consummation of marriage involves breaking the hymen and is followed by birth. Both involve the spilling of blood. (Tellingly, one's children are called one's 'blood'.) It has been argued that in this context, too, blood has a symbolic significance in that it culturally marks and helps build a relationship – also a relationship between groups. In the Indo-European conception of blood, this blood comes from the outside into the group of agnates, and shedding it helps incorporate the bride into the agnatic kin-group of her husband.[16]

Writing on feuding in nineteenth-century Corsica and other Mediterranean societies, Wilson points out a connection between the blood shed in feuds and the blood of virginity that the bride yields to her husband (and, by extension, also to his agnates) at marriage: 'Also of relevance, among the Bedouin, too, the shedding of blood of a virgin given in marriage to settle a feud was seen as a kind of symbolic vengeance, blood for blood' (S. Wilson 1988: 529 n. 222).

Peacemaking in feuds was similar among pastoral families in the Barbagia. About these 'symbolic' resolutions of the vendetta in contemporary Sardinia, Cagnetta notes:

> Le mode de conciliation le plus typique du pays est le mariage d'un homme du clan du victime et d'une femme du clan de l'assassin. Le sang virginal répandu présente en effet un caractère symbolique de rachat du sang versé au cours de l'homicide qui a précédé. (1963: 89)

> (The most typical form of reconciliation is marriage of a man from the clan of the victim with a woman from the clan of the killer. The virginal

blood that is spilled in fact presents a symbolic compensation for the blood spilled in the homicide that preceded it.)

We will come back to this point when discussing the concept of blood in feuding and peacemaking. Remember that the practice 'blood for blood' has distinctly homeopathic implications. Writing on ancient Rome, Barton argues that 'the Romans, unlike ourselves, were deeply accustomed to thinking in terms of homeopathic systems. Like things are cured by like (*similia similibus curantur*). This was true not only in sorcery and medicine but also in religion and law . . .' (1992: 180). In a note she refers to 'Plato's Pharmacy' (the *pharmakon* as poison and antidote, both sickness and cure), and recalls that Roman justice operated on the *lex talionis*, the principle of equivalent vengeance (*par vindicta*).

These connotations of the concept of blood may help to explain why in *mafia* networks, next to the bonds between brothers, relations between brothers-in-law are so important. *Mafiosi* draw on the idiom of kinship (with its implications of consanguinity) to constitute the units that make up Sicilian *mafia*. Loyalty to superiors in the families of the men of honour takes priority over commitments to one's own agnates if they fail to follow the rules prevailing among 'men of honour'. As a case in 1994 in Bronte (a town in the western foothills of Etna) illustrates, a *mafioso* may kill his *mafioso*-brother who 'talks': that is, reveals information about the organization to outsiders.[17]

This brings us to the imagery of blood in recruitment rituals. Since the mid-1980s and as a consequence of the so-called *mafia* war in which the *Corleonesi* wiped out many established *mafiosi* in Palermo and its hinterland, hundreds of *pentiti* (penitents)[18] provided the investigating magistrates with information about the organization of Cosa Nostra. As a consequence, today much more is known about *mafia* than before. One of the first and most famous *pentiti*, Tommaso Buscetta, mentioned that recruitment into a *mafia* family – initiation into the brotherhood or to be made a man of honour – involved a rite of passage the high point of which was a simple act and formula, as in many other secret societies.[19] Blood from his pricked finger was rubbed on a paper image of a saint, which was set on fire in his hand. As it burned, he repeated the following vow: 'May my flesh burn like this holy picture if I am unfaithful to this oath.'[20] Through these rituals of incorporation, blood assumes magical properties of mediation and social cohesion. But blood is also associated with impurity and can impede rather than promote social bonding. The polluting potential of blood is probably at least partly responsible for the often noted exclusion of women from these sodalities – and from secret societies in general.[21]

V

The blood symbolism is no less striking in the settlement of feuds and the imposition of sanctions. Vengeance and feuding are trademarks of *mafiosi*. We have already referred to retaliation and the principle of the *lex talionis* in the settling of accounts between *mafiosi*. As a form of negative reciprocity, retribution means the culprit is to suffer what he has done.[22]

Mafiosi are guided by sayings like 'blood washes blood', 'offences have to be washed with blood' and 'vendetta is the best forgiveness'. As in the case of shedding blood in the initiation ritual of *mafiosi* ('May my blood be spilled just as these drops are spilled', and so on), there is an element of what Frazer calls homeopathic magic in retaliation or negative reciprocity: 'Blood washes blood', or 'Like produces or kills like'.

As elsewhere in the Mediterranean (e.g. Sardinia, Corsica, Montenegro, Albania, the Moroccan Rif, and among the Bedouin), retaliation between *mafiosi* includes vendettas against an entire family in revenge for offences by single members.[23] In these feuds, the conception of blood assumes critical importance. Retaliation occurred on a large scale during the internal *mafia* 'war' of the early 1980s, when the *Corleonesi*, after first selectively killing a string of public officials in Sicily who interfered with their business, decimated the Palermo *mafia* establishment by murdering the leaders and their kinsmen, including twenty-one Inzerillos and eleven relatives of Gaetano Badalamenti (Sterling 1990: 209–10).[24] The way the *Corleonesi* waged this deadly (it has been said 'terroristic') campaign shows the flexibility and fluidity of *mafia* coalitions, the comparative ease with which alliances change according to circumstances. As Claire Sterling puts it: 'The Corleonesi had worked in from the outermost provinces, courting the envious, the voracious, the upwardly mobile. Now they had secret allies from Trapani to Agrigento to Catania to the heart of Palermo' (1990: 206). Commenting on the murder of the *mafioso* Vincenzo Puccio in prison in 1989 on Riina's orders, Stille summarizes the strategy of the *Corleonesi* as follows:

> The murder of Vincenzo Puccio [and the killing of his brother on the same day] in a sense closed the circle on the gruesome killings among the 'winners' of the great mafia war. Examined as a whole, the events that Marino Mannoia recounted looked like a 'food chain' in the grisly Darwinian struggle of Cosa Nostra, with each fish eating the other until the big fish, Totò Riina, finally swallowed them all. Filippo Marchese had been killed by Pina 'the Shoe' Greco, Greco had been killed by Vincenzo Puccio, and now Puccio had been eliminated by Marchese's nephews [Giuseppe and Antonino Marchese]. Then Riina had killed four birds with one stone, eliminating the Puccios, while making sure that their assas-

sins, the Marchese brothers, were out of the way. (1995: 308; cf. 305ff and 382)[25]

Already several years before his arrest in January 1993, however, Riina had become a victim of his own success:

> As the mafia wars have demonstrated, those most successful at destroying the 'honoured Society' have been its own members; first through the shootouts of the 1960s, and later through the vicious tactics of the Corleonesi. In challenging the Italian state by murdering its representatives, they forced the government to retaliate; in attacking their enemies with relentless terror, they generated a powerful resentment which would find its apotheosis in the declarations of Tommaso Buscetta. (Shawcross and Young 1987: 306)

Turning state's evidence contravened the most sacred rules of Cosa Nostra and triggered a violent response. Even though they were apparently safeguarded by a protection programme, many *pentiti* lost close kinsmen after they testified. The culture of blood feuds – the launching of vendettas against entire families in revenge for offences by single members – seems to fit the Indo-European notion that blood symbolizes the strongest and most enduring of human bonds.[26]

Blood is a powerful symbol: through its metaphorical and metonymical qualities it can stand for life and death, for defilement and purification, for mediation and social cohesion. This is obvious in the ethnography of blood revenge. The concept of blood helps define and reinforce relationships between close kinsmen: the ties between fathers and sons, the bonds between brothers, and, by extension, the bonds between blood-brothers. Blood symbolizes the life of an individual and that of a group.[27] Moreover, as a symbolic device, blood mediates between individuals and between groups, between insiders, and between insiders and outsiders, shoring up relationships that are inherently unstable, flexible and subject to change. In the context of retaliation, shedding blood is a powerful way to 'wash the stains of dishonour' and thus, to supersede the state of pollution and social exclusion.

Blood revenge, then, involves more than retaliation and deterrence. In her book on tribal origins and customs in the Balkans, Mary Durham suggests that revenge was taken on behalf of the soul of the victim, rather than to punish the actual killer (1928: 170). As Montenegrins viewed it, vengeance 'replaced' within the victim's clan the blood that had been lost (1928: 170).

An echo of this sense of loss (and the magical way to make up for it) also reaches us from older sources. As Burkert reminds us, at the funeral pyre of Patrocles, Achilles slaughtered several animals but also twelve captured Trojans:

> This can be understood as an outburst of helpless fury: 'If you are dead the others should not live'. Nevertheless, when it is related that 'about the dead man flowed blood such as could be drawn in cups', it is clear that the intention was for blood to reach the dead man in some way, to give him back life and colour . . . (1985: 60; cf. Burkert 1983: 53)

Very similar forms of retribution occur today, as evidenced by the Serbian General Mladic's remark after his troops conquered the Muslim enclave of Srebrenica on 11 July 1995. Addressing his soldiers and referring to Serbian civilians killed by the Muslim military in the area, Mladic is reported to have said: 'It is going to be a *meza* [a long, luscious feast]. We will kill so many of them that we will wade through their blood up to our knees.'[28]

Other aspects of blood revenge deserve mention. We have already referred to the liminal position of those who have been dishonoured and who are therefore expected, even socially obliged, to take revenge. Plunged into mourning, these victims have all the features of people 'out of place'. They are avoided, excluded, ostracized – until they have taken revenge. Only after they have 'taken blood' (and thus removed their defilement) is their mourning over and can they be reincorporated into everyday social life. This often happens in a festive way and they feel, as they say, reborn and sanctified, having moved from shame to honour, from defilement to purity – a symbolic equivalent of the transition from social death to life. Depending on context, the blood shed can have either a polluting or a purifying effect.

Vengeance in Calabria, we are told, works as a social regulator: by taking blood revenge, a man reasserts his status as a man and, as a consequence, the group recovers its fullness:

> Tant que la vengeance n'a pas eu lieu, on porte, d'une façon ou d'autre, le deuil, et l'on vit dans la honte. Par la vengeance, le groupe retrouve la vie: elle est saluée par une véritable fête. (Breteau and Zagnoli 1980: 49)

> (As long as vengeance has not occurred, one is in mourning, and lives in shame. Through vengeance, the group recovers life: it is greeted with a veritable feast.)

Blood vengeance implies far-reaching forms of reciprocity. Revenge aims at repairing the stained reputation of both the dishonoured person and his group. More is involved than metaphorical relations in practices that Frazer called 'homeopathic' or 'imitative' magic. This first branch of sympathetic magic is based on the principle of similarity. But the beliefs and practices concerning blood vengeance may also be understood in terms of metonymical relations: that is, in terms of contact and contiguity, as part–whole relationships. For this second branch of sympathetic magic, based on the principle of contact, Frazer used the term 'contagious' magic.[29] When people say they are 'in blood' and 'take blood' to make it 'flow back' to the victim and his group, to compensate for the lost blood, the relations are also conceived in terms of contact and are therefore clearly metonymical.[30]

Frazer's notion of sympathetic magic – especially its 'contagious' or metonymical variety – dovetails with what Lévy-Bruhl called 'participation': an ordering of reality that is not causal but mystical. As one commentator puts it:

> Participation can be represented as occurring when persons, groups, animals, places, and natural phenomena are in a relation of contiguity, and translate that relation into one of existential immediacy and contact and shared affinity. (In the language of semiotics, humans on the one hand and places, objects, and natural phenomena on the other, are represented as mutually representing one another 'iconically', and as transferring energies and attributes 'indexically'). (Tambiah 1990: 107)

Among other things, Tambiah refers to a south Italian village where grandparents speak of their ancient rootedness in their farms and villages of origin. He also mentions national monuments such as Arlington Cemetery and battlefields such as Gettysburg that 'are believed to enshrine a people's history or radiate their national glories'. In all these instances, writes Tambiah, we have manifestations of 'participation' among people, places, nature and objects. Moreover, 'people participate in each other as well: the bonding and the relation between parents and children, between kinsmen by the ties of blood and amity, [and] the transmission of charisma . . . are intimations of participation' (1990: 107–8).

Discussing kinship among Sarakatsani shepherds in Greece, Campbell downplays the metaphorical aspect of blood and refers to 'participation':

> The solidarity of the corporate family is symbolized in the idea of blood. In marriage a man and a woman mix their different blood to produce 'one blood' which is the blood of their children. One says of a child, 'he is my blood'. Relationships in the family are a participation in this common blood. (1964: 185)

Reciprocal vengeance killings, too, may be understood in terms of 'participation'. Campbell notes that Sarakatsani 'believe that in some way a killer absorbs the strength from the blood of the man he slays. "I shall drink your blood", is a phrase that threatens murder. . . . One avenger bathed his hands in the blood of the original killer and returned to show his mother "the blood of her son" ' (1964: 193).[31]

We have seen that similar customs prevailed in Montenegro. The people with whom first Durham and later Boehm lived had no term for what we call 'blood feud' – that is, 'a protracted state of homicidal aggression between two individuals or two groups that are consumed by bitterness and hatred' (Boehm 1984: 51). But they possessed a rich vocabulary for speaking of different aspects of blood vengeance. Most significantly, the words *u krvi* mean 'in blood', and designate a 'state of hostility where the purpose was to take blood revenge' (Boehm 1984: 51–2). According to Boehm the words describe a state of being, rather than a feud in the sense of a total event of a certain size, design and duration.

With the state of being 'in blood' (*u krvi* or *krvna osveta*) we have a manifestation of participation – the bonding between enemies who reciprocally take 'blood for blood'. Durham argues that *osveta*, the act of 'taking blood', goes beyond the punishment for a crime: one kills to replace the blood lost by the house or the group. *Osveta* has a religious quality, and Durham recalls that in Serbian the verb *osvetiti* means both to hallow or consecrate and to take blood in a feud.[32]

This type of bonding also surfaces in the interviews with Buscetta. For example, he compares the 'mentality' of *mafiosi* in the United States with his own attitudes, finding the younger generation more Americanized: 'They always talked about the rights and obligations of the individual. It was almost an obsession. At home in Sicily this "individual" did not exist. The "family" came first before everything else. Also before the real family, that of blood.'[33]

These considerations leave us with the question of whether we can actually speak of 'metaphorical' relations when people accept a certain identity between things of a different order. These relations can most usefully be understood in terms of participation or performance.[34] That way, one avoids seeing either too much or too little in other people's forms of ordering reality by simply imposing one's own categories – as happens when one mistakes the discourse of magic for that of science or pseudo-science.

VI

Finally, we should briefly look at the type of social structure that sustains those beliefs and practices connected with blood. The representations of blood and the corresponding ritual practices are especially prevalent in mountainous, remote regions of former empires and present-day nation-states, such as Sicily, Calabria, Corsica, Sardinia, the Moroccan Rif, Montenegro and other parts of the Balkans. In the absence of effective central control over the means of violence or by simply evading the law, people could for trust, loyalty and protection only turn to kin and quasi-kinsmen, however culturally constructed.[35]

These arrangements worked both ways in Sicily. Because forms of self-help[36] became – immediately after the unification of Italy – a force in their own right, the very existence of *mafia* coalitions made effective central control in these territories even more difficult. Parallel structures consisting of kinship, friendship, and patron–client ties developed in the interstices of the state.[37] These ties involved politicians from the highest echelons in local sociability and collusion – from being guests of honour at weddings and other parties at the home of their canvassers and henchmen, to membership in Masonic lodges.[38] Under these conditions a culture of blood feuds and atrocities prevailed at the local level. Peripheral and out of the way, the villages and towns in Sicily's western interior resembled remote communities in the mountainous border zones of large, declining (Ottoman, Habsburg, Russian and former Communist) empires.[39]

The pre-eminence of kinship bonds in *mafia* also reflects the origin of *mafiosi*: many come from small rural towns and villages within Sicily, in what may be called the periphery of the periphery.[40] In these remote rural areas lives were lived among kinsmen. Since the beginning of this century, several important *mafia* leaders, whose influence transcended the limits of their home towns (for which reason they erroneously acquired the epithet of *capo di tutti capi*), came from and often remained all their lives in relatively small, out-of-the-way communities.[41] Located in Sicily's western interior, these agro-towns rarely exceeded 12,000 inhabitants. Vito Cascio Ferro lived in Bisaquino, Calogero Vizzini in Villalba and Giuseppe Genco Russo had his residence in Mussomeli; Salvatore Riina came from Corleone, and his close friends Bernardo and Giovanni Brusca lived in the nearby town of San Giuseppe Jato.[42]

To summarize, blood symbolizes solidarity between agnates and affines as well as between friends and 'brothers' who are ritually (and through the medium of blood) turned into quasi-kinsmen. These practices prove especially important among people who conduct risky transactions and who cannot rely for protection on the institutions of centralized states.

Under these conditions, the vocabulary of blood and kinship is pervasive.[43] We find the term 'families' used for the most salient of *mafia* sodalities – the local groups that make up the entire network of Sicilian *mafiosi*. Members of the 'brotherhood' are often called *fratelli*, or 'brothers'.[44] A politician who protects his *mafioso* clients is referred to as *zio* ('uncle').[45] The term *padrino* ('godfather') for powerful *mafia* leaders is too familiar to require further comment. There is nothing artificial or irrational about these relationships. They attest to a holistic world-view and forms of interconnectedness that can perhaps best be understood in terms of 'participation'.

Blood is culturally associated with virginity and procreation, and therefore also imbues the bonds between in-laws. Finally, the imagery of blood governs relations between enemies and former friends since it is intimately related with conflict and the settlement of scores between *mafiosi*. Depending on context, shed blood can signify defilement or purification. Blood feuds show how kin-groups are decimated in vengeance for offences committed by single members. There is no getting away from the ubiquity of blood as a symbolic device.

6

The Meaning of 'Senseless' Violence

Violence is frequently called irrational. It has its reasons, however . . .
Girard, *Violence and the Sacred*

I

The comparative study of violence suffers from several handicaps. The most important is the dominant conception of violence in modern societies in which the means of violence have long since been monopolized by the state. Precisely because of the stability of this relatively impersonal monopoly and the resulting pacification of society at large, people have developed strong feelings about using and witnessing violence. They are inclined to consider its unauthorized forms in particular as anomalous, irrational, senseless and disruptive – as the reverse of social order, as the antithesis of 'civilization', as something that has to be brought under control.

The pacification of society and its acceptance as 'natural' lie at the basis of both scholarly and popular accounts of violence. If focused on the actual use of violence at all, the emphasis falls on the instrumental, most obvious aspects of violence.[1] The cultural dimensions of violence – its idiom, discourse and meaning – receive even less attention. Discussing violence in Northern Ireland, McFarlane notes that 'there is rather little discussion of violence per se in anthropology' (1986: 192). The reluctance of scholars to commit themselves to the study of violence is also evident in the historiography of the French Revolution: in her article 'Beheadings' Regina Janes argues that historians have systematically declined to discuss and explain popular violence.[2]

103

Another telling example of this avoidance behaviour provides one of the most famous pieces of anthropological literature. In a footnote at the end of his essay on the Balinese cockfight, Geertz mentions the mass killings on the island at the end of 1965 in a single sentence: 'in two weeks of December 1965, during the upheavals following the unsuccessful coup in Djakarta, between forty and eighty thousand Balinese (in a population of about two million) were killed, largely by one another – the worst outburst in the country' (1973: 452 n. 43). It was more than twenty years before a historian–anthropologist explored these events and the wider context in which they took shape.[3]

We want to understand violence primarily in utilitarian, 'rational' terms, in terms of means and ends. The question of what violence signifies, 'says' or expresses is at best of secondary importance. In this way, historically developed sensibilities serve as a standard in comparative research and are responsible for distorted views of both violence and society. This may help to explain why we speak of 'senseless' violence in cases where easily recognizable goals and obvious relationships between means and ends are absent. These dominant perceptions and representations of violence are all the more remarkable because modern societies include several domains in which unlicensed violence is part of everyday life and, what is more, far from disreputable.

Rather than defining violence *a priori* as senseless and irrational, we should consider it as a changing form of interaction and communication, as a historically developed cultural form of *meaningful* action. Frequently used qualifications such as 'senseless' and 'irrational' reflect a western bias and indicate how often cases of violence are divorced from their context. Without knowledge of their specificity and circumstantiality, without a 'thick description' of those cases, they cannot but appear as 'senseless' and 'irrational'. Ironically, then, these qualifications close off research precisely where it should start: with questions about the form, meaning and context of violence.

The phrase 'senseless violence' recently attained general currency in the media, in particular in comments on street violence and on related cases of violence in and around places of entertainment. Some commentators even propose to get rid of the expression altogether because its use implies that violence can also be 'meaningful' when all violence is 'senseless' by definition. I agree with Noel Malcolm who argues that 'the phrase "senseless violence" is a peculiarly empty piece of huffing and puffing. However repugnant deliberate violence may be, the one thing it is not is senseless.'[4]

We shall see that widely different forms of violence routinely labelled as 'senseless' or 'irrational' are governed by rules, prescriptions, etiquette and protocol. Ritualization characterizes any number of violent operations.

II

We shall take two cases of serious delicts that received some attention in Dutch newspapers: the so-called parking place killing in Leiden at the end of April 1991 and the killing with a knife of a train conductor in Frisia in early May of the same year. In both cases important information about the details and circumstances of the events was not reported in the newspapers. For example, we do not know what kind of verbal and non-verbal exchanges preceded the killings. In the first case, the ethnic identity of the offender was not revealed until much later, during the trial, when he turned out to be a young Turkish man. In the second case, the suspect was a young unemployed Moroccan.[5] Time and place, gender and age, cultural background – all these aspects were of course vital details and contextual aspects of the events. This also goes for the nature of the confrontations themselves. Consider gaze, gesture, posture and verbal exchange. To what extent are we dealing with offensive or disparaging attitudes and remarks and other forms of symbolic attacks on the person and violations of his territory that may have triggered the violent and fatal response?

In general very little about the details and circumstances of violent encounters is reported in newspapers. Distortion of events and context seriously hampers understanding and obstructs grasping any sense or meaning. Because violent events are represented only fragmentarily and largely out of context, it is not surprising that people define them as 'senseless'.

It is well known that many cases of homicide result from insults. We also know that sensitivity to insults varies with context and that some people are more sensitive to them than others. When inflicted in public, insults can be experienced as a serious form of verbal violence, in which injury mixes with insult. This is particularly true in cultures with a strongly developed sense of honour, as anthropologists have demonstrated for Mediterranean communities.[6] For men, the use of violence is the best way to obtain satisfaction for stained honour and to restore their reputation for manliness. It has been argued, therefore, that 'the ultimate vindication of honour lies in physical violence'.[7]

But this does not tell us enough about the context of the examples mentioned above. Both cases involved men from minority groups in confrontations with members of the autochthonous population. This element may have reinforced the existing tendency toward and sensitivity to condescending, arrogant and provocative behaviour.[8] Distortion of the context – through under-reporting and ignoring important ethno-graphic details, particulars about events and circumstances of delicts – can only produce defective perception and misunderstanding. These jour-nalistic practices may help to explain the popular and erroneous conceptualization of violence in terms of 'senseless' and 'irrational' behaviour. We should not exclude the possibility that circumstantial (or 'thick') descriptions of violent encounters are avoided because re-spectable newspapers consider them tasteless.

Examining accounts of violence confronts us with a paradox. The emotional value attached to violence in modern societies prejudges research and stands in the way of exploring the reason for and meaning of violence. Hildred Geertz's criticism of Keith Thomas's book on the decline of magic comes to mind. She blamed him for an uncritical use of indigenous categories as analytical tools.[9] In comparative studies of violent delicts a preoccupation with the classification of violence often dominates the participants' own classifications. The emphasis on num-bers leaves little room for the careful study of cases. Moreover, we are concerned with prejudices that dovetail with a public opinion more inter-ested in the increase or decrease of violence – in prevention, policy and control – than in ethnographic detail, form, meaning and context of vio-lence, which includes more than occasional references to the age, gender and occupational or ethnic background of offenders.

III

Rather than looking at violence through essentialistic or naturalistic lenses, it makes more sense to consider violence as a cultural category, as a historically developed cultural form or construction. How people conceive of violence and the meaning it has for them is contingent with time and place, varies with historical circumstances, and depends on the perspective of those involved – offenders and victims, spectators and bystanders, witnesses and authorities.

What we call the 'bullfight' is not defined in Spain as a fight but as a spectacle called *corrida de toros* (the running of bulls) in which the *torero* has to demonstrate in a stylized fashion his courage, daring, *gracia* and manliness.[10] Dutch society is divided over the issue of hunting and whether it involves acceptable violence: the *weidelijke* or 'decent', 'self-respecting' hunters, who strongly ritualize their relationship with game, on the one hand, and the larger public that, not hampered by much knowledge about the subject, rejects any form of hunting, on the other.[11]

That we have to consider violence as a cultural form or construction is also obvious from changing classifications and the definition of every-day crime. Street robberies, including snatching purses and handbags from women and elderly people, counted for a long time as theft, but were recently redefined as violent delicts. Interviews with convicts with long prison terms suggest that burglars have a code of their own and often differ from judicial authorities over the definition of violent delicts. In earlier days, violence against persons, including manslaughter, was considered less abominable and punished less severely than crimes against property, some of which were defined as capital crimes. In modern societies today, the law considers violence against persons as a more serious delict than crimes against property.[12] These shifts of meaning, which neatly fit the drift of the civilizing process described by Elias, can also be detected in the discourse on rape. Recent discussions on rape within marriage and in other contexts, including so-called 'date rape', reveal that we are again concerned with actions or aspects of actions that, for many people, have obtained a different meaning and that are now also formally defined as violent crimes.[13]

Rape illustrates the importance of meaning because it shows how meaning depends on context. So-called 'undesired intimacies', or sexual harassment (violations of privacy) at the workplace and elsewhere, concern social action that one would not accept from A, but might desire from B.[14] About such aspects of the context of micro-behaviour Goffman has reported extensively and admirably in 'Territories of the Self': 'The very forms of behavior employed to celebrate and affirm relationships – such as greetings, enquiries after health, and love-making – are very close in character to what would be a violation of preserves if performed between wrongly related individuals' (1971: 57–8). In his treatment of ceremonial violations in his earlier essay on deference and demeanour Goffman has already pointed out the possibility of inversion that all rituals include:

> The idiom through which modes of proper ceremonial conduct are established necessarily creates ideally effective forms of desecration, for it is only in reference to specific proper ties that one can learn to appreciate what will be the worst possible form of behavior. Profanities are to be expected, for every religious ceremony creates the possibility of a black mass. (1967: 86)

IV

Anthropologists have found it useful to distinguish between instrumental (technical) and expressive (ritual, symbolic, communicative) aspects of human behaviour.[15] The former involve expediency and practical reason, the relation between means and goals. The latter involve meaning: what do these practices 'say', what do they express? The emphasis is on cultural form rather than on means and ends. Both aspects are important and closely connected. It may be useful to see this relation in terms of a continuum: some actions are more instrumental, other actions are more expressive.

All social action, however, has potentially something 'to say'. In street robberies, for example, the instrumental aspects seem dominant. Yet it would be wrong to ignore the symbolic import, the meaning these operations have for both the victim (fear, humiliation, the loss of a loved object) and the offender (position, status, prestige, reputation in his own group). These are important matters and constitute precisely what symbolic action is all about. It is the task of cultural anthropologists to focus on what Leach calls the 'aesthetic frills' – how people operate and give form to social action and explicate the meanings implied.[16]

The analytical distinction between instrumental and expressive aspects of social action can be especially helpful in the study of violence. If the use of violence can be primarily understood in terms of symbolic action, this does not imply, of course, that we are dealing only with 'symbolic' violence. What it does imply, however, is that the effective use of physical force very much depends on its symbolic form. Like all performances, it turns on how it is carried out: it depends on the message, on what people want to say, to communicate. Hence the ritualization of violence. Although violence may be primarily directed at the attainment of specific ends, such as wounding or killing an opponent, it is impossible to understand these violent operations in terms of these easily recognizable goals alone. There are often more effective ways to obtain these results.

Liquidations in the world of the rural *mafia* in Sicily were often carried out by sawn-off shotgun, the weapon formerly used for hunting wolves. Hence the name *lupara* for this disfiguring and humiliating mode of killing. *Post mortem* mutilations of victims and dressing them up in grotesque ways also have specific meanings – as has feeding corpses to pigs. *Lupara bianca* denotes the elimination of opponents without leaving any traces. This more recent and rather unceremonious form of liquidation still permits mourning but excludes funeral rites and, therefore, underscores desecration and humiliation. From antiquity up to the present day, from Hector and Antigone to the anonymous victims of Srebrenica, we can detect the enormous value people attach to the integrated body and a proper burial in the numerous cases where dead bodies are mutilated and proper burials denied – both in the practices of official criminal law and in forms of popular justice. The symbolic import, the point of these cases, lies in the very absence of ritual.[17]

The church robberies in eighteenth-century Overmaas (the hinterland of Maastricht), for which the so-called *Bokkeryders* were held responsible, not only involved the violation of sanctuaries, but also included further profanations such as the theft of ceremonial objects and the celebration of a black mass.[18] The point of the bullfight is not that six bulls are killed and sent to the butcher, but how these dispatches are performed – how the matador faces the bulls, has them run, controls them, and so on.[19]

Ritualization characterizes a majority of violent operations, including sacrifice, hunting, cockfights, butchering, *charivari*, duelling, wars, judicial torture, public executions, the killing of sacred chiefs and kings (ritual regicide), tyrannicide, feuding, vendetta, head-hunting, terrorism, vandalism, pillage and organized crime.[20] All these forms of violence are, to a greater or lesser extent, tied to rules and prescriptions, etiquette and protocol. Their ritualization is evident from specifications of time and place, the presence of special persons in special outfits, the use of a special vocabulary – in short from their formalized, theatrical character. In all these instances more is at stake than the mechanical move towards a specific goal. If there are goals involved, they can only be reached in a special, prescribed, indeed *ritualized* fashion. If ritualization is absent in violent encounters, this may paradoxically underscore its importance.

Violent action involves major transitions, including crossing the boundaries between life and death. Special precautions serve to avoid or remove pollution.[21] One can detect in the ritualization of violence attempts to avoid moral responsibility for killing 'fellow' human beings. Special names for opponents and victims, like animal names ('dogs', 'cockroaches', and the like), offensive nicknames and other abusive terms serve to dehumanize them, set them apart from ordinary people and remove them from the moral community. Special times and places locate the action outside the moral community. Alcohol and drugs serve to exempt executors and offenders from moral responsibility for killing human beings.

We should therefore hesitate before defining violence as 'senseless' or 'irrational'. Moreover, the reason for and meaning of violence are also implied in the sanctions that come into play if the perpetrators commit errors or fail in the performance. People set great store by committing violence in a prescribed, formalized, theatrical fashion because deviation from protocol and scenario implies pollution and therefore often results in disqualification: the executioner who fails is punished himself (lynched by the spectators); the hunter who fails to observe the rules of *weidelijkheid* is excluded from his milieu; the man who refuses to give or demand satisfaction in a duel loses his membership in the 'good society'; the burglar who uses violence against victims is branded by his peers as an amateur; the football hooligan who uses unmanly means of fighting is looked down upon by his friends; the bullfighter who performs the prescribed moves without *gracia* or without taking risks – 'coming out before coming in' as Hemingway puts it in *Death in the Afternoon* – is scoffed at, called *asesino* (murderer) by the spectators.

Why the use of violence is so often ritualized and so unmistakably a cultural form is a problem in itself. Avoiding pollution and the issue of moral responsibility for killing fellow human beings have already been mentioned. This interpretation ties up with what Meuli and Burkert say about the *Unschuldskomödie* (comedy of innocence) in sacrificial and hunting rituals in ancient societies. In these cases one can see attempts to create a distance, to avoid and remove pollution, attempts at reconciliation with the victim, and, ultimately, to justify and legitimate violence.[22] Bloodshed is associated with transitions, the crossing of boundaries between life and death, this world and the next, culture and nature, and the like, which invariably imply pollution. For all these reasons, one can expect the use of violence to be surrounded by ritual.[23] This is also why the use of violence can have a purifying effect in vindication as 'washing the stains of honour' by 'taking blood for blood' testifies.[24]

V

That violence is symbolic action obviously applies to sacrifice. But it also applies to terrorism, which at least sometimes acquires the character of ritual sacrifice, as Zulaika argues in his study of political violence in the Basque country.[25] Terrorism is usually represented as irrational and senseless, especially when the victims are innocent and selected at random. A worse interpretation is hardly possible. The terror under the Zulu king Shaka has often been depicted as arbitrary and irrational; on closer inspection, however, there was method in Shaka's pitiless massacres.[26] The early nineteenth-century Zulu king and his European biographers already understood what long puzzled twentieth-century social scientists.[27] Zulaika recalls Aron's definition of terrorism as violence whose psychological effects are in no way commensurate with its physical results. He argues that what characterizes terrorism is the manipulation of the psychology of violence by inspiring fear among potential victims. Terrorism and ritual sacrifices share a fundamental feature: the victim (who encapsulates and embodies the aim and meaning of the action) has to be innocent. The innocence of the victims is implied in the randomness of terroristic attacks.[28] But we also know that some victims of Basque terrorism were neither innocent nor randomly selected.

The ritual character of public executions has recently been emphasized by various scholars and hardly requires further discussion. A few comments are, however, in order. To define death on the scaffold and the banishment of convicts as 'laborious' is to miss the point: a formalized, dramatic form of social communication concerning the removal of pollution. The ceremonies that accompanied the punishments, or of which the punishments consisted, cannot be understood in merely technical terms, as the mere physical elimination of criminals. Alongside their magico-religious import, public executions were 'spectacular' in more than one sense. They presented a warning aimed at deterrence as clearly specified in the verdict: 'to inspire fear and set an example'.[29]

In what took place in and around the scaffold, earlier scholars saw a ritual sacrifice. This point of view receives further attention in Girard's studies of the role of the scapegoat in collective violence.[30] Although public executions largely disappeared from modern societies in the nineteenth century, their form still holds a strong fascination for contemporary audiences as executions *in effigie* and the toppling of statues of hated rulers demonstrate. These practices are clearly expressive, communicative and magical. Iconoclasm and public exhumation, the carrying around and display of corpses, and further profanations of remains are usually directed against persons who themselves have become icons of a hated regime, an oppressive form of life, a dark epoch.[31]

VI

The main point of this essay is that violence should not *a priori* be dismissed as 'senseless'. On the contrary, it should be understood primarily as symbolic action, that is, as *meaningful* action. This is perhaps most evident in the emphasis on ritual and ceremony, status, identity and group membership. Violence makes statements, and it is the task of anthropologists to decipher them. They are greatly helped in this because violence often has the character of theatre and performance in which things are 'said' as much as they are 'done'.[32]

Ritual is no less prominent in 'everyday violence'. Football hooliganism in England and elsewhere in western Europe also abounds in symbolic activities and ritual performances. Confrontations between fans of different clubs provide young men (often from working-class backgrounds) with occasions to demonstrate their aggressive masculinity. Dunning and his collaborators, who studied the phenomenon in the United Kingdom, mention the repertoire of *symbolic demasculinization* and *ritual denigration* in the encounters between groups of supporters. They argue that *hooliganism* is rooted in the working-class subculture where fighting and open aggression are appropriate and desirable in certain situations, and serve – for an age category that has been cross-culturally identified as betwixt-and-between – as a means of acquiring status and prestige.[33]

The time and place of football vandalism are also symptomatic of its ritual character. It occurs on days and in locations that are unusual – on holidays and weekends, and in stadiums, special trains and buses. Ritual plunder by crowds has also been noted as an integral part of rites of passage, such as at the death of bishops and popes in early modern Italy. *Charivari*, or 'rough music', was, until recently, quite common in rural Europe. It provides another example of ritualized violence in which unmarried youngsters played a salient role.[34]

Ritual is also obvious in the violent struggle between Catholics and Protestants in Northern Ireland. Retaliation killings are rarely simple eliminations. Time and place are important. Sometimes opponents are shot dead in the presence of their wives and children. Territory can be so crucial that one scholar refers to *spatial formations of violence*.[35] Ethnic violence in the Balkans is not only a matter of physical harm and destruction; it also involves social and cultural destruction. The most grisly form of symbolic violence is ethnic cleansing. This expression is revealing because it shows once more how strongly the use of violence involves legitimation and the construction of an object defined as polluting that has to be purged. Elsewhere, as in Sri Lanka and South Africa, ethnic violence shows in all its details that much more is at stake than the physical elimination of opponents. Tambiah, who explored the ethnic war between Sinhalese and Tamils in Sri Lanka, writes: 'There occurs an increasing 'theatricalization', and an accompanying ritualization and polarization, in the escalating contents of violence between ethnic, religious, linguistic, or political minorities on the one side and the majority collectivities and established governments on the other' (1991: 116). What is at stake in all these tests of strength is epitomized in the classic European duel: identity, pride and meaning – and the group membership implied in them. What can be deployed and sacrificed for them, Simmel summarized long ago as follows: 'To maintain honour is so much a duty that one derives from it the most terrible sacrifices – not only self-inflicted ones, but also sacrifices imposed on others' (1983: 405).

One cannot explain and understand violence in terms of practical goals only. To justify hunting to their numerous critics, Dutch hunters point to their responsibilities for the preservation of game, the protection of agriculture and the conservation of nature in general. They emphasize the alleged utilitarian, instrumental, functional, practical aspects of their profession rather than the meaning and function that hunting has for them. Obviously, it is difficult to discuss these elements of a life-style and to explain how and why hunting also involves performance, sociability, entertainment and excitement.[36]

The discussion on violence is dominated by these taboos. Civilized persons may not show that they enjoy violence. In the course of the civilizing process a growing number of social practices have been defined and classified as violent and consequently proscribed and hidden behind the scenes, especially activities related to lust and pleasure, including sexuality, hunting, animal fights and duelling.[37] This may be why there has been little interest in the stylization of violence, the meaning and shifts of meaning for people involved in them – as if interest in these matters were also inappropriate.[38] There are many literary and forensic examples, however, that illustrate, for example, the complexity and ambivalence of incest and rape. The discussion of violence has run into a contradiction: on the one hand people pretend to know what violence is; on the other hand and under pressure from increasing democratization and civilization, they define and mark new areas of human action as violent.

VII

Violence is not an unchanging, 'natural' fact but a historically developed cultural category that we have to understand primarily as symbolic activity, as meaningful social action. To define violence as senseless or irrational is to abandon research where it should start: exploring meaning, interpreting symbolic action, and mapping the historical and social context of activities defined as violent. It is the task of the anthropologist or historian to find out what violence 'says' about honour, reputation, status, identity and group solidarity. The codes can be rather complex, but, fortunately for the researcher, there is much redundancy in ritual sequences.[39] Violence is interwoven with masculinity, and the human body often serves as a cultural medium, as a source of metaphorical material to symbolize power relations. As Campbell writes of Greek pastoralists: 'There is no more conclusive way of showing that you are stronger than by taking away the other man's life' (1964: 318). In her article on decapitations and parading severed heads on pikes during the first years of the French Revolution, Regina Janes notes: 'While severed heads always speak, they say different things in different cultures. . . . Cross culturally, taking and displaying an enemy's head is one of the most widely distributed signs of victory' (1991: 24, 47). A recent comparative survey on war attests to this pattern:

> By far the most common and widely distributed war trophy was the head or the skull of an enemy. The custom of taking heads is recorded from many cultures in New Guinea, Oceania, North America, South America, Africa, and ancient western Europe. The popularity of this practice is prob-

ably explained by the obvious fact that the head is the most individual part of the body. (Keeley 1996: 100)

Violation of reputation, humiliation, subjection – all these shows of strength are expressed most clearly through the medium of the human body: shaven heads, stigmas, brandings, mutilations, decapitations, exhumations, displays of corpses and denial of decent burial. In this regard, violence in ethnic confrontations, caste wars, tyrannicides, iconoclasm and public executions shows striking similarities. Physical violations tend to speak a uniform language, as Ranum points out in his essay on tyrannicide in early modern Europe. Both the violation and the vindication of honour are often represented in the idiom of the human body: the stained honour which can only be vindicated, 'cleansed' or 'washed' with blood (see chapter 5). The symbolism of the human body and the related issues of honour and identity loom large in violent confrontations. They raise the issue of family resemblances and cultural uniformities, which, alongside our focus on cultural specificity, deserves close attention in a world that is becoming increasingly interconnected.[40]

7

The Narcissism of Minor Differences

It is not the differences but the loss of them that gives rise to violence and chaos.

Girard, *Violence and the Sacred*

Nella stessa faccia, l'occhio destro odiava il sinistro.
(In the same face, the right eye hated the left.)

Sicilian saying

Ce sont les plus proches qui nous font mal.
(It is those closest to us who hurt us most.)

Bourdieu, Interview

I
We often attribute conflict between individuals or groups to growing contrasts between them. The larger the (economic, social, cultural) differences, the greater the chance of violent confrontations. But an outline of a general theory of power and violence cannot ignore the fact that the fiercest struggles often take place between individuals, groups and communities that differ very little – or between which the differences have greatly diminished. Civil wars are usually described as more merciless than other wars and the fiercest struggle is often between siblings. The archetypes are the biblical brothers Cain and Abel, one of whom was a shepherd and kept flocks, while the other tilled the soil. Hence the metaphorical use of the term 'fratricide' to describe a life-and-death struggle between groups or communities that are very similar, that are neighbours and maintain close ties.

115

Subtle distinctions, rather than great differences between individuals and groups, occasion many conflicts and ruthless struggles. Why should it be minor differences that move people to exclude others, to discriminate against them, to stigmatize them and subject them to extreme forms of violence? And to what extent have scholars recognized the role of subtle distinctions in explosive figurations?

II

One may begin with Freud (not with Marx, for he believed that the class struggle could only develop when the differences between entrepreneurs and workers, between capital and labour had increased: when all the means of production had come into the hands of the entrepreneurs). We start with Freud because he was probably the first to recognize the importance of small differences in understanding conflicts.[1] In at least four places in his work he discusses 'the narcissism of minor differences'. What does he mean by this phrase and what does he do with it?

The first time Freud discusses the narcissism of minor differences is in his essay 'The Taboo of Virginity' [1917]. He refers to a study by Crawley, who argues that people are separated from one another by a 'taboo of personal isolation', and that it is precisely the minor differences between people who are otherwise alike that form the basis of feelings of strangeness and hostility between them (Freud 1991a: 272). Freud writes: 'It would be tempting to pursue this idea and to derive from this 'narcissism of minor differences' the hostility which in every human relation we see fighting successfully against feelings of fellowship and overpowering the commandment that all men should love one another' (1991a: 272).

Some years later, Freud brings the subject up again. In 'Group Psychology and the Analysis of the Ego' [1921] he first refers to Schopenhauer's parable of the freezing porcupines who crowded together to profit from one another's warmth, but soon felt each other's quills and had to separate again. Freud then extends the comparison to the rivalry between neighbouring towns – known as *campanilismo* (from *campanile*, church bell): local or regional patriotism, a form of solidarity that develops in reaction against and contempt for a village or town in the neighbourhood: 'Of two neighbouring towns each is the other's most jealous rival; every little canton looks down upon the others with contempt. Closely related races keep one another at arm's length; the South German cannot endure the North German, the Englishman casts every kind of aspersion upon the Scot, the Spaniard despises the Portuguese' (1991b: 130–1). But Freud fails to recognize the importance of his discovery and even manages to reduce the heuristic value of the narcissism of minor differences by declaring immediately afterwards that we should no longer be surprised that 'greater differences should lead to an almost insuperable repugnance, such as the Gallic people feel for the German, the Aryan for the Semite, and the white races for the coloured' (1991b: 130–1). Did Freud misunderstand the quintessence of his own discovery?

The third time Freud focuses attention on the narcissism of minor differences is in his famous essay 'Civilization and its Discontents' [1930]. It adds little to what he already said about the subject and cites the same examples. Freud introduces the passage with an understatement. It is not easy for people to give up the satisfaction of their inclination to aggression: 'Sie fühlen sich nicht wohl dabei' (They don't feel comfortable with it). Referring to the earlier texts in which he discusses the narcissism of minor differences, Freud continues as follows:

> I once discussed the phenomenon that it is precisely communities with adjoining territories, and related to each other in other ways as well, who are engaged in constant feuds and in ridiculing each other – like the Spaniards and Portuguese, for instance, the North Germans and South Germans, the English and Scotch, and so on. I gave this phenomenon the name of 'the narcissism of minor differences', a name which does not do much to explain it. We can now see that it is a convenient and relatively harmless satisfaction of the inclination to aggression, by means of which cohesion between the members of the community is made easier. (1991c: 304–5)

Freud thus did not see much in his find. Little remained of the temptation he initially felt to pursue the idea.

At the end of his life, in his last essay, 'Moses and Monotheism' (1939), in which he tries to explain anti-Semitism, Freud comes back to the issue. He argues that the hatred of the Jews is primarily related to the circumstance that they live for the most part as minorities among other peoples,

> for the communal feeling of groups requires, in order to complete it, hostility towards some extraneous minority, and the numerical weakness of this excluded minority encourages its suppression.
> There are, however, two other characteristics of the Jews which are quite unforgivable. First is the fact that in some respects they are different from their 'host' nations. They are not fundamentally different, for they are not Asiatics of a foreign race, as their enemies maintain, but composed for the most part of remnants of the Mediterranean people and heirs of the Mediterranean civilization. But they are none the less different, often in an indefinable way different, especially from the Nordic peoples, and the intolerance of groups is often, strangely enough, exhibited more

strongly against small differences than against fundamental ones. (1990: 335)

The narcissism of minor differences continued to intrigue Freud, but his reservations and the expression 'strangely enough' suggest that he did not know what to do with it. This may be the reason why he hardly pursued the matter further. Yet considering the numerous conflicts that apparently go back to minimal differences between the warring parties that want to destroy one another, it should be clear that the notion of the narcissism of minor differences deserves further attention and elaboration. What will be explored in particular is how culture informs and shapes violent confrontations.

III
Freud's discovery links up with what other scholars have said about the importance of minor differences. First, Simmel's essay on discretion in *Soziologie* [1908] mentions the 'ideal sphere' that lies around every human being:

> Although differing in size in various directions and differing according to the person with whom one entertains relations, this sphere cannot be penetrated, unless the personality value of the individual is thereby destroyed. A sphere of this sort is placed around man by his 'honor'. Language very poignantly designates an insult to one's honor as 'coming too close': the radius of this sphere marks, as it were, the distance whose trespassing by another person insults one's honor. (Simmel 1983: 265; 1950: 321)

The expression 'coming too close' has both a literal and a figurative meaning here: approach too close and thereby also threaten, offend, dishonour.[2] It is also mentioned by Crawley (Freud's source), and we shall see how important propinquity is for understanding the narcissism of minor differences. Hence also Freud's reference to Schopenhauer's allegory of the freezing porcupines.

In their essay on primitive forms of classification [1903], Durkheim and Mauss argue that social differentiation constitutes the model for the classification of nature; animals, plants, celestial bodies, the seasons – all parts of the natural world are differentiated in terms of their relationship to the main social groups: 'It is because human groups fit into another – the sub-clan into the clan, the clan into the moiety, the moiety into the tribe – that groups of things are ordered in the same way. . . . And if the totality of things is conceived as a single system, this is because society itself is seen in the same way' (1963: 83). Lévi-Strauss further develops this idea in his studies of totemic classifications and shows how tribal groups such as clans and moieties, which share many features and are closely interconnected (in particular through intermarriage), articulate their differences by associating themselves with differences they find in the natural world:

> the differences between animals which man can extract from nature and transfer to culture are adopted as emblems by groups of men in order to do away with their own resemblances. [Men] have to assume the symbolic characteristics by which they distinguish different animals (and which furnish them with a natural model of differentiation) to create differences among themselves. (1966: 107–8; cf. 1969b: 155–64; and 1966: 115–17).

The importance of minor differences between groups has also been recognized by other anthropologists. Leach, for example, notes that 'The more similar the general pattern of two communities, the more critical will be the significance which is attached to minor points of reversal' (1976: 64). In an ethnographic analysis of a Cambridge college we find the following observation (of a famous historian who for obvious reasons prefers to use a pseudonym):

> It may be doubted whether any member of a Cambridge college would admit that his or her institution was typical – *campanilismo* is almost as strong in these bodies as it was in medieval Italian city-states, and one is encouraged, indeed expected, to see one's own institution as unique, a tendency which is strengthened by differences in local customs and titles. The head of most Cambridge colleges is called 'The Master', but King's has a Provost, Queens' a President, Newnham a Principal. There is a kind of narcissism in each college as in the University . . . (Dell 1987: 74)

In this essay, however, we will be mainly concerned with the role of minor differences in less peaceful confrontations.

The ethnographic literature on warfare in tribal societies suggests that violent confrontations usually take place in close circles: that is, within the limits of the tribe, between neighbours, friends or relatives – in short, between people who share many social and cultural features. As the Mae Enga in the western highlands of Papua New Guinea phrase it: 'We marry the people we fight.' Their ethnographer emphasizes that war among these mountain people is most frequent between neighbours and fraternal clans (Meggitt 1977: 28–9, 42). Exchange and war can be understood as two sides of the same coin. A recent synopsis of tribal warfare confirms this pattern and mentions propinquity as a major cause: people interact most intensely with their nearest neighbours, 'whether those interactions are commercial, nuptial, or hostile' (Keeley 1996:

122–3). Even in more complex societies, the feud is part of a network of reciprocity and offers groups the occasion to distinguish themselves within a common framework (Black-Michaud 1975: 208). The writer Milovan Djilas, a native of Montenegro, makes a similar point in *Land without Justice* (1958) when he reflects on the blood feuds that affected his own family:

> Though the life of my family is not completely typical of my homeland, Montenegro, it is typical in one respect: the men of several generations have died at the hands of Montenegrins, men of the same faith and name. My father's grandfather, my two own grandfathers, my father, and my uncle were killed, as though a dread curse lay upon them. My father and his brother and my brothers were killed even though all of them yearned to die peacefully in their beds beside their wives. Generation after generation, and the bloody chain was not broken. The inherited fear and hatred of feuding clans was mightier than fear and hatred of the enemy the Turks. (1958: 8)[3]

On the character of intertribal wars, Evans-Pritchard's observations on the Nuer in the southern Sudan are highly relevant. The Nuer feel closer to the Dinka than to other groups of strangers. At the same time, the Nuer show greater hostility toward the Dinka than toward other strangers. War between these two peoples amounts to more than just conflicts of interest. We are primarily concerned with a structural relationship because their animosity is deeply influenced by the extent of cultural differentiation between the Nuer and their neighbours:

> The nearer people are to the Nuer in mode of livelihood, language, and customs, the more intimately the Nuer regard them, the more easily they enter into relations of hostility with them, and the more easily they fuse with them. . . . The cultural cleavage is least between Nuer and Dinka; it widens between Nuer and Shilluk-speaking peoples. . . . Nuer make war against a people who have a culture like their own rather than among themselves or against peoples with cultures very different from their own. (1940: 130–1)

Similar structural relations, which provide a common framework of cooperation and distinction marked by the use of violence, are also evident in modern societies. Violent encounters between supporters of football clubs in western Europe provide an example. Rather than clashes of interest, we again see the articulation of minor differences between groups who share many features (age, gender, class, education, work, language, apparel, cultural interests and 'identity'). Moreover, these groups are part of other dualistic formations, including clubs, bars, neighbourhoods and cities. Fighting and aggressive behaviour have become part of 'going to the match'. As happened in duelling among the *jeunesse dorée* in western Europe until the late nineteenth century, arrangements are made for a time and place of violent encounters *extra muros*, outside the built-up area:

> On occasions, rival groups communicate an intention to meet at a particular location before or after the match. Such locations are chosen because the hooligan fans believe that this will enable them to avoid the attention of the police and give them a chance to establish, without outside interference or fear of arrest, which is the 'superior' crew. (Dunning et al. 1986: 168–71)

Next we come to Bourdieu, who illuminates two new aspects of minor differences between groups in his book on distinction – without, however, referring to Freud. In his book (translated into German with the apt title *Die feinen Unterschiede*), Bourdieu emphasizes the importance of minor differences for the formation and maintenance of identity and the threat to identity that comes from what is closest. Hence the importance of minor differences – the *narcissism* of minor differences – precisely when we are dealing with groups that are very close and similar. Bourdieu writes: 'Social identity lies in difference, and difference is asserted against what is closest, which represents the greatest threat' (1984: 479).

Bourdieu's book on cultural distinctions in twentieth-century France has obviously been influenced by the work of Elias on court society and the civilizing process. From these books we learn how, in the course of the civilizing process, more refined and differentiated codes of behaviour (originally designed at court to domesticate the nobility) enabled the same French aristocracy during the seventeenth and eighteenth centuries to distinguish itself from the upwardly mobile bourgeoisie. In this context, too, fine distinctions were at issue, important details, 'feine Unterschiede', 'minor differences', which played a crucial role in the establishment and maintenance of identity, social distance, and power. As Elias summarizes his view of civilizing processes and emphasizes that certain cultural differences do not merely reflect power differences but also help to shape and maintain them:

> Relatively stricter morals are only one form of socially induced self-restraints among many others. Better manners are another. They all enhance the chances of a superior group to assert and to maintain their power and superiority. In an appropriate configuration civilising differentials can be an important factor in the making and perpetuation of power

differentials, although in extreme cases they may weaken 'old' powerful groups to be more civilised and may contribute to their downfall. (1965: 152–3)

Most significant for our purposes is Girard's important study on violence and the sacred. On the basis of literary, historical and ethnographic material, Girard argues that the loss of differences between groups is the main source of extreme violence:

> A single principle is at work in primitive religion and classical tragedy alike, a principle implicit but fundamental. Order, peace, and fecundity depend on cultural distinctions; it is not these distinctions but the loss of them that gives birth to fierce rivalries and sets members of the same family or social group at one another's throats.
>   Modern society aspires to equality among men and tends instinctively to regard all differences, even those unrelated to the economic or social status of men, as obstacles in the path of human happiness. (Girard 1979: 49)

To illustrate his theory about 'differences', Girard discusses the role of twins and other sets of brothers. In some tribal societies, twins inspire a particular fear. It is not uncommon for one or both of them to be killed. Where differences are lacking, violence threatens. Girard points out the aspect of ritual pollution: when faced with biological twins, a common reaction of tribal communities is to avoid contagion. Therefore, the infants are 'exposed', that is, abandoned (1979: 56–8).

Girard ties up the theme of twins with that of brothers who are enemies. He refers to Kluckhohn (1968: 52), who argues that the most common conflict in myths is the struggle between brothers – a struggle that usually ends in fratricide. They are not always twins; they can be ordinary brothers who are very much alike and have been born shortly after one another. Even when the brothers are not twins, the difference between them is much less than between all other grades of kin relations. In many cases they occupy the same position with respect to other kinsmen, both close and distant relatives. Brothers have more rights, obligations and functions in common than is the case with other members of the family. In a way, twins are 'reinforced' brothers from whom the last objective difference, that of age, has been taken away: it is often impossible to distinguish them. We are inclined, Girard continues, to consider the fraternal bond as a model of an affective relationship ('brotherly' as synonym for affectionate and loyal). But the mythological, historical and literary examples that come to mind tell a different story: Cain and Abel, Jacob and Esau, Romulus and Remus. But it is not only in myths, writes Girard, that brothers are 'simultaneously drawn together and driven apart by something they both ardently desire and which they will not or cannot share – a throne, a woman or, in more general terms, a paternal heritage' (1979: 61–4).[4] This point can be taken one step further. As Sulloway convincingly argues in his detailed and masterful study of birth order, sibling rivalry and sibling relations can be best understood in terms of survival strategies; siblings compete with one another for parental attention and investment: that is why siblings seek to be different (1996: 55–118 and *passim*).

How can the narcissism of minor differences – the idea that identity lies in difference, and difference is asserted, reinforced and defended against what is closest and represents the greatest threat – clarify contemporary cases of extremely violent confrontations?

IV

The first example concerns the position of the Burakumin in Japan.[5] Formerly called Eta, the Burakumin do not differ in appearance from other Japanese. They were and still are discriminated against and considered as second-class citizens because of their profession (butchering and leather-work) and, therefore, lived in separate quarters. Their official emancipation in 1871 gave the Eta the same legal status and rights as other Japanese, but did not change the negative attitude toward them and their descendants. The state could not protect the civil rights of the Burakumin. In fact, these 'new ordinary people' lost the privileges they had enjoyed under the old feudal regime (the economic monopolies including slaughtering, butchering, skinning, tanning, and leather-work) without receiving any compensation. Local farmers persecuted the Burakumin for fear of being reduced to the status of these former outcasts: they believed that government policy aimed to turn them into Burakumin. This fear of losing their identity is evident from a number of incidents in which mobs of angry farmers used extreme violence against the Burakumin. In one major incident at the end of May 1873, the army had to intervene and arrested 400 people: 'According to official figures, 10 houses of government officials, 47 homes of village heads, 25 homes of policemen, 15 school buildings, and more than 300 Buraku homes were wrecked or burned. Eighteen Burakumin were reported dead and 11 badly injured. It was estimated that about 26,000 farmers joined the riot' (De Vos and Wagatsuma 1972: 37).

V

The mechanism of the narcissism of minor differences also played a crucial role in the American South after the abolition of slavery in 1865. Equality of ex-slaves before the law resulted (again unintentionally) in fierce discrimination and the use of extreme violence against them. The secret societies and the lynchings are post-Civil War phenomena – that is, after slavery had been abolished – and reached their climax in the decades around 1900. Persecution came, in particular, from poor and lower middle-class whites, who predominated in the secret societies, mobs and posses. They feared being put on a par with the former slaves, and derived their identity and self-esteem from their social distance from the black population. In *Caste and Class in a Southern Town* [1937], Dollard points out the importance of upward social mobility of blacks since the Civil War, their acquisition of middle-class status: 'The Ku Klux Klan and other more powerful secret orders were folk movements for the intimidation of Negroes and for the re-establishment of the social distance that formerly existed between whites and Negroes. Although the work of such orders differed in different regions, this function was invariable' (1988: 58). Visiting Atlanta in the 1980s, Naipaul discussed the still tangible results of the 1912 Forsyth County lynching with a local lawyer, who observed that

> to understand, it was necessary to remember that 120 years or so ago there had been slavery. For poor white people race was their identity. Someone well off could walk away from that issue, could find another cause for self-esteem; but it wasn't that easy for the man with little money or education; without race he would lose his idea of who he was. (1989: 29)[6]

Thus the theory of minor differences finds confirmation in figurations characterized by great differences. The one is the counterpart of the other. Where social distance is greater, where differences in power and cultural differences are more pronounced, the chance of conflict, struggle and extreme violence diminish accordingly (cf. Walter 1969: 15–16). Rather than overt forms of violence, we encounter subtle forms of passive resistance, recorded in 'hidden transcripts', as Scott has carefully documented in two important studies (1985; 1990). Of course, popular movements against established power-holders are not lacking in ethnographic and historical accounts, but such movements prove successful only if they can form coalitions with the rivals of their opponents.[7]

VI
Social distance and identity go hand in hand. Of the court nobility in France and Germany under the *ancien régime*, we learn that membership in the 'gute Gesellschaft' was closely linked to 'honour'. To be expelled, writes Elias, meant loss of honour, the loss of a constituent part of an individual's personal identity. In fact, a nobleman would put his life at stake often enough – either as challenger or as the one challenged.

He preferred to risk his life as a member of the 'gute Gesellschaft', for this meant to be elevated above the mass around him. Without this membership life had no meaning for him, as long as the power of his privileged class remained intact (Elias 1969a: 145–6). In his study of *satisfaktionsfähige* networks in nineteenth-century Germany, in which an upper-class Prussian could not withdraw from a duel, even if it would certainly end with his death, Elias describes the force of this aristocratic code of honour – to demand, and give, satisfaction – as follows: 'To give up and go away would not only have meant losing his position, but also losing everything which gave his life meaning and fulfilment' (1996: 70).

The duel is an example of stylized and refined violence between equals, one of whom has encroached on the 'ideal sphere' of another, who consequently gets the chance to vindicate his honour by putting his life at risk.[8] As a miniature, the duel shows how culture and cultural differences – between individuals, groups and national states – can be a matter of life and death.[9] Simmel understood that the ultimate vindication of honour lies in physical violence:

> as one can consider the specific accomplishment of religion to be that it made people turn their own salvation into an obligation, so one can claim, *mutatis mutandis*, that the accomplishment of honour is to have made man turn his social obligation into his individual salvation. That is why, with respect to honour, the aspects of right and obligation are interwoven and transitional: to keep one's honour is so much an obligation and duty, that one can derive from it the right to the most terrible sacrifices – not only self-imposed, but also sacrifices imposed on others (1983: 405, my translation).

VII

The civil war in the former Yugoslavia, where Croats, Serbs and Muslims fought each other in turn, provides us with another situation in which minor differences exacerbated the struggle between the warring parties. In the words of one author: 'Although long divided by history and religion, the South Slavs were both ethnically and linguistically one of the most homogeneous peoples in Europe. On the other hand, Tito never overcame the narcissism of minor differences which drove Croats and Serbs to harp on their essentially small divisions . . .'.[10]

In her observations on the disintegration of Yugoslavia and the revival of genocide, Bette Denich emphasizes the exaggeration of 'minor distinctions' between Croatian and Serbian variants of the literary language:

> The linguistic revisions provided an identity marker for 'good Croats', who were also expected to shed regional attachments in favor of Croatian

culture both unitary and non-Serbian. Regional identities were eliminated: Dalmatia was renamed 'southern Croatia'. As a further infringement upon Serbian status, the Latin alphabet was designated as the sole alphabet throughout Croatia, limiting recognition of the Cyrillic alphabet to communities with Serbian majorities. The new government took control of the media, turning television and newspapers into articulators of the linguistic innovations and other cultural constructions of the new Croatian state. (1994: 379)

The issue of minor differences between ethnic groups in the former Yugoslavia is also raised by another Balkan expert. Eugene A. Hammel distinguishes three primary elements of ethnic identification: kinship, language and religion. But these principles are not neatly related and do not result in clearly demarcated ethnic groups. Ethnic identity is a matter of labels: Serb, Croat, Muslim – especially in the context of civil war. Language is a tricky criterion. Obviously there are sharp distinctions between the Slavic speakers and Albanians, Hungarians, Turks, Greeks and others. But local people are often bilingual and linguistic distinctions among the Slavic speakers are gradual: 'Only minute attention to dialect makes ethnic identification possible. This dialect continuum has been segmented by internationally imposed political boundaries and the centralizing efforts of core states, and the intellectuals of such states have sometimes been busy erecting linguistic boundaries to serve nationalist interests' (Hammel 1993: 7). What this amounts to is that the three dimensions of ethnicity – kinship, language and religion – cross-cut each other. Religion cannot define ethnicity across the board of the major language divisions (e.g. no Catholic Croat claims common ethnicity with a Catholic Hungarian). In some cases, however, religion divides language communities into endogamous subsets, some of which have formed identifiable ethnic groups, like Catholic and Muslim Albanians. On the other hand, 'Catholic and Orthodox Slavs do not recognize common ethnicity, and no Croat peasants claim co-ethnicity with Serb peasants, and neither of these with Muslim Slavs, even when they speak the same dialect' (Hammel 1993: 7). Moreover,

> Croats, Serbs, and Muslims Slavs in Bosnia speak dialects that are only narrowly distinguishable. The dialect of the Bosnian Serbs is closer to that of most of the Croats of the region than it is to the Serbian of the core of Serbia. Similarly, the dialect of most Bosnian Croats is closer to that of the Serbs of the region than it is to that of the Croats of northern Dalmatia or the core of Croatia. The symbol that they use to differentiate themselves is religion, but religion fails in that task outside the region (for example with the Catholic Serbs of Dubrovnik). (1993: 7–8)

Hammel refers to recent homogenizing attempts of states to achieve a congruence of political borders and cultural qualities that were allowed under the Communist regime. As an example, he mentions how Tudjman stripped the *krajina* Serbs of the cultural distinctiveness and privileges they enjoyed under Tito. These efforts to limit symbolic expression had the same effect as under Maria Theresa and Joseph II – namely, armed rebellion (Hammel 1993: 8).

Once more, we see the working of the narcissism of minor differences: the erosion and loss of distinctions and differences result in violence. We also note the importance of concomitant circumstances: the absence of a stable, impersonal central power that is willing and able to protect minorities and their rights.

The view of the British war correspondent Glenny in *The Fall of Yugoslavia* is very close to the position taken in this essay. Glenny notes that from the beginning of the conflict in Croatia one particular question has intrigued people both in Yugoslavia and abroad: 'What causes this depth of hatred which has provoked atrocities and slaughter on such a wide scale over such a short period of time?' (1992: 168). It became obvious that the struggle in this area during the Second World War did not end with the establishment of the Communist regime under Tito. The conflict inside Yugoslavia between 1941 and 1945 'assumed such bloody proportions that, were it ever to revive, it was always likely to be merciless' (1992: 168). 'Even for people like myself,' writes Glenny, 'who have observed both the war itself and the political intrigue which led to it, the nature of the violence remains incomprehensible.' The conflict has complex historical and political causes; but the hatred has different origins. He notes that the wars of the Yugoslav succession have been nationalist in character: 'They are not ethnic conflicts, as the media would often have it, as most of those doing the killing are of the same ethnos. Indeed what is striking about Bosnia-Hercegovina, in particular, is just how closely related are the Serbs, the Croats, and the Moslems' (Glenny 1992: 168).

Hayden notes that the civil wars in the former Yugoslavia have taken place almost entirely within regions that were the most 'mixed' – with high levels of ethno-national heterogeneity and increasing rates of inter-marriage between members of different national groups. He writes that ' "mixed" marriages increased both in absolute numbers and in proportion to all marriages throughout most of Yugoslavia, but were particularly common between Serbs and Croats and between Serbs and Muslims in Bosnia Hercegovina' (1996: 788–9). But the author does not recognize that the resemblance between these groups and the blurring of boundaries lay at the roots of inter-ethnic violence in these areas.

Another Bosnia watcher, David Rohde, who traced the misfortunes of Srebrenica, corroborates this point of view. He notes that Bosnia ('the picturesque country of 4.3 million was 44 per cent Muslim, 31 per cent Serb, 17 per cent Croat, and 8 per cent "Yugoslav"') was the most ethnically integrated of Yugoslavia's six republics, and that intermarriage between Serbs, Croats and Muslims was common in cities and larger towns. All three groups are racially identical ('white Eastern European Slavs') and speak Serbo-Croatian with a Bosnian accent. Differences lie in their religious faith and naming practices: 'The only way a Serb, Croat or Muslim can distinguish one another is by their first or last name' (Rohde 1997: xi–xii).

Although religion has played a decisive role in dividing these people, it is not a confessional conflict. Glenny writes:

> For centuries, these people have been asked to choose between competing empires and ideologies, which have invariably been defined by religion.
> On occasions, great earthquakes have erupted along this powerful historical fault line. It is then that the Bosnians have been enlisted in the service of this or that great power. The Bosnian Serbs, Croats and Moslems have been adorned with many different cultural uniforms over the centuries by which they identify one another as the enemy when conflict breaks out. Despite this, underneath the dress they can see themselves reflected – it is the awful recognition that these primitive beasts [sic] on the other side of the barricade are their brothers which has led to the violence assuming such ghastly proportions in Bosnia. The only way that fighters can deal with this realization is to exterminate the opposite community. How else does one explain the tradition of facial mutilation in this region? How else can we account for the high incidence of women and children being killed in cold blood? The Orthodox, the Catholics or the Moslems can only claim victory when the heretics have been wiped out or expelled from their homes. (1993: 168–9)

The reflections of Glenny and Ignatieff come close to furnishing an explanation for the extreme violence in Bosnia and lead us back to the thoughts of Girard about the 'monstrous double' and, associated with it, his theory of ritual pollution and mimetic violence: the vicious circle of mutual violence that results from the erosion of differences. As the anthropological literature on symbolic classifications suggests, anomalies (if recognized) can invite either ritualization or suppression and eradication.

VIII

The narcissism of minor differences also governs the relations between Tutsi and Hutu in Rwanda. Since their first civil war in 1959 we have been aware of 'fratricide' between groups whose differences have, in the course of the twentieth century, been dramatically diminished through the agency of the former colonial power. Both groups developed from initial feudal patron–client relationships toward factions within their own elites: the Tutsi with support from the Belgian colonial government which administered the area through indirect rule; the Hutu first with support from the Mission, which favoured the formerly subaltern group and sent its children to school, and later, in the 1950s, with full support from the Belgian authorities, who encouraged ethnic equality and independence.[11] The diminishing of differences – economic, social, cultural – reinforced by the increase of mixed marriages, even led to confusion among anthropologists about the ethnic identity of Tutsi and Hutu.

Differences between Tusti and Hutu have in certain respects been far from extreme. Prunier describes Tusti and Hutu as 'the notorious rival twins of Rwanda'. They live side by side, 'on the same hilly slopes, in neighbouring hamlets – for better or for worse, for intermarriage or for massacre' (1995: 3). Although often called the tribes of Rwanda, they do not form separate tribes, nor do they have separate homelands. Tutsi and Hutu speak the same Bantu language, have the same religion, followed the same cultural practices (patrilineal kinship, polygyny), have lived side by side with each other, and have often intermarried. But at the time of first contact with European explorers they were neither similar nor equal. The Tutsi were originally cattle-herders and patrons of the Hutu; the latter were originally peasants who cultivated the land. Each group had its own dominant somatic type. The Hutu, who formed more than 80 per cent of the population, had standard Bantu physical characteristics and resembled the populations in neighbouring countries. The Tutsi were rather different: extremely tall and thin, they showed more angular facial features (Prunier 1995: 5).[12]

Between 1945 and 1959, Tutsi and Hutu became more similar, not only intellectually and as elites, but also in terms of property and wealth. By 1959 the average financial position of Tutsi and Hutu had generally become more equal. Well-to-do Hutu and poor Tutsi cancelled each other out on the economic average: 'under the banner of "democratic majority rule" on one side and "immediate independence" on the other, it was a fight between two competing élites, the newly developed Hutu counter-élite produced by the church and the older neo-traditionalist Tutsi élite which the colonial authorities had promoted since the 1920s' (Prunier 1995: 50). The loss of differences was also visible in their physical appearance. To understand this general loss of distinctions between both groups, we should look at the pattern of intermarriage. Frequent intermarriage between Tutsi and Hutu, writes Prunier, had produced many Hutu-looking Tutsi and Tutsi-looking Hutu (1995: 249).[13] Hutu refugees from Burundi considered the mixing of categories through intermarriage (Hutu intellectuals marrying Tutsi women) as breeding not life, but death: 'The 1972 massacre was seen as the historic culmination of such blurring of boundaries' (Malkki 1995: 86).

In the 1950s Maquet sketched a profile of Rwandese society as it probably existed around 1900. He observes that marriages between Hutu and Tutsi were not prohibited. In fact, according to his Hutu informants these marriages happened frequently. His Tutsi interlocutors, however, argued that such marriages were rare, but admitted that Tutsi often had Hutu concubines (Maquet 1961: 65–6). From this discrepancy Maquet infers that

> for a Tutsi to take a Hutu as wife in primary marriage entailed a loss of prestige. It was resorted to mainly because of poverty. Bride-wealth was lower in these inter-caste unions (not in the sense that the standard bride-wealth among Hutu was much lower) and a Hutu girl worked harder than a Tutsi. . . . A prosperous Hutu could marry a Tutsi girl, but then the bride-wealth was often greater than for a Hutu girl. It happened also that a Tutsi cattle-lord would grant a daughter to one of his Hutu clients. (1961: 66)

Later in his book Maquet comes back to these marriages which were much sought after by upwardly mobile Hutu: 'A Tutsi who did not own any cattle was still a Tutsi but a very poor one, dangerously slipping down in the social stratification, whereas a Hutu who possessed cattle was very near the aristocratic group and not infrequently could marry a Tutsi girl' (1961: 120). Prunier also believes that the clientèle system, through which a Tutsi patron transferred cattle to his Hutu client (a sign of wealth, power and prestige), offered the chance of upward social mobility:

> once endowed with cattle, the Hutu lineage would become dehutuised, i.e., tutsified. Similarly a very poor Tutsi who lost all his cattle and had to cultivate the land would in due course become hutuised. Marriage would tend to reinforce either trend, the children of the successful Hutu marrying into a Tutsi lineage and the children of the impoverished Tutsi marrying into a Hutu family. (1995: 13–14n.)

Gravel, who undertook ethnographic research in eastern Rwanda in the early 1960s, had also mentioned the blurring of distinctions between Tutsi and Hutu:

> Although the social system tends to keep the poor Tutsi out of poverty, either by helping them out or by making them Hutu, there are many Tutsi

of low rank and low status in every community. On the other hand, there are rich Hutu, who by dint of power and large family lineages, could oppose, or at least hold their own against, the encroachments and exploitations of the established Tutsi authority. In the past, such lineages, whose position could not be destroyed, were absorbed, and, although the newly rich generation was still regarded as Hutu, its sons could be 'Tutsi-ized' and its grandsons would be considered as Tutsi. (1968: 23)

It would be incorrect to argue, on the basis of this increasing mixture and overlapping of Tutsi and Hutu, that the categories 'Tutsi' and 'Hutu' are not indigenous concepts, but categories 'invented' by the former (Belgian) colonial authorities and imposed on the Rwandese population. Prunier observes:

Just as the 'different race hypothesis' has caused much crankish writing during the past hundred years, some modern authors have gone to great length in the other direction to try to refute this theory and to prove that Tutsi and Hutu belonged to the same basic racial stock. . . . Sober critics pointed out that this 'anti-racist' interpretation ended up being exceedingly racist . . . (1995: 16–17n.)

It is obvious that one cannot reduce the struggle between Tutsi and Hutu to a narcissism of minor differences. Other important conditions cannot be disregarded, most notably the rapid growth of population,[14] the eco- logical situation, the superior numbers of Hutu and their domination of the state, and the threat of the Tutsi army from abroad. But it is diffi- cult to ignore the relationship between the gradual dissolution of hier- archical interdependencies and the differences connected with them, and the extreme violence used by Hutu against Tutsi. It is quite possible that for the originally subordinate Hutu the historically dominant Tutsi, in a process of 'mimetic desire', had assumed the features of a 'monstrous double' – a figure that looms large in Girard's theory of violence. Gravel describes the rise of a Hutu politician shortly after the first civil war in Rwanda (November 1959), and the establishment of a pro-Hutu Belgian administration. Before terrorizing Tutsi in his community, this man had tried in vain to pass for a Tutsi of the royal lineage. Later he had tried in another community, likewise in vain, to marry the daughter of a local Tutsi leader (Gravel 1968: 191ff).

IX
These examples, which can easily be supplemented with others, show how the imminent loss of differences precedes the use of extreme vio- lence. Anti-Semitism in Germany intensified with the growing assimila- tion of Jews. As the anti-Semitic German scholar Carl Schmitt, who

collaborated with the Nazis (and who stood trial in Nuremberg), puts it in his post-war notebook *Glossarium*, 'The real enemy is the assimilated Jew.'[15] Anti-Semitism in Poland and the Ukraine in the nineteenth and twentieth centuries shows the same pattern: the pogroms came after the emancipation of the peasants and the Jews. Before, the latter had a separate, somewhat privileged position as mediators between gentry and servile peasants. Sometimes the violence of exploited peasants found expression in a *jacquerie* against representatives of this middle class of Jewish managers of large estates and, as happened in the peasant revolt in Moldavia in 1907, acquired an anti-Semitic character.[16]

The narcissism of minor differences may also throw light on the so-called 'Troubles', the struggle between Protestants and Catholics in Northern Ireland.[17] Conor Cruise O'Brien writes:

> The Catholics of Northern Ireland are physically indistinguishable from the Protestants; they speak one common language with the Protestants, and generally no other language; they live in the same sorts of houses and watch the same television shows. A stranger could walk through any working-class area of Belfast without having any idea of whether he was in Protestant or Catholic territory – until he looked at slogans on walls, testifying to the abiding politico-sectarian mutual hostility of the two look-alike communities. (1986: 442–3)[18]

Another example for further research is the struggle in South Africa between members of Buthelesi's Inkhata Freedom Party (with the support of over 6 million Zulus in Natal) and members of Nelson Mandela's African National Congress. Between September 1989 (after the abolition of *apartheid* and the inauguration of De Klerk) and January 1993 alone, this undeclared civil war claimed the lives of close to 10,000 people.[19]

Like many conflicts between arch-enemies, the struggle between Jews and Palestinian Muslims in Israel may easily be reduced to the issue of contested territories or 'competition over resources'. But in this case, too, political economy alone cannot explain their intense mutual hatred. For a better understanding it is worthwhile to explore what Jews and Muslims have in common (always anathema to warring parties, who narcissistically prefer to emphasize and exaggerate differences). Jews and Muslims are not only both 'Peoples of the Book', sharing many religious and cosmological views; there are also striking parallels in language (Semitic origins), physical appearance, ecological regimes (pastoral origins), food taboos, patriarchal structures of kinship and marriage, male circumcision and preoccupations with pollution.[20]

Another case of extreme violence worth exploring in terms of the narcissism of minor differences is the struggle between Tamils and Sinhalese
in Sri Lanka since the 1950s. The Sinhalese constitute more than 70 per
cent of the total population of about 14 million people. But there are
also regions where the Tamils are predominant. Although there are
important differences in language and religion, Tambiah describes the
civil war between these two groups as 'fratricide':

> Although the major identity components of the Sinhalese are their Sin-
> halese language and their Buddhist religion, and of the Tamils the Tamil
> language and their Hindu religion, both these populations share many
> parallel features of traditional caste, kinship, popular religious cults,
> customs, and so on. But they have come to be divided by their mythic char-
> ters and tendentious historical misunderstandings of their past. (1991: 5)

In various areas where both groups once knew peaceful coexistence,
Tamils were forced to give up their language and religion. Tambiah
detects an 'overdetermination' in the anti-Tamil attitude among certain
segments of the Sinhalese population: 'In these two cases, of coastal
peoples north of Colombo and interior peoples of the Eastern Provinces
who have shifted from a relaxed symbiosis to an imposed Sinhalese identity, we see one reason for the "overdetermination" in the anti-Tamil attitudes of certain segments of the Sinhalese population' (1991: 100–1).
The 'overdetermined' enmity toward Tamils is also present in the south-
western coastal plain of Sri Lanka. According to Tambiah this is likewise related to the disappearance of important cultural differences. In
the fervent religious nationalism of Sinhalese Buddhists, which entails
the rejection of Tamils as foreign 'others', one can see an attempt to reinforce Sinhalese identity and to stress contrasts, both imaginary and real,
such as physical differences and ethnic origin (Tambiah 1991: 100–1,
183–4).

These examples do not remotely exhaust the cases of extreme violence
between people who are (or have become) actually very close and
similar.[21] But this preliminary survey gives some idea of the connection
between extreme violence and threatened identity following the loss of
differences between groups. The narcissism of minor differences manifests itself in the emphasis on and the exaggeration of subtle distinctions
vis-à-vis others with whom there are many similarities. We are concerned
with forms of symbolic action par excellence in which social, cultural,
moral, mental and cognitive elements are closely interwoven. The theoretical purport of the narcissism of minor differences suggests that identity – who you are, what you represent or stand for, whence you derive

self-esteem – is based on subtle distinctions that are emphasized, defended and reinforced against what is closest because that is what poses the greatest threat. This leads us back to Simmel, who argues that to preserve honour people are prepared to make and demand 'terrible sacrifices'.

In a suburb of an English town in the Midlands, investigated in the 1950s, two adjoining working-class neighbourhoods were at odds with each other: the better-organized families who had lived there longer excluded and stigmatized the newcomers, who could not defend themselves because of their low degree of social cohesion (Elias and Scotson 1965). The established working-class families felt threatened by the newcomers and feared being put on the same level as their counterparts, who tolerated in their midst a small minority of deviant families. The people in the nearby middle-class neighbourhood (where some working-class families also lived) formed a reference group for the established working-class families, but were not bothered by the presence of the newcomers. For them there was no need to be concerned since the social distance was great enough for them not to feel threatened.

This example demonstrates, on a small scale, that stigmatization accompanies minor rather than great differences and that social distance, more control and a stable balance of power protect people against both contamination and fear of contamination.[22] *Les extrêmes se touchent*, also literally. In his book on seventeenth- and eighteenth-century court-life etiquette, Elias describes how ladies of the nobility could undress and bathe unceremoniously in the presence of their servants – a form of intimacy also found in other stratified societies, which qualifies Simmel's observations on discretion.[23]

The English example also shows that the narcissism of minor differences does not automatically result in violence. As pointed out above, other factors help to determine the colour and tone of relationships between rival groups. Next to demographic and ecological conditions, the political context – the role of the state – is critical. To what extent is there a relatively stable, effective and impersonal monopoly over the means of violence? In all cases where a loss of differences resulted in extreme violence we find unstable states: the minorities, their rights, their social and cultural identity remain unprotected. In some cases the state and the army more or less openly side with one of the warring parties, as in Sri Lanka, Bali, Rwanda and the former Yugoslavia.

X

To sum up, I have argued that the loss of differences – especially cultural differences – represents a threat and can lead to explosive situations. Hence the importance of the contributions of Girard – and those of

Freud, Simmel, Elias and others – in providing an outline of a general theory of power and violence. It is to the credit of Bourdieu that he has reopened the discussion on the narcissism of minor differences with an apt phrase. Social identity lies in difference, and difference is established, reinforced and defended against what is closest – and what is closest (in several senses of the word) represents the greatest threat.

We started with Freud and it is fitting also to conclude with him because he was well acquainted with the problem of the 'monstrous double' – also from his own experience. Freud and Arthur Schnitzler were both Jewish, lived in the same city, were both medical doctors, belonged to the same generation, and, moreover, were kindred spirits. For years, Freud had been aware of a strong similarity between his views and those of Schnitzler, but it was a long time before he decided to contact the famous playwright. In a letter to Schnitzler written in May 1922, he explains why:

> I have avoided you because of a sort of *Doppelgängerscheu* [fear of my double]. . . . Your determinism like your scepticism . . . , your being gripped by the truths of the unconscious, by the instinctual nature of man, your subversion of cultural-conventional certainties, the clinging of your thoughts to the polarity of loving and dying – all these things touched me with an uncanny familiarity.

Freud then continues in a more detached tone: 'I thus gained the impression that, through intuition – but really in consequence of fine introspection – you know all that I discovered about other people through toilsome work.'[24]

These reflections by Freud do not suggest that he suspected a close relationship between his *Doppelgängerscheu* and the narcissism of minor differences; but rather, that he did recognize the critical importance that people attribute to subtle distinctions in their everyday lives.

8

Explaining South Italian Agro-Towns

I

Peasant agglomerations, so-called 'agro-towns' that number several thousand inhabitants, are fairly common in southern Italy. This settlement pattern, which paradoxically separates the peasants from the land, is not restricted to the south of Italy. Often built on hilltops, agro-towns are characteristic of many countries along the Mediterranean.[1]

What kind of explanations are presented for the origin and continuity of these rural towns? In most cases the authors confine themselves to a distinction between nucleated and dispersed settlement and specify the conditions which are supposed to explain the differences. For example, Dickinson and Rochefort, both of whom carried out research in southern Italy, discuss the problem rather cursorily.[2] They mention 'age-long' insecurity in the countryside, the lack of roads and scarcity of drinking-water, the organization of large estates: conditions they hold responsible for the crowding of peasants into large agro-towns. But they do not discuss these conditions systematically. This is remarkable, because as early as 1927 the French geographer Demangeon had pointed out in a comparative essay on the subject the strongly variable character of these conditions. What we lack in most geographical accounts of these settlement forms is a distinction between historical, causal, functional and contingent relationships. In this chapter we will have a closer look at the nucleated settlement pattern in southern Italy and explore the links with its natural and human environment. Because scattered settlement is not entirely lacking in the area, there are possibilities for comparison so that both forms may throw light on one another.[3] Apart from the extensive literature on the subject, I shall also draw on field-notes made when I

136

lived for over two years, in the 1960s, in Contessa Entellina, a small agro-town in Sicily's western interior (see Plate 3).[4]

II

Demangeon is one of the few geographers who tries systematically to verify current general statements about the presence of agro-towns in southern Italy. He distinguishes between two main types of settlement – nucleation and dispersion – but acknowledges that social reality is too complex to be explained in only two terms: 'between the two terms, agglomeration and dispersion, reality shows us intermediary forms; between the village and the farm there is the hamlet' (1927: 112). He distinguishes a number of sub-types with the ratio of agricultural land to agglomeration of houses as a principle. One of these sub-types is '*le village à champs dissociés*' (the village with separate (i.e. distant) fields). Demangeon describes this 'extreme type' as follows:

> But the most curious aspects of the nucleated settlement pattern are to be found in southern Italy and in Sicily; the peasants crowd together in real towns which sometimes, as in Apulia, reach tens of thousands of inhabitants, such as Canosa, Andria, Corata, Biltonto, or as in Sicily, Caltanissetta and Caltagirone: large rural agglomerations swarming with life amidst the empty and desolate countryside. To reach the fields, the peasants must sometimes cover distances between twenty and thirty kilometres; often they must pass the week far from their homes, only to return on Sunday: example of a paradoxical settlement which alienates the agriculturalist from the land he cultivates. (1927: 4)

To explain the differences between agglomeration and dispersion, Demangeon identifies physical geographical factors (relief, soil, hydrology), social conditions (public security, health) and agrarian regimes (forms of land tenure, modes of cultivation, lease-contracts). One by one he checks to what extent current conceptions in the geographical literature may be valid. Through systematic comparisons he concludes that none of the following generalizations can be accepted:

1 if plains, then agglomeration;
2 if mountains, then dispersion;
3 if marshland, then dispersion;
4 if scarcity of drinking-water, then agglomeration;
5 if availability of drinking-water, then dispersion;
6 if insecurity, then agglomeration;
7 if large estates, then agglomeration;
8 if hydro-agriculture, then agglomeration.

a Entellina – Panorama

Plate 3 Agro-town, Contessa Entellina in the hinterland of Palermo, (Sicily), early twentieth-century

Today we are used to less simple ways of presenting the outcome of research and hesitate to accept ahistoric, law-like generalizations. It will not come as a surprise, therefore, to hear that in none of these cases can we speak of 'imperative rules': none of these conditions is singly responsible for the appearance of any settlement form. Demangeon argues that to account for these different habitats, we must consider an extensive range of conditions: 'To explain how certain people are used to living in agglomerations and certain others on isolated farms or in small hamlets, we must take into account all natural, social, and agricultural conditions' (1927: 23). Demangeon does not arrive at final statements; this has not been his intention. He only wants to present a preliminary classification and raise points for discussion (1927: 2). In the next sections we shall take up some of these points, restricting ourselves to the south Italian experience.

III
Although in many parts of southern Italy the peasant population lives concentrated around scarce sources of spring water, we must be careful in relating the two phenomena causally. Demangeon notes that in some areas with the same hydrological structure different settlement types developed. Yet for the geographers Ahlmann and Semple the subtropical Mediterranean climate with its long, hot and dry summers, on the one hand, and the soil conditions, on the other, have a powerful impact on settlement forms:

> Climatic conditions, expressed in the rarity of a reliable supply of drinking-water, forbade in general the isolated farm, just as they do today. . . . But where springs were more sparsely scattered, the population had to concentrate about them in fewer but larger groups, no matter how far might be the way from the home village to the outlying fields. . . . The longer the summer drought and the dryer the land, the sparser the villages in general. (Semple 1932: 539–40)

About Apulia, Ahlmann observes that the reason for the extreme concentration of the peasant population must be found (here as in Sicily and the rest of southern Italy) primarily in the scarcity of water. He also mentions other factors, but considers them only of secondary importance.[5] But his physical–geographical determinism does not fit his credo of evolutionism: Ahlmann argues that the oldest settlements must have been agglomerations.[6] Hence the Swedish geographer calls the nucleated pattern predominating in southern Italy 'primitive': only in a later stage would dispersion develop.[7] We are thus concerned with agglomeration and subsequent dispersion in the *same* physical environment. Nor are Ahlmann's ideas in agreement with the archaeological data about the prehistoric *nuraghi* in Sardinia, of which the oldest have been found in extreme dispersion.[8]

Scattered settlement, although certainly not a general pattern in southern Italy, shows itself in two forms. First, we find the so-called *masserie* (singular: *masseria*) – big, often fortified, farms that appear in the same areas as the agro-towns, including western Sicily where both forms go back as far as the fifteenth century. The *masserie* are large rent-capitalistic enterprises.[9] The owners often live elsewhere and lease them to middlemen, the notorious *gabellotti*.[10] Second, we find dispersed farmsteads belonging to smallholders:

> It is a mistake, however, to regard the dispersed farmstead situated in the midst of its own compact holding, and worked by the peasant cultivator, as absent in the South. There has been a steady increase in the areas of dispersed settlement over the last hundred years or more. Once the peasant is able to get secure tenure of a holding, adequate to support him, he ultimately moves out to it and builds a farm there. The crops he grows are naturally adjusted to the rhythm of winter rain and summer drought. (Dickinson 1955: 24)[11]

This less frequent pattern prevails, virtually by definition, in areas of intensive cultivation in Apulia, Calabria, Lucania, Campania and Sicily.[12] We may conclude, therefore, that socio-economic conditions are of as much importance as physical–geographical factors, if not obviously more significant. Hence it seems unwarranted to maintain that there is a simple connection between scarcity of water and agglomerations. But we cannot refute the thesis completely. Under certain socio-economic circumstances – specifically poverty of the peasant population – scarcity of water may force the peasants to crowd into agro-towns, because individual peasant families lack both the material and social resources to dig wells in the countryside, and build new homes there.

We know that understanding social phenomena requires recognition of complex linkages: only rarely are we able to formulate simple, deterministic propositions of the type 'if A, then B'. Phrased in social science jargon, multivariate propositions dominate over two-variate propositions (Zetterberg 1965: 63ff). This is also true for the problem of settlement patterns. The relationships between scarcity of water and agglomeration may be described as contingent: if there is scarcity of water, then there will be agglomeration, but only if there is also poverty. However, as we shall see below, things may be still more complicated. There are also situations in which different factors, or different combinations of factors, may independently have the same effect (that is, agglomeration). These cases of 'functional shift' are instructive and show the complexity of settlement forms that may escape us when we insist on formulating timeless propositions, even if qualified as follows: if A, then B; but if C, then also B – and when concerned with combinations of factors: if A and B, then C; but if D and E, then also C (and so on). At best, such propositions have a sensitizing or signalizing function.

We often find in geographical literature the idea that agglomeration may be explained by a set of 'possible relevant' factors. Although complexity is thus recognized, only rarely do we find spelled out which conditions may be considered necessary, sufficient or contingent. In a word, there are many statements and descriptions, but few analyses. Mere enumerations suggest that all factors mentioned are equally important or necessary conditions which, in combination, have the effect of agglomeration. This is not the case. Character, combination, significance and impact of various conditions vary in different situations.

IV

High summer temperatures, abundant concentrated rainfall (which on impermeable soils result in swamps) and deforestation make the coastal rim of southern Italy a favourable area for the malaria mosquito.[13] This factor is also related to the distribution of water. In this context, however, it is not a deficiency but a surplus of water that some authors, at least indirectly, consider important in the development of settlement patterns.[14] Kish's observations for Calabria may go for large parts of the south:

> The wars and invasions, the devastations and anarchy, that became the fate of Calabria when Roman imperial power was destroyed by the barbarian invasions left their mark on the land. The rivers ran unchecked to the sea, creating swamps in the lowlands; the forests having been cut on the mountains, erosion stripped the slopes bare; malaria made the seaside and lowland settlements unhealthy. (1953: 496)[15]

Le Lannou especially has stressed this point: the population does not abandon the plains because of malaria, but rather, the population abandons the plains (because of socio-political reasons) and only then does malaria develop.[16] The French geographer sees the presence of malaria as a consequence and not as an antecedent of social decline. He argues that the prevalence of malaria varies with the character of agriculture: where we find intensive agriculture ('*rapports permanents et intimes entre l'homme et la terre*') malaria will be most unlikely:

It is not surprising that malaria is so important in the Mediterranean, an area where the relations between the people and the land are so eminently unstable. Malaria is the most common consequence of somewhat sudden modifications in the physical environment in countries which, like the Mediterranean and the tropics, have a season warm enough to permit the rapid development of the sickness. In this way innovations and abandonment present grave dangers. (Le Lannou 1936: 134–5)

The poor upkeep of the fields and large estates on which extensive agriculture and sheep-breeding are carried out are, according to Le Lannou, in the whole of southern Italy, as elsewhere, the main causes of the development of malaria. That malaria should be considered an effect rather than a cause of the crowding of people into agglomerations has also been noted by other scholars.[17] Their findings leave little room for the hypothesis: if malaria, then agglomeration. But given malaria, would dispersion then not be extremely difficult? From a logical point of view this amounts to the same as maintaining agglomeration. Again, I believe, other circumstances must be taken into account before we have a more convincing answer. Along the coast of Calabria, Kish came across a number of settlements (*marine*) which had originated in the course of the last hundred and fifty years. The peasant population had left the traditional hilltop towns and villages in order to occupy the coastal zone. The construction of a railway along the coast may have promoted this migration: apparently the wish to live where work could be found and the desire for fertile land had overcome their fear of fever.

To summarize: malaria may obstruct dispersion, but should not be considered the cause of agglomeration in the hills and mountains. The case described by Kish demonstrates that economic and political factors may be decisive. Moreover, malaria has been wiped out in the south since the last war and is now efficiently under control in most areas. Nevertheless in many places agglomerations persist.

V

Security, defence and other strategic considerations have surely been of great importance in the construction of these nucleated hilltop towns. Virtually no author who writes of the geography of the Mediterranean neglects to mention this aspect: 'These plains are charged with history; the permanent insecurity during thousands of years has forced the agglomeration of people on fortified places' (Sorre 1952: 74); 'In many Mediterranean areas such as Sicily a man living outside the urban walls as rural worker and country resident is almost unknown. This is a product of centuries-long insecurity' (Weber 1962: 82). It would not be too difficult to collect a large number of similar statements.[18] Yet when we try to account for social formations, including agro-towns, we should distinguish between reasons for their origin and reasons for their continuity. What, then, keeps people in these large (paradoxical, as has been said) settlements? This question appears to be legitimate because insecurity has decreased significantly over the last hundred years, although in certain areas like Sicily and Sardinia it has not disappeared completely. For an illustration I shall again refer to Kish.

After the fall of the Roman Empire, Calabria (like other parts of the south) was characterized by invasions, raids and anarchy. The peasants took to the mountains. A map, made in 1759, shows only two main coastal towns: Reggio, protected by Messina, and Crotone, lying in the shade of a strong fortress. After the return of political calm, a part of the mountain population moved to the plains in the course of the nineteenth century.[19] This was very much a general pattern. Between 1861 and 1901 scattered peasant settlements in the south increased, not only in an absolute sense, but also in proportion to the increase of the urban population.[20] Nevertheless, we still find many agglomerations in largely pacified areas. Before we deal with this apparent anomaly, I wish first to consider the situation in which insecurity still prevails, as it does, for instance, in western Sicily.

As discussed elsewhere, scattered settlement as proposed and implemented by the government (construction of small farmsteads with allocation of small adjacent holdings) in the 1950s proved to be a failure in various Sicilian communes.[21] There are a number of reasons for the poor results of these reforms, and one of them, I believe, was that public security left much to be desired. Before and at the time of the reform (late 1940s and early 1950s) cattle-rustling, extortion, theft of crops and homicide were fairly common.[22] So people had good reasons for preferring to stay in their home towns, the traditional nucleated hilltop villages. Yet, as noted before, scattered settlement was not entirely absent and in fact has always been present in this area. Moreover, the *masserie*, the centres of the *latifondi* or large estates, have been there for centuries.[23] The owners and managers kept substantial herds of cattle and sheep. These enterprises were relatively prosperous in otherwise poverty-stricken areas. Only rarely were they pillaged. They had their own police force: feared armed men on horseback who, more often than not, extended their supervision to brigandage and protection of bandits, whom they would use to carry out large-scale rustling operations at the expense of less protected farmers and peasants. Against exaction from the law, the middlemen received protection from the estate owners.[24]

Insecurity does not always result in agglomeration. This holds true for other areas as well. Demangeon shows that in northern and central Italy isolated farms were fortified (1927: 16). We cannot, therefore, accept König's statement: 'the isolated farm may *only* (*überhaupt erst*) appear after pacification of the countryside and this is the reason that the farm is everywhere a relatively recent phenomenon' (1958: 35). Nevertheless, although insecurity does not seem to be a sufficient condition for agglomeration, it is doubtless a very important one.[25] It may be argued, however, that the relationship between insecurity and agglomeration is also reversible. The mere fact of agglomeration, ironically, creates favourable conditions for insecurity in the countryside. This is as obvious in the desolate interior of Sicily as in the centres of some American cities after dusk: no people, no social control.

To conclude this section let us dwell for a moment on the persistence of agglomerations in largely pacified areas. In such cases we must take other factors into account. It might be, as I indicated in reviewing the impact of scarcity of water and malaria, that the distribution of resources – that is, poverty of the peasant population – seriously discourages dispersion. On the other hand (and this seems to me a point entirely neglected in the literature on settlement patterns), agglomeration, for whatever reasons it is called into existence, may in the course of time generate conditions which make dispersion unattractive. Most specifically, an urban pattern of culture may entail contempt for both labour on the land and the countryman. As we shall see later on, this is the case in many parts of the Mediterranean area.[26] Functional shift may thus help to explain the continuity of agro-towns in pacified areas. We are dealing, then, with an example of what Darwin, in a response to criticism of his *The Origin of Species*, called the principle of 'functional change in structural continuity'.[27]

VI

Demangeon refers to several authors who believe in a direct relationship between the organization of large estates and the development of nucleated settlements. The big agro-towns of the south owe their existence to the strategy of large estate owners who wanted to concentrate their tenants in order to control them more efficiently (Demangeon 1927: 17). Moreover, the landlords were interested in avoiding permanent settlement of the peasants in the countryside for fear the peasant family would lay claim to the farmstead. Demangeon points to an exception: the situation in the Baltic states in the early nineteenth century described by Woeikof, who came across large estates in combination with dispersed settlements of the peasants. He offers the following explanation:

> The Lettish, particularly in Courland, have long lived on isolated farms and not in villages; there are maps and plans from the seventeenth century

proving this. After the abolition of serfdom (1816–1819), the noble estate owners judged that it was in their interests to encourage the peasants to live on farms, instead of in the small villages which existed in Estonia and in the north and east of Lithuania. They believed with reason that the peasants living on farms would prosper better and would pay revenues due to their former lords more punctually. The Estonians did not like dispersion, but the nobility employed a strongly German tenacity to achieve this end, and succeeded entirely in it. (Woeikof 1909: 15–16)

It seems that we are dealing here with two *ad hoc* explanations. Large estates would lead, on the one hand, to agglomerations (as in southern Italy) and, on the other, to dispersion (as in the Baltic states). Doubtless, other conditions have to be taken into account. I suspect that relations between both 'variables' may be contingent: if A (large estates), then B (agglomeration), but only if C (?). And the same would be true for dispersion. What should be read for C?

One of the important differences between the areas is the density of population, or, more precisely, population pressure. As appears from Woeikof's description, we have what Nieboer (1910: 385) calls 'open resources' in large parts of the Baltic countries: apart from the large estates there was land on which the peasants could practise shifting cultivation. The existence of these open resources may have induced the landlords to force the peasants into fixed places, in this case scattered homesteads. Moreover, according to Woeikof (1909: 16), shifting cultivation is not a favourable condition for agglomeration. In contrast, in southern Italy population pressure prevails: all arable land is occupied ('closed resources') and, with hardly any change in agricultural techniques, there is a population surplus that finds outlets in large-scale overseas emigration. In such circumstances – that is, closed resources – 'a landlord can always find free tenants who are willing to pay him a rent, and free labourers who are willing to work for him' (Nieboer 1910: 349). This was indeed the case in parts of southern Italy where large estates dominated. The agglomeration or, more precisely, the piazza of the agro-town served as a labour market, where the unemployed masses crowded to be considered for a short-term contract on terms dictated by the managers of the large estates. The persistence of agglomeration in the south also depended on the nature of the tenancy systems: short-term leases, which involved a yearly or two-yearly circulation of tenants, were the norm.[28] This system of tenancy was functionally consistent with the prevailing mode of crop-rotation: after the grain was removed, the stubble fields served to pasture the flocks of the owner or manager.[29]

It seems that we are now in a better position to know what may be read for factor C: population pressure, precarious employment, short-term tenancy systems and extensive modes of cultivation. We should recognize, however, that population pressure in the south is a fairly recent phenomenon. Between 1500 and 1800 a considerable number of nucleated villages were built in western Sicily by large estate owners because there was at the time a shortage of labour: they wished to colonize their unfarmed and underfarmed land.[30] Density of population, or population pressure, does not, therefore, appear of critical importance to the rise of settlement forms. To explain the difference in settlement between the Baltic and the Italian south we must focus on modes of agriculture, tenancy system, insecurity and, perhaps, other conditions that are not yet clear. Only a more detailed description of the history of Courland might provide a more definite answer.

VII

In southern Italy, as in other parts of the Mediterranean area, labour on the land is negatively valued. This has been noted in many studies. Banfield remarks: 'Manual labour is degrading in the southern Italian ethos, and labour on the land, together with personal service, is especially so' (1958: 69). Pitt-Rivers writes that Andalusian peasants lack 'a mystical attitude towards the land; they dwell in towns from which they go out to cultivate the earth, but they do not love it. This characteristic is typical of the whole Mediterranean' (1961: 46–7). In his book on a small town in Brazil, Harris argues that aversion to agriculture and to manual labour in general are elements of a complex of values, an urban ethos which 'is probably a fundamental part of Mediterranean and Latin American culture' (1956: 280–1). We find similar statements concerning the attitude toward the land in the work of Pitkin, who studied a rural community south of Rome:

> In Mediterranean Europe, among those who work the soil, there is not the strong tradition of independent peasantry in the sense of the individual cultivator closely attached to the soil and living according to the traditions of a folk culture that has been described for other parts of the world. In fact, a great many who live by the land have been day-laborers, not owner cultivators, and their attitude toward the land they work has often been more negative than positive. Even the small owner often attempts to relegate the labor of a part of his property to others so that he may enjoy the status of employer. And the large landowners generally absent themselves entirely from the scene, expending their energies on urban living. (1963: 127–8)

The cultural emphasis on an urban way of life brings us back to a question briefly touched upon before: what conditions may account for the continuity of agglomeration, for whatever reasons it may have come into existence? It is generally accepted that powerful forces in the past, especially insecurity, which was widespread throughout large parts of the Mediterranean, encouraged agglomeration. The idea suggests itself that large numbers of people, including the peasant population, living closely together over long periods of time, may have generated an urban pattern of culture which was strongly enough developed by the time these areas became pacified to make dispersion unattractive.

We have seen that dispersion is not entirely absent in the south. In some areas there is even an increase of scattered settlements. There is strong evidence for a close connection between dispersion and farm status. Banfield, who studied a 'fairly typical southern town', provides telling information:

> Three-fourths of the farmers live on outlying farms; the others live in town. Those who live in the country have much larger farms on the average (17 acres against 5); indeed, it is because their farms are so small that the town-dwelling farmers do not live on them. (1958: 46)

> The country-dwelling peasant is generally much better off than the town-dwelling peasant, in fact he lives in the country *because* he has enough land and livestock to require his presence there. (1958: 71)[31]

The village near the Pontine Marshes, studied by Pitkin, shows a similar pattern: poor peasants tend to live in the nucleated village and land-owning peasants prefer to live on farmsteads (1963: 172). Thus we have to consider the distribution of resources as a salient condition in understanding (the continuity of) agglomeration. The prestige of the town, the *polis*, carrying with it the peasant's distaste for agricultural work,[32] has a strong economic foundation. Yet cultural and economic conditions have to be kept separated, since the mere fact of living on the land and working it lowers the social status of the peasant, regardless of economic benefits.[33]

In the west Sicilian village where I studied the results of land reform, the new settlers showed little desire to live permanently on the small farmsteads that had been built for them in three outlying hamlets. One reason why this experiment failed was that the farms were too small and unviable. To supplement their income, some colonists turned to landlords for contracts; others left as migrant labourers for northern Italy and Germany. Where the allocated new farms were substantially larger, as for instance in Campania Felix, dispersion did succeed (Unger 1953: 522).

VIII

Closely related to the previous argument is the thesis put forward by Ahlmann and Demangeon. Both argue that there is an intimate relation between dispersion and intensive cultivation.[34] It is obvious that where the peasant lives on the land he will be able to devote more attention to his fields and crops. At least, he will not lose time and energy going back and forth between his home town and the land as does the peasant from the agro-town. In coastal regions of southern Italy (where we find irrigated fields and vast stretches of citrus trees), intensive cultivation is coupled with dispersion rather than with agglomeration. On the other hand, extensive grain cultivation and nomadic sheep-farming, which predominate in the inland regions where agro-towns are prevalent, do not require the permanent residence of peasants on the land. This mode of exploiting natural and human resources seems to be functionally consistent with nucleated settlement. We must, therefore, take into account the way in which resources are distributed. Dispersion seems to make sense only if the peasant is either owner of a more or less unified plot, or if, as a tenant, he enjoys a certain degree of independence regarding a similar piece of land. Traditionally, however, south Italian peasants are poor and lack security of tenure. If they own land it is often fragmented and scattered over great distances, a circumstance principally due to the prevailing practices of partible inheritance (this also reinforces agglomeration – residence in one, strategic place). Short-term leases are the norm, a fact that likewise helps to discourage capital investment and its corollary, dispersed settlement.

The advantages and disadvantages of dispersion and agglomeration respectively are set forth by several geographers. In land reform programmes, too, dispersion is often stressed. Less frequently do we hear that agglomeration fits existing patterns of land tenure, lease systems, inheritance practices and extensive modes of agriculture. Unless resources are reasonably redistributed and benefit the peasants living in agro-towns, dispersion is not attractive. In these cases it would be unwarranted, therefore, to speak of 'clear disadvantages of agglomeration'. We concur with Demangeon, who calls this settlement type paradoxical (1927: 4). Yet the paradox dissolves when one considers agglomeration in its larger social and historical context.

IX

It is sometimes argued that dispersion is unattractive because in southern Italy women are not accustomed to work on the land.[35] Especially in Sicily's interior, for women to till the fields was – and still is – both uncommon and restricted to only very poor families. Sicilian peasants pointed out that, given the difficulties of communication and the arduous nature of the work, female labour in the country would be unfeasible and unwise. This may be true, but there are yet other reasons why Sicilian peasants were unwilling to expose their women to work on the land.

The south Italian family has been characterized as 'father-dominated' and 'mother-centered'.[36] Masculine dominance and prestige find expression in, and are enhanced by, the male's economic role. As the head of the family the man is the main breadwinner. In this task he is usually assisted by his unmarried sons, but the responsibility is entirely his. The economic activities of his wife and daughters are confined to the home. Strong restrictions exist for the sexual activities of his wife and daughters, which he is supposed to control rigidly. A man who allows his women to work outside the home would jeopardize his honour in two ways: directly, by showing that he is not himself capable of supporting his family, and is thus failing in his culturally defined role of the superior male versus the subordinate females of his family; and indirectly, because he will be less able to control their sexual activities. Hence there is cultural emphasis on the seclusion of women: most peasant women are not only excluded from going out into the fields, they are rarely seen in public. As noted before, very poor families cannot live up to this ideal (though most peasant families try to do so by making important sacrifices) and, in order to make a living at all, must send their wives and daughters into the fields for light tasks such as gathering wood, or harvesting grapes and olives. In its association with low status and poverty, female labour on the land attains iconic importance.

X

This essay has explored the *raison d'être* of south Italian agro-towns. Conditions for the appearance of this settlement type have been often noted and described, but seldom systematically analysed and tested. Demangeon's essay, one of the few exceptions, was, predictably, unable to detect sufficient conditions: in most cases a range of circumstances had to be considered and their significance depended on context, on the circumstantiality of specific times and places. It proved useful to distinguish between conditions that played a role in the origin of agglomeration, on the one hand, and conditions that contributed to the persistence of agro-towns, on the other. Insecurity and the rent-capitalistic exploitation of land and labour remained powerful forces in the continuity of rural agglomeration: all three processes provide perfect examples of the *longue durée*, of intertwined 'structures of the long run'. But we also noted, in pacified areas, the working of the principle of 'functional change in structural continuity'. These functional shifts, in which a precariously employed peasantry long remained dependent on middle-men who managed the vast landed estates in rent-capitalist manner, together with the rise of an urban ethos, strongly discouraged the development of dispersion and kept the peasant population within the walls of picturesque hilltop agro-towns.

Postscript
Ritual Space in Sicily:
Town, Countryside and their Borderland

The compactness of south Italian hilltop towns, swarming with life, contrasts with the desolate countryside where vast grain fields alternate with pastures. Travellers from England, the Low Countries and Germany, where dispersed settlements are the norm, were struck by the abrupt transition between town and countryside south of the Alps and the Pyrenees. They wondered what might have kept the peasants in these towns after they had ceased to provide the rural population with the best means of defence and security.

Having explored the continuity of agro-towns in southern Italy, I shall now try to adumbrate how ritual space and time in Sicily's western interior helped to define and reproduce basic cultural categories and mediated major oppositions. Bearing in mind the lengthy discourse on the subject that has taken place in French and British anthropology, I understand ritual as practices that mark boundaries and help to bring about transitions between meaningful, clear-cut categories. Being unclear and ambiguous, boundaries and margins of all sorts invite ritual, which thus helps to order and structure a man-made, meaningful world.

One of the main distinctions made in Sicily's western interior is that between life in the village or town (*paese*), and life in the countryside (*campagna*). As noted earlier, in the Mediterranean area, labour on the land has been looked down upon. Consequently, peasants used to go to great length to avoid living in the countryside permanently.[37] The prestige of the town and the concurrent distaste for life on the land are historically related to the predominance of large estates, their absentee ownership and related rent-capitalist exploitation, and conditions of endemic insecurity (*mafia*, banditry). Until recently, the land was concentrated in a few hands, and those who tilled the fields as sharecroppers and labourers formed a landless proletariat rather than an independent peasantry.

In the hilly and mountainous countryside, grainfields alternated with pastures and fallow land, leaving little room for permanent vegetation. Roads and buildings were scarce and in constant need of repair, while permanent settlement was uncommon. This awesome landscape formed a striking contrast with the gregarious, cosy agro-town, where peasants lived in close proximity with kinsmen and friends, shopkeepers, crafts-men, landowners, and civil servants, *professionisti* and other members of the intelligentsia. Urban life included everything that was lacking in the countryside: sociability, information, leisure, education – in short, *civiltà*, or civility. It excluded everything that was associated with the countryside: desolation, work, toil, loneliness, animals, ignorance and wilderness. Living in the agro-town provided peasants with a strong sense of belonging, honour and identity. Participating, even vicariously, in urban life defined them as 'civilized' human beings, whereas living in the countryside would deprive them of regard and respect. Consistent with this orientation, women were virtually excluded from work in the fields. The opposition between town and country thus involved much more than ecological arrangements. It inspired a distinct form of life. How carefully the categories of urban and rural life were defined, reproduced and kept distinct is demonstrated by numerous verbal and non-verbal expressions in different contexts of everyday life. As men-tioned above, peasants made considerable sacrifices to exempt their wives and daughters from labour on the land. Common phrases to denote a bad woman included the abusive '*una donnaccia rurale*'. Some peasants went literally out of their way to keep the categories separate: they routinely avoided being seen in public when returning on muleback from work on the land, trying to reach their homes inconspicuously by taking longer and less travelled byways. These patterns are by no means restricted to Sicily's interior, and the symbolism of the urban/rural con-trast in this part of the Mediterranean can probably be best understood in terms of what Sherry Ortner has described as a 'root metaphor': that is, a key symbol with great conceptual power, since it 'formulates the unity of cultural orientation underlying many aspects of experience' (1973: 1340).

The distinction between urban and rural domains is particularly salient in the multifarious ritual activities that take place in the border-land separating *paese* and *campagna*, or urban and rural space. This intermediate zone is a true betwixt-and-between area, combining fea-tures of both domains and mediating a series of powerful oppositions.

Surrounding the agro-town, the *corona*, or rim, as it is appropriately called, consists of a zone of intensive cultivation. These fields differ in many ways from the vast estates that dominate the countryside. Culti-vated by the owners themselves, rows of vines alternate with stretches of fruit trees, and kitchen gardens.[38] Unlike the remote and grim *lati-fondi*, whose regime never tolerated much permanent habitation and vegetation, the *corona* is accessible and inviting. Its trees and bushes provide shade and coolness. An occasional shaded stream renders its aspect even idyllic, reminding the visitor of Alpine settings. Here, in a myriad of different plots, we find small vineyards, olive, almond, apple, peach, cherry, medlar, mulberry and other fruit trees. An occasional building, hidden behind a fig tree, provides temporary shelter. In a paradoxical way, we are here both inside and outside the agro-town: because of the proximity of the built-up area and because work on these plots assumes the character of leisure rather than toil.

Compared with the overwhelming importance of cereal production and animal husbandry in this part of Sicily, the type of farming carried out in the *corona* is also marginal from an economic point of view. An old man, who took me to his orchard in the *corona* to taste his mulberries and other fruits, illustrated this point. While I praised the cherries, he quoted an ancient Sicilian proverb, 'Sono buone le fighe e le cirase, ma guai allu stomacu che pane nun ci trase' (They are good, the figs and cherries, but unfortunate the stomach that does not get any bread).[39]

As mentioned before, women definitely belong to the inside and the domestic world. But in this intermediate zone, they can be seen at work: tending their kitchen gardens and picking grapes. Indeed, in this part of Sicily, the *vendemmia*, or grape harvest – subordinate to pastoralism and the production of cereals – is considered an outing, a festive affair. These inversions and reversals with respect to work, leisure, gender, time and place suggest that the zone of intensive cultivation surrounding the agro-town is an area of ritual space.

The rules concerning gender segregation are suspended once more during courtship – itself a transitional stage. When not confined to other transitional locations like windows, balconies and doorsteps, the liminal activities of *fidanzati* are also appropriately relegated to the ritual space separating town and country. Whereas in everyday life adult men and women are rarely seen together (also married couples avoid being seen in public together), fiancés and fiancées, and those who pretend to be engaged, meet at the outskirts of the town, along the roads leading into the intermediate zone.

The territory between habitat and countryside is the *locus* of other celebrations as well – ritual activities that likewise emphasize the transitional character of the *corona*, while at the same time helping to define and articulate major cultural categories. In the agro-town of Contessa Entellina, this borderland was the stage for the cult of saints. Virtually all the shrines and chapels devoted to saints, such as Santa Rosalia, San Calogero and San Antonio, were located at the periphery of the village and in the adjoining intermediate zone of intensive cultivation. The image of the local patron saint, the *Madonna della Favara*, stands in one of the main parish churches at the eastern periphery of the village. She is supposed to have appeared at a nearby well, which in the course of time became part of the built-up area. Devotion to the Madonna includes an annual pilgrimage and *festa* on 8 September, the day of the Nativity of the Blessed Virgin. Some chapels lie just outside the town area, while others have been constructed at a greater distance. The most striking aspect, however, was that they were placed neither in the town itself nor in the open countryside. Thus contact between the sacred and the profane, and supposed communication between this world and the next, between ordinary human beings and supernatural beings, took place in appropriate settings: the betwixt-and-between zone that separates urban from rural space. In this way, the cult of saints helps to shape the symbolic ordering of space and time, and emphasizes other major cultural distinctions with respect to work, leisure, recreation, civility, class and gender.[40]

This pattern of ordering experience is replicated in other symbolic activities. In the course of the nineteenth century, people in Europe stopped burying the dead in churches; the burial place was removed to outside the town. With the construction of the cemetery within the *corona* of Contessa Entellina, the intermediate zone became the scene of another set of ritual activities, including attending funerals and visiting the graves of relatives. These practices involve emphasis on and mediation between major cultural concepts, most notably life and death, this world and the next, and the living and the dead. Appropriately located in the marginal zone between town and country, the cemetery is also the main venue for the celebration of the annual feast of All Souls' Day (*Tutti i Morti*) on 2 November, when prayers are said for the dead.

Starting in the 1960s, the border zone between urban and rural space became a favourite location for *villeggiatura*, or country holidays (from *villeggiare*, to stay in the country for weekends and holidays). Local natives who have made successful careers in larger cities, especially Palermo, have built second homes in the countryside adjoining the town in which they grew up. Tellingly, these *nouveaux riches* only spend their holidays (which divide periods of work) in this location and thus emphasize its character of ritual space.

Most activities that take place in the area dividing urban and rural domains have a symbolic import. They mark borders of social space and time, transitions between life and death, the boundaries between the living and the dead, and between this world and the next; they help distinguish between work and leisure, and define categories of social class, age and gender. Indeed they turn the area into ritual space. Some activities structure the life cycle, creating intervals between major age categories, which they thus help to define and reproduce. Funerals do so with respect to life and death. Engagement marks the boundaries between children and adults. Other ritual activities structure annual cycles and symbolize time by creating intervals between periods of work and periods of leisure, between spring, summer, autumn, and winter. All these cultural categories are as much marked by stretches of 'no man's land' as by intervals of social 'timelessness'. Engagements, funerals, holidays, saints' days, pilgrimages, the grape harvest and other (predominantly) symbolic activities are all carried out and celebrated in this intermediate zone of intensive cultivation. Underscoring the importance of the urban/rural divide is the fact that the symbolic ordering of space and time, along with that of other major experiences, takes place in the liminal area between agro-town and countryside. The urban/rural opposition in Sicily's western interior looms large in the heads of its inhabitants. It both inspires and epitomizes an entire way of life.

9

Nicknames as Symbolic Inversions

Laughter and its forms represent the least scrutinized sphere of the people's creation.

Bakhtin, *Rabelais and his World*

Ma tutti i cognomi non furono in origine soprannomi?
(But were not all surnames originally nicknames?)

Sciascia, *Occhio di Capra*

I

Ignoring their ambiguity and contrapuntal thrust, the study of offensive nicknames as terms of reference has suffered from an overemphasis on social order. Drawing on comparative research, and Italian ethnography in particular, this essay explores various levels of ambiguity in this naming practice and argues that nicknames both reflect dominant cultural codes and reflect on them.

The use of derogatory, offensive nicknames as terms of reference in small communities across Europe, the Mediterranean and the Americas has drawn considerable attention from anthropologists and other students of the minutiae of social life.[1] Yet to account for this naming practice, most scholars have followed a rather limited approach, analysing nicknames in terms of their role in maintaining the local social system. The emphasis has therefore fallen on identification, classification, social integration, articulation of inter- and intra-community boundaries, and social control.

Although all these dimensions are relevant to the use of nicknames, I feel that the main point has been missed. The quintessence of nicknames

155

is their ambiguity. Nicknames provoke laughter and obviously belong to a parodic genre. This has often been noted, but it has as often been taken for granted. In a perceptive article, McDowell (1981) argues that the attitude toward the behaviour hinted at in the nickname is one of amusement rather than moral indignation. Far from only helping to define social groups, marking boundaries, expressing and fostering a sense of belonging, and reflecting the norms of the community, nicknaming also comments on the existing order of things, challenging, inverting or subverting prevailing moral standards. Nicknames are negative representations and can best be understood as a form of symbolic inversion.[2] Anthropology has sometimes been defined as a parodic pursuit; its practitioners have, then, a special licence to study discursive heterodoxies, 'designed to counter more standardized traditions of belief and practice' (Boon 1984: 170).

The ambiguity of nicknames resides on several levels, which can be briefly mentioned before discussing them at greater length later on. It is unfortunate (but interesting) that anthropologists have rarely discussed nicknames in relation to other naming systems, while those writing on names and naming usually ignore the issue of nicknames.[3] Yet as Geertz (1973d: 368–70) suggests, it is hard to discuss the one without referring to the other. Even in societies where nicknames are lacking, as seems to be the case in Bali, their absence is significant and may tell us a great deal about notions of self and personhood.

The oblique, equivocal, polysemic qualities of nicknames are most obvious when we contextualize them in the wider naming system and see how they, as derisive and offensive terms of reference, are juxtaposed in relation to formal, honorific terms of address. Pointing to some form of deviant behaviour or a physical defect of the referent, nicknames are used behind people's back, never in front of them – unless one's intention is to offend.[4] The person who is deferentially addressed, either by his Christian name, title, surname, kinship term, personal pronoun or a combination of these possibilities, knows that his nickname will be used as soon as he turns his back, leaves the scene or company (that is, when no close relatives or friends remain present). Nicknames are thus semi-public and semi-secret. In fact, they are public secrets, and this in itself renders them ambiguous.[5]

Since they focus on unfavourable or negative attributes of the referent – the dark or left side of people – nicknames contrast dramatically with official names. Writing on nicknames in the French village of Minot, Zonabend emphasizes this duality as follows:

> Tout ce que la censure sociale ne permet pas de dire directement, le sobriquet l'exprime à sa façon, sans tenir compte ni de l'ordre familial ni de

l'ordre social. Car, à l'encontre du patronyme et en partie du prénom, qui restent du ressort de la parentèle, le sobriquet est l'affaire de la communauté: il est laissé à la libre création du groupe social. Et dans cette distribution sont confondus les humbles et les nantis, les notables et le reste de la communauté. Mais si tous sont confondus, chacun est singularisé. Le sobriquet signale des traits particuliers, prend en considération la personalité de chacun, remarque les conduites et les comportements. Mais, tout en affirmant les différences, le group énonce l'absence d'une hiérarchie, il substitue un ordre à un autre, établit un ordre égalitaire pour tous les résidents au village. (1977: 271)

(Everything that social censorship does not permit us to say directly, the nickname expresses in its own way without taking into consideration the order of family or the social order in general. This is so because, unlike the surname and, up to a point also the first name, which belong to the realm of the family, the nickname is a matter of the community: left to the free creation of the social group. And in this distribution the low and the rich, the notables and the rest of the community are confounded. But if all people are mixed up, everyone is identified. The nickname signals particular features, takes into consideration the personality of everyone, comments on demeanour and behaviour. But by confirming the differences, the group proclaims the absence of hierarchy, it substitutes one order for another, and establishes an egalitarian order for all the residents of the village.)

In this juxtaposition lies also much of the comic character of nicknames. As attacks on control and formality, they provoke laughter. Indeed, as informal attacks on something formal (hierarchy, order, status, role, classification, etiquette – any dominant cultural code), a nickname can be understood as a play upon form: that is, as a joke or, rather, the punchline of a joke.[6]

The ambiguity of nicknames is still further evident when we realize that the reference to unusual, improper or deviant behaviour is mostly indirect and oblique. Often metaphoric and ironic, nicknames are allusive. In a roundabout way they seem to tell us what a person 'really' is as opposed to what he appears or pretends to be behind his mask of public fronts. Focusing on grotesque features of the human body, referring to organic aspects of human beings, and often challenging or blurring distinctions of species, class, age and gender, nicknames tend to emphasize 'nature' as opposed to 'culture'. They are part of the 'vulgar', popular, extra-official forms of speech, of what Bakhtin has described as the 'boundless ocean of grotesque bodily imagery', which

within time and space extends to all languages, all literatures, and the entire system of gesticulation; in the midst of it the bodily canon of art, belles lettres, and polite conversation of modern times is a tiny island. This limited canon never prevailed in antique literature. In the official literature of European peoples it has existed only for the last four hundred years. (1968: 319)[7]

Finally, the very use of nicknames, the nicknaming practice or custom, is ambiguous. As McDowell (1981: 12) argues, the behaviour the nickname depicts is considered improper, opposed to ideal patterns of behaviour, while the attitude toward this behaviour is one of merriment and benevolent amusement rather than disapproval or moral indignation. Highlighting unorthodox or deviant behaviour, nicknames paradoxically make for the integration of the referents rather than their expulsion.

The duality in naming practices reflects and articulates a more general dualism, which can be rendered as follows:

official names	nicknames
address	reference
deferential	insulting
front	back
public	secret
direct	indirect
hierarchy	equality
literal	metaphoric
outside	inside
state	community
written	oral
history	memory
formal	informal
elite	popular
good	bad
sacred	profane
culture	nature
order	disorder

In so far as the complexities of nicknames and nicknaming have been recognized, they have been more often explained away than accounted for. This is consistent with a long-standing, overall resistance to the study of negative representation and paradoxes. As Babcock has put it: 'by ignoring or minimizing negative representations, we fail in some basic sense to get at what symbolic processes are all about and, more importantly, how they function in any given social context' (1975: 156).[8]

Before discussing examples from the corpus of Italian (Sicilian) nicknames, let us briefly review the literature on the subject.

II

Since Pitt-Rivers (1961: 160–8) first described the use of offensive nicknames in the highlands of Andalusia in the early 1950s, anthropologists have reported strikingly similar nicknaming customs all around the Mediterranean as well as in several small communities elsewhere. In the pattern described, most men and only few women in the village or rural town are routinely referred to by derisive nicknames based on physical characteristics, personal habits, family background, occupation or local events. While not all such names might appear insulting to an outsider, all are deeply resented by their bearers and would ordinarily never be used in their presence. Hence the term *ingiuria*, or insult, for nickname in Sicily.[9] As suggested above, *any* form of naming can come dangerously close to shaming, to, literally, 'calling names'. Offending is a speech act *par excellence*. The uttering of an offence is not merely saying something; it is also a performative act *which does something*. Offending quite literally hurts, puts a person beyond the pale, etc.[10]

No concrete system seems to govern who receives nicknames, who thinks them up, or under what circumstances they are inherited. We know that their use is characteristic of small groups and face-to-face communities; nicknames fall into disuse with increased interpenetration of the community and the larger society (cf. Barrett 1978). Implied in their insulting qualities, most nicknames are funny to those who use them. They employ *double entendre*, word play, irony, metaphor and allusiveness, following virtually all the joke-techniques discussed by Freud, including brevity, condensation, displacement and representation by opposite. More often than not, they capture in one or two words controversial information of a story well known locally about a particular person. In his work on northern Spanish villages, Christian depicts the social context of nicknaming as follows:

> It is the aspect of the village as a stage, with its own characters and its own standing jokes, that every day solidifies the village, that is the living reality of this nebulous thing known as community. People's public personalities get away from them; they become stock figures just as well known and appreciated after their deaths as characters in the *Commedia dell'Arte*, remembered as the essential elements of scenes and incidents recounted around the hearth, in the tavern, at the portal of the church, or in the winter barns, in the long chains of stories and anecdotes that form the village's cultural legacy and the village entertainment. (1972: 26)

Anthropologists have several explanations for this naming practice. Some argue that nicknames serve to identify people with the same baptismal name and the same family name.[11] Owing to local endogamy, many people in small communities share the same family name. Baptismal names, too, are often few in towns and villages along the northern shores of the Mediterranean. This tendency stems partly from the custom of naming children after local patron saints in Roman Catholic areas. Moreover, first-born children in these communities are usually named after their grandparents, which produces the same Christian names both within and between generations. Given these naming practices, nicknames are indeed useful devices to distinguish people with the same name. Indeed, collecting nicknames is one of the first steps in ethnographic field-work in such communities.

Although nicknames do greatly help to identify people in this fashion, it does not explain the practice. First, we know that some people who share names do not have nicknames, while people with uncommon names often do.[12] Second, and perhaps more important, viewing nicknames as a device for identifying people does not help us to understand why most of these nicknames are derisive, derogatory and offensive, drawing attention to the least flattering features of the person involved. These names are not merely identifications; they are negative identifications and representations. As McDowell observes in his essay on nicknames among the Kamsá in south-western Colombia: 'Thus a man who might be identified by a score of positive attributes is identified in the ugly name in terms of negative attributes. Herein lies the fundamental discourtesy of the ugly name: the Kamsá ugly name is an unkind identifying description' (1981: 8). A second function of nicknames that has been singled out by anthropologists, and which is closely connected with identification, is that these denominations define people as members of the local community. In an early statement, Pitt-Rivers writes: 'The nickname defines a person in his relationship to the community, defines him by his origin, his family, his place of upbringing, his office or his outstanding characteristics in the eyes of the pueblo' (1961: 167).

These dimensions of nicknames – the person's identity relative to the local system of relationships and his integration into the local community – have been documented and emphasized by various ethnographers.[13] Such analyses are correct as far as they go, but like the first explanation, they fail to account for, or even to address, the negative identification inherent in our type of nicknames. Moreover, they ignore the comic aspect and tell us little about the ambiguities inherent in the paradoxical procedure of seizing on the deviant and the antisocial attributes of a person to define him as an insider rather than an outsider and make for his integration rather than his expulsion.

A third and related dimension highlighted in the literature on nicknames concerns their relation to social boundaries. Since nicknames define a person as a member of a local community, they foster a sense of belonging and help set the community off from its neighbours – or any in-group from the outside world. In his work on a central Italian village, Cohen in particular has emphasized this relationship between nickname and *campanilismo*, or local patriotism, and his phrase that such a village or town may be conceived as 'a community of nicknames' is felicitous (1977: 110). Other scholars have drawn attention to the intra-village boundaries marked by the use of nicknames and demonstrate that nicknames reveal tensions between rather than within families (Brandes 1975: 142–3; Gilmore 1982: 698).[14] These are, again, all important aspects of nicknames, and I have no quarrel with them. But they leave unexplained (if they mention them at all) the various ambiguities in the nicknaming custom, underplaying, ignoring or obscuring the significance of their metaphoric and comic aspects.[15]

Fourth and finally, we have the issue of social control. It has been argued that by drawing attention to and ridiculing deviant or socially unacceptable behaviour, nicknames operate as a mechanism of social control.[16] Most writings on the subject contain some version of this argument, and many authors seem to take its validity for granted. It is unclear, however, as Cohen observes, whether nicknames actually affect behaviour patterns. Writing on a central Italian village, he notes:

> There are any number of derogatory and insulting nicknames used in Collefiore. The mere fact that nicknames are derogatory or insulting does not imply their use as modes of community censure and control. . . . Obnoxious and odious nicknames neither enforce conformity to community standards nor do they serve as punishment for transgressions of the moral order. . . . If nicknaming operates as one means of social control, it does so only in the restricted sense of ridiculing and denigrating certain traits. In this restricted sense, some nicknames are one of the ways in which the moral codes and cultural ideals of the community are stated and affirmed. (1977: 106–7)

It may well be, then, that nicknames in this way help to spell out and reinforce the main values in local communities. But the criticism involved is often playful, indirect and allusive, and seems to be as much a commentary on those values as a support for them. Again, this approach, too, neglects the ambiguities so salient in nicknaming.

III

A more promising approach is suggested by Cohen's definition of nicknames. Taking issue with the social control argument, Cohen claims that 'the hallmark of the apt nickname is that deft touch of nuance, mocking humour, pungent wit, and droll equivocality' (1977: 107). This strikes close to the heart of the matter, addressing ambiguities pertaining in the use of nicknames. But Cohen does not pursue this lead. Instead, he considers nicknaming in the context of *campanilismo*, and concludes that nicknames 'operate as boundary-defining and boundary-maintaining mechanisms for groups to whom separateness, difference, and distinctiveness are of particular value and importance' (1977: 111).

Further helpful reorientations are offered in McDowell's essay, which starts out by reminding us that the term 'nickname' derives etymologically from the Middle English 'an eke name', that is, another name, suggesting that nicknames, properly understood, stand in opposition to other naming conventions and should, therefore, be studied in connection with those practices – most notably in opposition to formal modes of address. Considering nicknames as an example of informal performative nomination, McDowell argues that they earn their way into general usage on the basis of their semantic appropriateness, which he defines as 'the fit between the descriptive backing in the name and the social and biological identity of the name bearer'. The adoption of nicknames is further helped by their aesthetic qualities, which include brevity, acoustic texturing, allusiveness and piquancy (McDowell 1981: 9–13).

In discussing these aspects of nicknaming among the Kamsá in Colombia, McDowell underscores the ambiguities inherent in the use of nicknames. He recognizes that these so-called ugly names constitute a 'treasure of native metaphor' and convey in coded form a great deal of information (more than any other name) about the referent. More important still, these nicknames

> display a fundamental ambivalence toward the behavior they depict. On the one hand, these behaviors, taken collectively, comprise a Kamsá anti-world, an inventory of improperly guided behavior [standing] in opposition to ideal patterns of behavior. . . . On the other hand, the Kamsá attitude toward these behaviors is one of benevolent amusement rather than moral indignation. The very utterance of the name is a mildly deviant act, because of their marginal status and often obscene content. Moreover, the ugly names constitute in part a mocking of moral standards and exemplars of morality. There is an unmistakable undercurrent of celebration in the names, a recognition of the transcendent vitality of the community. (1981: 12)

McDowell also hints at the resemblance between the corpus of nicknames and the trickster cycle. Both genres are dedicated to the exploration of actual and possible modes of deviancy. The bearers of ugly names thus acquire through their names something of the aura of the trickster, a deviant figure who is nonetheless deeply expressive of the community's ethos. Significantly, the Kamsá exhibit the same response to the performance of both these expressive forms, one of enthusiastic mirth. (1981: 12–13)

This approach to the study of nicknaming is illuminating since it recognizes and tries to come to terms with its inverse and ambiguous qualities. In his analysis of Kamsá ugly names, McDowell goes further than telling us that nicknames criticize deviant behaviour. He argues that nicknames, as opposed to other naming practices, not only reflect the values of the community, but also comment on them. No previous study had taken this step of recognizing that nicknames as terms of reference should be studied in the context of the wider naming system, and that the opposition with formality provides an occasion for enjoying a release from control, creating the opportunity for realizing – as Mary Douglas wrote about the joke – that accepted classifications and standards of behaviour have 'no necessity'.[17]

To capture the implicit meanings of nicknames – their metaphoric quality, their double meaning and irony, their parody and play on words – requires further contextualization, which involves intimate knowledge of interpersonal histories and familiarity with local culture. Of all names, writes McDowell, the nickname tells us most about the identity of the name-bearer; compared with other names, nicknames convey substantial information. In their turn, nicknames can, therefore, tell us a great deal about the local and regional setting in which they have been coined, accepted and used. Taken as a whole, notes McDowell, the corpus of a community's nicknames provides us with a rich source of indigenous metaphors, pregnant with information both about the people to whom they refer and about the categories upon which they draw. Indeed, as Fortes observed some time ago, a name can be 'a document epitomizing personal experience, historical happenings, attitudes to life, and cultural ideas and values'.[18] More recently, Seeman explored the unconscious meanings of nicknames and other personal names, comparing them with associations emerging in dreams. She argues that many inferences can be drawn from knowledge of a person's name, which may explain why in some cultures it is kept secret (1983: 240–3).

IV
To see what complexities figure in Italian nicknames and to what extent these names should be understood as symbolic inversions or negative rep-

resentations, let us first examine two examples from the ethnography of the area.

One instructive example is reported by Eugene Cohen, who worked in a Tuscan village about a hundred miles north of Rome. He refers to the case of a limping woman there nicknamed *La Zoppa* ('The Cripple'). Like many nicknames, this one appears neither insulting nor humorous; the woman is a cripple, and the name clearly identifies her. Why should this nickname provoke laughter? Where is the 'pungent wit', the 'droll equivocality' that Cohen singles out as hallmarks of an apt nickname? As he rightly notes, however, there is more going on here than simple description. He speculates that the humour derived from the fact that this woman is 'renowned in village gossip for fleeing the village with her lover during the course of a passionate love affair'. The author seems to be unaware of the exact connection between the nickname and the adultery; he senses that one exists, though, and wonders whether the nickname *La Zoppa* 'mocks the passion that drove this disabled and not very good looking woman to abandon husband and community' (1977: 107).

Perhaps Italian folklore may shed light on the issue and clarify the semantic fit of the nickname as well as its aesthetic qualities. A Sicilian proverb suggests a connection between passion and limping women: '*Acqua di zotta, sticchiu di zoppa*', meaning 'Water from the pool [i.e. good water], cunt of a limping woman'.[19] In his essay '*Des boiteux*', Montaigne quotes an Italian proverb: 'Celui-là ne coignoit pas Venus en sa parfaicte douceur qui n'a couché avec la boiteuse' (He who has not lain with a limping woman does not know Venus in her perfect sweetness).[20] It is obvious that the nickname *La Zoppa* in the Tuscan village refers to this folk wisdom. The name would thus relate not only to the woman's physical imbalance (symbolizing her moral instability?), but also to popular beliefs surrounding it and the confirmation of those beliefs in her actual behaviour. Both the semantic fit and the artful elements of brevity, indirect reference and piquancy may help explain why this nickname was accepted and became part of the local oral tradition.

With the nickname *La Zoppa* we would seem to have an ideal case of nicknaming as social control. A woman who has transgressed a community norm is stigmatized by repeated, derisive reference to her deviance. But there is more going on as well, and such an approach would obscure all the implications of the apt nickname mentioned earlier. The accusation is not direct, but involves an indirect reference to a popular saying and belief, a wry *double entendre*. Moreover, its tone is not one of moral outrage, but of humorous delight. There may be nothing funny about a limping woman. But a limping woman who, in addition, is married and has fled her village with a lover is quite another case. Symbolizing sexuality, copulation and lasciviousness, limping belongs to the comic genre described as 'the grotesque image of the body' (Bakhtin 1968: 303ff). The Russian linguist and folklorist reminds us that

> the grotesque mode of representing the body and bodily life prevailed in art and creative forms of speech over thousands of years. From the point of view of extensive use, this mode of representation still exists today; grotesque forms of the body not only predominate in the art of European peoples but also in their folklore, especially in the comic genre. Moreover, these images predominate in the extra-official life of the people. For example, the theme of mockery and abuse is almost entirely bodily and grotesque. (1968: 318–19)

To dismiss the grotesque overtones of the nickname, to look only at its reference to a social transgression, is to miss the parodic thrust of this naming custom that distinguishes it from any ordinary, straightforward gossip or verbal scolding.

Like the sobriquet *La Zoppa*, nicknames based on occupations seem, at first glance, fairly innocent as well, and they have often been interpreted literally.[21] In the same Tuscan village of Collefiore, we hear about a schoolteacher nicknamed *Il Maestro*, which is a perfectly respectful term of reference for a schoolteacher. To appreciate the irony and wittiness of this nickname and to understand the insult conveyed by this denomination, one should know that this man was the worst and the least dedicated of the four schoolteachers in the village (Cohen 1977: 106). Many nicknames have such inverse qualities, containing backhanded insults in apparently innocuous references. Pitré reports, for instance, the case of a Palermitan physician nicknamed *Oravengo*, who, when sent for, always replied, 'Ora vengo' (I am coming), without ever showing up (Pitré 1978c: 382n.).

Next, let us consider some examples from a small agro-town in the interior of western Sicily, where I lived and worked for some years in the 1960s.[22] There, nicknaming closely followed the patterns reported by Pitt-Rivers, Brandes, Gilmore, Cohen, Antoun and other writers on Mediterranean communities. All nicknames were derogatory, satirical and offensive. They were, therefore, exclusively used as terms of reference. Various nicknames referred to occupations, but none of them was ever used as a term of address, however innocent it may have sounded to an outsider. The name *L'Avvucaticchiu*, for example, literally meaning 'Little Lawyer', referred to a friendly man of an upper-class family in decline, somewhat small of stature, who worked in the local tax office.

While the name seemed to refer to his physique, it also contained a veiled reference to the former grandeur of his lineage and to the fact that he had not finished law school. The title *Avvocato*, by contrast, referring to a real lawyer, is honorific and a formal term of address – emphasizing status and class, relationship with the outside world and the state rather than membership of the local community. Here again we find an equivocal insult in an apparently inoffensive designation. We also see how nicknames can tell us about local history and biography in an indirect, allusive way – and how ignorance about that history precludes interpretation of nicknames.

We know that things rarely are what they seem. Anthropologists, writes R. Murphy, make their living by showing that what seems to be one thing is actually something else (1990: 331). Consider the nickname *Fondacaru* for one of the bar-keepers and his family in this Sicilian agrotown. What appeared as a simple description of a profession turned out to be a term of abuse when used as a term of reference. The nickname derives from *fondaco*, a wayside inn with accommodation for horses and carts, where travelling people stayed for the night. The bar-keeper's father had been a *fondacaru* in the old days. The nickname was resented because the profession was looked down upon: *gente di fondaco* – 'a lower sort of people since they always dealt with travelling folk'.[23] When one of the bar-keeper's nieces – a single, ageing beauty – had again refused a proposal of marriage, the offended party commented on her *superbia* (haughtiness) and referred to her derisively as '*figghia di Fondacaru*' (daughter of the *Fondacaru*).

A much less obvious reference to occupation occurs in the nickname *Finíu Finau*. The man obtained his nickname because he would end every story he told (or heard other people telling) with the phrase '*Finíu finau*', meaning roughly 'And that was the end of it'. The importance of storytelling ability for social interaction in rural Sicily made this habit noteworthy in its own right. But yet another meaning was implied, as the man made his living as a grave-digger.

One of the landless labourers, of whom there were many in this *latifondist* settlement, was referred to as *Lu Mulu* ('The Mule'). Until the 1960s, mules were the main draught animals and the chief means of transport, and many landless labourers made their living as mule drivers on the large estates. The denotation was far from innocent, however, since it alluded to the man's civil status: he was an illegitimate child, his father being unknown. Mules are also bastards, the offspring of a mare and an (anonymous) donkey. This nickname was regarded as less humorous than most, but it was highly ambiguous and grotesque in metaphorically mixing human and animal images with respect to sexuality and reproduction.

Another man from the labouring classes – a mason – served for many years as an opposition leader, representing the local section of the Communist Party. Later on he became vice-mayor in a Socialist administration. He used to be very loud, preferring to shout everything he said, a habit he may have picked up as a local politician and mouthpiece of the opposition. This idiosyncrasy earned him the nickname *Campanazza*, meaning 'Bad Church Bell'. The nickname originated when one of the locals, annoyed by the man's loudness, snapped, 'Ci misi 'na campanazza' ('They have put a bad church bell on him'). The implications are obvious. Church bells call people to worship and, for a long period after the war, priests used to warn their parishioners against the 'dangers of Communism'.

Few women seemed to have nicknames. As Antoun, who worked in a Jordanian village, has observed, this is related to the fact that women are not public figures; usually they are attacked indirectly, that is, through their men:

> One might ask, then, why women, on the whole, do not possess nicknames. The answer is that they do not have public personalities and are consequently unneedful of public control; they are controlled directly by the men and their families, who speak for the common weal. A man wishing to curb the behavior of a woman almost invariably addresses the men of her house. In certain cases, e.g., widows and female orphans, direct contact with females is necessary, and it is exactly this necessity that makes such relationships fragile and difficult. Moreover, to use an invidious nickname for a woman is to attack her father, brother, or husband at the most sensitive point of his honor. When female nicknames are applied, they are applied by women to women, and the application is almost always in the presence of a very small and intimate group. (1968a: 166)

When women do become public figures, they may acquire nicknames. This is attested to in the Sicilian village where a married woman was called *Nina senza Paesi* or 'Nina without a Home Town'. We should not just take this denomination literally. Saying that she had no home town, that her origins were unknown, was a metaphor for a number of ways she was considered anomalous. Her father was from another town in the area and used to say 'Io non aju paisi' ('I don't have a home town'). Hence they called him *Ignazio senza Paisi*, a name subsequently transferred to his daughter. Nina herself had served on various occasions as a wet-nurse when she was breastfeeding one of her own children, which blurred private and public domains. Moreover, it was rumoured that not all of her children were from her husband, which brought her dangerously close to the category of a 'public woman', while her husband moved into the ranks of those who have failed to control their wives – an ultimate disgrace in this part of the world. All the same, she was much less circumspect in her relations with men than was customary in the area. Her case confirms Antoun's point about female nicknames, since Nina was a woman who had become publicly known.

Not only members of the popular classes were given nicknames. Four brothers of the landowning class of *burgisi* were called *I Torti* (singular: *Tortu, Mastru Tortu*), which has connotations of wrong, fault, twisted, blame, injustice, damage, deviance and impropriety. Violating basic rules of reciprocity and hospitality, the *Torti* were considered antisocial, misers, mean and miserable people, slow to pay for anything, in particular for the services of their employees.

Another man in the same Sicilian village had married a woman who had a house, land and some money. They called him *Maccaruni*, because some people said he had entered that house like a *maccherone*, like a string of maccaroni: with nothing but the clothes on his back. According to others, the man acquired his nickname because he liked maccaroni and always talked about it. Still others argued that this nickname was conferred on him because he was thin, and resembled a string of maccaroni. These interpretations do not exclude one another. Identifying a human being with this basic food, all designations comment on the scarcity of means and the ways to come to terms with that condition.

Many nicknames in the Sicilian agro-town used such references to bodily images. An obese woman was nominated *La Pignata* ('The Cauldron'), a pun on both her size and her appetite. A haughty and arrogant man who walked in a stiff, upright way was called *U Bicchirinu* ('Little Glass'), as if he represented a glass of liqueur filled to the rim. One of the local barbers, a rather pretentious man who was reputed to put on his white coat with much ostentation before starting his daily work in his shop on the piazza, was nicknamed *Barone Pilu* ('Baron Hair'). For the same reasons others called him *U Chirurgu* ('The Surgeon'). A strikingly fat peasant was known as *Peppe Zumili*, which derives from *zumili*, enormous baskets used to carry manure on muleback from the stables in the village to the countryside. Bakhtin regards representations of men with monstrous bellies as 'typical grotesque hyperbola' (1968: 328). It would be difficult to understand the nickname *Peppe Zumili* without some knowledge of the ecology and architecture in this area of agro-towns, where virtually the entire peasant population lives in nucleated settlements surrounded by narrow strips of intensive cultivation and an open countryside of pastures and fields of grain (see chapter 8).

Physical abnormalities (obesity, baldness, shortness, lameness) and speech defects (stammering, shouting) are the categories most frequently cited in the corpus of nicknames collected in Sicily. In addition to those already mentioned, we have *Peppe U Lungu* ('Joe the Tall One'), *Testa Sicca* ('Shrunken Head'), *Giuvanni Testa Grossa* ('John Big Head'), *Pupu di Lignu* ('Wooden Puppet'), *Rapacchiu* ('Wrinkled Head'), *Tignusu* ('The Bald One'), *Facciazza* ('Bad Face'), *Picchiacchia* ('Stammerer') and *Scioscia*, an onomatopoeic term for a woman who talked a lot in court-yards, the semi-public areas around the houses. Her voice was like the sound of grain being sieved.

Similar patterns have been observed elsewhere. Indeed, the image of the grotesque body looms large in offensive nicknames. This is one of the main reasons why they are comic – and why local literati regard the use of nicknames as a sign of backwardness and lack of *civiltà*.[24] Bakhtin writes:

> The theme of mockery and abuse is almost entirely bodily and grotesque. The body that figures in all the expressions of the unofficial speech of the people is the body that fecundates and is fecundated, that gives birth and is born, devours and is devoured, drinks, defecates, is sick and dying. In all languages there are a great number of expressions related to the genital organs, the anus, the buttocks, the belly, the mouth and nose. . . . Wher-ever men laugh and curse, particularly in a familiar environment, their speech is filled with bodily images. (1968: 319)

There are, then, various reasons why nicknames provoke hilarity. First, because they are, often in a dramatic fashion, juxtaposed to formal and deferential modes of address. Second, because they are a (meta-phorical) play upon form, in particular bodily forms, drawing on the comic genre of the grotesque and often employing the joke-techniques enumerated by Freud (see above). A third reason is because they often display 'acoustic texturing': that is, phonemic repetition and the alter-nating use of stressed and slack syllables. As McDowell (1981: 11) points out, these sound patterns reinforce the comic element, making the named person look particularly foolish.[25] In the literature on nick-names, examples of this variety have often and erroneously been recorded as 'semantically empty'. Let us briefly examine this aspect of nicknaming.

Apart from instances already mentioned (*L'Avvucaticchiu, Finíu Finau, Lu Mulu, Campanazza*), we have many examples of acoustic tex-turing which produce or heighten the comic effect of nicknames. *Ninuzzu Papa Ciuciu* refers to a man who stammers. *Ninuzzu* is a diminutive of

the name Antonino, while the second part of the nickname is onomatopoeic. Another stammerer was called *Picchiacchia*. Further, we have
Cicchitedda ('Little Bird') for a woman of small stature; *Peppe Schiri-
chití* for a man who had an ancestor with a deformed hand; and *Ignaziu
Pirituneddu*, which can be rendered 'Ignazio the Little Fart' or 'Ignazio
the Little Farter'.

To conclude this review of Sicilian nicknames, we shall briefly dwell
on the case of the husband of a local midwife. His nickname was
Mammalucco, which embraces widely different meanings, each of
them underlining the man's anomaly and ambiguity in the local setting.
As is well known, *Mammalucco* (Mameluke, mameluco) refers to a specific soldiery in the Ottoman Empire, originally composed of slaves and
prisoners of war from Central Asia. In Italian, the word has connotations of servitude, mixed origins, stupidity, foolishness and emascula-
tion. But why was this man, in the usual equivocal way, identified with a
eunuch?

People considered him unmanly in a number of respects since he
embodied an extraordinary complex of symbolic inversions and negative
representations. First, he was (like his wife) from a neighbouring town,
which set him apart from most villagers. Second, he did not bring anything with him when he married the midwife; he had no property and
no job. Third, he could not, as a consequence, support his wife. On the
contrary, his wife supported him, which produced a fourth anomaly.
Fifth, he stayed in the house like a woman, performing domestic (that
is, female) tasks. Sixth, his wife held a job and was consequently seen in
public. Moreover, she was a midwife, a profession closely bound up with
major transitions, most notably life and death. Seventh, he had no
offspring. Eighth, our man was married to a woman who dealt with
children that were not his. Finally there were the grotesque aspects. He
was a little man with a high-pitched, nasal voice, whereas his wife was
taller, imposing and more vigorously constituted. In all these regards,
the midwife's husband contradicted dominant cultural codes, in particular ideals of masculinity. But the nickname *Mammalucco* revealed a
fundamental ambivalence toward his behaviour. On the one hand,
the denomination evoked the man's numerous anomalies – a veritable
Sicilian anti-world; on the other hand, it epitomized them in an oblique,
metaphoric fashion, provoking mirth and laughter. In all its connotations
and allusions, the nickname *Mammalucco* played on dominant cultural
forms as much as it displayed them.

V

Most analyses of nicknaming have focused on its role in classification,
identification, integration and social control. Matched with an ahistori-

cal perspective was the neglect of the play of tropes in nicknames. Rather than recognizing their ambiguity, exploring their implicit meanings and assessing their aesthetic and comic qualities, anthropologists have emphasized the functions of nicknames and the various purposes they serve.

These aspects are by no means lacking in the nicknames discussed in this essay. But they are also rather obvious, and they have been spelled out often enough. By grafting nicknames on to people with unusual or deviant features, those who use them restate the cultural categories by which they live. The name *Mammalucco* embraces an inventory of Sicilian rules for gender distinctions, each underlined by the man's deviation from them. Likewise, the veiled references to *La Zoppa*'s infidelity, *Campanazza*'s loudness, the *Torti*'s stinginess and *Nina*'s improprieties provide vivid reminders of what is and what is not considered proper behaviour. In this sense Sicilian nicknames seem to reflect and reinforce dominant cultural codes.

In another sense, however, the nicknames undermine, subvert or contradict these codes. By defining people with deviant or unorthodox features in a comic fashion as insiders and incorporating them into the community rather than expelling them as outsiders, nicknaming also counters dominant cultural forms. As inversions and negative representations, nicknames create disorder and turn classifications upside-down. Bestowers and users of nicknames are not indignant at, or outraged by, the behaviour they single out for comment. They are often highly amused and seem to experience a release from the constraints of dominant cultural codes. They see in the deviations not a shocking departure from human behaviour, but an acknowledgement of the human condition beneath a person's public front.

Much as Antoun observes in Jordan, these Sicilians use nicknames to put down pretension, to demonstrate that despite differences in wealth, upbringing and status, the named person is after all no better than anyone else. As symbolic attacks on a person's cultural self and drawing on the grotesque imagery of the body, nicknaming is therefore also subversive of the cultural categories manifest in public fronts and deferential naming practices. Nicknames are offensive in more than one way. They offend people as well as the categories they seek to uphold. Pointing to social distinctions and cultural definitions, nicknames expose them – through the genre of the comic – as essentially arbitrary if not artificial. As tricksters of sorts, the users of nicknames participate in these challenges and subversions. Nicknames resemble the punch-lines of jokes. Something formal, dominant, official is exposed, commented upon, attacked, challenged, subverted by something informal and subordinate that is hidden or implied in it. Bound up with order as much as with disorder, playful and taunting, creative, colourful, poetic and mischievous, these naming practices shape personal identities as readily as they transform them. The evidence from Sicily and other parts of Italy confirms that while nicknames reflect dominant cultural codes and values, they also reflect on them.

10

Mediterranean Totemism: Rams and Billy-Goats

I

The problem as to why deceived husbands in European societies have been referred to, derisively, as 'cornutes', men who wear horns, has never been solved.[1] Nor do we know the reasons why the reference to horns in words or gestures is considered the worst possible insult. A comprehensive study of gestures in Europe and the Mediterranean rehearses no fewer than fourteen different 'theories' on the symbolism of horns and the vertical horn-sign (Morris et al. 1979). Although the authors have reasonable doubts about most of these explanations, they still believe that 'one day, some new evidence will come to light that will favour one above the rest' (1979: 121). As will be shown, however, the problem has less to do with a scarcity of ethnographic data than with the mistake of separating a code from its context.

Oddly enough, anthropologists writing on honour and shame in Mediterranean societies have fared no better than earlier folklorists and modern students of semiotics. Ignoring that 'the elements of symbolism are not things in themselves but "relations" organized in pairs and sets' (Leach 1973a: 48–49),[2] their emphasis has been on horns as such, on horns as a phallic symbol, and on horns as attributes of the Devil.[3] This leaves the question regarding the implicit meaning of the cornute completely open.

In the iconography and discourse of Mediterranean honour codes we are not concerned with horns as such, but with the horns of a specific animal, namely the billy-goat – a fact regrettably played down by Pitt-Rivers in his well-known monograph on an Andalusian town and in his essays on honour, and also completely disregarded in the aforementioned study of gestures. The deceived husband in Italy, Spain and Portugal is identified with the male goat (*becco, cabrón, cabrão*). The Italian term *becco* is a synonym of *cornuto* – the husband of an unfaithful woman. In Spanish, too, *cornudo* and *cabrón* denote a man who consents to his wife's adultery. The Portuguese *cabrão* is likewise synonymous with *cornudo*, with the double meaning of billy-goat and deceived husband or lover.[4] We may thus ask: why of all horned animals just the billy-goat?

The answer may be obvious for those familiar with certain characteristics of the behaviour of farm animals. Like deceived husbands, billy-goats tolerate the sexual access of other males to females in their domain, as I was able to observe when I lived for some years in a Sicilian village in the 1960s.[5] As I learned later, the etymology of the terms *becco* and *cornuto* for 'deceived husband' had already existed in standard and dialectical dictionaries in Italy since the mid-nineteenth century. For instance:

> *Becco, capro, caprone, irco.* The male of the nanny-goat. Said of whoever endures the shame which comes to him from his wife, having thus taken on the likeness of this animal's instinct. The beast does not become angry, unlike others, on seeing his mate lying with others.[6]

> *Becco.* Male of the goat (*capra*). Husband of an unfaithful woman. *Becco contento.* Deceived husband who consents.[7]

In his study of a Castilian rural community, Kenny reports:

> I was assured by a shepherd that when two male goats fight over a female the winner covers her first and then allows the loser to do so. To call a man a 'buck' or 'he-goat' (*cabrón*) is the worst possible insult, the important implication being that he consents to the adultery of his wife. When referring to a cuckolded husband, it is said that he has been given horns. (1966: 83)

These representations are not restricted to little communities and out-of-the-way places on the Iberian peninsula. In Andalusia, as throughout Spain,

> the predominant symbol of the cuckold is the *cabrón* and its *cuernos*, or horns. The term *cabrón*, in fact, has become so purely synonymous with cuckold that it is no longer usefully applied to the actual animal, who is referred to instead as a *macho cabrillo* ('little male goat'). . . . And the goat's horns have become so representative of the cuckold, as well, that the word *cornudo*, horned one, is employed interchangeably with *cabrón*. (Brandes 1981: 227)

Very similar sentiments govern the life of the husband in rural Portugal and very similar metaphors and metonyms are used to convey the disgrace of the deceived husband. The risk of his wife's adultery is the risk of perpetual dishonour: 'if it happens he will be forever a *cabrão* or *corno* (cuckold)' (Cutileiro 1971: 102, 141–2).

In his comments on an earlier version of this essay, the linguist Mario Alinei pointed out that the motivation of 'horns' for 'betrayed husband' appears in numerous national languages (other than Italian, Spanish and Portuguese), including Catalan, Rheto-Romance, Romanian, modern Greek, Turkish, Hungarian, Serbo-Croatian, Bulgarian, Czech, Polish, Russian and Dutch (1982: 771–2). They are linked to a pastoral context but there are also areas, both in the Mediterranean and in continental Europe, where the motivation of 'horns' does not appear in the national language and where other expressions exist to describe the deceived husband. In France, for instance,

> we have the famous *cocu*, originally 'cuckoo' (from the Latin *cuculus*), which extends, as a loan, to the English *cuckold* and which developed independently in the Old Catalan *cogul* and *cugul*. . . .
> The motivation of the 'cuckoo' also appeared in Germany. . . . [where] at present, the most common name for the 'betrayed husband' is *Hahnrei*, literally meaning 'castrated cock, capon'. (Alinei 1982: 772)

Regarding the choice for 'cuckoo' to designate a betrayed husband, Alinei notes that this bird is

> well known for its 'social parasitism', that is, the female cuckoo does not build a nest, but leaves each of her eggs in a different nest every time while the male cuckoo stands by. The *cocu*, then, is the betrayed husband, who calmly accepts the fact that his wife lies and gives birth in the bed of other lovers. (1982: 773–4)

This is a far more convincing interpretation of animal symbolism than that of Pitt-Rivers, who misunderstood this element of popular culture and confused the issue:

> In English, the word 'cuckoo' is thought to derive from cuckoo, the bird which lays its egg in the nest of another. Yet the word does not refer to him who plays the part of the cuckoo, that is, the cuckolder, but to the victim whose role he usurps. The same curious inversion is found in Spanish. The word *cabrón* (a he-goat), the symbol of male sexuality in many contexts, refers not to him whose manifestation of that quality is the cause of the trouble but to him whose implied lack of manliness has allowed the other to replace him. (1961: 116)

Far from dealing with 'inversions', however, we are concerned with *analogies* (between anomalous male behaviour of animals and humans) and with the distinction between normal and anomalous sexuality. Therefore, the view of the billy-goat as 'the symbol of male sexuality in many contexts' is also mistaken and leads nowhere. Along the northern shores of the Mediterranean, betrayed husbands are literally identified with the billy-goat. We are dealing, then, with one of the two main forms of totemic symbolism, namely 'metonymical totemism', which stresses the literal identification of the species from which a name is taken and the named individual or group.[8]

It is striking that the signifier and expression of 'horns' for 'betrayed husband' seems to be absent in France and particularly in Provence, which has been a typical pastoral area since antiquity. However, Alinei found that, first, without touching on the dialects, standard and popular French encompasses a whole series of terms based on the motif of 'horns' for the 'betrayed husband', from *cornard, cornardise, cornichon, cornette, encorner, cornifier, s'encorner, s'encournailler,* to *Cournuaille,* and Mr *Cornelius*; and second:

> in the southern, more distinctly pastoral area, we find that the 'betrayed husband' has completely different dialect names, as in Franco-Provençal and Provençal *banard, banaru, banyet, banichon,* all deriving from the local word for 'horn', *ban, bana* and its variants. This is probably of Celtic origin *banno* (we find it in the Irish *benn* meaning 'horn') and its field extends from southern France to Catalonia, where we find sometimes *banya* meaning 'horn' or *banyut* meaning 'betrayed (husband)'. (1982: 772)

These representations of the deceived husband have a long history and far-reaching implications in several countries both within and beyond the Mediterranean area. There are two restrictions. First, we do not know, as we do for Italian, Spanish and Portuguese, whether the expression 'horns' for 'deceived husband' always involves a reference to the billy-goat. Second, this imagery of horns (of the billy-goat) seems to be completely lacking on the southern shores of the Mediterranean. In spite of these limitations, we can explore the wider context of which this totemic animal forms part. Following Lévi-Strauss's view of the logic of the concrete, we can look for *sets* of animals and examine both external analogies and internal homologies. Next to metonymic totemism, this involves consideration of the other form of totemic symbolism, namely metaphorical totemism, that stresses the categorical nature of human thought.

II

In ancient Greece and Rome, the billy-goat was considered a lascivious and somewhat anomalous animal, epitomizing unrestrained nature. We should not be surprised, then, to find billy-goats, together with other anomalous creatures (such as nymphs, maenads, satyrs), prominent in the entourage of Dionysos and Pan. Remember, too, that the latter is a goat-god involved in pastoral activity and hunting, associated with wild places like mountains and forests, and holding sway on the borders of human space.[9] Summarizing the views of various classical writers, Keller remarks that 'already at the age of seven months, the billy-goat was able to procreate, and the extravagant voluptuousness, already visible in his eyes, uses the animal up so quickly, that he loses his strength in a few years, reaching senility before the age of six' (1909: 308).

These views are confirmed by recent scholarship. Discussing the etymology of the Greek word 'tragedy' (from 'tragos', billy-goat) and the sacrifice of billy-goats in ancient Greece, Walter Burkert reports that for the ancient Greeks the animal evoked lewdness and stench, and was sacrificed when his capacity to procreate diminished; a five-year-old billy-goat could be of no more use (1990: 19).

The anomalous character of the billy-goat remains implied in the semantic differentiation in Italian between the terms *becco* and *caprone*. Whereas the former, as we have seen, stands for betrayed husband, the latter, especially if preceded by *vecchio* (old), acquires the meaning of unrepentant womanizer or 'old goat' (Alinei 1982: 774n.). Obviously, the goat symbolizes sexuality out of place and out of control. This close association between goats and disorder is also suggested in the etymology of words like 'caprices', 'capricious' and 'caprioles' – and their equivalents in Romance languages (cf. Amiel 1987).

The meaning which these features of the billy-goat acquired in Mediterranean societies becomes more obvious when they are set off against those of its most natural counterpart. In several respects, the billy-goat differs sharply from another horned animal typical of the Mediterranean area, namely the ram. Unlike the billy-goat, the ram tolerates no rivals. Shepherds must regulate the number of rams with precision according to the size of the herd to prevent rams from fighting one another if the number of ewes decreases. Belonging to related species, rams and billy-goats share enough features to permit them to be compared.

Travelling with Provençal shepherds and their transhumant flock of over 2,000 sheep and goats from the plains of southern France to Alpine pasture lands 200 miles distant and 8,000 feet high, Moyal reports:

Like people, animals show an amazing variety of temper. Some rams are quiet and peaceful, others, glancing upward from under their lowered brows, will never miss a chance to butt you if you don't stare straight at them. Their tempers undergo a marked change in the mating season. Any September ram is an angry ram, and woe betide the man or dog coming between the proud male and his lady-loves. Shepherds have been butted and trampled to death while trying to interfere with the rams' fierce battles among themselves at this time of the year. (1956: 73)

Whereas two billy-goats are required to cover roughly fifty goats, one ram will serve at least the same number of ewes (Keller 1909: 308, 319). These figures from antiquity match those given by Moyal for the flocks he accompanied in southern France in the early 1950s (1956: 110). They also measure up to the ratios I discussed with Sicilian shepherds, one of whom kept roughly 200 ewes and five rams (*crasti*) to impregnate them between May and November. The biggest ram used to chase off the other rams – or tried very hard to make them stay away. These fights were dangerous and could also seriously harm humans when caught in the midst of them. In the end, however, as one of their owners pointed out, the ram would be *preso in giro*, tricked by his rivals, because he was unable to be on his guard all the time.[10]

From antiquity onwards and on both shores of the Mediterranean, the ram has been known for its virility, sacrality, beauty, strength and fierceness. In various European languages the verb 'to ram' still connotes one of the most striking features of this animal. Next to the bull, the ram was considered the most procreative of all animals.[11] No wonder then that these characteristics have qualified the animal as an appropriate symbol of rulers and kings and the most powerful and prestigious gods, such as Ammon, Zeus, Apollo and Poseidon, and that the Latin *aries* (ram) is related to the Greek *aristos*, the best one.[12] In all Great Traditions including Judaism and Islam that developed in the Mediterranean region, the ram was, as far as one can tell, the paramount sacrificial animal. The ram as Aries is also the first sign of the zodiac, the oldest and most sophisticated totemic classification to come out of the ancient world. Note, too, that a subordinated position in the zodiacal belt is left for Capricorn.

Rams' horns and rams' heads as attributes of rulers figure on Greek coins as early as the sixth century BC. We know of one such representation of Alexander the Great and an earlier example of a ram's head on a coin from the kingdom of Lydia in western Anatolia.[13] Similar qualities suggesting royal and heroic leadership and supernatural power have been ascribed to rams in ancient Egypt and in north-west Africa since prehistoric times where rams' heads have been depicted with discs, suggesting sacrality, kingship and a relationship with the sun.[14]

Although in ancient Mediterranean civilizations billy-goats are also associated with gods, these are nature-like, chthonic gods, such as Dionysos, Pan, Aphrodite and Artemis, known for their unrestrained, 'capricious', libidinous behaviour.[15] A rich iconography attests to these paired and complementary contrasts. The logic of the concrete is superbly rendered in a painting on an Attic vase dating from about 480 BC. It shows two sons of Zeus: the Olympian Hermes reclining on the back of a magnificent ram in juxtaposition to the chthonic Dionysos, who, with a beard and his long hair loose on his shoulders, is similarly installed on a billy-goat on the vessel's other side (Plate 4).[16]

Classical scholarship only recently developed an interest in animals and animal symbolism.[17] The billy-goats in the retinue of Dionysos provide an example. To illustrate his point that the sacrifice of billy-goats played an important role in the cult of Dionysos, Burkert presents a list of twenty-three Attic black vase paintings from the sixth century, and observes: 'These indisputable billy-goats in the entourage of Dionysos have found surprisingly little attention' (1990: 19, 33n.).

The evidence for the ritual prominence of rams and their close identification with male leaders and heroes are not only pictorial; it is also obvious in the myths and legends of Eurasian antiquity. To avoid being sacrificed by their stepmother, Phryxus and Helle, children of the king of Thebes, fled on a winged ram with a golden fleece which Phryxus had received from his mother. When crossing the sea, Helle fell from the ram and drowned (hence the name Hellespont), but Phryxus arrived safely in Colchis, where he sacrificed the ram to Zeus, who placed it in heaven as the constellation Aries, to become the first sign of the zodiac. A generation later, the ram's golden fleece, hanging from an oak tree in Colchis and guarded by a dragon, became the stake of a struggle between pretenders to the throne in which Jason and his companions – known as the Argonauts – prevailed. In a later development, Jason's uncle and rival, the usurper Pelias, was killed by his own daughters on the instigation (and by the intrigue) of the enchantress Medea, who had also helped Jason defeat the dragon. She persuaded Pelias' daughters that she had a charm to make their father young. To demonstrate her skills she cooked, in a cauldron of water impregnated with certain magical herbs, an old ram, who had been cut into thirteen pieces, and who reappeared as a tender he-lamb. Pelias' daughters were convinced and repeated the experiment with their father. But this time Medea was careful not to give them the right herbs, and Pelias regained neither youth nor life.[18] What strikes us in these tales is the mediating power of rams and their close association with heroic males throughout the narratives and the iconography (see Graves 1981: 203, 210).

(a)

(b)

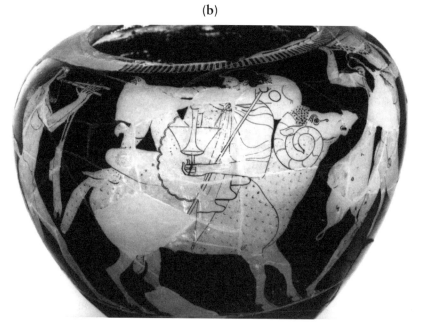

Plate 4 Two sons of Zeus, from an attic red-figure stamnos, c.480BC: (a) Dionysos on a billy-goat and (b) Hermes on a ram. Louvre, Paris/photos©RMN

In a brief discussion of the meaning of the Golden Fleece in his Malinowski Memorial Lecture, the anthropologist Anthony Forge reminds
us that, for Jason, the fleece was necessary to gain the throne of Colchis
and displace the usurper Pelias. Forge therefore considers the fleece 'as
a symbol of legitimate political power, of rightful hierarchy'. He finds
support for his interpretation in a later use of this symbol:

> In 1430 Philip the Good, Duke of Burgundy and Count of Flanders,
> founded the Order of the Golden Fleece, second only to the Garter in the
> European orders of chivalry. Contemporary accounts make it clear that he
> envisaged this foundation as an essential part of his campaign to organise
> a new Crusade under his leadership. (1972: 527)

A similar imagery is found in late medieval texts and pictorial representations. The art historian Gombrich draws attention to a moral treatise
composed by the fourteenth-century English friar John Ridevall, who
uses 'images' of ancient gods as starting points for the classification and
definition of virtues and vices. Jupiter (Zeus) stands in his system as the
personification of Charity or Benevolence, and is represented horn-faced,
that is, with the head of a ram:

> And this is indeed well in accordance with the virtue of Benevolence and
> Love which virtue stands at the head as the first among the other virtues.
> For the Ram (Aries) is called after the Greek word Ares which in Latin
> means virtue. And thus the head of the virtue is ram-like (*arietinum*) to
> signify the excess of dignity and perfection which belongs to Charity in
> the rank of all other virtues, a dignity about which Augustine treats in
> various places . . . (Ridevall, quoted in Gombrich 1978: 135)

Gombrich also found a rare translation of Ridevall's verbal picture into
an actual image in a fifteenth-century German manuscript, which shows
a figure of a man (Zeus?) surrounded by eagles with a ram's head above
his own and a billy-goat placed at his feet (1978: 136, Fig. 147).

In Homer, rams are closely associated with Olympian gods and heroic
leadership. Rams (as well as sheep and lambs) are offered to Zeus, and
Odysseus is compared to a 'thick-fleeced ram'.[19] *The Odyssey* describes
how the hero and the remnants of his companions managed to escape
from the cave of Polyphemos tied under the bellies of rams, 'well-bred,
thick-fleeced, fine, big animals in their coats of black wool'.[20] The biggest
and finest of the animals, which had carried Odysseus, was later sacrificed to Zeus as a thank-offering.[21]

The events on the island of the Cyclops show a close relationship
between rams and leadership on at least three scores. The biggest ram,
'the pick of the flock', carried Odysseus, King of Ithaca and leader of the

Plate 5   Odysseus under the ram. Escaping from the cove of Polyphemos. Greek vase painting by the Sappho painter, attic black-figure, c.510BC. Badisches Laroksmuseum, Karlsruhe/photo AKG London

expedition (see Plate 5). The ram was sacrificed to Zeus, the Father of Heaven. Rams themselves are also leaders, as suggested in the short speech Polyphemos addressed to the ram as he pawed over the animal carrying Odysseus when he left the cave.

Further attestations of totemic classifications (predicated on the contrasts between the emblematic rams and billy-goats and on the related opposition between sheep and goats) in ancient Greece are found in *Oneirocritica* of Artemidorus, who describes rams as symbols of powerful rulers and as leaders of the flock, while (billy-)goats are represented as bringers of misfortune, in particular storms; and since goats, unlike sheep, do not form flocks, they are not supposed to favour marriages, friendships and other bonds.[22]

The prominence given to the ram in sacrificial cults among the Berbers in North Africa is emphasized by several scholars.[23] Westermarck writes:

The domestic sheep has existed in North Africa from time immemorial, and the ram is known to have been a sacred animal in many of its pagan cults. The Egyptians held this animal sacred to the god Ammon; and at

Ammonium a Libyan god – the Zeus-Ammon of Herodotus – who was essentially a god of prophecy, likewise had the ram as his sacred animal. The worship of the Lybico-Egyptian god did not die out until Christian times. He was adopted into the Carthaginian pantheon under the name of Ba'al Haman, the word Ba'al being nothing more than the title 'owner' or 'master'; and the ram sometimes appears on the stelae of this Carthaginian god. But the ram also figures as a sacred animal farther west. At Bu Alem, in South Oranais, and at Zanaga, near Figuig, there are rock-glyphs of a ram, wearing something like a rayed disc, which have been supposed by some writers to represent the ram of the Egyptian Ammon, but according to another opinion are even more ancient than the latter. (1926, I: 100–1).

The same writer also points at the connection 'between the holiness of the ram and the *baraka* attributed to its whole species, whose extreme usefulness may have been the ultimate cause of the veneration of its propagator' (1926, I: 101). For the Berbers in Morocco, writes Westermarck, there is *baraka* in sheep, whereas the goat is considered a wicked animal. Moreover, they call a shepherd 'sultan' and a goatherd 'satan'. Rams are the meritorious animals for sacrifice (1926, I: 99–100; II: 302). In his essay on sacrifice and masquerade in the Maghreb, Hammoudi notes that the species of sheep provides the victim *par excellence*; the ram comes before the lamb and the ewe (1988: 169). These priorities have a long history.

In the three Great Traditions that, together with the classical heritage, helped to shape the Mediterranean world, a close identification obtains between rams and human males, especially male heroes. The events connected with the Golden Fleece are a case in point and also attest to the role of rams as mediators. Genesis (22: 9–13) describes the famous event where Abraham sacrifices a ram ('caught in the thicket by his horns') instead of his son Isaac. The tale of this offering 'has been widely taken as the foundation of sacrifice in the Jewish, Christian, and Islamic traditions' (Burkert 1996: 153). Abraham's substitution of a ram for the sacrifice of his son Isaac (Ismail) is every year commemorated in the Muslim world by a massive slaughter of sheep.[24] In Jewish religion the sacrifice of sheep forms part of the Passover or Paschal festival. In some form it also exists among Christian sects.[25] A rich iconography in both Christian and Islamic traditions also attests to the long-standing fascination with Abraham's sacrifice, but commentators often play down animal symbolism and, preoccupied with the appropriateness of the sacrifice of a child, neglect the fact that the ram in these Mediterranean Great Traditions figured as a mediator and formed an appropriate substitute for the son of a ruler.[26] Appropriate, because no other animal came so close to epitomizing the character of what was considered the ideal and quintessential male leader.

The notion of 'scapegoat', better rendered in the German word *Sündenbock*, originally appears in Leviticus (16: 1–34), which describes the rituals for the Day of Atonement. Two male goats serve for a sin offering and one ram for a burnt offering. The two goats are chosen to bear symbolically the sins of the people. The one chosen for the Lord is to be sacrificed as a sin offering; the other is to be driven into the wilderness to Azazel, an evil spirit or desert demon: 'Aaron shall lay both his hands upon the head of the live goat, and confess over him all the iniquities of the people of Israel, and all their transgressions, all their sins; and he shall put them upon the head of the goat, and send him away into the wilderness . . .' (Leviticus 16: 20)

What interests us in these representations of animals in Mediterranean societies is what Lévi-Strauss calls the working of the logic of the concrete: how sets of opposites in the natural realm – rams and billy-goats, sheep and goats – 'suggest a mode of thought' and are selected and enlisted to represent and articulate major contrasts in the cultural and social worlds, most notably differences between order and disorder, good and evil, grace and disgrace, honour and shame, high and low, and men and women.

This approach owes a great deal to the work of Lévi-Strauss, but cannot, of course, agree with his view that there is 'a sort of fundamental antipathy between history and systems of classification', a conviction that prompted him to say that this

> perhaps explains what one is tempted to call the 'totemic void', for in the bounds of the great civilizations of Europe and Asia there is a remarkable absence of anything which might have reference to totemism, *even in the form of remains*. The reason is surely that the latter have elected to explain themselves by history and that this undertaking is incompatible with that of classifying things and beings (natural and social) by means of finite groups. (1966: 232, my italics)[27]

I cannot agree either with his near-dismissal of content and meaning in favour of form, for which he was criticized as early as 1967 – that is, right after the publication of the English translation of *La pensée sauvage*.[28] Rams and billy-goats, and for that matter sheep and goats, are not only 'good to think': their relationship serves as a model for social and cultural differences, most notably gender differences. But their classificatory power cannot be separated from their great practical importance as objects of consumption and ritual. The choice of them has been far from arbitrary. As we shall see in a moment, practical reason must greatly have helped to motivate their role as signifiers and classifiers.

Of special relevance to totemic classifications in the Mediterranean world is the position of pre-eminence and *poste d'honneur* of the ram as Aries in the zodiacal belt and its duality with its counterpart Capricorn.[29] In their geocentric cosmology, the Greek mythographs and astrologers associated Aries (dry, male) with the ram with the Golden Fleece, whereas Capricorn (water, female) reminded them of Pan.[30] The zodiacal signs were, of course, primarily associated with time and space, in particular with the place and movements of celestial bodies. As natural emblems they helped to divide the year into twelve parts: Aries came up with the spring, Capricorn with the winter, and so on. There was also a connection with geographical areas:

> The early Greco-Roman divisions of areas of the world into zones with astral patrons were simply equivalents of older ideas about divine patrons. ... Manilius offers the oldest chorographic scheme to survive, which is a straightforward assignation of zodiac signs to zones. Here he refers to the worship of signs by regions, and his justifications rely on myth or other analogical associations. Thus the legend of the Golden Fleece explains the area over which Aries presides. (Barton 1994: 180–1)

Whereas Aries was associated with the East (Hellespont, Black Sea, Colchis), we find that Capricorn, according to the scheme of Manilius, had been assigned a place in the West (Spain, Gaul, Germany). Similar analogies and oppositions dominate the first Christianized zodiac that survived (from the fourth century): Aries and Taurus are linked with Christ as sacrificial victim (lamb and calf) whereas Cancer and Capricorn represent the variety of vice.[31]

As mentioned before, parts of the body are sometimes identified with zodiacal signs (and vice versa), as in Manilius, who links Aries with 'high' and Capricorn with 'low':

> The Ram, as chieftain of them all, is allotted the head, and the Bull receives as of his estate the handsome neck; evenly bestowed, the arms to shoulders joined are accounted to the Twins; the breast is put down to the Crab, the realm of the sides and the shoulder-blades are the Lion's, the belly comes down to the Maid as her rightful lot; the Balance governs the loins, and Scorpion takes pleasure in the groin; the thighs hie to the Centaur, Capricorn is tyrant to both knees, while the pouring Waterman has the lordship of the shanks, and over the feet the Fishes claim jurisdiction. (quoted in Barton 1994: 189–90)

Similar analogies and homologies – ram at the place of the head, billy-goat at the knees – are pointed out in Gombrich's study of symbolic images. He refers to two early sixteenth-century illustrations of the so-called Zodiac Man which 'sums up the astrological doctrine of the relation between the signs of the Zodiac and the parts of the body'.[32]

The geocentric astrologer's cosmology is rarely recognized as a (totemic) classification, but it has all the trappings of such a system, most notably the way in which meaningful differences in natural species (ram, bull, lion, goat, etc.) are adopted as emblems and used to articulate differences in both the natural and the cultural realm, and thus classify and help make sense of the world. Like totemic systems elsewhere, the zodiac taxonomy is based on the 'logic of the concrete' and the structural principle of complementary oppositions. It developed after hunters and gatherers in western Asia turned to animal husbandry and agriculture during the early Neolithic period, about 10,000 years ago. The earliest evidence comes from the Sumerians, who dominated Mesopotamia in the third millennium BC, and it was the Greeks who provided the final touch and contributed 'scientific' elements to astrology.[33] Zodiacal classification, then, developed in the very civilizations that made so much of sheep and goats for the ordering of their universe: Mesopotamia, Egypt, ancient Greece, the Roman Empire – that is, places where sheep and goats, most notably sheep, were the most numerous and the most important farm animals.

These animals also meant wealth. The Indo-European etymology of the word *pecunia* still recalls to what extent sheep (*pecu*) and money were coterminous.[34] In the Near East and the Mediterranean, early herdsmen and agriculturalists selected differences and similarities between animals and used them to articulate natural and cultural categories in homologous sets of a classification system that embraces a total universe, giving every element in it a meaningful place. It remains to be demonstrated to what extent the totemic classification explored in this essay is part of the astrologer's geocentric cosmology. After so many centuries, this 'failed' science, as it is sometimes called, still holds a strong popular appeal among millions of people in the modern world. It shows modern man's affinity with the logic of the concrete, with the quintessence of 'la pensée sauvage'.

The pairs of opposites – rams/billy-goats, sheep/goats – and the way these contrasts in nature have been utilized over time by pastoralists and peasants to make sense of their world, present us with a totemic classification of remarkable continuity. From Neolithic beginnings, when animal husbandry developed in western Asia, up to the end of the second millennium AD, when shepherds had been pushed toward the margins of the Mediterranean, sheep and goats, rams and billy-goats have proved 'good to think'.

Like totemic symbolism in tribal societies (about which much more is known), Mediterranean totemic categories involve more than cognitive ordering. As we have seen, they also have what is called affectual and evaluative meaning.[35] The classification of sheep and goats is imbued with strong cultural and social concerns. In their emblematic form, these animal categories mirror and reinforce gender roles, major moral concerns and notions about human destiny. Two more examples may suffice to illustrate this. In *Oneirocritica*, the book on dream interpretation composed in the second century, Artemidorus summarizes the collective representations of sheep and goats prevalent among the ancients:

> It was the opinion of previous writers that flocks of white sheep were auspicious and flocks of black sheep were inauspicious. I have observed, however, that sheep, whether they are white or black, are auspicious. But white sheep signify greater good than the black. For sheep resemble men in that they follow a shepherd and live together in flocks and, because of their name, they are analogous to advancement and progress for the better. Therefore it is most auspicious, especially for men who wish to stand at the head of the crowd as well as for sophists and teachers, to possess many sheep of their own and also to see and shepherd the flocks of others. Furthermore, a ram represents the master of the house, a magistrate, or a king. For early writers used the word . . . in the sense of 'to rule', and the ram is the ruler of the flock.
>
> Goats, whether they are white or black, are not good. They are all inauspicious. Black goats are more unlucky than white goats, especially for people at sea. For, in colloquial speech, large waves are called 'goats'. . . . The poet, moreover, uses the words 'boisterous, rushing' . . . , when he is describing a violent wind. . . . Goat dreams are not auspicious in regard to the contracting of new marriages, friendships, or partnerships or to the preservation of those that already exist, since goats do not live together in herds. But grazing apart from one another on crags and rocks, they make trouble for themselves and also for their goatherd . . .[36]

The totemic operation of this set of animals is particularly evident in a famous passage from the Gospels that is so well known that it has lent itself to proverbial wisdom. The way in which sheep and goats as contrasts in nature are enlisted and used for a meaningful organization of experience through articulating cultural differences and social divisions is neatly rendered in Matthew (25: 31–46) as follows:

> When the Son of man comes in his glory, and all the angels with him, then he will sit on his glorious throne. Before him will be gathered all the nations, and he will separate them one from the other as a shepherd separates the sheep from the goats, and he will place the sheep at his right hand, but the goats on the left. . . .[37]

Plate 6 The separation of the sheep and the goats. Matthew (25: 31–45) Sant'Appollinare Nuovo, Ravenna, early 6th century mosaic. Photo AKG London

This text from the Gospels on the Last Judgement has inspired an extraordinary mosaic in the church of Sant' Apollinare Nuovo in Ravenna, Italy, which dates from the beginning of the sixth century (see Plate 6). The metaphorical and metonymic relationships are retained and elaborated. Sticking to the images of sheep and goats in the fashion of a complementary opposition, the artists represented the Last Judgement in such a way that on Jesus's right hand the good people have their final place in heaven while on his left side the bad people have theirs in hell. In his role of emperor and judge, Jesus is assisted by two angels: one on his right who is attired in an orange-red apparel (suggesting dawn) with in front of him brightly white sheep; the other angel appears in midnight blue behind three goats.[38]

What makes this a totemic representation is, in particular, the resemblance between two systems of differences, the one natural, the other social and cultural in a context of meaning. As we shall see later on, sheep and goats have several features in common and form a distinct pair, but they also differ from each other. It is the combination of similarities and differences which, by itself, makes their choice far from arbitrary: that is, it shows why this particular natural opposition was chosen, rather than any plausible alternative, to serve as a model for a particular mode of social differentiation.

Apart from the differences already mentioned – and most significantly – these animals differ in the tendency to flock: sheep tend to flock whereas goats do not have a propensity to do so, which is why they are more difficult to control. These (and other) differences between the two species are used to articulate differences between human groups and between cultural categories: good people and bad people, people who are redeemed (elected, chosen) and people who are doomed, people in heaven and people in hell, people who sit at the right side and people who sit at the left side, that is, emblematic of 'right' and 'wrong'.

The pre-eminence of sheep (and the subordinate place of goats) is obvious in Christian discourse with its conceptual metaphors of God the shepherd (Psalms 23: 1); Jesus as the good shepherd (John 10: 1); Jesus, the ruler of nations, as shepherd (Matthew 25: 31–46), the priest-shepherd (pastor); kings and rulers as shepherds; the flock of the faithful; the lost sheep; the black sheep; and the representation of Jesus as the 'lamb of God', as 'Paschal lamb', as sacrificial victim (1 Corinthians 5: 7), and the 'scapegoat' (Leviticus 16: 20).[39] There is a structural connection between Abraham's sacrifice and the self-sacrifice of Jesus as *Agnus Dei*. Both involve a son and are identified with the same (mediating) animal.

These are not mere metaphors. We are concerned with conceptual metaphors, which structure experience and help define the way people see and construct the world.[40] They are by no means restricted to the People of the Book. The term 'good shepherd' was also used for Sumerian rulers (which suggests that they were also great sheep owners), and examples of shepherds' crooks as ceremonial attributes held by kings, as well as the notion of 'shepherd kings', have been reported for ancient Egypt.[41] Discussing the role of small livestock in ancient Greece, Richter observes: 'nur die *allgemeine* Vorstellung "Hüter einer Herde" ermöglichte auch die übertragene Verwendung auf Könige und Heerführer . . .' (Only the *general* representation of 'guardian of a flock' made it possible to transfer the use of the term to kings and rulers) (1968: 61).

On this point, the French ethnologist Haudricourt is also explicit. He argues that since Neolithic times, sheep-raising in the Mediterranean area provided a model for human action:

> L'élevage du mouton, tel qu'il était pratiqué dans la région méditerranéenne, me semble le modèle de l'action directe positive. Il exige un contact permanent avec l'être domestiqué. Le berger accompagne nuit et jour son troupeau, il le conduit avec sa houlette, il doit choisir les pacages, prévoir les lieux d'abreuvoir, porter les agneaux nouveau-nés dans les passages difficiles, et enfin les défendre contre les loups. Son action est directe: contact par la main ou le bâton, mottes de terre lancées avec la houlette. Son action est positive: il choisit l'itinéraire qu'il impose à chaque moment au troupeau. (1987: 278)

> The breeding of sheep as it was practised in the Mediterranean area seems to me the model of direct and positive action. It requires a constant contact with the domesticated creature. The shepherd is in the company of his flock night and day. He leads it with his shepherd's crook, he has to select pastures, to find watering-places, carry new-born lambs across difficult passages and finally he has to defend his sheep against wolves. His action is direct: contact by hand or the stick, clods of earth thrown with his crook. His action is positive: he chooses itineraries that he imposes on his flock at any time.

Haudricourt reminds us that Homer calls Agamemnon 'the shepherd of his people' and that it is no accident that in the Bible, as well as in the writings of Aristotle, the diad shepherd/sheep is the symbol of the relations between chief and people, god and humanity, master and slave, and thus favoured the development of certain modes of production: first slavery and later capitalism (1987: 300).[42]

On the basis of the evidence so far presented, there is little doubt that all over the Mediterranean, from the early Neolithic period when sheep and goats were domesticated, rams and billy-goats formed a distinct pair in the conceptual order of subsequent civilizations. Both natural sets of paired contrasts have been adopted and used to articulate differences between major social and cultural categories. The available evidence collected so far yields the following pattern:

rams	billy-goats
rams' horns	billy-goats' horns
sheep	goats
honour	dishonour
virility	impotence
virile men	cornutes
active	passive
strong	weak [*manso*, tame, domesticated, *dayyuth*]
first	last
men	women
male	female
pure	impure
superior	inferior
Olympian gods	Chthonic gods
heaven	earth
high	low
restraint	licence
good	bad
order	disorder
auspicious	inauspicious
gratitude	expiation (sacrifices)
wealth	poverty
day	night
light	dark
life	death
community	wilderness
God	Devil

As mentioned before, the choice of rams and billy-goats, and that of sheep and goats, are far from arbitrary. These animals definitely 'suggest a mode of thought', but their choice is also inspired by practical interests and should, therefore, also be understood in terms of their historical and cultural contexts. As Shore observes in his discussion of totemic symbolism, 'The classificatory powers of totemic animals cannot be separated from their inherent interest as objects of consumption and regeneration. . . . Their practical role can be said to "motivate" in part their meaning as classifiers' (1996: 172).

III

Returning from the *monde conçu* to the *monde vécu* of people who herded sheep and goats in the Near East and the Mediterranean, we have already noted that these animals differ in several respects but share enough features to form a distinct pair, which, as we have seen, makes them 'good to think' and their choice far from arbitrary.

First, both animals are ruminants and belong to the category of *small* livestock producing meat, milk, cheese, wool and hair, which sets them off from other domestic animals, like cattle, and in particular from the bull, who is often and erroneously identified as the animal associated with the vertical horn-sign.[43] Richter writes:

> Beide Tiere [i.e., Schafe und Ziegen] sind von den Griechen homerischer Zeit in engem Zusammenhang gesehen worden; das beweist die simultane Verwendung des Wortes '*μῆλα*' für 'Schafe *und* Ziegen' und 'Schafe *oder* Ziegen', das zumeist ohne weitere Erläuterung, aber bezeichnenderweise oft im Gegensatz zum Rindvieh begegnet und damit das 'Kleinvieh' als Gattung bezeichnet. Nicht immer ist deutlich ob der Dichter 'Kleinvieh' oder 'Schafe' sagen will . . . (1968: 53)

> (The Greeks in Homeric times considered sheep and goats to be closely connected, as the simultaneous use of the term '*μῆλα*' for sheep *and* goats and sheep *or* goats attests. In most cases this happens without any explanation or comment. Characteristically, this occurs often in contrast to the use of the term for cattle.)

Second, in the Mediterranean area, sheep and goats are far better suited than cattle to cope with heat, sparse water and poor pastures.[44] In comparison with sheep, goats are better adapted to harsh environments: they thrive and breed on a minimum of food and under extremes of temperature and humidity.[45] Third, sheep and goats have, compared with cattle, a considerably faster rate of regeneration and growth.[46] Fourth, as Richter points out in his essay on agriculture in Homer's time, sheep and goats are cheap, adequate, and productive enough also for the poorest sections of the population.[47] All these characteristics and circumstances help to mark out sheep and goats as a significant pair from other farm animals, most notably cattle.

The ancient Greeks had a special term, '*μῆλα*', for small livestock (sheep and goats), which reflects how closely they considered their relationship.[48] Already much earlier, during the third millennium BC, when the Sumerians held sway in Mesopotamia, sheep and goats were the dominant livestock in the countryside. Often grazed together, their partnership persisted when sheep-farming spread to Anatolia and Crete in the second millennium BC and later all over the Mediterranean area during the course of the first millennium BC with the expansion first of Phoenician settlements and, later, Greek colonization.[49]

Sheep and goats are also often mentioned together in sources.[50] Of the two species, goats always take a more modest position.[51] One may ask, then, why goats have never been replaced by sheep. The answer must be that, apart from their similarities, sheep and goats – very much like men and women in the Mediterranean – are different. At the same time very similar and very different, sheep and goats form an interdependent, although asymmetric, relationship. The animals complement each other on a number of scores.[52]

Although appreciated for their nutritive value (meat, milk, cheese) and as sacrificial animals, goats have always been of lesser value. The meat of sheep, especially that of lambs and wethers, is far superior to that of goats. Moreover, sheep are best known for their fine wool. These differences have been used to associate goats with the poor and sheep with the rich. However, the skins of goats are better suited for the processing of leather, especially for the manufacture of bags to carry oil, wine and water.[53] Before discussing the different products of sheep and goats in more detail, we shall look first at the interdependencies resulting from their differences in flocking and grazing habits.

The interdependence of sheep and goats manifests itself in flocking, and in the organization and movement of the herds between pastures and back and forth between settlements and fields. Flocks of sheep are often headed by goats or castrated billy-goats if no bell-wethers (castrated rams with bells) are available to lead the herds. Already in antiquity, the castrated billy-goat was recognized as *dux pecoris*.[54] When questioned about this practice, Sicilian shepherds pointed out that goats are more independent and intelligent than sheep. They have a better sense of place, can be trained and are able to return to the village by themselves. More *furbo* (cunning) than sheep, goats are compared to women – an external analogy that fits the internal homology goats/sheep = women/men. Discussing differences in eating habits between sheep and goats in Corsica (goats snatch and nibble the most tender shoots whereas sheep closely crop the grass), Ravis-Giordani mentions that goats are more difficult to pasture and refers to a local saying that stresses similarities between goats and women: 'Goats are like women: the latter embrace all the handsome men, the former eat all the beautiful flowers' (1983: 268–9).

In addition to what we already know about the various dimensions within which differences between sheep and goats are used to stress distinctions between men and women, differences in flocking between the two species may have been used to underwrite current representations of gender in the Mediterranean world. Because sheep have a natural tendency to flock which goats lack, the latter are more difficult to control. In folk beliefs across the Mediterranean, goats and (loose) women are often closely associated. About this metaphorical relation between women and goats in Castile, Kenny reports, 'In popular terminology a wife's looseness is reduced to the level of mating among goats' (1966: 83). Writing on the image of the goat and anomalous marriages and liaisons in rural France, Amiel recalls, first, that 'capricious' stems from *capra* (goat), and that the goat is the least submissive animal of the flock, quite different in this regard from the sheep. She further notes that the word *chèvre* in Finistère and *cabra* in Provence are used at meetings of adolescent girls who openly display their taste for boys. In seventeenth-century Italian, *capra folle* ('silly goat') indicates the *femme folastre* ('crazy woman') of easy virtue. A proverb from Alsace mocks feminine obstinacy: 'Alte Geisse schlecken noch gern Salz' (Old women [goats] do not easily give up on love). All over France, according to Amiel, the goat has been known for its precocious and excessive sexuality since antiquity. In French folklore the goat is generally associated with female anomalies.[55]

The arrangements in controlling the flocks are confirmed by Black-Michaud, who worked among the Luri pastoralists in western Iran:

> Luri pastoral capital takes two main forms. These are sheep and goats. Of the two species by far the least important is the goat. But whereas goats can be – and are occasionally – kept in flocks apart, sheep cannot be herded satisfactorily unless the flock includes two or three large buck goats. For in a country where sheepdogs are unknown a flock of sheep is, without goats to lead it, apt to disperse over the terrain, in which case a single shepherd can no longer control it. (1986: 41–2)

This seems to have been very much a general practice. Discussing the flocking of sheep in general, Ryder notes that goats are used as bell-wethers, a practice he traces back to Assyrian times (first millennium BC).[56] Referring to Moyal's study of transhumance in southern France, Ryder notes:

> The flock of 2,300 sheep accompanied by Moyal about 1950 was not part of a larger group, but had six shepherds, the one in charge being extremely experienced. Two walked at the head, two to the rear, and two patrolled the flanks on horseback. Where the route became difficult to follow, the trail was indicated by sheep droppings. Each flock was led by male goats (*menouns*) and wether rams (*floucats*) with bells. Moyal's flock had six of each and the *floucats* were left with tufts of unshorn wool to make it easier to catch them. (1983: 419–20)[57]

In his more recent study of transhumance in Provence, Schippers also discusses the part of goats in the movements of the flock and refers to the *menoun* or castrated billy-goat. Outfitted with the *sounnailles* (heavy bells), the *menoun* helps by leading the flocks of sheep on their way to the spring pastures.[58] Tellingly the complementary oppositions between rams and billy-goats, which inspired the *bricoleurs* of so many different civilizations in the area around the Mediterranean over several millennia, dissolves when both animals are castrated and, therefore, can be used as a substitute for one another.

In his *Prehistoric Farming in Europe*, the archaeologist Graeme Barker is also much aware of the asymmetric and complementary relationship between sheep and goats that existed over long periods of time. He notes that goats offer the same range of commodities as sheep except wool, but goatskin makes excellent leather; while the hair of goats is good for rope manufacture. He also points out that, in the Mediterranean region,

> goats have traditionally played a much more important role in the agricultural system than further north, because of their ability to thrive on desiccated scrub vegetation and to produce plentiful milk in the bargain. The Roman agronomists advised farmers to restrict goats to herds of 50–100 animals because of the difficulties of control and their depredations on vegetation. Many Mediterranean farmers today, however, will keep up half a dozen goats with their flock of 50–100 sheep not simply for their milk but also because of their ability on the walk to and from the day's feeding area to lead the way for the sheep to follow. This sort of proportion of goats to sheep is suggested by faunal collections I have studied from several Roman and medieval sites in Italy, and from many prehistoric sites in the Mediterranean as well. (1985: 43)

Considerable differences between sheep and goats regarding their milk yield have also been noticed by other observers. They never fail to point out the disproportion, as far as goats are concerned, between higher yields and poor pastures. Praising sheep over goats as producers of raw materials for technical processes, Zeuner emphasizes the sheep as a producer of wool and wonders why the goat has not been completely replaced by it. He believes that the goat 'as a browser prefers environments different from those liked by the sheep. It can thrive on desert scrub, and it yields more milk than its relative and rival' (1963: 151–2). Discussing animal husbandry in the ancient Greek *polis*, Hodkinson also dwells on differences between sheep and goats. He notes that goats yield more milk than sheep over a longer period, reproduce at a faster rate and are better adapted to the upland terrain and less likely to sicken in its cold winter environment.[59] Writing about the transhumant flocks in Provence, Moyal observes that 'while a goat may yield anything up to two pints a day, half a teacupful was the most they'd get from a ewe' (1956: 55).

In the rural economy of Mediterranean animal husbandry, sheep and goats form complementary oppositions in yet other respects. Shepherds in the Val del Belice, Sicily, where I conducted field-work in the 1960s, reported that, unlike goats' milk, the milk of sheep contains too much fat for direct consumption and is therefore processed into cheese and *ricotta*. This was confirmed a few years later by Ryder, who visited Sicily in 1972 and observed the making of cheese and *ricotta* on the western coastal plain near Marsala (a procedure which, as he notes elsewhere, had hardly changed since Homer, who in the story of Odysseus' visit to the cave of the Cyclops – supposedly located on the same island – provides a rare and detailed description of cheese-making). 'Sheep milk has more fat than that of any other animal. The sheep has 7.5 per cent, the goat 4.5 per cent, which is similar to the cow's 4 per cent . . .' (1983: 144, 721–2).[60]

Consistent with the complementary oppositions already mentioned, Mediterranean totemic classification includes the contrast between cheese and milk. Sicilian men rarely drink milk. In fact, they regard it as abominable.[61] Nor do women expect them to drink it. When it comes to dairy products, men prefer cheese. It is widely believed that milk (and *ricotta* to a lesser extent) is only good for women, children, the aged and those who are ill – that is, people who belong to the category of the weak. Since milk from sheep always has to be processed into cheese, while goats produce milk that can be directly consumed, the differences between cheese and milk are thus a particular instance of those between culture and nature, and both correspond to the social differentiation between men and women, between strong and weak, between healthy and ill.[62]

Other important differences between sheep and goats concern the use of wool and skins. Sheep are primarily praised for their wool, not for their skins.[63] Goats produce hair; and their skin, as mentioned before, provides superior leather. On his way to the island of the Cyclops with twelve of his best men, Odysseus took with him a 'goatskin of ruby wine, delicious wine' (which later served to trick Polyphemos). On the use of goats in ancient civilizations, Ryder notes that 'goatskins provided a universal inflatable container for oil, wine, or water' (1983: 100).[64]

Emphasizing their ecological interdependencies, Clutton-Brock sums up the main differences between sheep and goats as follows:

> Whereas sheep are grazing ungulates that inhabit hilly regions and the foothills of mountains, goats are browsers whose natural habitat is on the high, bleak mountain ranges. . . . Because of their adaptation to a particu-

larly harsh environment goats are perhaps the most versatile of all ruminants in their feeding habits, a factor that has greatly affected their success as a domestic animal. They are also extremely hardy and will thrive and breed on the minumum of food and under extremes of temperature and humidity. The goat can provide both the primitive peasant farmer and the nomadic pastoralist with all his physical needs, clothing, meat, and milk as well as bone and sinew for artefacts, tallow for lighting and dung for fuel and manure. Goats will complement a flock of sheep, which are perhaps usually rather easier to herd, by browsing on thorny scrubland whilst the sheep prefer the grass. Goats may have been of positive assistance to the Neolithic farmer in helping to clear land after the primary forest was burnt or cut down, and it is often argued that it has been the browsing of goats over the last five thousand years that has in great part caused the expansion of the desert areas of the Sahara and the Middle East. (1981: 57–8)

The complementary relationships between sheep and goats have been recognized and spelled out with particular acumen by the late Black-Michaud in his study of the Luri pastoralists in western Iran. After mentioning the role of castrated billy-goats as leaders in the flocking of sheep, he points out that goats are also kept for yet other reasons. First, goats produce hair which is used for the weaving of tents and as twine to fashion or strengthen ropes, nosebags and horse blankets. But hair of goats is in short supply, since a goat gives only one coat of hair in his lifetime (just before slaughter). Second,

goat skins are indispensable to the nomads, who use them for the conservation of milk products and the transport of drinking water. . . . Thirdly, goats are valued for their milk-producing capacity which is much higher than that of sheep. Fourthly, they are worth roughly 50 per cent less than sheep and therefore provide a cheap source of meat for domestic consumption, the entertainment of honoured guests and for birth, marriage or funeral feasts. Lastly, the very fact that they are little prized in monetary terms causes them to be kept in larger numbers by the poor than by the rich, although a very few extremely wealthy men do constitute entire flocks of both male and female goats in order that they should never be lacking in inexpensive meat for visitors. (1986: 42)

These interdependencies between sheep and goats are by no means restricted to nomadic pastoralists in present-day Iran. About Odysseus we learn that his house

was typical of the large self-contained farmsteads of the landed gentry. . . . Such a farmstead had about 150 acres of arable land, but the main wealth came from livestock which grazed the common land. Odysseus had 24 herds of pigs and goats and 23 herds each of cows and sheep, his estimated total livestock numbering about 30 000. (Ryder 1983: 143)[65]

In present-day Sicily's western interior, too, some big landowners keep large flocks of goats, which are grazed on available pastures of poor quality, like Rocca d'Entella, a table-like formation of about 60 hectares with an altitude of just over 550 metres, named after the ancient city of Entella, which oversees the River Belice.[66] This suggests another way in which sheep and goats formed a complementary pair. Their different grazing habits on the same or adjacent pastures – often marginal mountain areas – reinforced their interdependence and helped to set them apart from cattle. Writing about Homeric Greece, Richter notes that goats were less valued than sheep. The animal was appreciated for its meat and milk, and also played a role as a sacrificial animal. Yet goats were never completely replaced by sheep, who were always more sensitive but also more valuable because of their wool. In the flock community, the animals usually grazed together – a situation which has persisted in the Mediterranean area:

> Der Sammelbegriff μῆλα spiegelt diesen Zustand, und in der Tatsache, dass Schafe und Ziegen zwar nicht dieselben Weidengewohnheiten haben, wohl aber – im Unterschied zum Rind – auf demselben Gelände, und zwar auf dem steilsten und unwegsamsten, geweidet werden können und beide den Bergwald suchen – die Schafe zum Schutz vor der Sonne, die Ziegen wegen ihrer Vorliebe für Blattriebe – begründet die Zweckmässigkeit der Weidengemeinschaft. (Richter 1968: H60)

(The collective term 'meta' reflects this situation. Moreover, sheep and goats do not share the same pasturage habits, but they can – in contrast to cattle – be pastured on the same fields, that is, on the steepest and wildest stretches of land. Both species seek the mountain forests – sheep for protection against the sun, goats because of their preference for sprouts. All this provides the foundation of their combined herding.)

Since the 'dawn of civilization' in the early Neolithic period, sheep and goats – as a complementary and asymmetrical set – have formed a principal source of subsistence for all classes of people, first in the Near East and later on also on both shores of the Mediterranean. Apart from important exceptions, there is a general tendency to associate sheep with wealth and rich people and goats with poverty and poor people. Among the Sarakatsani pastoralists in Greece, writes the British anthropologist John Campbell, families with too high a proportion of goats to sheep lose prestige.[67] Only in recent times has the gradual expansion of agriculture at the expense of pasturage led both to the displacement of pastoralists to peripheral areas and to their stigmatization.[68]

These long-term transformations could not but erode the cultural world in which rams and billy-goats formed a union of opposites. In this way, the ram as one of the *imagines symbolicae*, as one of the main totemic categories in the Mediterranean, largely vanished from the mental world of people inhabiting the Mediterranean area – as it did literally from the horizon of a growing peasant and urban population (which may help explain the confusion of some contemporary scholars).[69]

Significantly, in regions with substantial pastoral zones, like the mountainous areas of Turkey and Morocco, rams retained their symbolic prominence. The word for 'ram' in Turkish, koç, for example, is used as a compliment for males, as in, for example, 'Koç gibisin' – that is, 'You are like a ram'. Moreover, Koç also figures frequently as a surname.[70] Although goats are still part of daily village life – a circumstance which may account for their persistence as a totemic category – the study of gestures mentioned earlier implies that none of the informants was aware that the vertical horn-sign referred to the billy-goat.[71] As suggested earlier, this account clearly suffers from an urban bias (and is thus unintentionally revealing), since there is abundant, though fragmentary, evidence (linguistic, lexical, ethnographic, folkloric, literary, iconographic) from rural areas attesting to the association between cornutes and billy-goats.

In everyday language, Sicilians rarely refer directly to the ram as a symbol of strength, virility and honour. Only once did I hear a shepherd, pointing at the head and beautifully curved horns of a ram, speak of *il vero maschio*, the real male. An implicit reference to rams is none the less contained in the standard expression *un uomo coi coglioni grossi* ('a man with big testicles'), used by Sicilians to denote an influential and powerful personage.[72] In the village where I stayed there lived a woman forced by circumstance to take care of things which are usually men's affairs. One male informant described her, favourably, as *una donna a chi mancano i coglioni*, that is, 'a woman who [only] lacked testicles to make it as a man'. He illustrated this phrase with a characteristic gesture: he moved both his fists downwards in a curve, holding them demonstratively in front of the lower part of his body – the movement and posture evoking the image of a charging ram.

One may expect that the symbolism of rams and billy-goats is best conserved in surviving pastoral communities on the margins of the Mediterranean region. Yet no ethnographer who worked in peripheral mountain communities in Corsica, Sardinia, Sicily, Andalusia, southern France, the Balkans, Turkey and the Rif makes any mention of it. Is it possible, then, that the ram as a symbolic image has become obsolete even among shepherds? It seems more likely that research interests were focused on other things, more on people and their relationship with livestock than on animals in their own right: their habits, characteristics and representations.[73]

Campbell, who studied the moral values of the pastoral Sarakatsani communities in north-western Greece in the 1950s, comes very close to identifying rams and billy-goats (and sheep and goats) as totemic animals. He briefly dwells on the attributes of sheep and goats. Among the Sarakatsani, Campbell tells us, sheep and men are opposed in a binary fashion to goats and women. Sheep are milked exclusively by men, while women usually milk the goats.[74] At this point Campbell refers to 'complementary oppositions'. But he does not push his analysis far enough to realize that sheep and goats, together with rams and billy-goats, provide a code, as may be seen from the following remarks:

For the Sarakatsani, sheep and goats, men and women, are important and related oppositions with a moral reference. Sheep are peculiarly God's animals, and their shepherds, made in His image, are essentially noble beings. Women, through the particular sensuality of their natures, are inherently more likely to have relations with the Devil; and goats were originally the animals of the Devil which Christ captured and tamed for the service of man. It is consistent with these ideas that sheep and shepherds in their respective animal and human worlds display ideal moral characteristics. Sheep are docile, enduring, pure, and intelligent. When the shepherd carries out a small veterinarian operation or when the ewe gives birth, the animal suffers in silence. To match this purity and passive courage shepherds ought to be fearless and devoted guardians, and clean in the ritual sense. After sexual intercourse a shepherd must carefully wash his hands before milking sheep and it is generally preferable that the two shepherds of the flock of milking ewes should be unmarried men. (Campbell 1964: 26)

Women and goats are conceptually opposed to men and sheep. Goats are unable to resist pain in silence, they are cunning and insatiate feeders. Greed and cunning are important characteristics of the Devil and Sarakatsani will often say that although Christ tamed these animals the Devil still remains in them. Sarakatsani keep some goats to exploit that part of their grazing land which is unfit for sheep. But as animals they are despised, and a *stani* with too high a proportion of goats to sheep loses prestige. Women are not, of course, simply creatures of the Devil but the nature of their sexuality which continually threatens the honour of men, makes them, willingly or unwillingly, agents of his will. It is consistent, therefore, that in the practical division of labour women rather than men care for the goats. (Campbell 1964: 31)

Consistent with what we already know about the points of comparison drawn between sheep and goats in Mediterranean pastoral communities to stress differences between men and women, we hear from the Sarakatsani about other paired contrasts, including silence and noise, rich and poor pastures, creatures of God and creatures of the Devil, honesty and cunning, purity and impurity, order and disorder. The Sarakatsani also refer to the deceived husband as a man who wears horns (*keratas*), but Campbell misses this clue in following the lapsus of Pitt-Rivers mentioned before.[75]

Discussing symbolic polarities in the written tradition of early Greek thought, Lloyd notes that, regarding 'male' and 'female', 'it is not only the case that the Greeks generally considered women inferiors, but the myth of Pandora, for instance, implied that women are the source of all evil: as Hesiod puts it, before Pandora, the first woman, appeared on earth, men lived free from evil, toil and disease' (1992: 42). Lloyd then moves to the Pythagorean Table of Opposites as rendered in Aristotle's *Metaphysica*, which includes 'ten pairs of opposite terms together in a single comprehensive schema which was evidently held in some way to represent the fundamental principles which underlie reality' (1992: 48–9). These associated oppositions include right/left, men/women, light/darkness, good/evil, white/black, Olympian/Chthonic, high/low, front/back, and gods/humans. In his later work on animal taxonomies, Lloyd also restricts himself to written sources (1983: 7–57). He fails to detect the importance of *sets* of *domestic* animals for a better understanding of early Greek cosmology, although he refers to the anthropological discussion on animal symbolism and recognizes that in ancient Greece, as elsewhere, ideas about species of animals presuppose a firm and intelligible classificatory framework. Yet that framework remains implicit. It is assumed and goes unchallenged: it is not the subject of deliberate inquiry or critical reflection (1983: 205).

The present essay tries to show that, when dealing with written and iconographic sources concerning the role of the imaginary in the ancient world, ethnographic field-work focused on local cultures and combining structural and interpretative approaches in anthropology elicits important clues regarding this implicit classificatory framework. Details attain great significance. One may understand, for example, why in the legend it was Helle and not her brother Phryxus who fell from the magical ram with the golden fleece, or, to mention another example, why on an Attic vase painting Patroclus' corpse over which Achilles and Hector are fighting has assumed the form of a sacrificial ram.[76]

Lévi-Strauss came close to sacrificing content to form and meaning to logic.[77] Setting out to demonstrate the importance of 'the logic of the concrete' in animal symbolism, he dismissed the links between totemism

and practical interests in animals as well as the importance of 'participation' between human and totemic species.[78] But his approach does not
necessarily rule out attention to content and meaning: classification and
participation are both fundamental aspects of totemic symbolism.[79] By
focusing on pairs, on unions of opposites, on systems of differences, we
were able to detect the 'natural' counterpart of the billy-goat, namely the
totemic ram, and bring to light *sets* of meaningful differences that turn
on a concept of honour closely associated with the use of physical violence. We shall briefly document the importance of the values surrounding this key element in Mediterranean communities before raising the
question in the final section of what may help to account for the *longue
durée* of this particular cultural focus.

IV

In his account of the Spanish expression *cabrón* for deceived husband,
Pitt-Rivers does not look for *sets* of animals, which explains his slip in
missing the most obvious analogies.[80] These flaws also invalidate the
comments of his critic Brandes (1981: 87–91), who, like Campbell before
him (1964: 152), follows Pitt-Rivers in regarding the billy-goat as a
symbol of sexuality (and horns as a phallic symbol), whereas local cultures clearly suggest a metaphorical representation of anomalous sexual
behaviour. It is precisely because rams and billy-goats (sheep and goats)
have characteristics in common and differ in other respects that they can
be classed in pairs of opposites and be adopted as emblems to encode
major social and cultural distinctions.[81]

The betrayed husband is dishonourable and ritually polluted on several
counts. His wife's adultery raises doubts not only about his sexual capacities but also about his capacity to protect her from the advances of other
men – that is, his ability to control and monopolize his wife, to ensure her
chastity and thus to guarantee the immunity of *all* his domains.[82]

Female virginity and chastity are signs. As tropes they suggest control
over domains (women, the family, livestock, land, crops) and represent
the immunity of an entire patrimony – the patrimony of patriarchal men.
Weakness in one domain signifies the lack of vigilance in another – and
invites further violations. Immunity (or sanctity) is the hallmark of
honour. Successful claims on a woman entail domination of the other
man, both from the point of view of the husband who jealously guards
his wife, and of the adulterer, who shows himself to be more powerful than the husband. Hence the domestication, the enclosure of
women, which is often regarded as one of the most salient features of
Mediterranean societies.[83]

In spite of their erosion by the impact of economic forces, the growth
of towns and the rise of national states, contemporary concepts of

honour, vested in an ancient totemic classification, are still primarily contingent on the use of physical violence. Not surprisingly this is especially the case in remaining pastoral communities located in remote and mountainous areas of the Mediterranean, including the Barbagia in central Sardinia, Sicily's western interior, the Zagori mountains in north-western Greece, rural Anatolia, the Andalusian Sierras, the Moroccan Rif and Kabylia in northern Algeria – that is, areas where state control has been either weak or absent.

The representation of the deceived husband as a cornute exemplifies how closely notions of moral and physical integrity are interwoven. First, the chastity of a woman is violated, which damages both her reputation and that of her husband and family. Second, the deceived husband cannot, without having rehabilitated himself through violence (physical force), easily show up in public domains dominated by competitive men. He is ritually defiled and consequently ignored, avoided, marginalized, excluded from ordinary social interaction and sociability. Only by shedding blood can the stains of dishonour be removed and cleansed.

Control over (the sexuality of) women was essentially the problem of Achilles with which *The Iliad* opens. His integrity or 'sense of self' was injured, shamed, mutilated, polluted in a most painful way through the seizure of his concubine Briseis by Agamemnon. The anthropologist and Indo-Europeanist Paul Friedrich, who reminds us of this theme, argues convincingly that three cases of dishonour, all involving struggles over women – the abduction of Helen, the seizure of the daughter of Apollo, and that of Achilles' beautiful concubine – 'unleash much of the force that drives this epic' (1977: 285).

According to a popular saying in Sicily, for the cornute to appear in public would 'hurt his horns'. Therefore, deceived husbands, like women (until recently), try to avoid the public realm, thus reinforcing their anomaly and aggravating their disgrace. Discussing public and private spheres among the Kabyles in Algeria, Bourdieu remarks:

All informants spontaneously give as the essential characteristics of the man of honour the fact that he *faces* others . . . (1979a: 128)

A man who spends too much time at home in the daytime is suspect or ridiculous: he is a 'house-man', who 'broods at home like a hen at roost'. A self-respecting man must offer himself to be seen, constantly put himself in the gaze of others, confront them, face up to them (*qabel*). He is a man among men. Hence the importance attached to the game of honour, a sort of theatrical performance, played out in front of others. (1979b: 141)

The strong emphasis in the concept of honour on virginity, chastity and the purity of women (and their subsequent enclosure to protect and control them) shows to what extent the discourse of honour in the Mediterranean world bears on the idea of immunity, physical integrity and physical violence.[84] In Andalusia, the popular term *hombría*, manliness, refers to courage and the capacity to resist claims and encroachments on what a man considers his property – women, land, livestock, etc. *Hombría* implies a direct reference to the physical basis of honour: those who live up to this ideal have *cojones* (testicles), while those who fail to show fearlessness are lacking in manliness and are considered *manso* – that is, symbolically castrated, tame. The term *manso*, also used in Sicily, is derived from the animal world, and is used to indicate a castrated ox or mule, which as a consequence of the operation, has become more tractable.[85]

In Sicily, too, the concept of honour is bound up with notions of virility and physical violence. *Mafiosi*, specialists in the use of violence, are called 'men of honour'. Many of them have a pastoral background.[86] Much of their vocabulary and violent practices is inspired by the idiom of this ruthless world. A notable aspect of their *habitus* is their gaze, which can best be described as 'nonchalant, roving, and yet steady'.[87]

Among the Sarakatsani, reports Campbell, adult males show themselves courageous and fearless: 'Manliness implies not only the condition of being courageous but the ability of a man to do something efficient and effective about the problems and dangers which surround him. The physical characteristics of manliness are important' (1964: 269). Therefore, adult males must be βαρβᾶτο, literally 'provided with a beard', but metaphorically,

> well endowed with testicles and the strength that is drawn from them. The word also describes a certain ruthless ability in any form of endeavour. Here again we see the 'efficient' aspect of manliness. . . . The manliness that is related to honour requires this physical basis, yet it must discipline animal strength and passions to its own ideal ends. (1964: 269–70)

A term similar to *manso* is used by Arab Muslims in rural Jordania to designate a deceived husband who is compliant. Antoun writes:

> The man preserves his honor, in great part, by protecting the modesty of his women. Among Arabs the man who does not do so is termed 'cuckold' (*dayyuth*), a term that in a religious context confers the strongest opprobrium in its meaning, 'reviled one'. In one of its popular meanings *dayyuth* refers to an animal that stands by and watches while other males make sexual connection with his mate. (1968b: 680)

Further lexical research reveals that the word *dayyuth* derives from *data*, meaning something that was or became soft, supple, easy. Hence the term *dayyuth*: he was or became a tame cuckold, without jealousy and regardless of shame, like a pimp to his own wife.[88]

In Sicily, as elsewhere in the Mediterranean region, honour is at stake whenever property rights are wilfully infringed: when the chastity of a woman is violated, when livestock or crops have been stolen, when part of the harvest is damaged, when cattle, sheep or goats are driven through another man's pastures or fields (*pascolo abusivo*), or when fruit trees or vines have been cut down. In all these cases the honour of the owner, proprietor or guard is impugned. Sometimes, these infringements are denoted by the term *sfregi*, affronts. Again we are concerned with the idiom of the human body, since *sfregio* literally means the disfigurement or mutilation of someone's face by cutting his cheek with a knife so as to leave a long, visible scar as a lasting mark of dishonour. *Un furto per sfregio* is thus a special kind of theft (sheep or cattle), carried out not to ruin the owner but to jeopardize his honour in revenge, to damage his reputation. This may explain the excitement and the violent encounters and exchanges that even 'little' damage or a 'small' offence can bring about. There is a parallel here with the so-called *point d'honneur* in western Europe under the *ancien régime*: on account of an 'insignificant' incident, men demanded satisfaction and challenged their opponents to fight it out in a duel. (These were, of course, by no means bagatelles for the people concerned, since an affront could imply that doubts had been raised about the group membership of the offended, without which his life had little meaning). Therefore nobles in early modern Europe were to some extent immune to offences from those who did not belong to the 'good society', and who consequently lacked *Satisfaktionsfähigkeit* – that is, the right to provoke a duel.[89] Very similar attitudes prevail in Kabylia and the Rif where certain marginal categories are excluded from violent exchanges and where the sense of honour finds its most total affirmation in physical violence, including murder.[90]

For the Sarakatsani, physical perfection is an important ideal, for both women and men. Campbell notes that 'maidens must be virgins, and even married women must remain virginal in thought and expression' (1964: 270); while 'a youth ought to be tall, slim, agile, and tough. Any kind of physical deformity is fatal to the reputation of a young shepherd' (1964: 278). In Mediterranean pastoral communities the moral and physical existence of transhument shepherd families depends on the capacity and readiness of men to defend themselves physically against thefts, insults and offences.

Since they lend themselves to anthropomorphic symbolism, the differences between the habits of rams and billy-goats (rather than any other pair or set of opposites) have been adopted to express the differences between strong, virile, courageous men and weaklings, those who fail to meet the demands of a pastoral life in which, according to Campbell's apt phrase, 'reputation is impossible without strength':

> Poverty is a mark of failure, not a virtue. Strength in sheep and men encourages others to respect a family's honour, it attracts dependent kinsmen whose support further extends influence and prestige. Honour and strength are linked. (1964: 317)

> Strength and prowess matter more than ethical goodness. Indeed a man is only good when he is also, by implication, able and strong. Although aimless violence is dishonourable there is no missing the pleasure it gives when a man is forced to kill; nor the prestige which it brings him. For there is no more conclusive way of showing that you are stronger than by taking away the other man's life. (1964: 318)

Pitt-Rivers stresses this intimate relation between honour and the physical person on several occasions (1965: 25–9; 1968: 505–6). He notes that honour is linked to the physical person 'in terms of the symbolic functions attached to the body: to the blood, the heart, the hand, the head, and the genitalia' and that 'any form of physical affront implies an affront to honour' while 'the ultimate vindication of honour lies in physical violence'. He does not pursue the question of why honour is symbolized in terms of the physical person and how this code has developed over time. Why, indeed, has the English word 'cornute', along with its equivalents in other western European languages, become obsolete – together with much of the vocabulary of honour[91] – while in southern Europe and other parts of the Mediterranean region, particularly in peripheral rural communities, these notions are still very much alive or had a longer lease of life?

The strong emphasis on physical integrity and physical violence in the Mediterranean discourse of honour suggests that the people who think in these terms cannot depend on stable centres of political control for the protection of their life and patrimony. In the absence of effective state control, they have to rely on their own forces – on various forms of self-help.[92] These conditions of the wider power fields put a premium on self-assertive qualities in men, involving the readiness and capacity to use physical force in order to guarantee the immunity of life and property, including women as the most precious and vulnerable part of their patrimony.[93] The extremes of this sense of honour are reached when even merely glancing at a woman is felt as an affront, as an incursion into a male domain, touching off a violent response. When might is right, women's virginity and chastity can become men's dominant concern, the physical integrity of women forming the linchpin of male reputation. Hence the intimate relation between honour and physical force as expressed in the idiom of the human body and symbolized in terms of a specific set of animals. Moral and physical integrity can be related to the point that 'to maintain one's honour is so much a duty, that one derives from it the claims to the most frightful sacrifices – not only self-inflicted ones, but also those involving others' (Simmel 1968: 405).[94]

During the past two centuries, the role of physical force in the western European concept of honour has lost much of its significance. In everyday language, the term 'honour' and its various derivations have acquired archaic and sometimes ironic overtones. In fact, cornutes have become 'cuckolds', a term in which the link with the physical person has gradually lost its explicit imprint, while women have become much less dependent on men for their protection and immunity. With the growing pacification and democratization of western societies, cultural forms of homage and chivalry have slowly been eroded. Apart from some important exceptions, to be discussed, the vocabulary in which differences of rank – especially those based on physical force – were expressed is disappearing from ordinary conversation. The notion of honour as a universal element of social evaluation is now phrased in other terms. One avoids the word honour. The impugned honour of yore has become the hurt vanity of today. Giving evidence of pride and self-importance is no longer appreciated. Those who indulge in it are now regarded as pompous and condescending, while in former times they were merely competing for points of honour. Insults are no longer felt to be injuries. Without 'losing face' one can often simply ignore them, the more so since insults have become more embarrassing and painful to the offender than to the offended. It has been noted that in our society 'the *reality* of the offence will be denied' (Berger 1970: 339).

In two widely different sectors of western societies, the notion of honour is still very similar to those prevalent in early modern Europe and the Mediterranean. One can understand why. First, it thrives in certain peripheral subcultures of 'men in groups', in bars, dockyards, prisons and the premises of organized crime, where rank, esteem and sanctions are matters of physical force. For obvious reasons, people who move about in these sectors cannot turn to the state for protection and help. Second, a code of honour intimately linked with the physical person is still conspicuous in the army as well as among sportsmen and certain members of the surviving aristocracy. In these sectors of society, honour not only concerns the bearing and physical feats of human beings, but also the power and prestige of the national state to which they belong, and which they represent. Indeed, since the French Revolution, the discourse of national honour has gradually appropriated the vocabulary of personal honour.[95] In particular matches and games, in diplomatic negotiations and in wars, national honour may be regarded as at stake. It has been rightly emphasized that the *point d'honneur* 'is still evident today in the intercourse between sovereign states' (Jones 1959: 35). Since the end of the sixteenth century, the functions of attack and defence and the corresponding loyalties and sentiments have step by step been transferred from local and regional levels to the national arena. Dynastic states have grown into national states, and the armies with which the European powers used to fight one another have become national armies. For protection and security, people have become much less dependent upon their own forces. Their self-help has given way to multiple forms of state control.[96] With the monopolization of the means of violence, a person's bearing and physical force have lost much of their importance to his social position, self-esteem, personal identity, pride and sense of honour.[97] With the expansion of scale, with the extension and differentiation of social networks, moreover, public opinion acquired other forms and functions: it became less *existenzbegründend*, less a foundation of social existence, than in the small-scale, relatively closed circles of herdsmen, peasants, university students and aristocrats, whose sense of honour and personal identity were largely and sometimes completely dependent on membership in those communities.[98]

I have argued that the symbolism of the horns of the deceived husband or cornute should be understood in the context of an ancient totemic classification and as an integral part of an originally pastoral code of honour, predicated on virility and physical force. Mediterranean totemism (and the concept of honour it entails) revolves around the complementary opposition between rams and billy-goats (sheep and goats). These sets of animals with their resemblances and differences – and their enduring fundamental economic importance in Mediterranean societies – have been adopted as emblems to encode major social and cultural contrasts, most notably the unions of opposites between male and female, strong and weak, honour and shame, order and disorder, and good and evil.

The anthropological literature on Mediterranean communities contains only fragments of this cosmology. This state of affairs is partly due to ecological and political discontinuities within the Mediterranean region – the *monde conçu* of rams versus billy-goats and sheep versus goats no longer agrees with the *monde vécu* of people who have gradually turned away from pastoralism – and partly to a lack of historical depth in anthropological studies. Despite their attention to the so-called material basis of Mediterranean cultures, anthropologists have neglected the minutiae of the behaviour of domesticated animals and the meaning they had for local people. The interest in animal symbolism in tribal societies, greatly stimulated by Lévi-Strauss's studies of totemic classifications in the early 1960s, never found its equivalent in the study by anthropologists of complex societies. *Pace* Lévi-Strauss's argument about a 'totemic void' in complex civilizations, Mediterranean totemic symbolism and the embedded concepts of honour persisted in pastoral and peasant communities that remained for centuries only nominally integrated into state societies. If my interpretation of these codes is correct, new light may be thrown on an old problem: how structural and historical analyses can be fruitfully combined.

11

Female Rulers and their Consorts

> By becoming male, the female escaped subordination.
>
> Marina Warner, *Joan of Arc*

I

Why are women leaders often single – either unmarried or widows? And if they are married, why is their husband often unknown or politically insignificant? Historical examples, such as Joan of Arc, Elizabeth Tudor, Catherine de Medici, Christina of Sweden, Catherine the Great, Maria Theresa, and the Chinese Empress Wu are mirrored by more recent figures: Dolores Ibarruri, Sirimavo Bandaranaike, Indira Gandhi, Golda Meir, Bernadette Devlin, Margaret Thatcher, Cory Aquino, Benazir Bhutto and Violeta Chamorro.

The individualities of female leaders have often been noticed, and the historical circumstances in which they rose to power have been described in numerous biographies. But it is impossible to understand their careers in terms of local contexts only, since that would leave unanswered the question of the recurrent features in their careers: why are they often single – either *de facto* or symbolically? To see whether one could discover a more general pattern underlying the careers of female leaders and rulers, I began collecting biographical information on them, building up what would grow into a sizeable portrait gallery. In the process I have drawn on the writings of Hastrup (1978), Denise O'Brien (1977) and Heisch (1980), who, in different ways, have pointed to the relevance of ambiguous gender classification and its relationship to power.

Hastrup has convincingly argued that whereas men are just men all the time, women go through different stages – such as virgin, wife and

210

widow – that can be used as social markers. Joan of Arc, for example, would probably never have succeeded in her campaigns and obtained such a large following among men had she not been really or symbolically a virgin, but just a woman. The same holds true for Bernadette Devlin, whose power diminished after she had a child.

Among the Shilluk of Sudan, the king's daughters had a high political status and could not become wives and mothers, but were allowed to become 'female husbands' and have lovers. Similar arrangements (in which a woman takes on the legal and social roles of a husband and father by marrying another woman of whose children she becomes the legal father) existed among at least thirty other African populations. Female husbands were especially prominent among the Shilluk, the Nyoro in western Uganda, and among various southern Bantu populations, where women could become political leaders. They were treated like men, ruled as chiefs, and were not allowed to become wives and mothers.[1] Women who have become social males by moving into extradomestic statuses of high prestige have been described as 'honorary males',[2] and the phrase is apt. Regarding the marital status of these female leaders, one finds, in varying degrees, an 'emphasis on the mutual exclusiveness of the roles of political leader and wife and on the necessity for a leader to be a husband'.[3] Because of its explicitness concerning the mutual incompatibility between leader and wife, the case of autonomous female husbands may help us to understand the role of female leaders elsewhere.

II

In the summer of 1989, when I began this research, one could hear about the ascendancy of the 'charismatic' leader of the Japanese Socialist Party, Takako Doi (aged 61), former professor of law at the University of Kyoto, and for many Japanese an acceptable Prime Minister. She is unmarried. Another woman leader, from an entirely different part of the world, is Intassir Al-Wazir (47), who has been elected as a member of the board of Al Fatah, the most important faction in the Palestinian Liberation Organization. She is the widow of the Palestinian leader Abu Jihad, who was killed by Israeli commandos in August 1988. Third, we have Violeta Barrios de Chamorro (61), a widow, and owner and editor of the Nicaraguan opposition paper *La Prensa*. Early in September 1989 the opposition party in Nicaragua, the Union of National Opposition (a fractious coalition of fourteen political parties), elected her as a candidate for the presidential elections scheduled for February 1990, which she won. Mrs Chamorro went into politics shortly after her husband, the politician Pedro Joaquin Chamorro, was assassinated in 1978 (presumably on the orders of the dictator Somoza).[4]

Other examples of single women leaders include the unmarried Agatha Barbara, who was President of Malta between 1982 and 1987, and her contemporaries M. Eugenia Charles, Prime Minister of Dominica and Vigdis Finnbogadottir, President of Iceland. Both Charles and Finnbogadottir are single mothers. There is also Ursula Koch (48), a 'flamboyant' local politician in Zurich, nicknamed 'Saint Patron' and 'The Red Witch' by friends and enemies respectively.[5] Dora Bakoyannis, the widow of the Greek politician Pavlos Bakoyannis, who was killed by terrorists in September 1989, announced she would pursue her husband's political goals.[6] At the end of February 1991, Khaleda Zia (46) won the national election in Bangladesh and could choose between the prime-ministership and the presidency. She is the widow of General Ziaur Rahman, who was President of Bangladesh until he was assassinated in 1981. After Mrs Zia was persuaded to take up her husband's mantle, she reportedly transformed herself in less than a decade from a self-effacing wife of a powerful general to a formidable political leader in her own right. In the elections she defeated her rival, Sheik Hasina Wazed, the daughter of Bangladesh's first Prime Minister, Sheik Mujibur, who was assassinated in 1975.[7] Three new prime ministers in 1993 provide further examples of gender inversion among female leaders. The Polish Hanna Suchocka (47) is single; Kim Campbell (46) in Canada is also single (twice divorced); and though the wealthy Tansu Ciller (47) in Turkey, a former university professor and minister of economic affairs, is married and has two sons, she has kept her own name and convinced her husband that he should bear her name (at the urging of her father, a provincial governor, who deplored not having a son to continue the family line).[8]

While there is a great deal of attention paid to the particulars in the biographies of female leaders, the implicit affinities between these women – their 'family resemblances' – often go unnoticed and have never been systematically explored. Most cases of woman leaders are dealt with by area specialists, who are usually more interested in differences, in historical and cultural particularities, than in spelling out structural resemblances. Obviously, the discovery of similarities and commonalities requires a comparative approach. But comparative research seems out of fashion. As N. Thomas (1991) argues, it has suffered from the justified criticism of an old kind of positivistic comparison that sought to establish law-like generalizations, ignoring cultural and historical contexts. Moreover, comparative reasearch suffers from a time-honoured research agenda of anthropologists in which the exploration of unrecognized cultural differences between societies (in particular between western and tribal societies) is still the foremost priority: the presentation of other cultures in exotic terms still 'retains canonical status within the discipline'.[9] Thick descriptions make for thin comparisons. But even a better understanding of cultural differences cannot do without some form of comparison, for we can only know about differences and similarities after comparative research.[10] And it remains an important task to explore both: 'Much of the creativity of anthropology derives from the tension between two sets of demands: that we explain human universals, and that we explain cultural particulars.'[11] Let us, therefore, take a closer look at a number of female leaders, search for their differences and similarities, find out to what extent and in what forms we are dealing with gender-inversion, and assess how each case provides a commentary on the others.[12] Such efforts may also help to reorientate comparison in cultural anthropology – and contribute to transcultural understanding.

III

Lü Zhi became Empress Dowager of China at the beginning of the second century BC after the death of her husband, Emperor Liu Bang, founder of the Han dynasty. She eliminated the successor and his mother, and placed her own son, Zhao Di, on the throne. He was still young and malleable, and in fact Lü ruled the empire. She was able and courageous but also 'ruthless' (a common characterization in the biographies of female rulers). When her son became adult, she killed him and replaced him with another boy whom she took from the ranks of the palace children. In the words of the biographer from whom these data are obtained: 'In his gorgeous robes he was a puppet; she was the ventriloquist.'[13] After Lü's death, the bureaucrats and military killed her entire family and restored acceptable male leadership.[14]

Of all the female rulers of Imperial China, Empress Wu (625–705) was probably the most colourful.[15] She was the daughter of a general and reputedly very beautiful. At the of age thirteen she came to the palace of Emperor Tai Zong as a junior concubine. When the Emperor died in 649, Wu was already involved with his son and successor, Gao Zong. As a favourite of the new Emperor, Wu enlarged her influence. Before she was thirty she had a son, had eliminated her female rivals from the palace, and replaced the childless Empress Wang. Having become Empress herself in 655, Wu removed, banished or executed all bureaucrats and military whom she did not like or whom she had reason to suspect. She was helped by her husband, a weak and incompetent figure who let her take over the administration. About their relationship Terrill observes:

> When the Emperor gave an audience, Wu sat beside him on a throne equally elevated but, in deference to the tradition that women should keep out of politics, hidden by a screen. The official historians reluctantly noted

the real situation: 'The whole sovereign power of the Empire passed into her hands; life or death, reward or punishment were decided by her word. The Son of Heaven [Emperor] sat on his throne with folded hands, and that was all'. (1984: 310)

Actual power thus resided with Wu, who ruled the Empire ruthlessly but also very competently. Helped by a new generation of officials, Wu continued the consolidation of China that her father-in-law had begun. When the Emperor died in 683, his oldest son succeeded him. After a month he was deposed by his mother and replaced by her second son, who ruled only in name. In 690 Wu usurped the throne and became Emperor herself, which proved a unique event in the history of China. Fitzgerald writes:

> Wu Chao had now achieved the impossible; for the first time in Chinese history and, as it proved, for the last also, a woman had ascended the Throne of the Emperors and had been recognized, not as Empress or Empress Dowager, titles which were not sovereign, but as Emperor – since Chinese terminology and Chinese mentality were alike incapable of finding a different title for the unique phenomenon of a female monarch. (1968: 128)

Wu had entirely dominated her husband, Emperor Tai Zong: 'Weak, ill, and stupid, he was no match for her, and he knew it.'[16] But she had always been faithful to him. All historians, including those who were not favourably disposed toward her, seem to agree on this. Yet her love life had uncommon aspects. Wu had been the concubine of two emperors, in this case father and son, which was regarded as incest. Later on, when she had become a widow, she began to favour attractive, virile young men, of whom the pedlar Xue and, afterwards, the brothers and carpenters Zhang were best known. When Xue became increasingly overbearing, Wu had him strangled by palace women. The favourites Zhang were killed in a conspiracy in 705. Old and ailing, Wu was then forced to retire, after having ruled China for nearly fifty years.[17]

Apart from important differences, the life of the Chinese Empress Ci Xi (1838–1908) shows striking similarities with that of Wu. Like her predecessor, Ci Xi began her career as a concubine of the Emperor. She also reinforced her position when she bore the Emperor a son (the only one) and further made herself useful by helping the Emperor with administration. After his death in 1861, her son succeeded to the throne as Emperor Tong Zhi. As Empress Dowager, however, Ci Xi became the effective ruler. Together with the brother and the first wife of the former Emperor, she formed a co-regency and enforced peace and unity by modernizing the school system, reorganizing the military and suppressing two great rebellions. When her son became adult in 1873, Ci Xi continued her regency, and when he died two years later she replaced him with a young nephew whom she had adopted as a son and who, as Emperor Guang Xu, became her marionette. In the early 1880s, one of her co-regents, the first wife of the former Emperor, died, and after her brother-in-law had been eliminated Ci Xi was able to assume total power. Like Wu, she reigned for almost fifty years. She is also supposed to have ruled with competence and ruthlessness – again a recurrent theme in the iconography of female rulers. Her death in 1908 coincided with that of her nephew, Emperor Guang Xu. As one of her biographers, on whose work I have extensively drawn, phrases it: 'The coincidence of the deaths of the tragic [Guang Xu] and the tyrannical woman who had adopted him as her son was indeed remarkable.'[18] At any rate, Ci Xi had, shortly before her death, appointed her third child-emperor, a boy of two, who was to be the last Emperor of China.

In the rule of Catherine de Medici (1519–89), who became Queen of France through her marriage to Henry II, we also find the widow who effectively rules for her sons who are sovereigns only in name. After the death of her husband in 1559, Catherine acted as Regent for two of them. They died young, and Catherine remained influential since her third son, Henry, who became King, was incompetent and showed little interest in state affairs anyway. At the time, France was rent by religious wars. Catherine aimed at reconciliation and national unity, trying to consolidate royal power, but she did not live to see her numerous attempts result in peace between the warring Catholic and Protestant factions.

Her contemporary Elizabeth I (1533–1603), who was Queen of England between 1558 and 1603, remained single despite various attempts to have her married and provide a successor. Possibly she avoided marriage because she was more interested in ruling: to become the consort of a king would have severely diminished her authority.[19] Like the female rulers mentioned above, Elizabeth was a competent sovereign and her reign lasted several decades – an epoch to which she lent her name. Doubtless, these circumstances have contributed to the formation of the legends and cults surrounding her. She also encouraged this by presenting herself as an extraordinary woman: virgin queen, bride of England, mother of all Englishmen, learned and scholarly, intelligent and erudite, but also courageous and martial, as suggested in her famous speech of 1588 at Tilbury, where she said: 'I know I have the body of a weak and feeble woman, but I have the heart and stomach of a King, and a King of England, too.'[20]

Marie de Medici (1573–1642) was married to the French King Henry IV. After his assassination in 1610, she became Regent for her son Louis

XIII. When the latter came of age in 1614, Marie retained power and was strongly supported by her favourite, Concini, who sought to humiliate and eliminate the young King and came close to replacing him. Marie's rule came to an end in 1617, when her Italian friend was murdered in an aristocratic plot favouring the King.[21]

Christina (1626–89) was the daughter and only heir of the Swedish King Gustav Adolph. After his death in 1632 she was, on instructions left by her father, brought up like a prince. She became Queen of Sweden in 1644 and abdicated voluntarily in 1654. She never married but reputedly had several lovers. She is described as a competent ruler and as a learned woman (hence her nickname 'Minerva of the North'), who promoted the arts and sciences, first in Sweden (where she hosted Descartes) and later also in Italy, where she spent most of the rest of her life.

Catherine the Great (1729–96) was a poor German princess from Stettin who went to Russia when she was 14. One year later, she was married to the heir to the throne, Grand Duke Peter, a weak and sickly young man who had few social skills. No one regarded him as the father of Paul, the son who was born only after nine years of marriage. Whereas the Grand Duke idolized everything related to Prussia and mainly occupied himself with drilling his troops from Holstein, Catherine familiarized herself with Russian culture and society. As Troyat characterizes her: 'If she did not eclipse all the other women at court by her beauty, Catherine easily outshone them by her broad culture and piquant conversation.'[22]

Her husband had, as Tsar Peter III, ruled Russia for barely six months when a coup in the summer of 1762 by Catherine's palace guard forced him to step down and accept arrest. The same day Catherine replaced her unpopular husband and was proclaimed Empress. A week later Peter, who was put under house arrest, was killed by two of the coup leaders, brothers of Catherine's lover Orlov. After her coronation in Moscow later that year, Catherine ruled as sovereign, not as Regent for her son, whose regal claims to the throne she was to ignore until her death. She remained unmarried, entertaining throughout her reign of well over thirty years intimate relations with a succession of several young and dashing favourites, virtually all of them recruited from the palace guard, and of whom Orlov and Potemkin are probably the best known. Regarding this aspect of her patronage, a recent biographer writes:

> Except for Zavadovskii all her main choices singled out Guard officers, a blatant example of her assiduous attention to them as a mainstay of her rule. From a practical angle, moreover, Guardsmen were especially likely to catch her attention in view of their youth, robust physiques, their ubi-

quity at court, and their employment in all manner of government duties. Since all her favorites came from fairly obscure noble families, their rise thus reminded the nobility of the rewards that state service (servicing the autocratrix in this instance) could gain for an individual and his relatives. In one sense Catherine used her selection of favorites to restock the elite, prompting newcomers and rescuing old families fallen from eminence in recent decades. Never did she choose a favorite from an already prominent noble clan. To have done so would have risked inciting the jealous ire of other established families. (Alexander 1989: 223–4)

Under her rule Russia extended its frontiers to the south and the west, but there were fewer social reforms than one might expect on account of her 'legislomania' and manifold contacts with French intellectuals. Catherine turned out to be a typical enlightened despot – more despotic than enlightened.[23] As a female ruler and legislator she was considered an anomaly, 'Cathérine Le Grand', as she was sometimes called. Her androgyny was further marked by a tomboy youth and preference for horseback riding, hunting, and wearing military uniforms. She loved, on occasion, to appear on horseback in the uniform of her guardsmen, a performance that had proved so successful during her acclamation right after the coup.[24] Struck by her masculine looks, a British envoy observed: 'A man's dress is what suits her best; she wears it always when she rides on horseback. . . . It is scarce credible what she does in that way, managing horses, even fiery horses, with all the skill and courage of a groom'.[25]

Sexually, too, Catherine set herself apart from other women. Her preference in this regard and the way she had attained and maintained power earned her the nickname 'The Semiramis of the North', coined by her admirer Voltaire and recalling the legendary Assyrian Queen who ruthlessly secured the throne from her husband and infant son and indulged in unparalleled sexual exploits. Time and again, Catherine's contemporaries were intrigued by her ambiguity. As an English (male) visitor noticed: 'Indeed, with regard to her appearance altogether, it would be doing her an injustice to say it was masculine, yet it would not be doing her justice to say it was entirely feminine.'[26]

The characteristics recurring in these sketches of female rulers emphasize in various degrees their identity as social males and their relative autonomy, in particular their independence *vis-à-vis* a husband. Quite often the man is absent, either *de facto* or symbolically. In so far as he is present at all, he does not dominate. On the contrary, the husband is dominated by his wife and has accepted a subordinate position. This also applies to other men in the immediate (public) setting of the female leader, such as her male descendants, who sometimes rule in name or are about to do so.

IV

A common way of marking the extraordinary quality of things and people is by symbolic inversion.[27] This seems to have happened to female leaders virtually everywhere. To a greater or lesser extent, they are regarded, represented and treated as men – and have to present themselves accordingly. When women leaders have spouses, we are confronted with a double gender inversion: women assuming male roles and statuses – a switching of codes that is complemented by husbands adopting female roles.

The female leaders discussed so far distinguished themselves from other, 'ordinary' women by their beauty, foreign origin, tomboy youth (the mentor of Takako Doi described her as 'big, loud and pushy'), chastity, promiscuity, philandering, cruelty and ruthlessness, transvestism, scholarly interests, and other pastimes defined as masculine like hunting and horseback riding.[28]

In the iconography of female rulers two main features stand out: being single and donning male apparel. To Joan of Arc, an archetypal female leader, both symbols were of fundamental importance. In her fine biography, Warner dedicates an entire chapter to the meaning that wearing male dress had for Joan and the resistance it provoked in her environment, in particular from her judges.[29] Warner writes:

> That a particular woman contravened the destined subordination of her sex when she wore men's clothing underlies many of the prohibitions against it. Transvestism does not just pervert biology; it upsets the social hierarchy. . . . [T]he disguise constituted a rejection of parental authority and, more precisely, of male domination. By becoming male, the female escaped subordination. (1981: 147, 158)

But the most dramatic turn in the choreography of female leaders and the most effective and frequently used device was and still is the actual de-emphasis of the role of wife and mother. Defined as female and domestic, these functions prove virtually everywhere difficult to combine with the position of leader or ruler. This may explain why, in so many cases of women leaders, the husband has become superfluous. The example of the 'female husband' from various African countries proves instructive for a better understanding of female leaders elsewhere. It highlights the point that women who move into extra-domestic statuses of high prestige must also move into the social category of 'male' – since the subordinated role of wife would be incompatible with a position of high status. In the conclusion of her essay on 'female husbands', Denise O'Brien writes: 'By their need to reject the roles of wife and mother normatively associated with women in the domestic sphere, and to assume the roles of husband and father, these female chiefs and queens are but one more demonstration that persons who occupy power positions in male-dominated societies must be males' (1977: 123). Being single – free from male patronage – may also explain why female leaders are often represented as either chaste or promiscuous. These are powerful symbols, and as attributions of anomaly they are consistent with patriarchy, with 'hegemonic masculinity', with what some anthropologists call 'the universality of female subordination'.[30] In her biography of Eva Perón, Taylor writes: 'Virtually all societies exclude women from their formal ranking and regulations, positions and goals, relegating them to the realm of domesticity outside official structures. The roles and power ascribed to women are informal and uninstitutionalized in contrast with the culturally legitimized statuses and authority attributed to men' (1979: 13).[31] It would be more correct to say that in all societies women are virtually excluded from formal positions, etc., because this would explain why individual women who reach such formal positions are regarded as anomalies and defined as social males.

Consider how the logic of gender relations also governs the cultural practices of modern nation-states. From the autobiography of Golda Meir it appears that her husband, Morris Meyerson, had trouble with his health, held mostly odd jobs, and took care of the children while his wife was politically active and spent most of her time outside the home. Gradually they grew apart. Later she regretted this and acknowledged that it had been impossible for her to combine domestic and public roles.[32] Yet after she became a widow in 1951 and Foreign Minister in 1956, she marked these transitions by changing her name to the Hebrew Meir.

Indira Gandhi was also married and had children as well but became a widow early in life, well before she rose to become Prime Minister. Her marriage was considered unusual in several respects, not least because she always remained closer to her widowed father Jawaharlal Nehru, whom she adored and for whom she acted as official hostess, than to her husband, Feroze Gandhi, with whom she indeed rarely cohabitated. He had a different social and religious background, and although he later became a prominent politician in his own right, he never overcame his 'subsidiary status' as the husband of the Prime Minister's daughter. Condemned to anonymity and condescending recognition, he died of a heart attack in 1960 at the age of 48.[33]

Creating a distance from the statuses of mother and wife is not in conflict with the collective and spiritual motherhood that has often been ascribed to female rulers. In fact, several of them are represented as 'mothers of the nation'. Newspaper reports on Violeta Chamorro, who has four children, refer to her 'radiant smile and motherly concern'.[34] To many in the nation, Indira Gandhi was known as *Amma* (mother), and to the impoverished masses she was *Mataji* (revered mother).[35] Catherine the Great was called *Matiushka* (little mother) by her soldiers, and many saw in Golda Meir a kind of grandmother. In all likelihood this would also have happened if these female leaders had not been biological mothers, as is attested by the case of Queen Elizabeth I of England, who remained single and considered herself the mother of all Englishmen.[36] About the childless Eva Perón we learn that 'she was mother to the children of Argentina. More than that, she was mother of the nation as a whole, particularly to the common people and the poor and needy of Argentina' (Taylor 1979: 75). The description 'mother of the nation' has also been attributed to Winnie Mandela, another female leader. This happened when she had reached a climax in her struggle against apartheid and was 'single', her husband Nelson being away in prison on Robben Island. Things began to change in 1990, after her husband's release, at the very time she was having to defend herself against criminal charges involving assault and kidnapping boys. Indicted, divorced from her husband, and fallen from grace in the ANC as well, she faced obscurity. As one journalist described her demise, which was imminent early in 1991: 'In two years, South Africa's Eva Perón, revered by her followers, had been transformed into its Imelda Marcos.'[37]

V

The political success of female rulers depends on the real or symbolic absence of a husband or any other close male associate. This is evident from the consistency with which males in their entourage have been resisted, domesticated or eliminated. This illustrates again the contradiction of female power in a patriarchal order. It tells us to what degree women leaders had, and still have, to adapt their appearance and imagery to the pattern of 'hegemonic masculinity' and, in the process, help to perpetuate it.[38]

Where female leaders are not forbidden to marry (males) and have children – a proscription which, as we have seen, existed for princesses in certain East African societies – the dialectic of gender relations in patriarchal societies enforces other arrangements. One can refuse to marry (Joan of Arc), one can avoid marriage (Elizabeth I, Christina, Doi), or one can resist marriage and postpone it as long as possible (Benazir Bhutto).[39] Once married, one can abandon the husband or separate from him (Ibarruri, Meir, Gandhi). One can also have the husband killed (Catherine the Great) or simply wait for his death – a much-used 'strategy' in view of the large number of widows among female leaders.

From this perspective there is no better husband than a dead husband, especially since the martyrdom of the husband can provide the widow with considerable political and cultural capital. If there is something like a 'deep structure' of female leadership, then we have to look for it here. Not only a husband-politician but also a father-politician who has been killed or who has simply died can help legitimize the rule of a female leader (Indira Gandhi, Benazir Bhutto). Suffering arrest or years of solitary confinement after the martyrdom of a revered husband or parent may also give female rulers legitimacy.[40]

At this point we should not underestimate the symbolic value of violence and death. As Valerio Valeri has argued, sacrificial violence 'creates a strong impression and therefore a *memory*' (1985: 69–70). Assassinations of husbands and fathers, in particular when they are public or publicized, symbolize in a spectacular and memorable fashion the autonomy of female heirs.[41] Moreover, their death, like that of martyrs and saints, can become a source of considerable (magical) power, also providing the successor with the means to mediate between this world and the next. When running for President, Cory Aquino did much to present her slain husband Ninoy as a martyr. At the time, she was described as an almost religious figure, very similar to the *baylan* or spirit medium:

> Cory Aquino has consistently presented herself as a medium of her assassinated husband, whose spirit is invoked in almost all her speeches. But, as always, native spirits have merged with the Christian faith. . . . The commonly held belief that Cory Aquino did not seek the presidency, but was guided to it by Ninoy, or even God, is one of the strongest foundations of her power. It makes her the greatest and possibly only unifying force in the country.[42]

We have encountered similar forms of mediation – and similar representations – of female leaders in the cases of Chamorro and Zia.

Finally, rather than doing without their husbands, female leaders can tolerate them. What we have then is a complete gender inversion because the husband also participates in the role switch. This variation now deserves our attention because, rather than conflicting with the argument of this essay, it confirms it in a surprising way.

VI

Not all female leaders are unmarried or widows. As we have seen, quite a few of them had considerable influence long before they became widows, and some ruled effectively alongside a (weak) king or emperor. But what can one say about married women who were rulers in their own right like Maria Theresa and, more recently, Margaret Thatcher in England, Benazir Bhutto in Pakistan, and a number of English and Dutch queens in the nineteenth and twentieth centuries?

In all these cases the pattern of gender inversion turns out to be even more distinct and complete, since *both* partners switch roles. Rather than conflict with the general pattern that is unfolding in the material under discussion, they further illustrate and confirm it. The prince consort usually figures in the background; he forms a striking contrast with his female counterpart or first lady.[43] Sometimes he is unpopular, like the French husband of Maria Theresa.[44] At other times he is taken to task and ridiculed, as was Denis Thatcher.[45] In many cases he is virtually unknown abroad. The history of prince consorts suggests that their survival depends on their low profile. Apart from important exceptions to be discussed later on, it seems that in modern societies, too, married female leaders cannot dispense with male symbols to mark their role as leaders.

Dolores Ibarruri, 'La Pasionaria' (1895–1989), the indomitable Basque co-founder of the Spanish Communist Party, who won international fame during the Spanish Civil War as a fiery orator and organizer, came from a poor miner's family in the mountains near Bilbao. At the age of 20, she married Julian Ruiz, a miner from Asturias who had migrated to the Basque country. She had six children, but only two of them survived childhood. In the 1920s, after she had helped to found the Spanish Communist Party, Ibarruri emerged as a spellbinding orator and organizer. The more she became involved in politics, the more the bonds of marriage weakened. In the 1930s, she separated from her husband and moved to Madrid. In those years she also visited the Soviet Union (where she had sent her two surviving children for schooling). During the Civil War she became the most visible Spanish Communist and acquired the reputation of a fearless woman. She left Spain in 1938 for the Soviet Union, to return only after Franco's death. In her autobiography she says very little about her husband.[46]

As mentioned above, an intriguing figure in the setting of the married female leader is the domesticated husband, the male consort who has accepted a subordinate position, also often literally a place in the background. This is even true of constitutional monarchies like those of Great Britain, Denmark and the Netherlands where sovereigns do not hold much power and are mainly ceremonial figures. At best the prince consort can make himself useful somehow. But he cannot escape some degree of humiliation. Nor can he, with impunity, entirely withdraw from the female role imposed on him that entails, in the first place, accepting that his children do not inherit his name but their mother's. Significantly, his role involves other restrictions with respect to his civil rights and public appearance.[47]

The subordination of these males may have been for many of them an embarrassing, even tragic, experience. But the symbolic inversion in which they willy-nilly played their part is entirely consistent with gender differentiation found in all societies – the fundamental distinction all people make between male and female, however much the notions of masculinity and femininity may vary according to their specific cultural and historical contexts. Moreover, this role reversal fits gender hierarchy, the near-universal pattern of the public dominance of men over women. The role switching which we see occurring in all varieties of female leadership does not effectively change the definition of gender roles themselves, although the latter may be challenged and called into question in the process.[48]

VII

From the biographies of female leaders there emerges a well-known theme: a man who marries a queen or a crown princess will never become a king himself, but a woman who marries a king or crown prince will always become a queen.

It is tempting to see in the operation of this principle a sign of the subordination of men rather than of women: tempting, but of course incorrect, because it confuses personal with social levels. In fact, this asymmetric arrangement suggests the opposite: an affirmation of male supremacy and the subordination of women in marriage. *Mésalliance* always tend to include more restrictions for women than for men. There is, in general (not only in India), a greater sensitivity toward hypogamy than toward hypergamy.[49] The former (a woman marrying below her status) is an anomaly, for it is in conflict with the patriarchal order in which women are both persons and currency. The latter form (a woman marrying above her status) fits patriarchal arrangements quite neatly, and is, therefore, also more prevalent.

In their role of ruler, chief or sovereign, men are powerful enough to make their wives publicly prominent (or allow them to be so), without violating the logic of gender classification (male/female, strong/weak, dominant/subordinate, public/private). Consider the profiles of Eva Perón, Jiang Qing, Elena Ceausescu, Winnie Mandela, Imelda Marcos, Nexhmije Hoxha and other first ladies who came close to replacing their husband rulers. But women as 'queens', as political leaders in their own right, have to present and represent themselves as males, since tolerating a powerful man next to them would force them back again into the role of a (subordinate) female. Hence the switching of roles – and hence the striking 'singleness' among women leaders.[50]

Through marriage to a male leader, a woman can become a 'queen'. But a man can never expect to become a 'king' by marrying a female leader. On the contrary, he becomes weak, insignificant (if he had not been so from the start), and he sometimes has reason to fear for his life.

What at first sight appears to be a privilege of women turns out to be an instance of the persistence of patriarchal relations. Even societies where the power balances between the sexes have become considerably less unequal, as has happened in certain western democratic nation-states, evince a structural opposition between first ladies (strong, male, public) and prince consorts (weak, female, private).

Female rulers can be seen as 'normal exceptions', as extreme cases which illuminate dominant cultural codes.[51] The androgynous symbolism of female leaders can then serve as an index of patriarchal relations. If there is no need for a female leader to mark her role with masculine symbols, it may reflect a pattern of more equal gender relations. This seems to be the case in Norway, where for several years the Prime Minister was a woman. Gro Harlem Brundtland (b. 1939) is from an elite family in Oslo. She studied medicine and obtained a Ph.D from Harvard. She is married and has four children. Her husband, Arne Olav, whose name she adopted, has a similar background and is also a prominent politician. They share domestic chores. Significantly, nearly half the members Brundtland's cabinet (1985–9) were women, who also form an important contingent in the Norwegian Parliament.[52]

Various women have become powerful as the consort of a male ruler or sovereign. Among female rulers we see the reverse. If their husbands were not weak and insignificant from the start, they inevitably became so in the course of their careers, as is also evident from the dynastic history of constitutional monarchies in western Europe. Where a woman in the position of consort can develop into a political figure in her own right – or at least becomes a 'first lady', the opposite awaits a male consort: he gets enveloped in a process of social atrophy, suffering a loss of identity no one can stop, reverse or avoid.

The asymmetry between first ladies and prince consorts, and the ambiguity of female leaders, are also reflected in the terminology. As Denise O'Brien has correctly reminded us, the meaning of the word 'queen' is wider than that of 'king', since 'queen' refers both to the wife of a king and to the woman who is sovereign or ruler in her own right.[53] Ruler-queens may, in Great Britain, for instance, have husbands, but they may not have husbands who are kings. Queen Elizabeth I of England, being unmarried, was both king and queen, as one of her advisers reminded her. A marriage would have turned her into a queen consort, which would have presented a considerable loss of power and status.[54]

Thus the logic of gender relations also governs the life and career of the female leader as upstart: the 'queen' or 'first lady', or the woman as the consort of a male leader. At first sight this variation seems to contradict the general pattern, since these women have assumed positions of power and have become political figures in their own right under the patronage of their husband-rulers. But their ascendancy to power often coincided with the gradual withdrawal, absence, indifference or demise of their husband, or anticipated his departure, as happened with Wu, Catherine the Great, Eva Perón, Jiang Qing, Imelda Marcos, Winnie Mandela and Nexhmije Hoxha.

On closer inspection, therefore, these first ladies bear a strong resemblance to other female rulers, most notably the widows who loom so large in our portrait gallery. First, their position is similar to that of the widows before they lost their husbands. Second, neither the widows nor these first ladies were subordinated, controlled or dominated by men. These similarities were not lost on Jiang Qing, who, in anticipation of Mao's death, studied the careers of famous Chinese empresses.[55] As mentioned above, a significant feature in the political tableau of first ladies is their relationship with a ruler who is unwilling or not in a position (because he is absent, ailing, aged or enfeebled) to subordinate his wife.

The autonomy of first ladies can indeed become considerable.[56] Their sway is evident not only from the actual power positions some of them have obtained, but also from the way they actively plan to succeed their husband after his death. In some cases the succession seems to have been taken entirely for granted. Hence the reference to 'dynasties'. It was assumed that Elena Ceausescu, already Deputy Prime Minister and member of Romania's Politburo, would take over when her husband's rule came to an end.[57] Imelda Marcos entertained serious ambitions to succeed her husband as President, and at one point criticized Mao's widow Jiang Qing for her wrong timing. As one report phrased it:

> If things had worked out for Imelda, Marcos's virility would have founded a dynasty in the Philippines. Two of her children have held office, and Imelda herself apparently harbored ambitions of succeeding her husband as president. Years ago she criticized Mao Zedong's widow Jiang Qing, for allowing power to slip through her fingers. 'She didn't move fast enough', said Imelda. But then the Marcos regime collapsed, like one of her own airy fantasies.[58]

A similar situation existed in Albania, where it is generally believed that the wife of Enver Hoxha ran the country with Ramiz Alia (who later became Hoxha's successor) during the illness that marked the last ten years of her husband's life.[59] Other first ladies who have assumed the characteristics of wicked queens and wielded great power behind the throne include Mirjana Markovic, the wife of Serbia's President Slobodan Milosevic, and Agathe Habyarimana, wife of the former President of Rwanda, who allegedly masterminded and led the genocide in 1994.[60]

Although seriously ill, but strongly supported by the *descamisados*, Eva Perón tried to become Vice-President in 1951, but her attempts were thwarted by the army. More than twenty years later, Perón's second wife Isabel was more successful, and when the dictator died in the summer of 1974, she succeeded him as President. But within two years an army coup terminated her (disastrous) political career.[61]

A more recent example of the rise and fall of an aspirant first lady is provided by Winnie Mandela in South Africa. She owed much of her stature as a female leader to her charismatic husband and his spectacular absence. Reportedly, she harboured ambitions to succeed him. It is significant that her trial and conviction, which foreshadowed her political demise, coincided with the return of her husband.[62] The case of Winnie Mandela is of particular interest for understanding the symbolic realism of female leaders, since it demonstrates, almost in an experimental way, the critical importance of the absence of the husband for successful female leadership.[63]

Semra Ozal is the wife of Turkey's late President Turgut Ozal. She was his favourite candidate to head the Istanbul branch of the Motherland Party he founded in 1983 and led for six years as Prime Minister. The proliferation of Ozal's brothers and in-laws in positions of power fed charges of dynasty, and Semra's candidacy has sparked off charges (which she denied) that she desires to become Prime Minister herself one day.[64]

VIII

The social background and upward mobility of female leaders may help account for their popular bent and enormous appeal. Like the actress Camila Perichole in Thornton Wilder's famous tale, several female leaders came from poor and marginal families and had worked in entertainment and show business before rising to power and demonstrating their sense of performance in the political arena. No less significantly, some of these women grew up in peripheral areas before moving to metropolitan centres.

Wu and Ci Xi had started their careers as concubines.[65] Eva Perón was an actress and came from a humble family in the little town of Los Toldos, where her unwed mother allegedly ran a poorly disguised brothel. Isabel Perón had a similar background. She was an itinerant dancer and later worked in night-clubs. It was in one of these cabarets, in far-off Panama, that she caught the eye of the exiled Perón.[66] Jiang Qing had also been an actress in a travelling theatre group, and had acted in films before she met Mao.[67]

Although from a class of landed elites (in the southern area of Leyte), Imelda Marcos had, as a young girl, known relative poverty and humiliation. Later she moved to Manila and became a singer and beauty queen, in which capacities she drew the attention of the successful politician Marcos, who married her within days after their first meeting.[68] Her life was 'marked by a series of transitions – from relative poverty to relative wealth, from countryside to city, from clerical obscurity to cover-girl prominence' (Rafael 1990: 287). Imelda's vicissitudes contain all the materials for the fashioning of a Cinderella, a motif which cannot have been lost on the Philippine masses.[69]

IX

Female leaders find themselves in an intermediate position on a number of scores. Obviously women, but occupying positions normally held by men, they are both male and female, yet also neither. As social males they defy classification, yet help sustain asymmetric gender relations.[70]

Their ambiguity is further enhanced by their age. Many of them have been older and hence less sexually specified. But their ambiguity is most dramatically symbolized by their rejection of the roles of wife and mother.[71] Virtually everywhere, female leaders have been 'single': that is, unencumbered by male control and tutelage. They cannot, therefore, but present themselves as men, adopting, in various ways, male attributes and symbols in order to assume and be invested with the socially defined male functions and legitimize their position as leaders.

The style in which they present themselves (and are represented by others) and the iconography of their rule vary with the context within which they operate and are also, of course, an expression of their personality. But behind the idiosyncrasies and cultural particulars epitomized in nicknames, like 'Maid of Orleans', 'Iron Lady', 'Woman with the Whip', 'Semiramis of the North', 'Pasionaria', 'White-Boned Demon', 'Saint Cory' and 'Steel Butterfly', loom specific and recurrent features, structural similarities and family resemblances, all of which suggest the existence of a more general pattern that cannot be fully understood in terms of local contexts only.

What connects all these cases of female leaders with one another is their relative autonomy from a husband and consequent anomaly and ambiguity. As widows, virgins and viragos, either *de facto* or imagined, they represent single women. The secret of female leaders lies in their relationship to masculinity rather than in their relationship to men. Not dominated or subordinated by a husband (or father), they have become, socially, culturally and politically, men in their own right. Moreover, they derive power, specifically magical power, from the contradiction inherent in being androgynous women. Hence their propensity to fascinate (from *fascinum*, spell), to cast a spell. Discussing the charm of Imelda Marcos as a female performer, Rafael remarks:

Charm suggests the ability to fascinate, to compel the attention of others as if by magic. Its Latin root, *carm* (song or magical formula), points to the necessarily performative, even theatrical nature of that which is charming. Because of its association with ritual magic, the power to charm in one sense can be understood as the ability to present oneself as both source and object of desire. As various accounts indicate, Imelda's body and voice forced people to watch and listen in rapt expectation. (1990: 288)

Their ambiguities may help to explain why many female leaders have enchanted millions of people and often assumed legendary proportions while still alive. As Naipaul has pointed out, of Eva Perón there remains only the legend. And there is no lack of materials for legends in this realm. The Cinderella motif marks any number of female leaders. One learns about beautiful young women who have miraculously risen from a poor and marginal existence and have, often by way of the magic of the performing arts, become veritable fairy queens, amassing and displaying immense fortunes. Naipaul writes: 'The display of fairy-tale wealth – wealth beyond imagination coming to someone who was poor – added to the Evita legend' (1980: 168). Conspicuous consumption also pertains to other first ladies, most notoriously and recently Imelda Marcos, whose extravagances stretch the imagination and will remain enshrined in the synecdoche of her baffling collection of shoes.[72]

The ambiguity of female leaders can also help us to understand why many of them are credited with a strong charisma. Almost invariably, they are described as charismatic leaders. Like the terms 'charm' and 'fascination', the term 'charisma' (from the Latin *charis*, favour or grace) is derived from the religious sphere. Since Max Weber's coinage, it has been used to designate a form of leadership in which – usually under circumstances of social disruption – supernatural, extraordinary powers or qualities are ascribed to individuals who, one way or another, set themselves apart from ordinary people. Weber understood charisma to refer to

> an *extraordinary* quality of a person, regardless of whether this quality is actual, alleged, or presumed. 'Charismatic authority', hence, shall refer to a rule over men, whether predominantly external or predominantly internal, to which the governed submit because of their belief in the extraordinary quality of the specific *person*. . . . The legitimacy of their rule rests on the belief in and the devotion to the extraordinary, which is valued because it goes beyond the normal human qualities, and which was originally valued as supernatural. The legitimacy of charismatic rule thus rests upon the belief in magical powers. . . . (Weber 1958a: 295–6)[73]

Quite a few female leaders have come to power in situations of social disruption and upheaval, and it seems likely that such circumstances have contributed to facilitate their rise to power if not helped to legitimate their leadership. In periods marked by conspiracies and coups, by revolts and civil wars, by faction fights and political assassinations, the leadership of these women often appeared the only option. Consider late sixteenth-century France (the age of Catherine de Medici), nineteenth- and twentieth-century China, Spain in the 1930s, post-war Argentina, the Philippines, India, South Africa, Nicaragua, Bangladesh, Sri Lanka and Pakistan in our own time; but consider also the divided realm of early fifteenth-century France, which formed the stage for the appearance of the 'Maid of Orleans'. She is perhaps the most prototypical female leader – ideal of (and model for) numerous aspirant female leaders, even beyond Europe, who could see in her refusal to marry and her determination to wear only men's clothing an attempt to break away from the bonds of female subordination. About these two powerful symbols, Warner writes in her biography of Joan of Arc:

> The concept of virginity which she embodied – literally – had enormous power in her culture. Juxtaposed to the vivisected and dismembered body of the kingdom, her virginity provided an urgent symbol of integrity. By synecdoche, Joan's sexuality stood for the whole of her, and in the ambitions of her supporters, for the whole of France. (1983: 50)

> Through her transvestism, she abrogated the destiny of womankind. She could thereby transcend her sex; she could set herself apart and usurp the privileges of the male and his claim to superiority. At the same time, by never pretending to be other than a woman and a maid, she was usurping a man's function but shaking off the trammels of his sex altogether to occupy a different, third order, neither male nor female, but unearthly, like the angels whose company she loved. (1983: 152)[74]

The ambiguity of female leaders explains not only their charisma, their acknowledged claims to supernatural power; it may also account for their sustained and frequently successful performance as mediators between warring parties in a divided realm. Sometimes, their mediation was cast in the idiom of sainthood. At other times it resulted in remarkably long reigns, like those of the Chinese empresses Wu and Ci Xi, the queens Elizabeth I and Catherine de Medici, the empresses Maria Theresa and Catherine the Great, and the reigns of the constitutional queens Victoria and Wilhelmina.

X

My thesis that female leaders have to be single, either *de facto* or symbolically, for classificatory reasons, is also confirmed by two comparative studies that came to my attention while revising this essay. I have

already referred to the work of Fraser (1989) on warrior queens, most
of whom turn out to have been widows, unmarried or otherwise free
from male domination (the relevance of which, however, is lost on the
author, who insists on seeing them as 'appendages' of men). Kelly and
Boutilier (1978), who studied the careers of about twenty active political women, find very similar patterns and conclude as follows: 'The
women in our study who became politically active (1) waited until their
husbands died, (2) had husbands who strongly supported their efforts,
or (3) did not get into any long term family involvement with men at all'
(1978: 157).

Some similarities in the lives and careers of female leaders have been
recognized by female leaders themselves. Their observations further
attest to the general pattern outlined in this essay, although the protagonists, like their biographers, are more inclined to emphasize differences
and unique features. Both Indira Gandhi and Cory Aquino identified
with Joan of Arc. While accompanying her father during a visit to Indira
Gandhi in June 1972, Benazir Bhutto could not help but notice her host's
prolonged staring at her. Guessing at the meaning of Indira's gaze, she
writes in her autobiography: 'Perhaps she was recalling the diplomatic
missions on which she had accompanied her own father, I thought to
myself. Was she seeing herself in me, a daughter of another statesman?'[75]

Reflecting on the similarities American journalists had observed
between Cory Aquino and Benazir Bhutto, the latter acknowledges that
they both came from landowning families, had both been educated in
the United States, and had both lost beloved family members to dicta-
tors. But she insists on the relevance of important differences, like the
support of the military and the church that Aquino had enjoyed and she
had lacked.[76] Empress Ci Xi liked to compare herself to her contemporary, Queen Victoria, whom she admired.[77] As mentioned before, Jiang
Qing began comparing herself to various Chinese empresses when Mao
was growing older and the issue of succession had to be addressed.[78]
Imelda Marcos recognized a certain likeness to Jiang Qing, but was not
flattered when compared to Eva Perón.[79]

In the biographies of female leaders, comparisons are no less rare.
Similarities are at best hinted at in a random fashion and usually miss
the point. But I found useful suggestions in the reviews of Buruma (1986;
1987) and the work of Terrill. Both have a comparative consciousness
and an eye for historical and cultural parallels. As Terrill observes in his
biography of Jiang Qing:

Her story is one of extraordinary will. Wolves, men, illnesses – she was
always doing battle with an enemy. At the age of nineteen, she cut all past
ties to go alone to one of the world's biggest, most dangerous cities and

try her luck in the arts. Always she felt poised on the tightrope of her will. Fame and power lay waiting on one side; infamy and subjection glared from the other. Like Joan of Arc, she was focused upon herself and she saw visions. Like Eva Perón, she watched almost as a spectator her performances before the masses who were her audience. Like Eleanor Roosevelt, she displayed single-mindedness and belief in herself in picking up power that slipped from a weakened husband. (1984: 18)

Like Joan of Arc and Catherine the Great before them, Eva Perón and Imelda Marcos have themselves become icons. Discussing Winnie Mandela's trial and undoing, one reporter observes that within two years, 'South Africa's Eva Perón, revered by her followers, had been transformed into its Imelda Marcos'.[80] In Turkish newspapers, images have been drawn of the politically ambitious wife of the Turkish President, Semra Ozal, as a latter-day Eva Perón or Imelda Marcos.[81]

In a fine study that the anthropologist Julie Taylor has written on the myths of Eva Perón, she occasionally ventures into comparisons, suggesting certain similarities, but is cautious in this regard: 'But from the mass of detail concerning different images of Eva emerge suggestions that links may exist among these disparate cases of powerful women. Only by amassing similar detail concerning such women and others can these links be examined or new ones postulated' (1979: 11). This is what I have tried to do in these notes on the symbolic realism of female leaders. The limiting case of the 'female husband' among the Nyoro and the Shilluk proves instructive. Because of the explicit rejection of the roles of wife and mother and assumption of the social and legal rights of a father, her leadership clarifies the position of female rulers elsewhere.

Many questions remain, but perhaps we may be certain about this much. These female leaders are all singular women. Yet they resemble each other, each being governed, to a greater or lesser extent, by the dialectics of gender in patriarchal societies, and having to convey and symbolize their singularity as social males by some form of singleness.

12

Rediscovering *Ars Moriendi*

He turns toward the wall, lying on his side with one hand on his cheek,
instinctively imitating the classical attitude of the dying when they had had
enough of the world.

Ariès, *The Hour of our Death*

I

Because she believed that anthropologists know a great deal about other
cultures, a Dutch friend of mine asked me some time ago whether
euthanasia and assisted suicide are practised in other societies, and if so,
which forms they assume and what light that may throw on medical decisions and practices concerning the termination of life in our society.

We commonly associate euthanasia with a gentle, easy death, with the
act of painlessly putting to death a person suffering from an incurable
and painful disease or condition, or with the assisted suicide of a person
who is terminally ill and suffers unbearably. Euthanasia can be active or
passive, direct or indirect, practised with or without the approval of the
patient. Although defined as major offences in the Dutch Criminal Code
(Articles 293 and 294), both euthanasia and physician-assisted suicide
are *de facto* legalized in the Netherlands – a country that also takes pride
in its social policy of pragmatic tolerance toward abortion, prostitution
and drugs. Legislators and medical specialists in the Netherlands today
recognize only one form of euthanasia: the situation in which a doctor
kills a person who is suffering intolerably and hopelessly, at the patient's
explicit request. Among other things, the physician has to report the case
to the judiciary.[1] As we shall see, things are more complicated because
cases of abstinence[2] and pain relief are often difficult to distinguish from

232

active euthanasia, while the termination of life without an explicit request is defined as 'normal medical practice'.[3] Moreover, the scale is huge and reporting rates remain low. Of 2,700 cases in 1990 only 18 per cent were reported. Of the 3,600 cases in 1995 just over 40 per cent were reported. Medical termination of life without an explicit request in that year amounted to almost 40,000 cases.[4]

Scanning the ethnographic literature on euthanasia and assisted suicide in other societies yielded few results. We know a great deal about rites of passage, which essentially mark transitions between one social status and the other (birth, initiation, marriage, death). In particular we are well informed about funeral rituals, mourning practices and attitudes toward death. But anthropologists are strikingly silent (reluctant?) about the subject of euthanasia. Some of them argue that euthanasia only occurs in the modern world.[5]

The lack of systematic attention from anthropologists tells little about the nature and frequency of euthanasia practices. Sometimes the interests of scholars are out of step with the importance of a phenomenon. The question, then, is why euthanasia has received so little attention in the ethnographic literature. Some answers suggest themselves.

II

First, until recently, anthropologists neglected the place in society, and treatment, of the elderly, although these people were often their main informants. This lacuna may be related to the modest role of elderly people in economic activities in which anthropologists were always primarily interested – a preference that is still reflected in prevailing classifications of societies (hunting and gathering, horticulture, pastoralism, agrarian, pre-industrial, and so on). But their bias may also have been due to the low regard for older people in their own society.[6]

Second, euthanasia is notoriously difficult to pinpoint. We are not only concerned with things people prefer to hide from outsiders. At issue are matters that are located in the border zone of homicide and suicide, and practices that stand midway between doing and abstaining. Every society offers numerous possibilities and forms of non-treatment, abstinence, silent neglect and 'accidents': not only in the heart of the community – the domestic domain – but also in public places and enclaves like hospitals and prisons. I am reminded of an old, demented widow in the Dutch village where I grew up in the 1940s. She was no longer called for supper and pined away in a dark barn, mocked and chased around by the children of the neighbourhood. Another example that comes to mind is the death of Don Lopez in Buñuel's film *Tristana* (1970). Instead of calling the doctor, the heroine opens the windows to allow cold air into the room.

Plate 7 *Death and the Maiden*, or Death as Lover. Hans Baldung Grien. About 1515. Ocffentliche Kunstsammlung *Kunstmuseum Basle*, *Switzerland*

Not only elderly people but also children, especially girls, died because of insidious neglect by kinsmen.[7] Partly for these reasons, ethnographers may have brought cases of euthanasia under different categories and classified them as homicide, gerontocide, senilicide, infanticide, neonaticide, suicide, assisted suicide, or death from natural causes. Harris, for example, believes that infanticide 'is widely practiced among low-energy primitives'. He also offers an explanation: 'Severely handicapped infants and children do not normally survive to adulthood among low-energy primitive groups, precisely because such groups cannot afford to support adults who do not contribute their full share of subsistence and defense' (1971: 287). Similar reasons are mentioned to explain cases of gerontocide.[8] In his comparative survey of dying in tribal societies, Simmons notes that 'suicide by the aged might result from neglect, abandonment, or any other trying circumstance' (1970: 229).[9]

In modern societies, too, transitions between these categories are gradual. In the Netherlands, as we have noted, the legislator defines euthanasia and assisted suicide as criminal offences. Yet criminal proceedings are waived when doctors follow a well-defined procedure, and meet the so-called 'requirements of careful practice'. However, in his participant research on decision-making processes about the issue of dying in a Dutch hospital, the anthropologist Pool shows how hard it is to distinguish between a palliative-abstaining treatment, pain medication, euthanasia and assisted suicide – and how 'euthanasia' as a separate category of practices is constructed (1996: 154–5).[10] Pool's findings confirm Chabot's views on the proximity of abstinence (from life-prolonging treatment), pain medication and euthanasia (Chabot 1996: 25–7). It should be remembered that in the United States abstinence and pain relief in this context are categorized as 'passive euthanasia', whereas in the Netherlands, as previously mentioned, the same medical interventions are defined as 'normal medical practice'.[11]

III

But the main reason why so little is known about the practices of euthanasia in other cultures is that anthropologists have focused on *post-mortem* beliefs and practices rather than on the issue of dying and dying people. In their survey of the literature on death, Palgi and Abramovich write: 'When reading through the anthropological literature in one large sweep, one is left with the impression of coolness and remoteness. The focus is on the bereaved and on the corpse but never on the dying' (1984: 385).[12]

Other scholars, too, argue that research into dying is just beginning.[13] Elias suggests that this reluctance to confront dying goes back to the strong taboos with which the subject is surrounded in western societies.

Everything related to death, in particular the process of dying and the dying themselves, has been placed behind the scenes of social life in the course of the civilizing process:

> Closely bound up, in our day, with the greatest possible exclusion of death and dying from social life, and with the screening-off of dying people from others, from children in particular, is a peculiar embarrassment felt by the living in the presence of dying people. They often do not know what to say. (1985: 23)

> They find it difficult to press dying people's hands or to caress them, to give them a feeling of undiminished protection and belonging. Civilization's overgrown taboo on the expression of strong, spontaneous feelings ties their tongues and their hands. (1985: 28)

This distancing from the human realities of dying also pervades ethnographic research on death and funerals. Hence the scarce attention given to euthanasia, assisted suicide and kindred forms of death-hastening practices.[14] Hence also the likelihood of *under-reporting* and the possibility of creating a blind spot in ethnography.

The strong feelings evoked by euthanasia in western societies fit a particular cultural–historical development, in which everything related to the organic aspects of human life – not only eating, sleeping, sexuality and the use of violence, but also death and dying (with their unmistakable aspects of violence) is removed from public life and pushed behind the scenes.[15] The dying are left alone. Death is denied and no longer a subject of discussion.[16] In this regard, western medicine became a victim of its own success. Physicians fight a battle against death rather than against diseases.[17] Unintentionally, and not without irony, advanced medical technology has produced a prolonged dying process that entails much suffering and pain. In the medicalization of death, dying is no longer a natural event; it has become a condition to be fought with the most advanced means. In the apt phrase of Ariès, 'death is denied by masking it with disease'.

IV

In a comparative study of medical practice in the United States and China, Sankar shows that western attitudes toward death contributed to the physician's aversion to elderly people. (As we shall see, deterioration of physical appearance is an important determinant of contempt for elderly people.) From the perspective of the physician, old age is the ultimate incurable disease. There is no hope of recovery. This is an important fact; it is at odds with the goals of modern medicine. Hence the tendency to avoid elderly patients and the reluctance to treat them when they visit the doctor's office: 'When the incapacitated, incontinent nursing-home resident who has been ignored by the medical profession for years starts to die, the most sophisticated and expensive medical technology is called into play and heroic efforts are made to save a life. Death is not a natural occurrence, but one to be treated "aggressively"' (Sankar 1984: 274).

In the Chinese system, on the contrary, people go out of their way to treat pre-terminal patients and to reduce their suffering. They surround them with devoted care. Pain and stress are treated seriously, including that of family members. But as soon as someone is dying all medical efforts are stopped and one lets the patient die.[18]

This form of passive euthanasia (abstaining, non-treatment, stopping life-prolonging therapies) accords with a society where people are familiar with death, where the living and the dead are less separated and life and death less polarized, where the dying are not abandoned but surrounded by kinsmen, where the will and the means to extend the life of the dying in anonymous ways are lacking.

More active forms of euthanasia are found in tribal societies, including the Inuit and the Tiwi in northern Australia. Examples from within Eskimo communities are well known. If elderly people could no longer help others or sustain themselves, they were abandoned or killed. As long as an old woman could make herself useful by chewing frozen garments into softness she was a respected member of the community. If her teeth wore down and she could not do this job any longer, she usually withdrew and committed suicide by exposing herself on the ice to the cold.[19] Referring to Rasmussen (1908) and Hutton (1929), among others, Simmons describes the way in which the elderly among the Eskimo were treated:

> Old women too feeble to travel stayed indoors, attended household chores, repaired garments, tanned leather – chewing it to make it soft – and shredded with their worn teeth the sinew of dried caribou and narwhal. . . . Enfeebled Labrador Eskimo women eked out a meager existence at indoor jobs such as plaiting straw hats and baskets, caring for wearing apparel, and attending to the family boots. When a pair of boots has been worn for some time, during a few hours in warm weather they absorb moisture and become nearly half an inch thick on the soles. When taken off they must be turned inside out and dried, then chewed and scraped by some old woman who is only too glad to have the work for the two or three biscuits she may receive as pay. (1970: 83–4)

Gerontocide and suicide did not take place among all Inuit people to the same extent, and, moreover, involved only elderly people with serious handicaps. About north-western Alaska Burch remarks: 'Abandonment occurred in situations [of the most extreme hardships] in which old people had to be sacrificed or everyone would have starved to death' (1975: 149).[20] Of the central-eastern Eskimo, Graburn reports: 'Often the old people would ask to be left behind or even killed if they felt they were useless' (1969: 73). Guemple found the same duality among elderly people among the Eskimos he studies. Elderly people experience a

> marked reduction in both respect and affection when they are no longer able to make a useful contribution. As they grow older and are increasingly immobilized by age, disease and the like, they are transformed into neglected dependants without influence and without consideration. . . . To alleviate the burden of infirmity, the old people are done away with. (1969: 65, 69)

According to Freuchen, Eskimos do not have a fear of death, 'they only know love of life' (1961: 145). Among the elderly of this people one finds more cases of suicide than neglect. Freuchen points at the aspects of honour, reputation and reciprocity:

> When an old man sees the young men go out hunting and cannot himself go along, he is sorry. When he has to ask other people for skins for his clothing, when he cannot ever again be the one to invite neighbours to eat his game, life is of no value to him. Rheumatism and other ills may plague him, and he wants to die. (1961: 145)

The anthropologist Rasing provides more precise information about suicide among elderly Inuit in his research of a case of assisted suicide among the Inuit in eastern Canada (the area of Baffin Island and Melville Peninsula), which took place in December 1962.[21] A leader of about 69 who had fallen seriously ill and felt his strength giving away made it known that he wanted to die and obtained help from others: one got the gun, another loaded it, and a third handed him the weapon. In this extended case study Rasing discusses in detail the circumstances and the implications of the event. He argues that suicide among the elderly of this people has to be understood against the background of an unfriendly climate and a number of compelling rules. There was an expectation that each adult would make a contribution to the survival of the group. Nobody was allowed to monopolize the natural resources; animals did not belong to anyone until they were caught, and hunters were obliged to share their catch with others. The Canadian authorities could not, of course, accept this case of assisted suicide, and Rasing points at the tensions between the survival strategies of the hunters and the rules of Canadian law.[22]

Only fragmentary information is available about other nomadic peoples. Among the Tiwi, when hard-pressed, one disposed of old and sick people by burying them up to their necks.[23] As among other Australian peoples, it sometimes happened that elderly persons expressed the desire not to live any longer and requested to be abandoned.[24] About this custom, the Berndts write: 'Aborigines on the whole treat their old people fairly well. But there are cases of neglect; and in desert regions during bad seasons, when a horde is on the move, it may be forced to leave its old people behind to starve or die of thirst' (1988: 210).[25]

Severe circumstances also play a role in the practices of active euthanasia among agrarian people, including those in northern Japan. Exposing elderly and sick people to the elements by carrying them up to a high mountain is the subject of the Japanese film *Narayama Bushi-ko* (1983), directed by Shokei Imamura.[26] These forms of senilicide, gerontocide, death-hastening practices, suicide and voluntary withdrawal show family resemblances with what in the western world is described as abstaining, assistance with suicide and euthanasia.

For the loaded word 'euthanasia' no euphemism has yet been found. Chabot points at the 'indelible pollution' of the concept by the Nazis.[27] The term 'death-hastening practices', coined by Glascock, suggests itself as a fitting alternative. These practices form the counterpart of the prolonged terminal phase that has become an integral part of medical practice in the modern world.[28] Pool argues convincingly that the distinction between euthanasia (on request) and assisted suicide is somewhat artificial: 'Since in both cases the individual takes the decision to terminate his or her life, one may use the term "suicide", that is, if one has to choose a single term' (1996: 224–5).

The boundaries between voluntary euthanasia and suicide were blurred even more after the death of the 66-year-old Australian cancer patient Bob Dent in September 1996. He is allegedly the first person in the world who died as a consequence of legal active euthanasia or assisted suicide. His physician Philip Nitschke applied an IV injection after which Dent himself pushed the computer button to inject the lethal dose.[29]

Apart from the similarities between death-hastening practices there are also, of course, important differences. But what strikes us in the examples from tribal and agrarian societies is the self-evident character of, and the extent of institutionalization associated with, these forms of dying. Termination of life – in whatever form – is part of the culture in question. Rather than punishable practices, we are concerned with established, sometimes honorific, customs by which people are guided and with which they go along.

V

It would be naïve to neglect the question of the constraints of others (family members, friends, colleagues) in any form of so-called voluntary practices. Also in our society a request for euthanasia may result from social pressure, and be initiated by the wish 'not to be a bother to other people'. In his research in Dutch hospitals, the sociologist Hilhorst concludes that family members, doctors and nurses often exercise pressure on patients to move them to request euthanasia.[30] Chabot suggests the possibility of an increasing number of assisted suicides (in cases of terminal suffering) resulting from pressure from family members, physicians or caretakers.[31] Exploring the context of dying in hospitals, Pool offers several examples of pressure of family members on physicians, which, however, had little effect.[32] Yet Pool has few doubts about the power of physicians: in all his cases the physician takes the decision about life and death. In one remarkable case the patient made it quite clear that the physician had to take this decision.[33]

Patients who are terminally ill and suffer unbearably and who therefore wish to end their lives, as well as those who want to assist them, run up against the resistance of the legislators, meet with contradictions in the criminal code and are confronted with a strongly divided public opinion which permeates medical care and criminal law. As mentioned above, in the Netherlands, euthanasia and assisted suicide are tolerated (*gedoogd*) but not legalized. They are criminal offences unless specific 'requirements of careful practice' are met. The criteria are laid down by Dutch courts and the Royal Dutch Medical Association (KNMG).[34] In 1993 they were included in a law that stipulates that physicians who do not follow these guidelines will be prosecuted. Briefly, the requirements include the following criteria: (1) the patient is terminally ill and suffers unbearably; (2) the patient's request is voluntary, explicit, serious and sustained; (3) a second opinion is obtained from another physician; (4) the use of the right euthanaticum; and (5) correct information on the cause of death at the judiciary. Physicians following these guidelines will not be prosecuted.[35]

In principle, then, both parties have appearances against them and lack the benefit of the doubt. Their practices are controversial and lack general consensus and respect. Physician and patient operate in the margins of the moral order, partly because euthanasia 'is still killing', partly because dying itself is a liminal event, and partly because there is a large 'grey' area in which increasing palliative care passes easily into death-hastening practices with or without the request of the patient.[36] The evaluation of reporting euthanasia also suggests that the boundaries between deliberate termination of life, on the one hand, and palliative care and fighting symptoms, on the other, are often difficult to draw.[37]

There is an important difference between the position of the physician and that of the patient. While one side requests euthanasia, the other side can honour the request or reject it. In both cases the physician demonstrates his power over the patient and the procedure.[38] For example, the physician may feel that the 'unbearable suffering' which would help justify euthanasia has not yet started.[39] In a report on the Dutch Society for Voluntary Euthanasia, we hear about ignoring critical requests and delaying help: 'Even if a patient meets all the requirements, it is often impossible to find a physician willing to perform euthanasia.'[40] This statement is in accord with the observation of Griffiths et al., who write:

> It seems pretty clear that a patient whose request meets all the legal criteria sometimes experiences great difficulty in finding a doctor willing and – in the light of the limitation to doctors with an established treatment relationship – legally able to carry it out. The whole complex of problems surrounding the availability of euthanasia has yet to receive adequate legal attention. (1998: 108)

To be considered for euthanasia in the Netherlands, a patient (with a bad prognosis) has to go to great lengths – after first overcoming the cultural resistance in him- or herself. A so-called euthanasia certificate, or advance directive, is not sufficient: 'The doctors concerned', writes Griffiths, 'are of the view that such a document "can never take the place of the doctor's judgement about the patient's situation", although they are prepared to take its contents into consideration.'[41] Chabot mentions two reasons why medical doctors are reluctant to accept advanced directives from elderly people who do not want to prolong their unavoidable deterioration. First, dementia does not meet the requirements of 'unbearable suffering'. Second, the demented person is no longer the same person he was when he drew up the certificate. These patients find themselves in a Catch-22 situation:

> 'No' you have and 'no' you can get. If I want to die now, then unbearable and hopeless suffering is not the issue, hence the doctor is not justified in helping me killing myself. If I wait until the diagnosis and my situation is hopeless, then my request is no longer deliberate. (Chabot 1996: 99)[42]

This dilemma – and the power of the physician – are also discussed in one of Pool's descriptions of the decision regarding the request to die (1996: 141–56):

> 'So you could take seriously his request for euthanasia?'
> 'Sure. He was not dementing in a way that would prompt me not to take him seriously in that regard.'

'And why do you think it was not discussed?'
'I believe because his condition was relatively good. That is to say, a good condition, or an acceptable condition.'

Pool's study of decision-making processes concerning euthanasia in a Dutch hospital also shows how education and class influence the relationship with the physician and the treament of the patient. Discussing two cases of young men suffering from AIDS, Pool writes that this ward of the hospital included young and educated people who were well informed (often more so than the physicians) about their illness, the prognosis, the treatment, and the stages through which to obtain euthanasia. Their negotiating position was therefore much stronger than that of the older cancer patients from working-class neighbourhoods who were less verbal and less well organized (1996: 182–3).

The power of the physician *vis-à-vis* the legislator is obvious from the latitude he has in reporting the cause of death.[43] The physicians in the hospital where Pool carried out his research preferred, for instance after increasing morphine, to issue a certificate of natural death to avoid the 'rigmarole' when reporting euthanasia.[44] We mentioned before that Hendin came upon several thousands of cases in which termination of life was the main or attendant goal of palliative care. Yet these cases were all defined in terms of normal medical practice – even if they lacked an explicit request from the patient.[45] Hendin emphasized that the information about euthanasia in the Netherlands suggests that only a minority of the physicians who carried out euthanasia reported the cases correctly. Since then, physicians have reported euthanasia and assisted suicide more often. But in 1995 more than half of the cases went unreported, while termination of life without a request from the patient was hardly reported at all.[46]

These developments led many people to advocate legalization of euthanasia and assisted suicide. This appears most recently from the founding of a new organization, the Society of Voluntary Life (SVL), which aims at a 'legal recognition of the right to kill oneself and of the right to obtain the means to that goal'.[47] Yet it is questionable whether legalization of euthanasia and assisted suicide are the panacea for the various dilemmas. It does not seem likely, for example, that the proposed amendments of the law will ensure the autonomy of the patient or diminish the power of the physician over the patient.[48]

Hendin believes that the practice of euthanasia in the Netherlands sprang from the idea that the power of the doctor over the patient had to be reduced. Ironically, however, it has in fact enlarged his power.[49] Moreover, Hendin expects that legalization of euthanasia will further extend the power of the physician and diminish the autonomy of the patient.[50]

VI

The issues of euthanasia and help in dying (assisted suicide) have confronted society with the dilemmas inherent in a paradoxical medical ethics that has its roots in the denial of death and its related medicalization.[51] In the practice of euthanasia, physician and patient, each in his own way, demonstrate unintentionally how pervasively the taboo on dying has taken root in our society. Palliative care leaves much to be desired and support in the dying process is weakly developed – even in the 300-odd nursing homes of which the Netherlands can boast. This country of over 15 million people has only one hospice (since 1994, and of which a foreigner is a director).[52] There is no social space, no language, no scenario for dying. Strangely enough, in a society in which the dying process has become longer, cultural forms for dying are lacking: there are no prescriptions, no blueprints for dying, indeed, no *artes moriendi*.[53]

This situation forms the setting for a growing interest in the practice designated by the term *versterven*, or 'to let oneself die'. The patient retires, refuses all treatment, abstains from food and drink, and dies without any substantial help from others but with some measure of composure and decorum.[54] There is nothing new about fasting until death follows. In fact, this form of self-help among elderly people is possibly the most frequent (and least studied) form of euthanasia and death-hastening practice in the world.[55]

Versterven by refusing food (also called *inedia*) was, like many other things, already known in antiquity. In his study of self-killing in classical antiquity Van Hooff discusses the practice of *versterven* by refusing food among elderly Greek philosophers and Roman notables.[56] He considers these suicides as cases of 'stylized euthanasia' and emphasizes the aspect of distinction. *Inedia* gives proof of determination and perseverance, and evoked admiration. This form of self-killing was considered honourable and a perfect way to 'lead oneself from life' (1990: 46–7). In antiquity, the way of dying had to be a dignified fulfilment of one's existence and one should not be surprised to find that this preoccupation with *dignitas* was most pronounced among the elite. Among Roman senators, *inedia* was the most frequently used self-killing device (1990: 241).

In a recent dissertation, Pikaar discusses *versterven* by refusing food (*endura*) among the medieval Cathars in the south of France.[57] The Cathars reacted against Roman Catholic orthodoxy and distinguished themselves by their belief in reincarnation and redemption, which they believed could be attained through a sober and ascetic lifestyle and the *consolamentum* – baptism by imposition of hands. In keeping with their lifestyle of moderation and abstinence, the Cathars encouraged *endura* for seriously ill and dying people to reduce their suffering by hastening death. Taking contemporary figures for suicide in the Netherlands as a point of departure, Pikaar suggests the possibility of a modern *endura*, implied in a growing number of cases of the deaths of elderly people (mainly women) by *marasmus*, or undernourishment.[58] She notes that people of the third and fourth age (that is, between 60 and 80 and older than 80 years old) who refuse food are not always suicidal but may be regarded as people who want to die with dignity. Pikaar emphasizes that elderly people who elect to die in this fashion may have been prompted by their loss of status and their social isolation, and the prospect of being taken to a nursing home: 'le cauchemar de l'entrée dans une maison de retraite ou dans un centre hospitalier' (1996: 61–2).[59]

Versterven among elderly intellectuals in India is known as *samadhi*, the last stage of yoga, which can be regarded as 'a well-considered act of the disposal of the body'. We may recall the case of one of India's most venerated personalities, the 87-year-old social reformer Acharya Vinoba Bhave, a religious ascetic, whom many Indians regarded as a Hindu holy man. The *Acharya* (teacher) refused all food, water and medicines after he had had a heart attack ten days earlier.[60] *Samadhi* implies concentration, contemplation, meditation. The term also refers to the grave of a holy man whose body has reached the end-stage (*dehanta*). The idea is that the holy man is liberated from the circle of rebirths.[61]

In his book *Death in Banaras* (1994), especially in the last chapter entitled 'Asceticism and the Conquest of Death', Jonathan Parry mentions *samadhi* and describes this as 'a timeless state of non-duality in which there is neither birth nor death nor any experience of differentiation' (1994: 25). His remarks about a 'good death' also deserve attention:

> Death must be a voluntary relinquishment of life, a *controlled* evacuation of the body. In the paradigmatically 'good' death (*sumaran*), the dying man forgoes all food for some days before death, and consumes only Ganges water. . . . Having previously predicted the time of his going, the dying man gathers his sons about him and – by an act of concentrated will – abandons life. He is not said to die, but to relinquish his body. (1994: 158)[62]

Apart from the obvious differences, there are also striking similarities with the *endura* among the ascetic Cathars, who believed after receiving the sacrament of *consolamentum* that they would escape from their earthly chains and die without falling back again into a new cycle of reincarnation. Both traditions emphasized the idea that by renouncing the world, by ascesis and abstention, by controlling natural processes to which the human body is subjected, they were able to cancel, overcome and conquer the duality of life and death. As in antiquity, both *modi moriendi* implied the elements of respect and dignity, which are also central to the modern *endura*.

About *versterven* and death-hastening practices among the Aborigines in eastern Arnhemland we are informed by Eastwell, a medical doctor who examined forty cases between 1969 and 1980.[63] He found that next to psychosocial factors, somatic conditions played a significant role (in so-called 'voodoo death'), specifically dehydration by refusing to drink. When because of witchcraft or a terminal disease a person does not have any chance of recovery, he or she is considered socially dead. Kinsmen (and often also the patient himself) recognize that death is unavoidable and imminent. As part of the last rites, people sing songs of the ancestors, all medical help is denied, and the patient does not get any water, which means that he or she dies within days. As Eastwell reports:

> The ideology of clanship in Arnhem includes the concept of recycling the individual soul through future generations of the clan. This implies a quality of timelessness to individual life which aids the acceptance of death. The terminal patients often show great relief once the rites have begun. . . .
>
> Maku was an old widow, probably in her late 50s. After a vertebra collapsed (probably from tuberculosis) she was hospitalized for bedrest. We did not think she would die. One morning an old man appeared and said he dreamt she was going to die. He brought singers and dancers who began outside but she was left alone in the room. From that time she was not given water and we were asked not to help her. The health workers did what the old man ordered. Her tongue was misshapen from thirst and she died the next day. There was running water in the hospital room but she made no attempt to reach it, although she could have if she tried. (1982: 13)

Another case Eastwell summarizes as follows:

> D., male, born around 1900. Warner [1937] mentions him as embarking on a political career in which he acquired eight wives. Five of these were sitting at a respectful distance from him in his dying days. His physical disease was prostrate cancer. 'May 16: No fever. Given only small amounts of fluid. May 18: Very little water. May 20: No fever. Died.' *The aspect of euthanasia with the prevention of suffering was paramount in this case.* Three hundred people attended his funeral, with burial five days after death. (1982: 16, my italics)

In a recent essay, the Dutch psychiatrist Chabot also discusses the respectable and relatively painless way of *versterven* in the Netherlands. He explores the connotations of *versterven*, including *afsterven* (to die off), *wegsterven* (to die or fade away, to pine away), and wilfully abstaining from earthly pleasures. He also mentions the prestige attached to this way of dying in antiquity and challenges some prejudices. Referring to recent research, Chabot argues that dehydration 'if going together with good care of the mouth and palliative care can, in seven out of eight cases, go together with well-being' (1996: 182). Chabot is therefore surprised to find out that 'in the Netherlands one rarely hears that many dementing elderly people and terminally ill patients choose spontaneously the way of *versterven*, and especially that this alternative can be made bearable if it goes together with good care' (1996: 189). Referring to the research of a colleague, Chabot wonders why patients who have asked for euthanasia do not themselves take the initiative by abstaining from food. This brings us back again to the finely woven research of Pool into the decision-making around euthanasia in a Dutch hospital. He also found cases of patients who had explicitly and consistently requested euthanasia, but who none the less continued taking their meals and their medicines (1996: 156–8). To explain these contradictions, Pool distinguishes different discourses and different levels of discourse with one and the same patient: an explicit discourse in which the patient explicitly and consistently asks different people for euthanasia and an implicit discourse through which the patient sends signals that he (or she) does not want to die (1996: 219–22).

A Dutch medical doctor and Socialist Member of Parliament points out that little is known about the meaning of requests for euthanasia. He suggests that research should focus on the considerations, wishes and experiences of those who are directly involved – patients and their surviving relatives:

> One should investigate why some people ask for euthanasia, why others who suffer unbearably and hopelessly do not ask for it, and why still others ask for it and later change their mind. We simply do not know this. We know about these things only indirectly, from the point of view of the physician. What we do know is that many requests for euthanasia are not requests for euthanasia, but involve questions of an existential nature.[64]

Opposed to a stylized, dignified *versterven* is the gruesome death Buñuel describes in his autobiography: 'A death that's kept at bay by the miracles of modern medicine, a death that never ends. In the name of Hippocrates, doctors have invented the most exquisite form of torture ever known to man: survival' (1982: 256). Chabot would not have much of a problem with this characterization of high-tech dying. His book with the telling title *Dying Adrift* (1996) can be read as a warning against the unintended prolonging of the dying process. Chabot argues that where medical care is highly developed, the dying process has become longer. He considers this high-tech dying as the main driving force of the euthanasia debate that over the past few years has pervaded the consciousness of the western world. He notes that dying with high-tech care has become a prolonged process of deterioration (1996: 24–9). It looks as if we are dealing with the same paradox Sahlins notes in his essay 'The original affluent society': 'This is the era of unprecedented hunger. Now, in the time of the greatest technical power, starvation is an institution. Reverse another venerable formula: the amount of hunger increases relatively and absolutely with the evolution of culture. . . . The world's most primitive people [hunters and gatherers] have few possessions, *but they are not poor*' (1974: 36–7).

Information about dying and termination of life are rare in the ethnographic literature, including the medical–anthropological literature. The data are mainly anecdotal and research is rarely systematic. For reasons discussed earlier, the subject is hardly *thematisiert*. The main place where one finds information on the subject of dying is in studies of elderly people (also a relatively recent specialization).

In the slipstream of the pioneering work of Simmons, *The Role of the Aged in Primitive Society* [1945], Glascock has significantly contributed to a better understanding of what he calls 'death-hastening behaviour'.[65] Based on the Human Relations Area Files, his comparative–statistical research suggests that death-hastening practices prevail in non-industrial societies and are directed against elderly people who find themselves in a situation of deterioration. Glascock distinguishes three forms of death-hastening behaviour: neglect, abandonment, and killing of the patient by members of his or her group. He holds that the distinction between 'intact' and 'decrepit' – and the transition of elderly people from the former to the latter category – has long been known in anthropological literature. But the connection with death-hastening practices has only been studied more recently. Simmons already recognized that,

> Among all people, a point is reached in aging at which any further usefulness appears to be over, and the incumbent is regarded as a living liability. 'Senility' may be a suitable label for this. Other terms among primitive people are the 'overaged', the 'useless stage', the 'sleeping period', the 'age grade of dying', and the 'already dead'. (Simmons 1960: 87, quoted in Glascock 1990: 52)

To this Glascock adds that all actions in which capable elderly persons are respected and supported while moribund elderly persons are neglected, abandoned or killed are opposed to the values of western societies and, for that reason, remain hidden or difficult for the western anthropologist to detect.[66] Both Glascock (1990) and the Maxwells

(1982) found that death-hastening behaviour prevails in areas with a harsh climate, where the population is mobile and applies a simple technology that offers few possibilities for storage of food. These populations include hunters and gatherers, shifting cultivators and nomads. More sedentary, technologically more advanced societies included specialized caring institutions for elderly people. The reason for death-hastening behaviour is always the enfeeblement of physical strength and health which turns elderly people into liabilities for the other members of the group. But not only physical and mental deterioration are involved. The Maxwells found, to their surprise, that deterioration of appearance also played a key role in the marginalization and contempt awaiting this category of elderly people:

> The results of the multiple regression suggest that family support systems are the elderly's first line of defense against contempt. That loss of physical strength should be an important determinant of contempt is to be expected, but it is surprising that the deterioration of appearance should outweigh it. In our own society, too, appearance may be an extremely important component of one's social self, but it is one that no one likes to talk about. The paucity of studies in the behavioral sciences dealing with the differential destinies of beautiful and ugly people may be another expression of this disinclination. (1980: 370)

It looks as if physical decay, and deterioration of appearance in particular, are powerful synecdoches and universally considered portents of death.

VII

Let us return to our initial question: can death-hastening practices in tribal and agrarian societies throw new light on euthanasia in the modern western world? Glascock also discussed this issue and believes that there are both similarities and differences (1990: 55–6). First, these practices are directed against elderly people who are dealing with serious deterioration of their physical and mental health. Second, people are killed who are considered a liability – for themselves, their family and the community. Third, the decision to kill or to hasten death is difficult and concerns family members and often also the patient him- or herself.

The differences are striking. First, in tribal and other pre-industrial societies death-hastening practices are part of accepted cultural arrangements. The intervention is open and widely accepted. In western societies euthanasia is highly problematic, controversial and seriously debated. If accepted, it is carried out in enclosed settings under the direction and control of medical specialists. (The aspect of disguise requires further attention.) Second, the persons who decide to intervene and carry out the intervention are different in both worlds. In tribal societies, the family decides, often openly and in dialogue with the patient. Euthanasia in western countries can only be decided and carried out by a physician or the medical staff of a hospital, although the patient and his or her family have a say in the matter. Third, there are differences in technological achievement – the main difference, according to Glascock. Death-hastening practices prevail in societies where people live on the margins of existence: there are no food supplies on which one can draw for all members of the community in case of shortages.[67]

Another major difference concerns the absence in tribal societies of a 'class of priests' (to whom also belong the medical specialists), who in more differentiated societies have a monopoly (also recognized by the state) over the means of orientation. Priests and doctors control the border areas between life and death, ill and healthy, this world and the next. No wonder the strongest resistance to euthanasia and assistance with suicide comes from their side.[68] Where the absence of priests leaves room for death-hastening practices, the presence of religious and medical specialists goes hand in hand with a prolonged dying process.

The situation in pre-industrial societies also raises questions about the status and identity of people in our society who are no longer productive or useful or have any input in the realm of social and cultural capital from which they could derive recognition. It is well known – *even by the elderly themselves* – that elderly people in the modern world are associated with unfavourable characteristics. We noted that this is one of the reasons why the study of elderly people and the dying process received so little attention. The growing number of *seniors* (a recent euphemism that illustrates the strong taboos that surround the subject) has become a source of concern with the growing costs of ageing and illness.[69] In ten years, the densely populated Low Countries will have more elderly people than any other western country[70] – and fewer young people to contribute to the cost of ageing. Tellingly, this information is only rarely brought up in discussions on euthanasia. In his article 'Australia ponders the right to die', Michael Richardson writes: 'The debate [on doctor-assisted suicide] in Australia, where an increasingly large segment of the population of 18 million is over 60 years, is being closely watched overseas by advocates and opponents of voluntary euthanasia, especially in Western countries and Japan, where societies are also aging quickly.'[71] Both subjects are closely related but usually dealt with in different contexts. In this respect, too, knowledge of views and customs in other societies – where elderly people are spatially and socially less isolated, accept their mortality and have the space to prepare themselves for death – can invite reflection on modern society where the right to live and the right to die are measured by different standards.

A comparative perspective on elderly people and well-being opens up a number of homologous contrasts and inversions. In the modern world we encounter increasing marginalization of elderly people irrespective of their capabilities, on the one hand, and, on the other, intensification of medical care when these people reach the dying stage. In more traditional, less differentiated societies, elderly people are respected regardless of their age; they often have power or influence because of their knowledge and social skills. But when they deteriorate physically and mentally, death-hastening practices prevail: they are neglected, abandoned or killed. The contrast between death-hastening and death-delaying practices finds a parallel in another contrast: cultural acceptance of death versus denial and medicalization of death. Whereas Montaigne in his *Essais* could still frankly write about death, his seventeenth-century countryman La Rochefoucauld, in a maxim that became famous, recognized that one cannot stare at the sun or at death: 'Le soleil ni la mort ne se peuvent regarder fixement' (Neither the sun nor death can be steadily looked at). At the end of the nineteenth century, Tolstoy was one of the first writers to identify this trend. *The Death of Ivan Ilyich*, first published in 1886, shows that denial and acceptance of death can coexist in the same society, even in the same household. The juxtaposition is beautifully rendered in this sombre tale, which is really more about dying than about death. Ivan's bourgeois wife and friends feel only repulsion and contempt for him and keep a cool distance. But the valet Gerassim, who is of peasant origin, accepts death and takes good care of his master and helps him in every possible way:

> Ivan Ilyich would sometimes call Gerassim and get him to hold his legs on his shoulders, and he liked to talk with him. Gerassim did everything easily, willingly, simply, and with a good nature that touched Ivan Ilyich. Health, strength and vitality in other people were offensive to him, but Gerassim's strength and vitality did not fret but soothed him.
>   What tormented Ivan Ilyich most was the pretence, the lie, which for some reason they all kept up, that he was merely ill and not dying. . . . He saw that no one felt for him, because no one was willing even to appreciate the situation. Gerassim was the only person who recognized the position and was sorry for him. And that was why Ivan Ilyich was at ease only when Gerassim was with him . . . (1960: 142–3)[72]

VIII
The context of dying in tribal and agrarian societies shows, as far as one can tell, a greater variety of cultural forms than is the case in the modern western world where, in more than one sense, dying happens elsewhere:

it concerns others and is banished from public domains. Moreover, dying is preferably associated with other, less pacified societies that are often torn apart by civil wars: peripheral areas of Europe and North America, the African continent and the border areas of various Asian states.[73]

Furthermore, there is a lack of prescriptions: both the *artes moriendi* and the *ars moriendi* have disappeared. There is no scenario, no decorum or etiquette; neither is there autonomy or dignity of the patient. Distance, denial and disguise also govern the practices of medical doctors, who are rarely actually present when patients die:

> Artz und Abgehörige verhalten sich so, dass der Sterbende eigentlich gar nich sterben darf. Gefühle der Angst und Trennung werden bagatellisiert und das entscheidende Problem der unabänderlichen Trennung und die damit verbundenen Gefühle werden aus der Kommunikation ausgeklammert.[74]

> (Doctors and relatives behave in such a way that the dying person is not in fact allowed to die at all. Feelings of anxiety and separation are played down and the decisive problem of the definite separation and the feelings that go with it are excluded from communication.)

In *Seduced by Death*, Hendin argues against the medicalization of death. Physicians should not resort to extraordinary measures to prolong life, nor should they encourage people to choose a premature death (1997: 149–51). We have to accept that 'dying is an inevitable part of the aging process, not simply the product of a disease that can be prevented or cured' (1997: 215). Hendin points at the importance of palliative care and argues for a better training for physicians with respect to easing the pain and discomfort of terminal patients. He also believes that there is a need for prescriptions for dying and seems to say that with the introduction of *artes moriendi* one may encourage the development of a new *ars moriendi*:

> We need public courses in which you learn how to give shape to the last years of your life – courses that cover every aspect of aging, terminal illness, advance directives, and the right of anaesthesia when pain cannot be treated. These courses should involve not only physicians, but also civil servants, lawyers, and specialists on ethics. (1997: 218)

This call links up with a suggestion of Ariès: 'Dying must be made bearable, either by allowing the natural dignity of the dying to reappear, as in the case of Mélisande, or by means of a training which is *learned like an art*, a training such as Elisabeth Kübler-Ross gives at the University of Chicago' (1981: 592, my italics).

It is obvious from the ethnographic literature on death that anthropologists could, for a long time, ignore the conventions with which dying in their own society was surrounded. For them, too, dying happened elsewhere, outside their scope of interest. Hence the development of a blind spot in ethnography: an area where knowledge and insight are lacking.

In a recent study of ageing, illness and dying on the Indonesian island of Nias, located off the west coast of Sumatra, Klasen points at the lack of attention paid to dying in the ethnographic literature, but deals with the subject only cursorily herself on a single page. What she writes about it confirms what is already known: ageing people are respected, they accept death and they die in a familiar setting surrounded by relatives. These brief notes are phrased in general terms and suggest that they are based on what she has heard, rather than what she has seen or observed.[75]

The unplanned long-term processes of individualization, secularization, pacification, professionalization and medicalization have eroded the social and cultural context of ageing and dying in the modern world and divested both stages of meaning and significance. The question arises as to whether we are concerned with part of a more general ritual impoverishment which some anthropologists consider characteristic of western societies.[76] The marginalization of ageing people is where the isolation of dying people starts.[77] The lack of cultural forms to mark these transitions is tellingly illustrated in a popular and commonplace metaphor for retirement: 'Then you drop in a black hole.' One gets the impression that in the modern world elderly people and their well-being can only be talked about in ironic ways.

Versterven constitutes an exception, and perhaps also a reaction, to this situation. This traditional form of voluntary termination of life appears, if the signs of the times do not betray us, to be experiencing a renaissance and can, if properly supervised, go together with well-being. Because of its emphasis on abstinence and control, its rejection of intervention, especially from the state, the Church and the medical profession, this form of *ars moriendi* epitomizes a high degree of individualization. *Versterven* represents, therefore, both the most simple and the most civilized *modus moriendi* that is known: in tribal societies because of the lack of means; in more differentiated societies as a mark of distinction of an elite which values a dignified, controlled and stylized form of dying. A lifestyle characterized by abstinence and control finds its continuity and apotheosis in an ultimate form of abstinence and self-control. This way of dying, then, reflects a form of life with which it is both metaphorically and metonymically connected.

On the basis of comparative examples, this essay used the strategy of cross-cultural ethnographic juxtaposition.[78] As a strongly contrasted alternative to prolonged dying, so characteristic of the modern world, we find a short terminal phase – death-hastening practices – in tribal and agrarian societies. This difference implies other structural contrasts, including marginalization of elderly people as opposed respect for the elderly, denial and medicalization of death rather than acceptance of death, inverse notions of a 'good' and and a 'bad' death, and lonely, anonymous dying as opposed to dying among kinsmen and friends. It was my intention, through ethnographic juxtaposition, to make familiar things strange and to reflect on current customs surrounding dying in the modern world and connect then to new developments. This form of what Magritte called *dépaysement* prompts reflection on and critique of the way of dying in the modern world. The argument links up with a renewed interest in the time-honoured practices of *inedia* – dying by refusing food. Can one, as Montaigne suggests at the end of his most famous essay, learn from tribal wisdom? A recent report suggests as much when it states in a somewhat different context, 'If modern life deprives us of the basic moral principles that make us fully human, help is at hand in the margins of the modern world.'[79] The example of *versterven* points in that direction.

Notes

Introduction

1 This celebrated phrase is often misquoted and misread (e.g. Lévi-Strauss 1967: 24), which may help explain why its *portée* is still badly understood (cf. Blok 1992: 121–2).

2 Quoted in Dreyfus and Rabinow (1982: 187); Ortner (1994: 405, n. 18). This is analogous to Darwin's theory on evolution. Gould identifies the obstacle to its acceptance in the radical content of Darwin's message. Darwin argued that evolution has no purpose: 'Individuals struggle to increase the representation of their genes in future generations, and that is all. If the world displays any harmony and order, it arises only as an incidental result of individuals seeking their own advantage – the economy of Adam Smith transferred to nature' (1991b: 12). Spelling out the theoretical implications of the unintended consequences of intended human interactions arouses similar resistance from sociologists and politicians who firmly believe in planning and control. Entrenched attitudes and beliefs in the malleability of society and social engineering prevent social theory from coming full circle: from Adam Smith and Malthus to Darwin and back.

3 'The Modernist world view', writes Daniel J. Singal in his study of Faulkner's work, 'begins with the premise of an unpredictable universe where nothing is ever stable and where human beings accordingly must be satisfied with knowledge that is partial and transient at best. . . . [The Modernist believes] in a universe governed entirely by chance where the only thing a person could count on was change and impermanence' (1997: 12, 59). A similar view comes from another Modernist. In a series of conversations about his films, Buñuel remarked: 'Je crois que dans la vie tout est hasard. . . . Les petits détails peuvent changer une vie, et même l'histoire' (Pérez Turrent and De la Colina 1993: 308–9).

254

4   As Bourdieu phrases it in a different context: 'Ce sont les plus proches qui nous font mal.' Interview on the occasion of the publication of his book *La misère du monde*. See *Libération*, 19 March 1998, 44.

5   Because much of the practice approach has an uneasy relationship with the study of historical processes (if it does not ignore them entirely), there is a certain irony in the final remarks of Ortner's essay on theory in anthropology when she notes that she could imagine that instead of the practice model many would have chosen a different key symbol of eighties' anthropology: history (1994: 402).

6   For a detailed criticism of the *homo clausus* model, see Elias (1978a: 104–33).

7   As Peirce long ago recognized, Darwin's theory of evolution introduced the principle of chance: 'Natural selection, as conceived by Darwin, is a mode of evolution in which the only positive agent of change in the whole passage from monkey to man is fortuitous variation' (1992: 358; cf. 213–24 and *passim*). For more recent accounts of the role of chance in Darwin's view of evolution and his distinction between 'laws in the background and contingency in the details', see Gould (1991a: 288–91; 1991b: 11–33; 1994: 148–9).

8   The illuminating and therapeutic effects of drama are well known. Under the title 'The Writer's Insight', the following notice appeared in *Time Magazine* of 29 November 1971: ' "Imaginative writers", Freud once wrote, "are valuable colleagues; in the knowledge of the human heart, they are far ahead of us common folk". That view is accepted at Brown University in Providence, R.I. For the past three years, the university has been offering a unique course in psychiatry that uses the insights of gifted playwrights to teach premedical students about emotional disturbances they may some day encounter in their patients. In alternate weeks, the course replaces conventional classes with professional performances of excerpts from such plays as O'Neill's *Long Day's Journey Into Night*, Williams's *A Streetcar Named Desire* and Ibsen's *Hedda Gabler*. Before each 15- to 20-minute performance, the students are briefed by an English professor on the theme of the play and by a psychiatrist on psychological traits to be observed in the characters. Afterwards students, faculty and the actors themselves take part in a two-hour discussion.'
    A related example that comes to mind is Jules Henry's account of disturbed families in *Pathways to Madness*. Henry understands these families 'as Greek tragedies without gods': 'They seem destined to misery and even to catastrophe because they were locked in by their past and by the configurations of love, hate, anxiety and sham which became established in the home, rigid as the walls' (1973: xx). Henry views these families 'as helpless to change their destiny without outside help as Agamemnon was helpless to change his destiny without a god' (1973: xxi).

9   In his book on violence among the Gabusi in New Guinea, Knauft explains that he was prompted to obtain systematic data on mortality and sorcery not by a preconceived research design (he had not planned to study sorcery), but 'by the fact that in the course of giving genealogies, informants casually mentioned a surprising number of cases in which the person in question had been executed as a sorcerer' (1985: 114).

10 A telling example from my own discipline may help illustrate this trend. Two
    outstanding members of the international anthropological community, the
    American Clifford Geertz and the Norwegian Fredrik Barth, worked in
    Balinese villages, the former before and the latter after the massacres follow-
    ing the unsuccessful coup of 1 October 1965 in Jakarta. In less than a year,
    between 500,000 and one million people were killed. The most savage mas-
    sacre took place on Bali where in two weeks in December 1965 more than
    80,000 people were killed (Hughes 1967: 184–94; Robinson 1995: 273–4).
    What do these anthropologists have to say about these events? Geertz briefly
    mentions them in a footnote at the end of his essay on the cockfight (1973c:
    452) and refers to Hughes (1967), an American journalist who was in
    Indonesia at the time. In his latest book, *After the Fact* (1995: 4–11), Geertz
    mentions the massacres, again in passing, as part of another story, and
    includes material concerning Pare, the town in east-central Java, where he
    worked in the early 1950s. About the actual killings in Pare, Geertz quotes
    an eye-witness account (1995: 8–9). About Bali, where according to Hughes
    'the most savage massacre took place and the troops had to call the people
    off' (1967: 188), we learn that the upheavals took just over two weeks, to
    which Geertz adds, between parentheses: 'in my Balinese village it took one
    night, during which thirty families were burned alive in their houses' (1995:
    8). Barth, who studied two villages in north Bali, is similarly reluctant to deal
    with the subject. Most villagers did not wish to discuss the events with him.
    He does not tell us why (but see Robinson 1995: 275). Barth limits his com-
    ments on what people there call the 'National Tragedy' to less than a single
    page. He includes the account of a man who helped kill, with his sword and
    spear, thirty-four people – men, women, and children – in one hamlet on a
    single night (1993: 125). It would take a historian to reconstruct and make
    sense of the two weeks of collective violence in Bali. Robinson (1995) dis-
    cusses the massacres themselves but also places them in the larger contexts
    in which they occurred. He criticizes the work of both Clifford and Hildred
    Geertz for their 'lack of attention to time, place, or historical and political
    context beyond the village level' (1995: 7–9) and makes short work of exist-
    ing accounts of the massacres that emphasize 'the ostensible harmony, order,
    and equilibrium of Balinese culture' and thus 'divert attention from broader
    political and historical processes, thereby distorting rather than enhancing
    our understanding of what happened' (1995: 275–80).
11 Cf. Peirce (1992: 305–7); and Gould (1991a: 288–91; 1991b: 11–13).
12 'Zadig's method', after Voltaire's eponymous oriental tale (1961 [1747]).
    See Ginzburg (1989: 116), who also mentions the success of aphoristic rea-
    soning and the relevance of the term 'aphoristic' (a clue, a symptom, a lead)
    and recalls that *Aphorisms* was, in fact, the title of a famous work by
    Hippocrates (1989: 124). See also Eco, who observes: 'Scientific discover-
    ies, medical and criminal detections, historical reconstructions, philological
    interpretations of literary texts are all cases of *conjectural thinking*'
    (1988: 205).
13 Cf. Peirce (1998: 95, 107, 205, 216–17). See also Sebeok and Umiker-
    Sebeok (1988: 24–5) and Muir (1991: xvii–xix).

14   Two Italian proverbs neatly suggest the anthropologist's main goals (to explain cultural particulars and to explain cultural universals): '*Paese che vai, usanza che trovi*' [Different countries, different customs] and '*Tutt'il mondo è paese*' [The whole world is (like) your own country].

15   Even Geertz, who perhaps most strongly encouraged the study of local cultures in their own terms and for their own sake, admits that '[t]here is no opposition between general theoretical understanding and circumstantial understanding, between synoptic vision and a fine eye for detail. It is, in fact, by its power to draw general propositions out of particular phenomena that a scientific theory – indeed science itself – is to be judged' (1973b: 51–2).

16   This belief was recently underlined by Sherry Ortner in her work on young people in North America and their anxieties: 'Finally I reminded myself of the cardinal rule of ethnography: the informant is always right' (1998: 427).

17   Cf. E. Wolf (1964: 88–93).

Chapter 1   Social Banditry Reconsidered

1   During a trip by Minghetti to Camporeale in Sicily, at the time when he was Prime Minister, the local priest presented himself to him:
Priest: I should like to commend to you a poor young man, who needs your protection.
Minghetti: And why? What does he want?
Priest: Nothing, only he had an accident, he has killed a man.
Quoted in Alongi (1891: 50). Marco Minghetti was Prime Minister of Italy from 1873 to 1876.

2   We should remember that unsuccessful bandits are less likely to be recorded, for they do not live long enough to get widely known, let alone reach the annals of history. Hobsbawm does not make clear whether this category belongs to his universe, since he does not mention it at all.

3   See also Eberhard (1965: 100–6). The alliances between delinquents and local nobles throughout modern European history still await full sociological treatment.

4   Cf. Wolf (1966b: 1–11); Landsberger (1969: 1–8).

5   Cf. D'Alessandro (1959: 97). This important study is regretfully not utilized by Hobsbawm. It might have induced him to revise some of the ideas on *mafia* as expressed in *Primitive Rebels*, especially the notion that *mafiosi* can be understood in terms of social rebels. In *Bandits*, Hobsbawm refers to the Sicilian *mafia* as those 'unofficial political systems and networks, which are still very poorly understood and known' (1969: 33). See, however, Romano (1952; 1966); and Pantaleone (1966).

6   During the nineteenth and twentieth centuries, Sicilian brigandage provided alternatively an *instrumentum regnum* and a staff of large landowners to control the peasants. See Romano (1952: 279–86); and D'Alessandro (1959: 123–42).

7   For a valuable case study of Giuliano's career, see Gavin Maxwell (1957). The part played by brigandage in post-war Sicily has been covered by Sansone and Ingracsi (1950) and Gaja (1962).

8   The atmosphere in which Leggio (also spelled 'Liggio') operated is described in Dolci (1963: 25–50). See also Pantaleone (1966: 113–22). For his later career as the main *capo-mafia* of the Corleonesi, see Sterling (1990: 54–66, 143–55, 203–14); and Stille (1995: *passim*). For the concepts of terror and zone of terror, see Walter (1969: 5–7).

9   See the observations in Wolf (1966b: 92; 1969: 294); Moore (1968: 479); and Landsberger (1969: 57).

10   See Mack Smith (1950) on Sicily and Eberhard's discussion of the various stages of banditry in medieval China (1965: 101–2). Similar complexities are described for early nineteenth-century Banten in north-western Java (Sartono 1966: 109–27). The heterogeneity of the *déclassé* and floating population of which bandits are part raises specific problems in revolutionary movements. The role of external power-holders who challenge the power that constrains the peasants is discussed by Wolf (1969: 290–1). At least one Chinese bandit managed to become emperor. This was Liu Bang, who successfully fought against the Confucianists and founded the Han dynasty. See Witke (1977: 464). We should appreciate, however, that in China (as elsewhere) there are no rigid lines of demarcation between bandit leaders and warlords. For the very different impact Pancho Villa and Emiliano Zapata – who both remained tied to regional views and interests – had on the Mexican Revolution, see Wolf (1969: 3–48, esp. 31–7) and Hobsbawm's brief remark (1969: 93).

11   Cf. Bloch (1961: 145–9) and J. Schneider (1971). See also Niermeyer (1959), who traces the semantic shifts of the term '*honour*' in medieval European societies. For a more recent discussion, see Stewart (1994).

12   'Since human beings have an infinite capacity for self-conceit, reality can only be reached by exposing their illusions.' This is, according to Alexander Parker, how the early seventeenth-century writer Francisco de Quevedo focuses on the problem of the delinquent in his novel *La vida del Buscón*, the masterpiece of the picaresque genre. See Parker (1967: 56–74).

13   See, for example, Pereira de Queroz (1968: 112–22) for a discussion of the career of the Brazilian bandit Lampião, who operated in the 1930s in the north-eastern part of the country.

14   See Mack Smith (1968: 419).

15   In Bourbon Spain, bandits could obtain pardon from the king and pass into royal service (Pitt-Rivers 1961: 180). See also Brenan (1962: 156). For data on Mexico, see Friedrich (1962, 1965). Van den Muyzenberg discusses the role of the Huks in central Luzon (1971). The new development of brigandage in Sardegna in the 1960s is too easily dismissed by Hobsbawm (1969: 76). He fails to recognize the part played by shepherds and outlaws in kidnapping and extortion and to note the rapid and violent ascent of both rural and urban bourgeois in recent years. See Brigaglia (1971: 299–314) and a recent autobiography by Graziano Mesina (1993).

16   See Chandler (1979); Slatta (1987); Joseph's detailed review of the literature on Latin American banditry (1990); and Slatta's comments (1991). For reports on banditry in European and Mediterranean areas, see Blok (1988: 89–140); and Fiume (1984) on Sicily; Raggio (1990: 194–226) on

the Genoese Republic in the sixteenth and seventeenth centuries; Koliopoulos (1987: 239–92) on nineteenth-century Greece; S. Wilson (1988: 335–76)
on nineteenth-century Corsica; Hart's (1987) review of the literature on banditry in nineteenth- and twentieth-century Morocco and other parts of the
Middle East that demonstrates the irrelevance of Hobsbawm's model and
also shows that not even all fictional bandits were Robin Hoods; cf.
Bourqia's (1991) critical review of Hobsbawm and Hart on the basis of
Moroccan materials; Cobb (1972: 181–211; 1975: 141–210) on revolutionary France; Egmond (1986; 1993) on the Dutch Republic; Blok (1995a)
and chapter 2 of this volume on the eighteenth-century Dutch frontier; and
Siebenmorgen and Brümmer (1995) on early modern Germany.
17 See Hobsbawm (1974: 143; 1981: 17–18).
18 See Joseph (1990: 15).
19 See Cobb (1975); and Egmond (1986).
20 See Blok (1995a) and chapter 2 of this volume.
21 Slatta (1987: 196).
22 See John F. Burns, Bandit Queen returns, an angel to the oppressed. *New
York Times*, 23 February 1994. See also Sen's biography (1995).

Chapter 2   Bandits and Boundaries: Robber Bands and Secret Societies on the Dutch Frontier (1730–1778)

1 Most of the surviving court records are preserved in the State Archives at
Maastricht (RA LvO). For a detailed account of the sources, see Blok
(1995a: 235–445).
2 Cagnetta's sketch of the *bardana* (razzia) in Orgosolo, Sardinia (1963:
90–102) provides a good example of the momentary and transitional character of banditry. These aspects are also given emphasis in Vittorio De Seta's
film *Banditi a Orgosolo* (1962). See also S. Wilson's superb account of
feuding and banditry in Corsica (1988: 335–76).
3 On the military and political history of the Lower Meuse, see Wouters
(1970); Haas (1978); and Gutmann (1980).
4 For the importance of the gentry in the Lower Meuse, see Wouters (1970:
325–8); Haas (1978: 202–6, 234–6); and Janssen de Limpens (1982).
E. P. Thompson writes that ruling-class control in eighteenth-century
England 'was located primarily in a cultural hegemony, and only secondar-
ily in an expression of economic or military power' (1978: 254).
5 The quintessential role of secrecy in social life was long ago recognized by
Simmel, who regarded the secret, the hiding of realities by negative or
positive means, as one of man's greatest achievements (1950a: 330, 345–6).
6 In some European areas the skinner remained a social outcast until the end
of the nineteenth century (cf. Weiss 1946: 113).
7 On the subversive role of taverns and inns, see Scott, who writes: 'Here subordinate classes met offstage and off-duty in an atmosphere of freedom
encouraged by alcohol' (1990: 121–2). See also Burke (1978: 109–11). On

the pivotal role of *cabaretiers* in the *Bande d'Orgères*, see Cobb (1972: 191). For the influence of innkeepers in Dutch village life, see Wichers (1965: 37–8). On the leading role of shoemakers in popular movements in early modern Europe, see Hobsbawm and Scott (1980).

8   The vicissitudes of the Eta in Japan, a despised occupational group that specialized in butchering, tanning and leatherwork (which in a Buddhist society are considered defiling pursuits), were, in this respect, very similar to those of the skinners in the Lower Meuse. They were prosperous during the period of civil wars when their services were much in demand. But the Eta suffered during the relative peace of the Tokugawa period (1603–1868) when their trades lost the importance they had held during the civil war and discrimination against them intensified (cf. Price 1972).

9   In eighteenth-century France (and elsewhere), surgeons were the primary medical practitioners and have been called 'the physicians of the poor'. The development of their profession was stimulated by the rise of the standing army in the seventeenth century. See Wellman (1992: 16–17, 29).

10   On the genesis of the *Freikorps* in the German territories in the mid-eighteenth century, see Childs (1982: 119).

11   The *Carolina* (1532) specifies punishments for these forms of sacrilege (Radbruch 1960: 172ff). For similar cases of theft from churches in eighteenth-century France – and similar punishments, see Ferrand (1989: 65, 71–3), on which I have drawn in some detail.

12   In his remarks on the symbolism of the body, Firth (1973: 227) distinguishes between three bodies of Christ: the physical body, the mystical body and the eucharistic body.

13   There is little doubt about the presence of elements of protest and parody in the way a successful theft from a church was celebrated. Cf. Thompson (1974: 387 and 1978: 254). For an extensive documentation of more covert forms of protest and resistance, see Scott (1990: 136ff).

14   This belief seems to have been common in early modern Europe: 'Die vom Galgen abgeschnittene Diebshand sichert, beim Stehlen angezündet, das Gelingen des Raubs [The thief's hand, cut off from a corpse on the gallows, when lit during the robbery, assures success]' (Danckert 1963: 42). See also Bächtold-Stäubli (1929/30: 229–31). On the luck-bringing power of the *Diebsdaum*, see Angstmann (1928: 93–4). For a general account of the magical power of liminal material, see Leach (1964a; 1976: 33–6, 61–2 and *passim*).

15   Courts in western Europe had long since lost interest in demonology (Levack 1987: 170ff). This was particularly the case in the Low Countries, where there were few witch trials anyway, and which dropped the subject long before its heyday in Germany and France. The sentences in the Lower Meuse that contained explicit references to the oathtaking phrased this profanity invariably in terms of blasphemy or sacrilege, that is, 'de godslasterlijke eed'.

16   Two contemporary reports refer to the denomination '*Bokkeryders*', but they merely record the use of the term and the associated folk belief, while expressing personal reservations; see Mengels (1887[1773]: 269); Sleinada (1972[1779]: 61–2). One cannot, of course, exclude the possibility that for

some people the initiation rituals of the robbers and the term *Bokkeryders* included references to representations current during the witch trials in the sixteenth and seventeenth centuries.

17   Ginzburg, quoted in Luria and Gandolfo (1986: 108).

Chapter 3   Infamous Occupations

1   See, for instance, Danckert (1963); Brunschvig (1962); Le Goff (1980); and Price (1972). I am using the past tense, because most of the evidence regarding these occupations bears on historical rather than contemporary situations.

2   *Infamia*, from *fama*, fame, good reputation. For the complicated semantics of the term *infamia* in legal contexts, see Peters (1990) and Stewart (1994: 55–8).

3   For a perspective from the members of these professions themselves, see De Vos and Wagatsuma (1972) on the Burakumin in Japan; Fontaine (1996) on itinerant merchants from the Alps; Khare (1984) on the Chamars in Uttar Pradesh, India; Van Nieuwkerk (1995) on female singers and dancers in Egypt; Ensel (1999) on the Haratin in Morocco; and Scott's comparative studies of subaltern populations (1985; 1990).

4   Gerholm (1980: 86–7); see also Kramer (1971).

5   For the use of the concept of 'family resemblances', see the famous passages in Wittgenstein's *Philosophical Investigations* (1967, para. 65ff) and my discussion of this approach in comparative research (Blok 1976).

6   Cf. Beneke (1863: 134–5); Danckert (1963: 39, 168). For examples from Japan, see Ninomiya (1933: 98, 99, 109), who discusses restrictions regarding the Eta and Hinin: 'The privilege of dressing the hair in conventional manner and of wearing the *geta* (wooden clogs) was denied to the *eta*. . . . In 1723 the Shogun issued a decree which forbade all *hinin*, other than their chiefs, to wear the conventional headdress, any headgear, and to coil their hair. Furthermore, the women of the *hinin* class were not to shave their eyebrows or to blacken their teeth.' As metonymic signs, all these restrictions served to emphasize 'nature' at the expense of 'culture', thus setting the Eta and Hinin apart from ordinary people as more 'animalic'. See also Passin's remark on what the Eta could and could not wear in Tokugawa Japan (1955: 41). On headgear as a metonymic sign, see Leach (1973a: 227–30).

7   Quoted in Wissell (1971: 104).

8   In this context '*rechtelös*' did not involve being an outlaw, but it meant to be deprived of certain civil rights, specifically the rights resulting from membership of a *Stand* (estate) and corporation, with which the notion of *Ehre* (honour) was intimately connected. As the *Schwabenspiegel* (1276) conceptualized this connection: 'Rechtelöse lüd dat synt de de an ere bevlecket synt' ('Outlaws' are people who are tainted). For interpretations of this phrase, see Danckert (1963: 9–12) and Spruit (1969: 55ff). On the limited civil rights of the Japanese Eta and Hinin, who specialized in leather-work and entertainment and who were also classified with criminals, see Ninomiya (1933); Passin (1955); and J. Price (1972). On the *infamia* of

actors (*mimi*) and prize fighters (*gladiatores*) in ancient Rome, see Spruit (1966); Richlin (1983: 99–100); and Wiedemann (1992: 26–30; 102ff), who points out that the gladiators were recruited from the ranks of condemned criminals and were classified in Roman legislation together with prostitutes, pimps and actors: all sold their bodies for the delectation of others, which tainted them with *infamia*. For a different view on the attitudes toward gladiators, see C. Barton (1993). Regarding the position of actors and actresses in China, we learn that both were looked down on socially: 'Even in cosmopolitan Shanghai of the 1930s they were lumped together with butchers, criminals, vagrants, and prostitutes ...' (Witke 1977: 99); cf. Mackerras (1990: 15–16).

9   On the South Asian Kanjar and Qalandar, see Berland (1982; 1987a). On the related Dom in Bihar and Pakistan, a despised lower caste of smiths, musicians and leather-workers, see Michels-Gebler (1984: 45–58). See also Sakata on the real or assumed foreign origin of (the despised) musicians in eastern Afghanistan (1983: 76–8). Other examples of nomadic artisans and entertainers who belong to ethnic minorities are discussed in Rao (1987).

10   See Eliade (1978: 87–109), who also emphasizes their itinerancy, or 'nomadic condition' (1978: 25); and the résumé in Danckert (1963: 268–71). For more recent discussions of the position of smiths in African societies who combined iron-working (smelting and forging) with other occupations, see Michels-Gebler (1984: 73–135); McNaughton (1988); Herbert (1993: 25ff, 160); and Van Beek (1992), whose approach is similar to the one followed here.

11   See Van Beek (1992) and Abbink (1987).

12   Danckert recognizes that this explanation fails because it 'takes symptoms for causes' (1963: 13). But see Jones (1955: 6) with respect to millers in late medieval and early modern Europe. Jones also suggests: 'One might ask why equal scorn was not heaped upon the other trades and crafts originally performed by serfs' (1955: 6). In his recent study of gladiators in ancient Rome, Wiedemann also refers to the paradox of the stigmatization of important and indispensable work. He takes issue with the attempts to explain the *infamia* of gladiators and their trainers in terms of the foreign (i.e. Etruscan) origins of the gladiatorial contests (1992: 30ff). Wiedemann emphasizes the relationship with death: 'Instead of seeing a gladiatorial combat as a public display of killing, it might be useful to see it as a demonstration of the power to overcome death' (1992: 34–5). On this point, see also C. Barton (1994), who recalls the self-immolation of the Roman hero Mucius Scaevola and the bold intensity and steadfastness of his gaze.

13   For examples from Japan, see J. Price (1972: 22) and Passin (1955: 261–2), who refer to not particularly dirty tasks like the making of baskets from willow branches, wooden-clog making, etc., as special monopolies of the Eta.

14   Similar attitudes prevailed in pre-industrial German towns, where people charged with tracking down and guarding criminals were considered *unehrlich*. See Danckert (1963: 57–63).

15   Richlin (1983: 99). For a detailed study of the Roman gladiators and their infamy (which was also related to their status as condemned criminals), see

Wiedemann (1992). For a somewhat different interpretation of the position of the gladiator, see C. Barton (1992).

16 On the luck-bringing (i.e. magical) power of sweeps and their related liminality, see chapter 4. On prostitutes as luck-bringers in Europe and India, see Duerr (1988: 302). In his monograph on prostitutes in nineteenth-century rural Sweden, Frykman (1977: 222–3) also emphasizes their luck-bringing power. We shall come back to this point below.

17 See Bloch (1973); and compare Mauss (1975 [1903]: 29–30) on various (infamous/magical) professions and people in positions of authority. As far as European kings are concerned ('more godly and priestly than they are magical'), Bloch would later prove him wrong.

18 See Bloch (1973). For the term 'low, taboo status', see Barth (1960: 123–4); see also Radcliffe-Brown (1952); Leach (1964a; 1976).

19 Cf. Mauss (1975: 28–9). In the most comprehensive account of infamous occupations, Danckert (1963) uses a notion of taboo that includes both the sacred and the unclean for understanding the *Unehrlichkeit* of these occupations. But he insists on a search for origins and survivals of older, pre-Christian sacrality in them to explain the entire complex of the proscribed occupations. By focusing on the magical aspects of these professions, but always trying to fit his material with his survival theory, one might say that Danckert was right for the wrong reasons. The essays of Le Goff (1980; 1988), while ethnographically interesting for their emic views and their focus on merchants and usurers in late medieval France, suffer from a lack of theoretical consistency. Indulging in piecemeal explanations, Le Goff refers to taboos about blood, impurity, dirt and money as if these are all categories of the same logical order, rather than sorting them out. He calls them 'ancestral taboos' and 'the taboos of primitive societies', and seems unaware of the comparative literature on the subject and of discussions in anthropology regarding classification, taboo, magic and ritual, which go back to the fundamental work of his countrymen Mauss and Van Gennep. These flaws are all the more baffling when one realizes that Le Goff wrote the Introduction to a new edition of Marc Bloch's *Les rois thaumaturges* (1983) and is a staunch advocate of historical anthropology, as is attested by a section in one of his books entitled 'Towards a historical anthropology' (1980b: 223–87). The volume on marginal groups edited by Vincent (1979), although useful, is poor on theory, comparison and occupational marginality.

20 See Van Gennep (1960); Douglas (1966; 1970; 1975); Leach (1964a; 1976); Ohnuki (1981: 105–32); Jansen (1987); Parry (1982; 1985); and Lambek (1992: 246–8).

21 See the critical remarks of Parry (1985), who leaves the issue unresolved. Tambiah's notion of 'invading' and his emphasis on the relative rarity of intrusions are helpful but do not explain why some anomalies are auspicious and other ominous (1985a [1969]: 202–4). But the case of the prostitute (who, depending on context, can be either) suggests, together with other cases (e.g. the executioner), further theoretical adjustments.

22 'Maskings, roles, symbols, special times and places – all attest to the distance of ritual events from social processes. And because rituals are

264 Notes to pp. 50–52

performed "as if not for the first time", scholars have spoken of re-enactments, repetitions and the like . . . this curious quality of ritual embedded in
the life of society, yet separated from its own references in respect to both
place and time' (Mack 1987: 18). This formulation is important, since it
highlights the ambiguity of ritualization: members of the despised occupations were segregated (separated) from and yet part of (embedded in) the
communities they served. See also Rappaport's discussion of ritual. He
emphasizes formality, performance, instrumentality: 'ritual not only com-
municates something, but is taken by those performing it to be "doing something" as well' (1979: 177). See also Tambiah (1985b: 60ff) for the
performative (illocutionary) aspects of ritual – and, by implication, of magic.

23   Dumont (1980: 48), quoted in Ohnuki (1984: 289). Kolenda (1978: 47–8)
speaks of the lower castes' absorption of pollution on behalf of their high-
caste jajmans. The notions of impurity and pollution, as Dumont and others
have pointed out, are thus closely connected with that of purity, especially
the purity of high-caste women and priests. The same is true for the concept
of *Unehrlichkeit* (infamy), which is impossible to understand without reference to its opposite, *Ehre* (honour).

24   See Leach (1964a); Bulmer (1967); Tambiah (1985a: 169–211); Douglas
(1975: 278–318); and the helpful discussion in Ohnuki (1981: 105–32).

25   On the ritualization of twins, see Evans-Pritchard (1956: 129–32); Lévi-
Strauss (1963: 79–82); and Firth (1966).

26   Cf. Douglas (1966: 168–79; 1975: 33–44, 285ff).

27   In some areas (e.g. the Low Countries), the work of the chimney-sweep has
sexual connotations, as is attested by the Dutch phrase, 'having her chimney
swept'.

28   Cf. Douglas (1966; 1975: 213–14); Leach (1964a: 37–8); and Ohnuki
(1981: 126–7). As Leach phrased it, 'the exudations of the human body are
universally the objects of intense taboo – in particular, faeces, urine, semen,
menstrual blood, hair clippings, nail parings, body dirt, spittle, mother's
milk. Such substances are ambiguous in the most fundamental way. . . . So
strong is the resulting taboo that even as an adult addressing an adult audience, I cannot refer to these substances by the monosyllabic words which I
used as a child but must mention them only in Latin' (1964a: 38). This may
be true, but the emphasis on what is defined as dirt differ both between and
within cultures. As is well known, laundering is especially polluting in India
and so is saliva. In Japan, the collection of human excrement was a
respectable business, less strictly hemmed in by taboos than everything relating to death (cf. Passin 1955: 262). Within the same cultural areas one may
find significant differences in bodily controls between social classes (and over
time), as Elias has shown for western Europe (1978b). For other examples
of what may be called the 'diversity of dirt', see below.

29   Elias has addressed these issues in his *magnum opus* on the civilizing process
(1969b). For a return to universals as far as nakedness and shame are concerned, see Duerr's (1988; 1990) ponderous critique of Elias. But see also
Corbin (1986b) and Vigarello (1988), who deal with changing sensibilities
regarding bodily smells and dirt in France. It seems that we remain caught

between orientalism and ethnocentrism, between creating alterity and imposing our categories on others – unless we commit ourselves to a true comparative and historical anthropology.

30 For a concise picture of the medical spectrum under the *ancien régime*, see Huisman (1989).

31 For the stigma on barbers, cuppers, tanners, weavers, sweepers, nightmen and scavengers in Islamic societies, see Brunschvig (1962). In Buddhist areas, where killing animals and the consumation of meat are proscribed, all butchers were untouchable, as were people working with leather and fur (Sjoberg 1960: 133–7; Passin 1955: 251–3; Donoghue 1957; J. Price 1972; and De Vos and Wagatsuma 1972). In the German territories skinners, who worked with dead animals, were considered *unehrlich*, while the butchers (who had killed the animals), tanners, shoemakers and saddlers did not suffer from any opprobrium. For the generally low social position of shoemakers (cobblers) in early modern Europe, see Hobsbawm and Scott (1980), who focus on the background of their prominent role in movements of social protest. Whereas in Germany skinning and tanning were worlds apart, it seems that these occupations were considerably less differentiated in England. On Denmark, see Rockwell (1974). Egardt (1962) has discussed the taboos connected with killing horses and eating their meat for Scandinavian cultures. On medieval and early modern France and Flanders, see Le Goff (1980; 1988), who looks at these occupations from the perspective of the clergy, who, at one time, were rather severe in their condemnation of butchers, soldiers, and so on, by classifying virtually all non-agrarian (i.e. 'non-productive') professions as dishonourable, ignoble, contemptible or otherwise illicit. Le Goff recognizes a close connection between urbanization and the revival of commerce, on the one hand, and the erosion of the opprobrium on trading and banking, on the other.

32 For further details and references, see Blok (1995a: 153ff).

33 See Angstmann (1928: 90ff); and Von Hentig (1958: 200–2).

34 On the role of the executioner as healer and magician, see Angstmann (1928: 90ff), who recognizes both the 'negative' and 'positive' sides of his power, and who stresses his role as luck-bringer: 'das Volk glaubt an magische, auf jeden Fall ausserordentliche Kräfte, die dem Henker durch sein Amt, durch seine ständige Berührung mit Hingerichteten, zufliessen' (People believe in the magical – or in any case extraordinary – powers bestowed on the executioner because of his office, because of his constant contact with executed persons) (1928: 90). See also Von Hentig (1958: 200ff) and the statement of Mauss in his paragraph on magicians, where he discusses the role of magic in various occupations: 'And we find that executioners are individuals who have access to spells and charms. . . . They are magicians' (1975: 29). The first part of Angstmann's dissertation is called 'Die Namen der Henker' (1928: 1–73) and deals with well over a hundred different names by which this profession was known in the German territories, including the surname of the author. This unusually large number of names and nicknames betrays a strong ambiguity and supports the view of Mauss, who wrote: 'There is, of course, one profession which separates a man from

his fellows more than any other – particularly as it is usually performed by a single individual on behalf of the whole society, even a large-scale society – this is the role of the executioner' (1975: 29). When reading 'a single individual on behalf of the whole society, even a large-scale society', one is immediately reminded of the figure of the king. As persons with respectively low-taboo status and high-taboo status, executioners and kings share several features. We have already mentioned the healing powers ascribed to both of them. Moreover, with his sword the executioner symbolized the authority of the king, and his proximity to rulers in Asian and African societies has often been noted. On the affinity between kings and executioners in German folk tales, see Angstmann (1928: 80–2).

35   For the German-speaking areas, see Danckert (1963: 37–41). For similarities and differences between executioners and skinners in early modern Germany, see Wilbertz (1979).

36   Corbin (1986a: 210–12). For the prostitute as the repository of impurity, see also the Scriptures (Proverbs 23: 27). About the association between death and sexuality, Corbin remarks: 'As putrid body and emunctory/sewer, the prostitute maintains complex relations with the *corpse* in the symbolic imagination of these times. This fact is not surprising; after all, psychoanalysis links the death drive with the desire that overwhelms the prostitute's client' (1986a: 211). The relationship between prostitutes (including promiscuous women) and disease, in particular the children's disease rickets, has also been attested in relation to nineteenth-century rural Sweden. See Frykman (1977), who also discusses the prostitute's affinity with other marginal people who were credited with the same qualities of disease and impurity. These attributions of supernatural danger served as a boundary and barrier between the 'established' and 'outsiders'. For a further discussion of these terms and the critical notion of *Berührungsangst*, or fear of contamination, see Elias and Scotson (1965).

37   On the wet nurse and midwife (also layer-out) in northern Burgundy, France, see Verdier (1979: 83–156). For the position and relatively good reputation of midwives in four cities of the Dutch Republic, see Van der Borg (1992).

38   But compare Mauss, discussing the qualities of the magician: 'There are other individuals destined to become magicians who are brought to public notice by fear or suspicion, or through their physical peculiarities or extraordinary gifts – jugglers, ventriloquists and tumblers are examples. Any infirmity suffices, such as a limp, a hump or blindness' (1975: 27–8). One is reminded of the proverbial blind beggar, the mythological blacksmith Hephaistos, who limped, and several examples of 'shamans' discussed in the work of Carlo Ginzburg (1992). In more recent anthropological work, it has been recognized that 'the contrast between man and not-man provides an analogy for the contrast between the members of the human community and the outsider' (Douglas 1975: 289). On this point, see also Leach (1982: 118). For an early and massive documentation of this point, see Elias (1978).

39   See Ninomiya (1933: 115–16, 123). Passin writes: 'This conception of the "base" people as less than human – evidenced in the word *Hinin* itself (which means "not human", "non people") – has been a persistent theme

in Japanese social history. During Tokugawa days, the Eta were frequently counted with the classifier used for animals (*hiki*) instead of people. . . . Often they were not included in the census tabulations, or they were listed separately from "people"' (1955: 254).

40　Mauss dealt better with the magical aspects of anomalies, which remain off-centre in the work of Douglas, who has always been primarily interested in problems of classification, 'how anomalous beings may be treated in different systems of classification' (Douglas 1975: 282).

41　See the remarks of Willems (1970: 530–1) on the situation in early nineteenth-century Cologne, Germany. On the agricultural fringes of cities in the Middle East, see Lapidus (1984: 86), who, referring to late medieval Damascus, observes: 'expanding cities sometimes englobed villages lying just outside the old city into a continuous agglomeration'. For what has been called the 'de-ruralization' of the towns in early modern England, which involved the shrinking of gardens and orchards and the disappearance of trees, see K. Thomas (1983: 250).

42　'Master status' has been defined as a 'status that overrides all others and provides a continuing focus of identification, however unfair or inappropriate' (B. Jackson 1978: 262). On the German guilds, see Walker (1971) and Wissell (1971).

43　Pirenne (1936: 54). See also K. Thomas (1983: 243–4) on the symbolism of town walls (security, civility, human achievement). On the restrictions regarding travelling on the European continent, which lasted until the end of the eighteenth century, see Laermann (1976: 71–7).

44　On the social and spatial segregation of low-status occupational groups in pre-industrial cities, see Sjoberg (1960: 91–103); and Lapidus (1984: 79ff). On the peripheral location of prostitution in towns and cities in nineteenth-century France, see Merriman (1991: 62–5).

45　On peripatetic artisans and entertainers, see the pioneering work of Berland (1982; 1987a; 1987b) and the important volume edited by Rao (1987).

46　For further details see the brief overviews of Price in the volume edited by De Vos and Wagatsuma (1972: 6–30); Passin (1955); and the account of Ninomiya (1933). I have also consulted and learned from the work of Donoghue (1957) and the more recent writings of Ohnuki (1984; 1987) on Burakumin monkey performances in contemporary Japan.

47　See the important essay of Laermann (1976).

48　Writing about the criminalization of the working class in eighteenth-century England, E. P. Thompson observes that 'their only crime was that they did not have any property', which is a far cry from – and possibly a pun on – that famous nineteenth-century phrase, ascribed to the anarchist Proudhon, '*La propriété c'est le vol*' (Property is theft). In his work on marginal and mobile people in late medieval Paris, Geremek (1987: 276ff) has also emphasized the significance of the 'lack of a fixed abode' and its implications. His focus is more on crime and criminals than on (infamous) occupations. The chapters on prostitutes, beggars, students and traders show how closely the worlds of these people were associated with crime of one sort or another.

49   In the Dutch Republic (as probably elsewhere in early modern Europe), the sentence of banishment invariably included the phrase 'op poene van zwaarder straf', which meant that a premature return of the convict (if any return was allowed) would be followed by a more severe punishment – usually hanging. For examples and further details, see Spierenburg (1984) and Blok (1995a: 153ff). On banishment, see also Geremek (1987: 19–21).

50   For summaries of their legal status and further details, see Spruit (1969: 55–62) and Salmen (1983: 23–6).

51   See Faral (1910: 28–9); Casagrande and Vecchio (1979: 916); and Salmen (1960: 61–2; 1983: 25–6).

52   Quoted in Spruit (1969: 59) from a sixteenth-century text printed in Leipzig.

53   See Wiedemann (1992: 46–7) on the associations between *infamia* and (social) death in ancient Rome.

54   Salmen (1983: 26), who refers to Adorno for the concept of 'mimetic taboo'.

55   See Leach (1961: 132–6) on the association between rites of passage and symbolic reversals. See also Needham (1963) and Babcock (1978).

56   See Huizinga (1955: 27).

57   See Berland (1982, *passim*); Sakata (1983: 76ff) describes similar inversions for the Dalak in eastern Afghanistan (see below).

58   Casagrande and Vecchio (1979: 917). As Le Goff (1980) has shown, the clergy in medieval France entertained, at least for some time, a negative view of virtually all professions that did not fit the world of 'the three orders'.

59   Casagrande and Vecchio (1979: 919–23).

60   The connection with fairs and weddings may be obvious (cf. Burke 1978: 97 and Spruit 1969: 29ff), but the structural relations or 'homologies' between these transitions and the liminality of the entertainers – and their implications for the reputation of these professions – are often ignored.

61   Fabre-Vassas refers to the description of the performance of the tall, red-haired *châtreur* in Carlo Levi's well-known *Christ Stopped at Eboli* (1963: 189–92), and, referring to Verdier (1979: 46–9), points at the ambivalence of reddish and sandy-coloured hair.

62   See Fabre-Vassas (1983: 31), who, in this connection, also stresses the gender ambiguity of the *châtreur*.

63   Fabre-Vassas (1983: 6).

64   Finally, the reputation of the *châtreur* as a magical healer may also have been related – as in other cases of peripatetics – to his status as a stranger. Van Gennep recognizes that in many cultures 'a stranger is sacred, endowed with magico-religious powers, and supernaturally benevolent or malevolent' (1960: 26). Simmel's remarks on the ambiguity of the stranger are also pertinent in this context, in particular his observation that the stranger who moves on 'often receives the most surprising openness – confidences which sometimes have the character of a confessional and which would be carefully withheld from a more closely related person' (1950b: 404). For a more negative image of this profession, see Danckert's notes on the German *Sauschneider* and *Nonnenmacher* (1963: 189–95).

65   See Sakata (1983: 76–105). The barber, who often also specialized in phlebotomy or blood-letting, circumcision, scarifying, etc., was deeply despised

in Islamic societies. See Brunschvig (1962: 47–9), who fails to explain why these professions, along with their practitioners, were considered infamous.

66 See Barth (1960: 123–4, 139–40), and references in Sakata (1983: 80–1).

67 See Kyrova (1994: 58); cf. De Jongh (1995: 16–18 and *passim*).

68 See the overview in Jones (1955).

69 See Beneke (1863: 1ff, 12–13); Danckert (1963: 127–8); and Jones (1955: 11).

70 Danckert (1963: 127–8); Beneke (1863: 12–13). The infamy of the linen weavers may have been related to their handling urine, which they needed for the soaking and bleaching of their raw materials.

71 Pourcher (1989: 98–9).

72 For the location of urban mills in medieval Amalfi, see Del Treppo (1977: 45–51). For an example of a twelfth-century guild of millers in Lucca, see Guidi (1912: 179–80, document no. 1196). Marc Bloch (1935: 554–61) has argued that mills in late medieval and early modern France and Germany were resented in areas where they were part of a manorial system: rather than grinding their grain at home with hand mills for free, peasants were forced to use the water mills of the landlord who enjoyed *droits de banalité*. I am indebted to Paolo Squatriti for these references.

73 By the 1960s, the water mills had been abandoned and replaced by electric mills in the towns. The millers belonged to the *burgisi*, the relatively prosperous rural middle class of farmers and landowners (cf. Blok (1988) and chapter 8 of this volume).

74 Herbert (1993: 160).

75 See Michels-Gebler (1984: 47ff, 179).

76 See Michels-Gebler (1984: 98–9, 179).

77 Herbert (1993: 134, 159–60). For more on the '*Roi-Forgeron*', see Herbert (1993: 131–63).

78 Burkert (1996: 3).

79 Myerhoff (1982: 109).

80 Burkert (1996: 4).

81 See Faral (1910: 128–42); Salmen (1960: 90–111; 1983: 24–9); Krickeberg (1983: 119); Danckert (1963: 252–62); and Spruit (1969: 95–126).

82 Favoured by seclusion on three levels (organization, language and space), the practice of the medical profession evolved from a low-taboo to a high-taboo status. These transformations still await their historian, but see, for France, Foucault (1973); Gelfand (1980); and Ramsey (1988); for the Dutch Republic, see Frijhoff (1983) and Nieuwenhuis (1994).

83 An important exception should be made for scavenging, which has been defined as the collection and disposal of culturally defined waste materials. For an overview of the literature, see Blincow (1986), who draws attention to a cultural division of labour where specific ethnic groups constitute the sole or major elements of scavenger populations. The author points at the relationship between polluted and stigmatized ethnic status and the defiling nature of scavenging work (1986: 101–2).

84 See K. Thomas (1983: 143ff) and Frykman and Löfgren (1987: 42–87). See also Wiedemann on the meaning of *venationes* (hunting and the killing of

wild animals in the arena): 'in a pre-industrial world, any sign of control over the natural world is reassuring to society at large' (1992: 64).
85 See Honigmann (1964).
86 E. Weber (1977: 5), who reminds us that 'Civilization is urban (civic, civil, civilian, civilized), and so of course is urbanity; just as polity, politeness, politics, and police spring from *polis* – the city again.'
87 See chapter 8 of this volume; Silverman (1975); Freeman (1979); and Blok and Driessen (1984).
88 Freeman (1970: 179–80).
89 I am grateful to Abram de Swaan for suggesting this expression after reading an earlier version of this essay.

Chapter 4   Why Chimney-Sweeps Bring Luck

1 See Mayhew (1968, II: 338–78); Spiesberger (1974, based on Reketzki 1952); and Lafranchi-Branca (1981).
2 See Lafranchi-Branca (1981: 37–41); and Bühler (1984: 169–70).
3 See Mayhew (1968, II: 346); Pitsch (1949, I: 97–9); and Eloy (1983: 51–2).
4 See Lafranchi-Branca (1981: 45–82); and the biographical sketches in Martin (1981) of retired sweeps from the Vallée de Rhêmes, a lateral valley of the Val d'Aosta near the French–Italian border. In a recent study of the history of pedlars from Alpine valleys, Fontaine discusses itinerancy from the point of view of the home communities and the local structures supporting it (1996).
5 See Bianconi (1980: 49–56); and Lurati and Pinana (1983: 93–103).
6 See Bovenkerk and Ruland (1984); and Heering (1985: 33–41).
7 This question is raised (but not answered) by Bühler (1984: 170, 174). See also Cole and Wolf (1974: 111).
8 See Danckert (1963: 214–20); Küther (1983); and Fontaine (1996: 164–82).
9 See Danckert (1963: 202); and Mayhew (1968, II: 364).
10 See Lurati and Pinana (1983: 93ff).
11 For reports that confirm these patterns, see Martin (1981: 33–6 and *passim*).
12 See Egardt (1962: 294).
13 For England, see some notes in George (1966: 161); Phillips (1962); and Phythian-Adams (1983: 97).
14 See Martin, who writes about the sweeps from the area of Aosta: 'Plusieurs maitres-ramoneurs achetaient aussi des cheveux des femmes. Ils appellaient "cavei del pentou" les cheveux qui restaient attachés au peigne lors de la toilette du matin. Pour avertir les femmes de leur passage, ils criaient: "Oii...câveii del pêntou...due lire all'etto". Cela se passait encore dans les années 1910–1915' (Several master sweeps also bought women's hair. They called the hairs that remained attached to the comb after the morning toilette 'cavei del pentou' [hairs of the comb]. To announce their arrival to women they shouted 'Oi...hairs of the comb...two lire for one ounce'. This still happened during the years 1910–1915) (1981:

28). The hair was collected in a little cotton bag and sold in Turin on Saturdays.

15   See Pitsch (1949, I: 99); and Palmer and Palmer (1980: 135–9, especially 183–5). The frontispiece of this book is a callotype image, taken in the early 1840s probably somewhere in England, representing a young sweep with a top-hat and an eighteenth-century, guitar-shaped hurdy-gurdy. The picture is probably the oldest photograph of a chimney-sweep.

16   See Mayhew (1968); Pitsch (1949; 1952); and Lafranchi-Branca (1981: 10, 14).

17   See Niederer (1980: 82–4).

18   Photos by courtesy of Dr Fernando Bonetti, Archivio Cantonale di Bellinzona, Switzerland.

19   See Mayhew (1968, II: 370); Palmer and Palmer (1980: 135–7); and Spies-berger (1974: 27).

20   See Mayhew (1968, II: 344–5); Eloy (1983: 86–90); and Hoffmann-Krayer and Bächtold-Staubli 1932, IV: 940–1).

21   See Stoett (1935); and Eloy (1983: 33, 38).

22   I should like to thank Dionigi Albera, who kindly provided me with this text.

23   See Reketzki (1952: 210–85); Lurati and Pinana (1983: 93ff); and Heering (1985: 37–9).

24   See Mayhew (1968, II: 367); Spiesberger (1974: 20); Lafranchi-Branca (1981: 53); and Bovenkerk and Ruland (1984: 29).

25   See Spiesberger (1974: 9–11, 24). Spiesberger also notes a remarkable marriage pattern among Viennese sweeps. Older widows sometimes married young apprentices, who, in their turn as older widowers, married young women. It was just such anomalous marriages that, in early modern Europe, attracted local criticism in the form of *charivari*. See Thompson (1972; 1981); Davis (1975: 105–7); and Le Goff and Schmitt (1981).

26   See Bühler (1984: 175).

27   See Danckert (1963: 22); and Casagrande and Vecchio (1979), who also point out that prostitutes and jugglers belonged to the same category of the infamous, since both gave up their honour for profit (*guot umb êre nemen*), disguising, contorting, showing and selling their bodies in public for money.

28   Mayhew (1968, II: 357, 364).

29   See Mayhew (1968, II: 357).

30   See Lafranchi-Branca (1981: 51–3); and Bovenkerk and Ruland (1984: 3).

31   On the ritual significance of costume and headgear, see Leach (1973a: 227–30) and his observations elsewhere: 'But once a particular uniform comes to be habitually associated with a particular rite or with a particular social office associated with that rite, then any characteristic part of the uniform may be used as a metonymic sign for the rite or office' (1976: 56). See also Hobsbawm's suggestion, that 'traditions' and pragmatic conventions or routines are inversely related. . . . The wigs of lawyers could hardly acquire their modern significance until other people stopped wearing wigs' (1983: 4).

32   Frank Bovenkerk, personal communication.

33   Compare Goffman (1968: 15).

34   See Eloy (1983: 31–40); and Bregenhoj (1978: 38–41).

35 In a famous essay, Leach (1964a: 37–40) presents an outline of a general theory of taboo that derives from Durkheim and Mauss (1963), Van Gennep (1960) and Radcliffe-Brown (1952), and converges with the essays of Douglas (1966; 1975) on boundaries, pollution and anomalous animals. See also Leach (1976), and Leach and Aycock (1983: 15–16). Whatever or whoever does not fit accepted social categories, writes Leach, is marginal, ambiguous and credited with the (magical) power of mediating. He maintains that such ambiguous categories attract the maximum interest and generate the most intense feelings of taboo. Whatever is taboo has ritual value, is sacred, valuable, important, powerful, dangerous, untouchable, filthy, unmentionable. Leach illustrates this with exudations of the human body (faeces, urine, semen, menstrual blood, hair clippings, nail pairings), which are universally objects of taboo. Earlier (1939), Radcliffe-Brown had advanced the idea that anything which is the object of ritual avoidance or taboo has ritual value (1952: 138–9), which does not explain much. The term 'liminal' was introduced into anthropology by Van Gennep (1960) and further developed by Turner (1967: 93–111; 1969; and 1974: 231–71).

36 See two unnumbered New Year's well-wishing cards, one from 1871, the other from 1889, reproduced in Spiesberger (1974).

37 See Eloy (1983: 32–6).

38 See Hoffmann-Krayer and Bächtold-Staubli (1932, IV: 940–1); and Brown (1960: 190).

39 See also Lévi-Strauss's seminal essay 'La structure des mythes', in particular his phrase: 'et le rôle de porte-bonheur attribué, en Europe, aux ordures (vieux souliers), aux cendres et à la sui (cf. le rite du baiser au ramoneur)' (and the role of luck-bringer attributed, in Europe, to dirt (old shoes), to ashes and to soot (cf. the ritual kissing of the sweep)) (1958: 250).

40 For an instructive discussion of the ladybird as a luck-bringing mediator, see Mooyman (1986).

41 See Tambiah (1985a) and Douglas (1975: 27–45, 276–318).

42 From a structuralist point of view, marriage and funeral ceremonies have a great deal in common. Hertz (1960: 80) already recognized their similarities, in particular a painful departure, before Van Gennep published his famous treatise. Cf. Van Gennep (1960: 190).

43 Quoted in Bühler (1984: 173). See also 'Il mondo dello spazzacamino', special issue of Eco dell'Ossola. Risveglio ossolano, Domodossola, Italy (29 July 1982, p. 5), which also contains a heartrending picture of such a pranzo di spazzacamini.

44 See Judge (1979: 9–27).

45 See Phillips (1949); Judge (1979: 35); Phythian-Adams (1983: 97–101).

46 A comprehensive study of marginal groups that completely ignores the ritual value of marginal persons, as well as the connection between marginality, mediation and magical power, is the otherwise valuable essay of Graus (1981). This is a serious omission, since these connections also help clarify what the notion of infamy (Unehrlichkeit) was all about. It has been the merit of Danckert (1963) to have recognized the importance of these dimen-

sions, but his interpretation in terms of pre-Christian survivals remains
unconvincing.

47 See Hoffmann-Krayer and Bächtold-Staubli (1932, IV: 940).
48 On the mediatory functions of domestic fire (hearth) between sky (sun) and
    earth, and the equivalence of the female–male polarity and the sky–earth
    polarity, see Lévi-Strauss (1969: 285–99, esp. 293–4).
49 On the tasks of the barber in Swat, see also Barth (1965: 47–8).
50 Weavers hardly seem to belong to this company. Yet some of them, most
    notably fullers, handled human exudations, namely urine, which contained
    ammonia and was used for the preparation of cloth.
51 See Danckert (1963: 37–44; and Wilbertz (1979: 47–99).
52 On the executioner as a magician, see Angstmann (1928: 90ff), and the per-
    ceptive remarks of Mauss (1975: 29).

Chapter 5   The Blood Symbolism of *Mafia*

1 See also Arlacchi (1987: 196ff, 221).
2 For the terms 'organizational flexibility' and 'structural fluidity', I have
   drawn on Berland (1982: 84–93 and *passim*), who explores the social structure of the peripatetic Qualandar (service nomads in western Pakistan) and
   stresses the importance of the sibling group: 'of all interpersonal relationships, the most valued, loved, and respected are those between brothers and
   sisters within a tent' (1982: 92).
3 *Mafia* families take their name from the territories they 'protect' and control:
   for example, the 'family of Santa Maria del Gesù' in Palermo once headed
   by Stefano Bontate; the 'family of Passo di Rigano' led by Salvatore Inzerillo; the 'family of Corso dei Mille' led by Filippo Marchese, etc. In the hinterland of Palermo, almost every town has its eponymous family. For maps
   of the territories of Sicilian *mafia* families, see Sterling (1990); Stille (1995);
   and the sketch of Buscetta in Arlacchi (1994: 106–10).
4 There are good reasons to argue against the 'monolithic theorem' that,
   according to some, has served as a useful instrument in judicial politics. In
   a recent review article entitled 'How organized is organized crime?', Martin
   Clark points out that anthropologists and sociologists traditionally had
   a different view of the Sicilian *mafia*: 'Far from being a unitary organization, to them "The Mafia" is a fluid network of competing "families", each
   loosely organized and subject to constant conflicts and reversals of fortune
   and alliance' (*Times Literary Supplement*, 1 September 1995, p. 7). See also
   Stajano (1986: 24, 41–9); Gambetta (1993: 153–5); and Stille (1995: 364).
   Insider Buscetta also takes issue with the notion of a centralized leadership:
   'Cosa Nostra non ha una vera e propria testa, ma un centro di gravità col-
   locato tra Palermo e Trapani' (Cosa Nostra does not have a true, real chief,
   but its cantre of gravity is located between Palermo and Trapani), quoted
   in Arlacchi (1994: 106–7). After the arrest of Salvatore Riina in January
   1993, hierarchical tendencies gave way to a cellular model: that is, a segmentary system. This is the view of the Chief Public Prosecutor in Palermo,
   Giancarlo Casella, professed in June 1997 after the arrest of Pietro Aglieri,

the alleged number two of Cosa Nostra and considered one of the people to have been entrusted with this reorganization. See *La Repubblica*, 7 June 1997, and *NRC Handelsblad*, 10 June 1997.

5 For a sketch of this war, see Stajano (1986: 17–37); Sterling (1990: 203–35); and Stille (1995). Buscetta conveyed his premonitions in his talks with Arlacchi: 'that many of these killings [in 1979 and 1980 of prominent people] were carried out by the *Corleonesi* without warning and without the authorization of the Commission' (Arlacchi 1994: 222–3).

6 Sicily has a total population of about 5 million people.

7 Some early examples are discussed in Blok (1988: 103ff). Sterling recognizes the importance of sets of brothers in the network of *mafiosi* running the international drug trade (1990: 287).

8 Cf. D. Schneider (1968: 49–54; 1984: 165–201).

9 See also Benveniste (1973) and Friedrich (1979: 201–52).

10 *Corleonesi: mafiosi* from Corleone, a rural town in the hinterland of Palermo, but also including their allies from the neighbouring town of San Giuseppe Jato and some families from Palermo and Catania. From the late 1970s until their demise in the early 1990s (following the arrest of Salvatore Riina in January 1993 and the death of Luciano Leggio in November that year), the *Corleonesi* dominated the Sicilian *mafia*. As mentioned before, in the second *mafia* war (1981–2), they decimated the ranks of their more traditional rivals in Palermo and some neighbouring towns. For details, see Stajano (1986: 16–37); Shawcross and Young (1987); Sterling (1990: 54–66, 203–35); Follain (1995: 95–175); and Stille (1995).

11 See Sterling (1990: 200). Another example of matrilineally transferred leadership among *mafiosi* concerns the brothers Calderone from Catania. It seems that the older brother, Giuseppe, followed in the steps of one of his mother's brothers, a man called Luigi Saitta. See Arlacchi's biography of Antonino Calderone (1992: 10–20).

12 Sterling (1990: 199–200). Her source, which I could not consult, is Giusto Sciacchitano (1982). See also Shawcross and Young, who note that 'In the mid-1970s the Sicilian branch of the Gambino family was up to its neck in heroin trafficking mainly through the clan headed by Salvatore Inzerillo and Rosario Spatola, both relatives of the Gambinos [i.e. the cousins Rosario and Carlo Gambino]. It has been estimated that by the late seventies the Inzerillo–Gambino–Spatola network was smuggling $600 million worth of heroin into America each year' (1987: 77–8).

13 In January 1996, Tommaso Buscetta was interviewed by the lawyers of Giulio Andreotti who was accused of having protected *mafiosi*. One of the lawyers, Franco Coppi, asked Buscetta why Gaetano Badalamenti would have met Andreotti. Buscetta answered: 'Per interessamento nella soluzione del processo del cognato Filippo Rimi' (Because of his concern with the outcome of the trial of his brother-in-law Filippo Rimi). (*La Repubblica*, 11 January 1996, p. 7.) For more examples of intermarriage between *mafiosi*, see Stajano (1986: 33).

14 Cf. J. Schneider (1971) and Meeker (1976).

15 Cf. Goody (1983: 6–33).

16   See Linke (1985: 357–61). See also Herzfeld (1993: 28–34), who drew my attention to Linke's work.

17   We also know of fraternal rivalry coming close to fratricide: in the spring of 1981, a resentful brother may have had a hand in the murder of Stefano Bontate, one of Palermo's most important *mafia* bosses. See also Buscetta's observations on loyalty to the 'family' in Arlacchi (1994: 157–8), and chapter 7 of this volume.

18   The term *pentito* (plural: *pentiti*) can perhaps be best translated as 'crown witness' or a person who, under a protection programme, has turned state's evidence.

19   See La Fontaine (1985: 58–80). Cf. Buijtenhuijs (1971: 255–85); Blok (1995a: 102–11; 129–32); and chapter 2 of this volume. Buscetta did not consider himself a *pentito*: 'Non sono un pentito'. See Arlacchi (1994: 3).

20   Quoted in Shawcross and Young (1987: 34–5). See also Stajano (1986: 43) and Arlacchi's interviews with Buscetta (1994: 35–8). For more examples of how men of honour are 'made' (including the mixing of blood between old and new members, which implies notions of strong solidarity), see Gambetta (1993: 262–70); the testimony of Vincenzo Marsala from Vicari in Stajano (1986: 63–6); and the description of Antonino Calderone from Catania in Arlacchi (1992: 52–61). Discussing the organization of bandit bands in nineteenth-century Greece, Koliopoulos points at the close relationship between banditry and foster-brotherhood (1987: 263–5). He refers to the tradition of the mixing of blood of foster-brothers and argues that the 'foster-brotherhood created bonds that transcenced those of kinship, and like kinship rendered the band an instrument in the quest for security' (1987: 264–5). For ancient examples of oath rituals that enact irreversibility, see Burkert, who mentions an oath ceremony in *The Iliad*: 'as Agamemnon cuts the [sheep's] throats, the other participants pour wine to the ground from their goblets and pray: "Whoever does wrong against the oath, his brain shall flow to the ground as does this wine, his and his children's, and their wives shall be given to others". Flowing blood, flowing wine, flowing brain are brought together; as the one is enacted, the other is conjured to follow suit' (1996: 173).

21   See Buscetta's observations on gender relations among *mafiosi* in Arlacchi (1994: 159 and *passim*); cf. Shawcross and Young (1987: 76–7). On menstrual taboos, see the collection edited by Buckley and Gottlieb (1988: 28–9). Following Douglas, they argue that menstrual blood is seen as polluting only 'when it symbolically encodes an underlying social-structural ambiguity regarding women'. On the conspicuous absence of women from nineteenth-century Greek bandit bands and from the world of bandits in general, see Koliopoulos (1987: 283–4). The monosexual character of *mafia* organizations is the subject of a recent book (Siebert 1997).

22   On negative reciprocity, see Gouldner (1960); Sahlins (1974b: 191–5); Blok (1983); Di Bella (1992); and Burkert (1996: 133).

23   See Durham (1928: 63–92, 147–84); Cagnetta (1963); Black-Michaud (1975); Jamous (1981: 75, 78–87); Boehm (1984: 191ff); S. Wilson (1988); and Peters (1990: 59–83). See also De Seta (1962); Pigliaru (1975: 131ff);

and Ruffini (1978) on the *ius talionis* among Sardinian shepherds in the Barbagia.

24   See Stille (1995). Intra-*mafia* violence is by no means exceptional. For Calabria, Arlacchi mentions that 'of the 244 mafia-type murders committed in [this region] between 1970 and 1979, some 176 (over 70 per cent) arose from conflicts among mafia groups; and of these 176, at least 141 can be traced back to clashes between mafia family/enterprises struggling for economic and territorial supremacy' (1987: 157).

25   Several popular expressions attest to the common practice of betrayal and betrayals within betrayals (cf. Maxwell 1957). In the biography of Tommaso Buscetta, the protagonist observes: 'L'uomo che ti sta accanto ti può portare a una festa come alla tua tomba. L'amico più caro può essere il tuo assassino' (The man who stands beside you can bring you to a party as likely as to your tomb. The closest friend can become your murderer.) (Arlacchi 1994: 155). For a discussion of Sicilian proverbs conveying the ambiguities of friendship, see Blok (1999).

26   Once Tommaso Buscetta had become *persona non grata* and had moved to Brazil in January 1981, within two years several close kinsmen, including two sons and one brother-in-law, disappeared and were not heard of again. Another brother-in-law, a son-in-law, two grandchildren, and a brother and his son, were also killed. As Buscetta pointed out, none of these nine people was a *mafioso*; their only fault was that they had his name or were related to him through kinship. See Arlacchi's biography (1994: 236–43).

27   For a brief documentation of the close relationship between blood and life, see Camporesi (1984). Cf. Di Bella (1992).

28   Roy Gutman, 'Dutch Reveal Horrors of Mission Impossible' (*Newsday*, 25 July 1995); quoted in Danner (1998: 67), who refers to the massacre of Serb civilians near Bratunac in December 1992, for which the young Muslim commander in Srebrenica, Naser Oric, was held responsible. For detailed accounts of the fall of Srebrenica and the previous fighting between Muslims and Serbs in this area, see Rohde (1997: 215–17 and *passim*) and Sudetic (1998: 147ff and *passim*).

29   Frazer (1957, I: 16ff and 49ff).

30   Involving a system of messages and signs, *mafia* violence can be understood in terms of culture and communication. This is not always recognized by Italian sociologists and historians. See, for example, the discussion in Siebert (1997: 35–9 and *passim*). She shows little patience with 'folkloristic explanations' and seems completely unaware of the anthropological discussion on ritual and the ethnography of feuding in the Mediterranean area.

31   See also Durham (1928: 164); Boehm (1984: 51ff); and S. Wilson's ethnographic sketch of the idiom of blood in Corsican feuding (1988: 408–10). His observations on the real and figurative meaning of 'taking blood' in reciprocal fashion – for example, 'in Corsica as in Albania, it was felt necessary to literally replace the blood which the kindred had lost through a murder of one of its members by making offerings of blood in a variety of ways, of which vengeance killing was only one' – easily fit the metonymic paradigm of 'participation'. Sicilian examples are mentioned

by Siebert (1997: 37–8, 247 and *passim*), who, however, dismisses them as 'folklore'.

32   Durham (1928: 162, 170). Durham suggests that the swearing of blood brotherhood when settling a blood feud also denotes a replacement of lost blood (1928: 170).

33   Quoted in Arlacchi (1994: 157–8).

34   See Huizinga (1955: 25), who discusses this issue in his book on play: 'When a certain form of religion accepts a sacred identity between two things of a different order, say a human being and an animal, this relationship is not adequately expressed by calling it a "symbolical correspondence" as *we* conceive this. The identity, the essential oneness of the two goes far deeper than the correspondence between a substance and its symbolic image. It is a mystic unity. The one has *become* the other.... We must always be on our guard against the deficiencies and differences of our means of expression.'

35   The case of the transhuman Sarakatsani shepherds in the Zagori mountains of north-western Greece confirms this. Although the idea of feuding is very real and the Sarakatsani have a taste for violence, they have a notably low incidence of vengeance. Their ethnographer Campbell relates this pattern to the well-organized and omnipresent Greek police (1964: 194–5).

36   See Steinmetz's definition of *Selbsthilfe* (self-help): 'Wo und wann der Einzelne aber von ihm [dem Staat] und seinen Organen entweder im Stich gelassen oder umgekehrt erstickt zu werden droht, tritt die Selbsthilfe als Rettungsmöglichkeit wieder auf' (Where and when the individual, however, threatens to be abandoned or, conversely, suffocated by the state and its institutions, self-help appears once more as a saving device) (1931: 22). See Boehm (1984: 65–6, 173) for a more recent view of self-help.

37   See E. Wolf (1966a).

38   See, for example, *Dossier Andreotti* (1993); Buscetta's view in Arlacchi (1994: 206–9); and Stille (1995: 390–412). On the 'faccia pulita' of the *mafia*, see also Stajano (1986: 43).

39   I draw here on a passage in Misha Glenny's article 'Why the Balkans are so violent' in the *New York Review of Books* (vol. 43, no. 14), 19 September 1996, pp. 34–9, esp. p. 36.

40   The *pentito* Vincenzo Marsala (from the 'family' of Vicari near Termini Imerese) emphasized in his testimony that the *mafia* has its strongholds and main recruitment areas in the little towns of Sicily's agrarian *retroterra*. See Stajano (1986: 69).

41   The expression 'capo di tutti capi', which is often uncritically used in the popular press whenever an important *mafioso* is arrested, unwittingly underscores the distinctly segmentary character of Cosa Nostra. For critical comments on the expression '*capo di tutti capi*', see also Buscetta's observations in Arlacchi's biography (1994: 106–7).

42   On the modest living quarters of the famous Genco Russo in Mussomeli, see Buscetta's description of his visit in the 1950s. He emphasizes stereotypical representations including 'sleeping with the mule at home' and the lack of privacy with respect to defecation. See Arlacchi (1994: 16–17).

43 The concepts of blood and kinship overlap in the colloquial *meo sangue* ('my blood'), a term of endearment mothers use when they hug their young children (cf. Campbell 1964: 185).

44 See, for example, Buscetta's references in Arlacchi (1994: 153, 219, 228 and *passim*).

45 See Buscetta's comments on the denomination of 'uncle' in Arlacchi (1994: 209, 225). On the use of kinship terms outside the realm of kinship, Goody notes that in 'Christianity, kin terms were used not only for addressing the gods and the priesthood, but also for addressing all the fellow-members of the sect, and later those specially chosen as spiritual kin or godkin. God the Father is served by priests and helpers who are "fathers" and "brothers", "mothers" and "sisters". The Head of the Church is *il Papa*, the Pope, the head of the monastery is called the Abbot, again a "father", derived from the Aramaic *abba*' (1983: 194).

Chapter 6   The Meaning of 'Senseless' Violence

1 The social sciences have usually been more interested in social order than in violence and chaos – a bias that is closely connected with the pacification of western societies: the means of violence have long since been monopolized by the state and have in most part moved 'behind the scenes' (cf. Elias 1978b: 191ff; Blok 1995b).

2 This is a strong statement, which does not do justice to the work of the English historian Richard Cobb (1972; 1975).

3 See Robinson (1995). See also p. 256 n. 10.

4 'The uses of violence', *Times Literary Supplement*, 16 January 1998, p. 7.

5 On this hypocrisy and self-censorship for fear of being branded as politically incorrect or racist, see the article by Koos Van Zomeren in *NRC Handelsblad* (17 August 1991) on the trial and the deliberately distorted reports in two leading Dutch dailies. Publicity on the ethnic background of offenders was still a controversial subject when this essay first appeared (cf. Bovenkerk 1991).

6 For a summary of the literature, see Gilmore (1987). The related code of honour among aristocrats is discussed in Elias (1983: 94ff); Pitt-Rivers (1977: 1–17); and Nye (1991).

7 Pitt-Rivers (1977: 8). The relationship between honour and violence is explicitly addressed in Campbell (1964); Bourdieu (1979a); Jamous (1981); Nye (1991); and chapter 10 of this volume. Pitt-Rivers in anthropology and Goffman in sociology have, independently, drawn on the fundamental insights of Simmel.

8 For an inventory and discussion of the repertoire of offensive performances, see Goffman on 'territories of the self' and 'remedial exchanges' (1971: 28–61 and 95–187). About the person as a ceremonial object and the symbolic actions related to this sacredness, see Goffman's famous essay on deference and demeanour (1967: 47–95) and his book *Stigma* (1963). Cf.

Simmel (1950a: 320–1) on discretion, distance, honour, and the 'ideal sphere': 'Although differing in size in various directions and differing according to the person with whom one entertains relations, this sphere cannot be penetrated, unless the personality value of the individual is thereby destroyed. A sphere of this sort is placed around man by his "honor". Language very poignantly designates an insult to one's honor as "coming too close": the radius of this sphere marks, as it were, the distance whose trespassing by another person insults one's honor' (1950: 321).

9   H. Geertz (1975), quoted in Tambiah (1990: 22–3).
10   See Hemingway (1977); Pitt-Rivers (1983); and Marvin (1986).
11   See Dahles (1990: 14–15 and *passim*); K. Thomas (1983: 160ff); and Elias (1986).
12   Van de Brink (1991: 101).
13   Estrich (1987) and Brownmiller (1975) argue that rape is not a sexual but a violent crime. Attitudes in the Netherlands are also changing. In September 1991 the Dutch government initiated a four-year publicity campaign to help change the sexual behaviour of boys and men in order to diminish sexual violence against women. Current ideas about sexual violence had been investigated before. Forty per cent of those interviewed define all intimacies carried out against the will of partners and others as sexual violence. Thirty per cent prefer to restrict the use of this term to rape and assault.
14   Because the concept of 'undesired intimacies' would wrongly imply that one is concerned with intimacy, some prefer the term 'sexual intimidation' (*NRC Handelsblad*, 19 October 1991), which links up with the current term 'sexual harassment' in English. The expression 'undesired intimacies', however, best captures all the uninvited advances and passes short of sexual intimidation. These terminological changes alone suggest that violence constitutes a cultural category and refers to historically developed practices, representations, perceptions and attitudes that are closely bound up with (although not reducible to) the largely unplanned shift in the balance of power between the sexes in favour of women. These developments illustrate modern anthropology's belief that culture makes people as much as people make culture.
15   Cf. Radcliffe-Brown (1952: 143); Leach (1964b: 10–14; 1966; 1976: 9). For a slightly different appreciation of the distinction between expressive and instrumental behaviour, between 'saying' and 'doing', see Rappaport (1979: 175ff); Geertz (1980: 120, 134–6); and Tambiah (1985b: 77ff and 123ff).
16   Leach (1964b: 12).
17   See Blok (1995a: 153–76) and chapter 2 of this volume.
18   See Blok (1995a) and chapter 2 of this volume.
19   See note 10, above.
20   On sacrifice, see Girard (1979); Burkert (1983); Hamerton-Kelly (1987); Valeri (1985); and De Heusch (1985); on ritual regicide, see De Heusch (1997); on hunting, see Howe (1981); Itzkowitz (1977); Elias (1986); Dahles (1990); and the special issue of *Etudes rurales* (1982); on butchering, see Vialles (1994); on *charivari*, see Le Goff and Schmitt (1981); Blok (1989); and Rooijakkers (1994); on plunder, see Dekker (1982); Ginzburg (1987);

and Blok (1995a); on football hooliganism, see Dunning et al. (1986); Stokvis (1991); and Bromberger et al. (1995: 229–95); on feuding, see Black-Michaud (1975) and Boehm (1984); on head-hunting, see Rosaldo (1980); on the Sicilian *mafia*, see Blok (1988) and Gambetta (1993); on duelling, see Kiernan (1988); Billacois (1986); Elias (1996: 44–119); Nye (1991); McAleer (1994); and Frevert (1995); on terrorism, see Walter (1969); Zulaika (1988); Douglass and Zulaika (1990); and Feldman (1991); on tyrannicide, see Ranum (1980); on public executions, see Linebaugh (1975); Schild (1980); Gernet (1981); Spierenburg (1984); Von Dülmen (1984); and Blok (1995a); on war, see Koch (1974); Meggitt (1977); McNeill (1992); and Keeley (1996: 59–69); and on judicial torture, see Langbein (1977). Collective violence during revolutions is often less spontaneous and more 'directed' than has generally been assumed; see Aya (1990).

21   Cf. Gernet (1981: 265–6).

22   Cf. Meuli (1975b, II: 952ff and 1004ff) and Burkert (1983: 35ff). Some scholars view the so-called *Henkersmahlzeit* (last meal of the condemned) as an attempt at reconciliation (see Von Hentig 1958). In a French documentary on deer-hunting shown in Aix-en-Provence in the autumn of 1997, a man who had shot a deer lifted its snout and placed a brief kiss on it. The custom of blindfolding convicts before executing them is also consistent with the idea of distance and reconciliation: the killers do not have to face, look in the eyes of, those they are killing. Blindfolding (like putting on a mask) removes convicts and killers symbolically from the place of execution. 'le bourreau ne veut pas croiser le regard de la victime . . . parce qu'il voit des yeux, un miroir des siens propres, alors que cet autre doit être autre. On bande les yeux de celui qui va être fussillé, on lui tire dans la nuque, pour ne pas croiser son regard' (The executioner does not want to meet the gaze of the victim . . . because he sees these eyes as a mirror of his own. . . . One blindfolds the person who will be executed, one shoots him in the nape of the neck in order to avoid meeting his gaze) (Nahoume-Grappe 1996: 320).

23   See Meuli (1975b, II: 952) and Burkert (1983: 22–34 and *passim*). On the ritual pollution of warriors in antiquity, see J. Redfield (1975: 222). For a modern variation, see Zulaika (1988: 86–101). On prototypical territorial violations that entail ritual pollution, see Goffman (1971: 50–2).

24   See chapter 5.

25   Cf. Zulaika (1988: 206, 326) and Douglass and Zulaika (1990: 225), who emphasize the innocence of victims in sacrifice: 'Some societies resort to the institution of drawing lots to assure the ritual innocence of the victim. To kill someone for an offence is an act of justice; to kill someone to placate an angry god is a ritual sacrifice in which the innocence of the victim has to be made patent through random selection.' See also Burkert (1983: 35–48); Girard (1979: 314); and Simmel (1983: 405). Unlike English and French, the Dutch language retains in the word *slachtoffer* (victim) the connection with the concept of sacrifice.

26   For the strategies underlying Shaka's violence, see Walter (1969: 131–2, 133–77).

27   Cf. Walter (1969: 171).

28 See references to Zulaika's work in n. 25. Walter argues and demonstrates that in the terror process innocence is irrelevant: 'Anyone may be a victim, no matter what action he chooses' (1969: 26).

29 For discussions of seventeenth- and eighteenth-century public executions in the Dutch Republic, see Spierenburg (1984) and Blok (1995a: 153–76). For Germany and England, see Von Dülmen (1984) and Linebaugh (1975). Gernet discusses public executions in ancient Greece and observes: 'The victim of *apotumpanismos* is *exposed* as an object of public indignation and cruel laughter. The victim is also an *exemplum*, since agony is more telling than a dead body' (1981: 267).

30 See Von Amira (1922); Girard (1979); and Hamerton-Kelly (1987).

31 For sixteenth- and seventeenth-century examples, see Ranum (1980); for the ritual killing of the Dutch politician De Witt and his brother in The Hague in 1672, see Rowen (1978: 61–84). For our time, recall the fate of Mussolini. Some years ago, Haiti was the stage of *post mortem* profanations of the remains of the tyrannical President François Duvalier, who died in 1971. For the exhumation and desecration of the remains of *religieuses* and ecclesiastics during the Spanish Civil War, see Lincoln (1985). More recent and less harsh examples of these forms of symbolic violence are found in the iconoclastic wave in eastern Europe after the fall of Communist regimes.

32 Hence the term 'performative action' for ritual. For ritual as performance, see Rappaport (1979: 176–97); and Tambiah (1985b: 77ff and 123–66). Ritual action not only 'says' something, but also 'does' things, brings them about. This implies a further refining of the distinction between instrumental and expressive aspects of human behaviour.

33 See Dunning et al. (1986: 170–8); cf. Stokvis (1991) and Bromberger (1995: 221–95). On the relationship between adolescence, transition and violence, see Van Gennep (1960) and the following note.

34 Cf. Davis (1975: 152–87); Ginzburg (1987); Le Goff and Schmitt (1981); Blok (1989); and Rooijakkers (1994).

35 Feldman (1991: 17–45).

36 Cf. Dahles (1990), who describes how hunters justify their activities to themselves (in terms of *weidelijkheid* or ritualization) rather than to a critical outside world (in terms of social usefulness). For a candid report on hunting, see the interview with a young Dutch hunter, a student at the University of Amsterdam, in *Folia Civitatis*, 4 October 1991. It is significant, however, that the title of the interview, 'Hunter replaces lynx and wolf', again highlights the utilitarian aspects of hunting. In the densely populated Low Countries, hunting is a flourishing business. Of the total area of the Netherlands, about 75 per cent is open to hunting, which occurs in many areas virtually all the year round. The number of hunters (almost exclusively men) has increased during this century from about 7,000 in 1900 to 20,000 in 1950 and over 30,000 at present. See Dahles (1990: 13–14), who also notes that the image of hunters has become more negative over the past few years. The same applies to fox-hunting in England. Popular resistance against hunting in the Netherlands is growing: over 90 per cent of the Dutch population are in favour of abolishing all hunting, and Parliament in Sep-

tember 1997 proposed new laws that would restrict hunting to just a few species.
37 See Elias (1978b); Blok (1995b); and K. Thomas (1983). For the growing sensitivity to domestic violence, see Brinkgreve and Van Daalen (1991).
38 Kiernan's book *The Duel in European History* (1988), for example, is a study against, rather than about, the duel. The author shows little understanding of the meaning and context of duelling and totally ignores the anthropological and sociological literature on honour. In his book, one looks in vain for thick descriptions of famous duels such as Nabokov offers in an extensive note to his annotated edition of Pushkin's *Eugene Onegin* on the duel fought on 27 January 1837 near St Petersburg between the poet and his challenger, Baron Georges Charles d'Anthès, a protégé of the Dutch ambassador Van Heeckeren. See Nabokov (1975, II, 2: 43–51).
39 See Leach (1966: 404; 1976: 10–11), for whom redundancy is a hallmark of ritual.
40 Appadurai points out that violence inflicted on the human body in ethnic conflicts is never entirely random or lacking cultural form: 'Wherever the testimony is sufficiently graphic . . . , it becomes clear that even the worst acts of degradation – involving faeces, urine, body parts; beheading, impaling, gutting, sawing; raping, burning, hanging, and suffocating – have macabre forms of cultural design and violent predictability' (1999: 308–9).

Chapter 7   The Narcissism of Minor Differences

1 Hobbes and Tocqueville have drawn attention to the close relationship between equality, similarity and conflict. For a more recent exposé, see Dumont (1980: 13–20, 262–6), who draws heavily on Tocqueville.
2 About personal territoria and territorial violations, see Goffman (1971: 28–61).
3 Quoted in Boehm (1984: 60–1).
4 The theme of fratricide is not only mythical. The history of the early nineteenth-century Zulu kingdom, for example, includes several cases of fratricide among despots. The terrorist regime of Shaka came to an end in 1828 through a conspiracy between his brothers Dingane and Mhlangana. Later, Dingane killed Mhlangana and succeeded Shaka as king of the Zulus. Dingane died in 1840 after his brother Mpande turned against him in a revolt (Walter 1969: 174–5, 209–11). According to a recent survey, about 10 per cent of homicides in agrarian societies involve fratricide (Daley and Wilson 1988: 25, quoted in Sulloway 1996: 437). But brothers do not always fight and kill each other. In tribal societies, matrilocality entails internal peacefulness, while patrilocal societies often include 'fraternal interest groups', which are responsible for a high degree of open aggression (Thoden van Velzen and Van Wetering 1960; cf. Koch 1974: 166–71); see, however, Knauft (1987: 471–3; cf. 1985), who shows that the Gebusi of New Guinea lack fraternal interest groups and yet have an extremely high rate of inter-

nal violence. The loyalty between brothers and other agnatic kinsmen is also important among Sicilian *mafiosi*, in particular in the struggle between 'families' (Blok 1988). Yet close kinsmen can easily end up as antagonists, as happened in the so-called second *mafia* war in the early 1980s that ended in victory for the Corleonesi, who double-crossed many closely related opponents (Stajano 1986: 16–37; Stille 1995: 99–120 and *passim*). In those days, as one newspaper puts it, within the same family one brother feared the other, and sons were afraid of what their father had in store for them. These cases illustrate the popular saying, 'Nella stessa faccia, l'occhio destra odiava il sinistro' (In the same face the right eye hated the left one) (*La Repubblica*, 7 June 1997, p. 2). Other expressions, like 'Fratelli, coltelli' (Brothers, knives), '*Cugini, assassini*' (Cousins, killers), 'Genitori, traditori' (Parents, traitors) and 'Per gli amici mi guarda Iddio' (God protect me from my friends), likewise suggest familiarity with the other side of affection and friendship (cf. Blok 1999).

5 This sketch is based on De Vos and Wagatsuma (1972: 33–67, esp. 34–8).

6 For a recent anthropological interpretation of lynching in the American South, see Brundage (1993). See also his notes on the Forsyth County case (1993: 43, 315, n. 87). Cf. Dumont (1980: 262–4, 425, n. 26).

7 See, for example, E. Wolf's study of peasant revolts (1969) and Aya's reflections (1990: 106–22).

8 For recent studies on the development of the duel in Germany, see Frevert (1995) and McAleer (1994).

9 Culture can be a matter of life and death. I owe this formulation to Rod Aya.

10 Richard West, *Tito and the Rise and Fall of Yugoslavia* (1994), quoted by Michael Ignatieff: 'The politics of self-destruction', in *New York Review of Books* (2 November 1995, p. 17). See also Ignatieff's statement in his review article 'The Balkan tragedy', in *New York Review of Books* (13 May 1993, p. 3): 'Freud once argued that the smaller the difference between two people the larger it looms in their imaginations. This effect, which he called the narcissism of minor differences, is especially visible in the Balkans.' Ignatieff returned to this theme in greater detail in his book *The Warrior's Honor: Ethnic war and the modern conscience* (London: Chatto & Windus, pp. 34–71), which appeared in the summer of 1998 when the present essay was in press.

11 This outline is based on Prunier (1995). For a view of the relationship between Tutsi and Hutu around 1900, see the reconstruction by Maquet (1961: 129–72 and *passim*).

12 For a detailed account of these different racial types, see the photographic essay by Maquet (1957). On the proximity of Rwandese Tutsi and Hutu, and their linguistic, religious and cultural unity, see Vidal (1996: 335–7, 356–7).

13 In his description of the genocide in the spring of 1994, Prunier notes that distinguishing Hutu and Tutsi in the countryside was not a problem because the identity of the villagers was generally known. However, 'It was not the same thing in the towns and even more in Kigali where people did not know each other. There the *Interahamwe* manning the road-blocks asked people

for their identity cards. To be identified on one's card as a Tutsi or to pretend to have lost one's papers meant certain death. Yet to have a Hutu ethnic card was not automatically a ticket to safety. . . . And people were often accused of having a false card, especially if they were tall and with a straight nose and thin lips. Frequent intermarriage had produced many Hutu-looking Tutsi and Tutsi-looking Hutu. In the towns and along the highways, Hutu who looked like Tutsi were often killed, their denials and proffered cards with the "right" ethnic mention being seen as a typical Tutsi decep-tion' (1995: 249).

14 See population figures in Prunier (1995: 4), who comments on the rapid growth in population (from 1.5 million in 1934 to approximately 7 million in 1989): 'Grim as it may seem, the genocidal violence of the spring of 1994 can be partly attributed to that population density' (1995: 4).

15 Quoted in Mark Lilla, 'The Enemy of liberalism', in *New York Review of Books* (15 May 1997, p. 39). In his essay on the psychology of prejudice, Ernst Kris notes that the assumption that the greater the differences between groups the more intense will be the prejudice is not born out by the facts. On the contrary, he found that 'even the smallest difference can be stressed and overstressed and may become a focal point around which prejudice may crystallize. One can go even further: propinquity seems to invite such overemphasis; thus a slight deviation in accent or pronunciation in one and the same language can be experienced as indicating a wider gulf between groups than the use of a different language; "brethren in blood", like the Spanish and the Portuguese, can hold against each other no less embittered prejudices than people of different coloured skins.' Kris then further argues: 'If one difference tends to disappear or to lose its importance, i.e., to appear less crucial to group members, another is called upon to take its place. Hence, when in western and central Europe during the 19th century Jewish assimilation proceeded rapidly, so that ever more persons of Jewish descent became indistinguishable from the dominant groups, and, simultaneously, the religious distinction was felt by many to be less decisive, it was suddenly claimed that the difference between Jews and non-Jews rested upon racial inheritance; racial reasons were called upon to supplement religious reasons for segregation and discrimination' (1975: 467–68). Cf. Gay (1988: 14–21; 1978: 18–19) on Jewish emancipation and assimilation in Vienna in the nineteenth century. Zizek, too, argues that the anxiety about the resem-blance between Jews and Germans was a key fact of anti-Semitism (Zizek 1989: 128–9). Discussing the connection between anti-Semitism and nation-alism in Germany, Goldhagen (1996: 45, 55–62, 487n.) fails to recognize the unintended consequences of Jewish emancipation (legally, politically and socially). The emancipation of the Jews, in combination with the develop-ment of Germany as a nation, produced the forms of anti-Semitism that led to the 'final solution'.

16 On the development of this uprising, which became the most important peasant revolt in the history of eastern Europe and which was suppressed by the army (with much bloodshed), see the summary by Chirot (1976: 150–5) and the detailed study by Eidelberg (1974).

17   An indication of this can be found in an analysis of the first disturbances: 'The problem is one of the working class. There have been no riots in the prosperous areas of Belmont or the Malone Road in Belfast. Here the well-to-do middle classes are protected by their own mobility. They know that they have the resources to get up and go if they have to – and more of them are now contemplating it – to a calmer part of the province, to the Republic, or across to England. But for the poverty-stricken ghettoes of the Shankill and Falls areas of Belfast, or the Bogside and Fountain districts of Londonderry, no such option is open. With a generally low level of industrial wages, high unemployment and an acute shortage of low-cost housing, the people trapped by their economic circumstances in these slums are ready victims of gut emotion whenever they feel a threat to what little stability they can cling to. It is those who have least to lose in material terms who most need to hug what they do have' (H. Jackson 1972: 5).

18   Akenson (1988) also aptly illustrates my argument, but came too late to my attention to be used here.

19   Source: State of the Nation Report, South African Institute of Race Relations, January 1993, quoted in *New York Review of Books* (13 February 1993, pp. 24ff). On the fierce fighting within the Zulu faction itself – a case of fratricide within fratricide – see Meredith (1997: 419–33).

20   Huntington, who makes much of differences between civilizations, especially along their fault lines and in the realm of religion which he describes as 'possibly the most profound difference that can exist between people' (1996: 254), recognizes that the long-standing and violent conflict between Islam and Christianity 'also stemmed from their similarities' (1996: 210–11). But it is precisely along these fault lines and borders, where conflicts are particularly bloody, that one may expect to find transcultural similarities that result from proximity and what Dumont in his essay on the relationship between Muslims and Hindus calls 'cultural osmosis' (1980: 206).

21   From this point of view, the events in Bali in December 1965 deserve further investigation. In less than two weeks, about 80,000 people were killed ('largely by one another') in the aftermath of the unsuccessful coup in Jakarta on 1 October. See Geertz (1973c: 452) for a marginal note and Robinson (1995: 273–313) for a detailed report on the post-coup massacre in Bali. The mass killings between Muslims, Hindus and Sikhs in the Punjab shortly after India and Pakistan became independent in 1947 ('the twins born from the same egg', as one author puts it) provide another example of violence following the imminent erosion of minor differences – minor differences that were previously respected under British rule, but now lost their self-evidence under the impact of the ideology of social equality. On the western side of the new border, Muslims killed Hindus and Sikhs, on the eastern border, Hindus and Sikhs massacred Muslims (*NRC Handelsblad*, 9 August 1997). Violent confrontations between Muslims and Hindus have long been an issue in India itself. To account for them, scholars often follow native views and emphasize the differences between the warring parties and neglect their similarities. In a review of the French edition of Dumont's book, Yalman writes: 'The problem however is not merely that the ultimate principles of Hinduism

and Islam differ. In the Indian context, on the contrary, *the real issue is the extraordinary cultural similarities between Hindus and Muslims*. The general ideology may express the polarisation but does not, in Dumont's definition, take care of the nuances, particularly on the Muslim side' (1969: 128–9, italics added). The narcissism of minor differences can also help us understand why in modern urban settings many victims of violent crimes are killed by friends, relatives or acquaintances. A recent survey of 1,156 women, who died from crimes between 1990 and 1994 in New York City, mentions that almost half of the victims whose relationship with their killer could be traced were killed by their present or former partner (*International Herald Tribune*, 1 April 1997). We are dealing here with structural relationships characterized by the diminution of hierarchical and cultural differences between men and women that coincide with a growing mutual involvement. Knauft analysed in great detail the paradoxical coexistence of affectionate friendship and extreme violence (typically within the community) among the Gebusi in New Guinea, who have rates of homicide that are among the highest reported for any human society (1985: 116–17). He notes that 'the same pattern (although to a much reduced degree) is evident in marital or lover relationships in our own society: intense positive affects hold an underlying potential for extreme anger or violence when the relationship fails or when one party feels ultimately betrayed. . . . In Western countries, physical violence and homicide have been documented as most frequent between spouses – the marriage tie being the most intimate and most highly valued in our society' (1985: 182–3). Knauft argues convincingly that, among the Gebusi, 'it may be precisely the intense valuation of the ideal of "good company" that ultimately leads to violence', and observes that, in a sense, 'the violence that stems from Gebusi sorcery attributions is not the antithesis of "good company" but its ultimate culmination' (1985: 111–12). Knauft further notes that 'among men, coexistence of amity and lethal aggression has been ethnographically documented in a number of politically decentralized societies, particularly those with strong norms of harmony and cooperation' and 'a general lack of adult male status differentials' (1985: 337).

22   Compare Dumont's comparative view, which he summarizes in a number of aphorisms in a paragraph on American racism with the title 'From hierarchy to discrimination'. For instance, 'Make distinction illegitimate, and you get discrimination' and 'Segregation has replaced etiquette as a mode of social distance' (Dumont 1980: 262ff).

23   Elias (1969a: 77n.). In his essay on the 'nonperson', Goffman quotes a passage from Mrs Trollope's *Domestic Manners of the Americans* (1832) about the intimate association between masters and slaves: 'I once saw a lady, who, when seated at table between a male and a female, was induced by her modesty to intrude on the chair of her female neighbor to avoid the indelicacy of touching the elbow of *a man*. I once saw this very young lady lacing her stays with the most perfect composure before a Negro footman' (1959: 151–2).

24   Letter from Freud to Schnitzler, 14 May 1922, quoted in Scheible (1976: 119, 121).

Chapter 8   Explaining South Italian Agro-Towns

1 For useful overviews and helpful maps, see Dovring (1965: 10ff) and Houston (1964: 450–63, 499–544, and *passim*). See also Monheim (1969); Driessen (1981); and Blok and Driessen (1984).
2 Dickinson (1955) and Rochefort (1961: 101–3).
3 See, for example, Rochefort's map of the dispersed population in Sicily (1961: 100).
4 Exploring the *raison d'être* of agro-towns was part of a larger research project that resulted in a study of the development of the local *mafia* (cf. Blok 1988).
5 Ahlmann (1926: 113–15).
6 Ahlmann (1925: 259–60).
7 Ahlmann (1926: 108).
8 Cf. Le Lannou (1938: 103). It has been assumed for a long time that the *nuraghi* were tombs, but Le Lannou feels on reasonable grounds that they were dwelling-places ('habitations des vivants').
9 Bobek describes rent-capitalism as a form of capitalism predicated on leases and sub-leases: rather than 'linked with production, it was satisfied with skimming off its proceeds' (1962: 236–7); cf. Wolf (1966b: 55). For a detailed description of rent-capitalistic enterprises in western Sicily, see Blok (1988: 53–84). Writing on labour, poverty and underemployment in southern Italy, Dickinson pinpoints the system of leases and sub-leases in the following terms: 'This form of parasitism is an accepted and respected way of living' (1955: 64–5).
10 Singular: *gabellotto* (from *gabella*, lease). The *gabellotti* formed the backbone of the rural *mafia* (cf. Blok 1988).
11 On modern dispersion in Spain and Portugal, see Houston (1964: 240–5).
12 Maranelli (1946); Unger (1953: 506–25); and Rochefort (1961: 100–1). Houston notes for Sicily 'a close relationship between areas of dispersed settlement, fruit crops and the distribution of alluvial and marine terraces and terra rossa'. On the same map (Fig. 211), he points at 'the markedly nucleated pattern of large villages over the Pliocene clay lands with their cereal monoculture' (1964: 542–3).
13 Le Lannou (1936: 113–36).
14 In this respect, Vöchting notes that 'southern agriculture suffers more from an abundance than from a shortage of water' (1951: 19).
15 On the complex causes of deforestation in the Mediterranean area, see McNeill (1992: 266–7); cf. Braudel (1972: 142, 238).
16 Le Lannou (1936: 121–6).
17 Maranelli (1946: 26–8) and Compagna (1963: 78).
18 See, in particular, Braudel's detailed account of the impact of banditry and piracy (1973: 734ff, 865ff and *passim*).
19 Kish (1953: 499). A similar pattern can still be recognized in Corsica. The bigger towns on the coast – Ajaccio, Bastia, Bonifacio – are all fortresses.

The largest inland town, Sartène in the south, is a fine example of a hilltop agro-town.

20   Maranelli (1946: 28).

21   Cf. Rochefort (1961: 109–17), and Blok (1966).

22   See discussion and map in Rochefort (1961: 46–53), and, for one town, a summary in Blok (1988: 233–43).

23   A similar settlement pattern has been noted in the Great Hungarian Plain (Alföld). See Den Hollander (1960/1). In this part of Europe we also find isolated farmsteads (*tanyák*) and large nucleated villages, 'big enough to call urban yet with a rustic air: the streets are unpaved, the houses are of one storey only, and the occupations of the people are largely agrarian. These peasant towns are a feature almost peculiar to the Alföld; nowhere else in the world are there so many large agglomerations of this type' (Den Hollander 1960/1: 74–5). The south Italian experience sets a limit to the claim of uniqueness of the Alföld settlement type. Yet two minor differences between the forms must be mentioned. The Hungarian *tanyák* arose as a temporary home during the busy season, only to become a fixed peasant family settlement unit afterwards. The Sicilian *masseria* was never permanently inhabited by peasant families: it was a big farm, situated at the centre of a *latifondo*, where supervisors and agricultural personnel (who had their homes in the agro-town) stayed temporarily. Like the *tanyák*, it included stores and stables.

24   For a detailed description and analysis of these arrangements, see Blok (1988).

25   The close relationship between insecurity and peasant agglomeration has also been observed in some African societies. See W. Watson (1958: 75) and Bascom (1955).

26   For early statements, see Weulersse (1946: 173); Pitt-Rivers (1961: 47); and Redfield (1960: 65–6). See also Caro Baroja (1963), who traces the prestige of the *polis* and the low regard for the countryside to antiquity.

27   Quoted in Gould (1992: 143).

28   Cf. Maranelli (1946: 27–8). McDonald observes that 'Italian literature is rich with accounts of cultivators of the "typical" South abasing themselves before the more wealthy in order to get share-cropping contracts' (1956: 446).

29   For further details on rotation systems, share-cropping and the exploitation of the *latifondi*, see Blok (1988: 58–84).

30   Cf. Garufi (1946: 81–3); and La Mantia (1904).

31   The large proportion of peasants of this town living outside its walls somewhat weakens Banfield's statement that the place is typical of southern Italy (1958: 11).

32   Cf. Redfield (1960: 66).

33   Cf. Moss and Cappannari (1962: 289–90). See also Silverman on the situation in central Italy and the comparison with the south (1968; 1975).

34   Ahlmann (1926); and Demangeon (1927: 23).

35   Sartorius von Waltershausen (1913: 23–7); and Carlyle (1962: 106).

36   Moss and Thompson (1959: 38).

37   I am mostly using the past tense, because much has changed in the area since my research in the early 1960s.

38 This is very much a more general pattern in southern Italy (cf. Dickinson 1955: 23–4). See also Blok and Driessen (1984).
39 I have translated one verb rather freely: *trase*, from *tràsiri*, meaning 'enter' or 'penetrate'. See Biundi (1851).
40 A similar pattern exists in Tunisia, where this intermediate zone is called the *'ceinture chaude'* (personal communication, Mohamed Kerrou).

Chapter 9   Nicknames as Symbolic Inversions

The original version of this essay was co-authored with Andrew S. Buckser.

1 For the most detailed accounts, see Pitt-Rivers (1961: 160–7); Antoun (1968a); Bernard (1969); Collier and Bricker (1970); Dorian (1970); Eberhard (1970: 217–22); Brögger (1971: 87–92); Christian (1972: 23–30); Pilcher (1972: 105–14); Manning (1974); Brandes (1975); Cohen (1977); Barrett (1978); Fox (1978: 66–81); McDowell (1981); Breen (1982); Gilmore (1982); Mewett (1982); Busse (1983); de Pina-Cabral (1984); Skipper (1986); Tak (1988); and Jacquemet (1992). I have also profited from work on other naming practices, e.g. Goodenough (1965); Lévi-Strauss (1966: 172ff); Price and Price (1972); Geertz (1973d: 368–89); Zonabend (1977; 1980); Isaevitch (1980); Barnes (1982); Maybury-Lewis (1984); Rosaldo (1984); and R. Watson (1986). I do not know of any comparative or comprehensive account of nicknaming practices, but a valuable, annotated bibliography on nicknames has been compiled by Massolo (1987). Despite a strong interest in problems of identity, anthropologists have shown relatively little attention to names. See, however, Zonabend (1977; 1980) and the special issue of *L'Homme* (1980, vol. 20, no. 4) on forms of nomination in Europe, and Tooker's (1984) slim collection on naming systems. For a useful annotated bibliography on personal names and naming, see Lawson (1987).
2 Following Babcock (1978: 14), symbolic inversion may be defined as 'any act of expressive behavior which inverts, contradicts, abrogates, or in some fashion presents an alternative to commonly held cultural codes, values, and norms be they linguistic, literary or artistic, religious, or social and political'. The notion of symbolic inversion is similar to what Wertheim (1964: 23–37) has described as 'counterpoint'. Suggesting that no human society is a completely integrated entity, Wertheim argues that 'in any community there are hidden or overt forms of protest against the prevalent hierarchical structure. . . . Beneath the dominant theme there always exist different sets of values, which are, to a certain degree, adhered to among certain groups and which function as a kind of counterpoint to the leading melody' (1964: 26). See also Scott's treatise (1990) on 'hidden transcripts'.
3 The article of McDowell (1981) and the work of Zonabend (1977; 1980) and Bromberger (1982) are important exceptions. See also Goodenough (1965); Price and Price (1972); Rosaldo (1984); and R. Watson (1986) for brief references to nicknames.

4   Eberhard's point about Chinese nicknames may hold true in many other
    places. 'There is a tendency to define a nickname as one used to designate
    an individual when talking *about* him, but not when talking *to* him. It would
    be difficult, in Chinese society, to keep the knowledge of the nickname secret
    from the person who has been given the name. Nicknames always seem to
    refer to members of a certain social group, such as a gang, a school class,
    a work crew, and so forth' (1970: 218). There are, however, exceptions,
    like the longshoremen discussed by Pilcher (1972: 102–13). These work-
    ers in Portland, Oregon, use offensive, derogatory nicknames as part of
    joking behaviour, but do so reciprocally and exclusively among themselves:
    'It is a *faux pas* to use a man's nickname outside of the [longshore] ingroup
    context, but in the absence of women it is only a *faux pas* and not a
    serious offense' (1972: 105). For similar patterns of nicknaming, see
    Skipper (1986) and D. Wolf (1991: 75–7). Sometimes nicknames become
    widely known because their referents are famous, like those of Roman
    emperors ('Caligula'), medieval monarchs ('Charles the Bold'), and
    Brazilian soccer players ('Socrates'). The genre of historical nicknames is
    amply documented by Frey (1887). The nickname is often the only name
    by which these people are known. In such cases nicknames may lose much
    of their offensive intent. Obviously, many surnames have developed from
    nicknames. In fact, the Latin *cognomen* and the Italian *cognome* stand for
    both family name and nickname. Consider Verga's *I Malavoglia*. As Scias-
    cia observes: 'Ma tutti i cognomi non furono in origine soprannomi?' [But
    were not all surnames originally nicknames?] (1990: 102). See also Just
    (1988: 149–50).

5   On the sociological significance of secrecy, see Simmel (1950a: 307ff).
    Taboos surrounding the use of personal names are widely known; cf.
    Radcliffe-Brown (1952: 146–7); Frazer (1957: 321–45); Lévi-Strauss (1966:
    183ff); Price and Price (1972); Maybury-Lewis (1984: 1–2); and Geertz
    (1973d: 368ff), who explains why Balinese personal names are treated as
    though they were military secrets. In Imperial China, one could not use the
    personal name of the Emperor (Fitzgerald 1968: 12). But the taboo on the
    sacred character of personal names is not restricted to tribal and pre-indus-
    trial societies (cf. Hand 1984). There are close connections between naming
    and power. Personal names do not only identify individuals, but also help
    to change and transform them (cf. Maybury-Lewis 1984: 7; R. Watson
    1986: 622). A personal name can become the 'aural equivalent of the person'
    (Gilmore 1982: 696) or a 'part' or an 'extension' of people's selves. The
    resemblances and contiguities between persons and their nicknames may be
    conceived in terms of magical links between them. Using nicknames is then
    not merely describing or saying something, but also 'performing an act': that
    is, doing something. Considering the metonymical and metaphorical con-
    nections between a person and his (nick)name, the taboo on naming betrays
    a belief in the magical power of names. Reflecting on the dangers of naming,
    one is also reminded of what Simmel (1950a: 321) wrote about the 'ideal
    sphere' that lies around every human being, and of Goffman's work on 'ter-
    ritories of the self' and 'territorial offences' (1971: 28–61; 1972: 47–95).

6   Drawing on Freud, Douglas defines jokes as a 'play upon form' (1975: 96). See also Gilmore (1982: 695), who points to the burlesque features of nicknames in Spain and also explains the intense pleasure they provide in terms of displacement. Thanks are due to Don Handelman for suggesting that a nickname can be understood as the punch-line of a joke.

7   For massive evidence of this statement, see the work of Elias on the civilizing process (1978b) and Burke's study on popular culture in early modern Europe (1978).

8   Cf. Babcock (1978: 26–7).

9   See also Sciascia (1990: 102) and Chapman (1971: 236–8). *Ingiuria* (insult) has a Latin root in *injury*, which makes sense since injuries can signify insults, attacks on one's reputation. The word *insult* (from the Latin *sultus*, *saltus*) implies the notion of 'damage to the body'. On the meaning of *sfregio* (disfigurement, affront) in Sicily, see chapter 10 of this volume. See also Goffman (1968: 11) on the original literal meaning of the Greek word *stigma*.

10   On performative acts, in which the uttering of a sentence is, or is part of, the doing of something, see Tambiah (1985b: 77–85), who refers to Austin's famous treatise on speech acts (1962).

11   See, for example, Breen (1982) and Mewett (1982).

12   See Cohen (1977: 106) and Gilmore (1982: 689).

13   Brögger, who worked in a Calabrian village, writes: 'The most characteristic feature of the peasant system of person identification is the use of nicknames' (1971: 87). See also Brandes (1975); Cohen (1977); de Pina-Cabral (1984); Skipper (1986: 136–7); and Wolf (1991: 76–7).

14   How the *reciprocal* use of offensive nicknames as terms of address in small face-to-face groups expresses and reinforces social solidarity is described by Pilcher (1972: 105ff); Busse (1983); Skipper (1986); and D. Wolf (1991: 75–7).

15   The emphasis on the obvious is striking even in recent accounts of nicknames. Writing on western Ireland, Breen goes at great length to demonstrate that 'nicknames were of primary importance in setting up relationships of difference between households in a situation in which there was an extensive overlap of surnames and forenames' (1982: 711).

16   This aspect has been emphasized by most anthropologists writing on nicknames. For example, in his article on Spanish nicknaming Brandes observes that 'offensive nicknames are one of the most effective community mechanisms for the maintenance of social control. For they openly place socially unacceptable traits up to ridicule and operate as a constant reminder of the kinds of behavior which will not be tolerated without resistance' (1975: 146).

17   As mentioned above, a nickname can be understood as a joke, as a 'play upon form'. Douglas writes: 'The joke merely affords opportunity for realising that an accepted pattern has no necessity. Its excitement lies in the suggestion that any particular ordering of experience may be arbitrary and subjective. It is frivolous in that it produces no real alternative, only an exhilarating sense of freedom from form in general' (1975: 96). See also Gilmore (1982: 695).

18   Quoted in Price and Price (1972: 341). See also Skipper (1986), who, referring to the etymology of the word nickname, observes that nicknames
'provide a richer and more explicit denotation. Nicknames tell us more
about an individual than just the fact that he is Harold Jones. Sometimes
they serve as thumbnail character sketches or illustrations of aspects of an
individual's personality, physical appearance, or mannerism' (1986: 135).

19   Sciascia (1982: 11) recalls a slightly different version of this proverb in
which *roccia* (rock) replaces *zotta*. Both versions carry the same meaning.

20   Montaigne (1958, III: 278 [1991: 1170]), who adds that the saying applies
to both male and female. Cf. Davis (1983: 118–22) and Sciascia (1982: 11)
on the limping Martin Guerre. Pitrè's volumes on Sicilian proverbs do not
contain any reference to this saying on limping, nor to any other proverb
dealing with bodily functions – which attests to the considerable distance
between this Victorian gentleman-folklorist and his peasant and working-
class interlocutors. Writing on learned collectors of proverbs in the sixteenth century, Davis observes: 'Not only had they put their sayings into
a "common" French, not only had they excised those with unseemly
metaphors, but also they envisaged different uses for proverbs from those
that they had among the peasants (and even perhaps from those they had
among the *menu peuple*. . . .)' (1975: 242–3). The connection between
limping and sexuality in popular discourse also appears in contemporary
Spain and rural France. Referring to the amorous reputation of limping
women, Verdier (1979: 47) quotes a local proverb, 'Les boiteuses, c'est des
bonnes baiseuses' (Limping women are good kissers), with the implication
– in French – that they are good in bed. Also recall the explicit eroticism of
the limping heroine in Buñuel's *Tristana* (1970). The detail of Tristana's
amputated leg fascinated both Buñuel and Hitchcock (cf. Pérez Turrent and
De la Colina 1993: 207). Asked about the erotic attraction of the limping
Tristana, Buñuel replies: 'Oui, il y a une relation sexuelle perverse. Je le dis
dans *Tristana*. Pendant la guerre d'Espagne j'allais au café de la Paix, où
j'avais rendez-vous avec des gens pour parler de questions politiques. J'ai
souvent vu deux jeunes filles d'une vingtaine d'années qui bottaient, très
grandes, très belles et maquillées. Elles se promenaient aves leurs béquilles,
elles ne cachaient pas qu'il leur manquait une jambe. C'étaient des prostituées et elles avaient toujours des clients, elles avaient un énorme succès'
(Yes, there is a perverse sexual relationship. I say it in *Tristana*. During the
Spanish Civil War, I went to the Café de la Paix, where I met people to talk
about political questions. I have often seen two young girls in their twen-
ties who were limping, very big, very beautiful girls, and dressed up. They
walked with their crutches and did not hide that they missed a leg. They
were prostitutes and always had clients. They had great success) (Ibid., p.
210). At the end of Buñuel's *Viridiana* (1961), it is, of all the beggars, *Le
Boiteux* ('Hobbly') who tries to rape the heroine and benefactress.

21   See, for instance, Pitt-Rivers (1961: 163), who too readily assumes that references to occupations in nicknames are little more than descriptive (or
hereditary). But why then would people take offence and why would such
nicknames provoke laughter?

22   For detailed information on the history and social structure of this community, see Blok (1988).

23   The *Encyclopédie de l'Islam* (1977) describes the term *funduk* as a term of Greek origin, particularly used in North Africa, to denote hotels for animals and travelling people: 'Ces hôtelleries n'étaient guère fréquentées que par les pauvres gens; les autres s'efforçaient d'éviter l'inconfort, la promiscuité avec les animaux et, dans bien des cas, le voisinage des prostituées, car elles occupaient souvent plusieurs chambres où elles accueilaient les voyageurs de passage' (These hotels were only frequented by poor people; others tried hard to avoid the discomfort, the promiscuity with animals, and, in many cases, the proximity with prostitutes, because these women often occupied several rooms when they received travellers passing through). See also Raymond (1985: 248ff). I owe these references to Jean-Charles Depaule, CNRS-IREMAM, Maison Mediterranéenne des Sciences de l'Homme, Aix-en-Provence.

24   This attitude has been expressed toward outsiders, including the visiting anthropologist, and reflects once more the ambiguity with which nicknaming is surrounded. Pitt-Rivers writes: 'There is a feeling, not only among the officials but in the pueblo, that nicknames are degrading and their use is a sign of barbarity. People feel slightly ashamed that a foreigner should wish to inquire into such matters, and fear that the pueblo will be made to sound backward and uncivilized by this feature' (1961: 162–3).

25   Compare Freud's observation on 'pleasure in nonsense', *Zittersprache*, and 'pleasurable effects, which arise from a repetition of what is similar' (1960: 153–7).

Chapter 10   Mediterranean Totemism: Rams and Billy-Goats

1   See Barakat (1973); Brand (1877); Cocchiara (1977); De Jorio (1832); Elworthy (1958); Onians (1951); and Sittl (1890). The most common word for deceived husband in English is 'cuckold' (French: *cocu*), which derives from 'cuckoo' (Latin: *cuculus*), a bird well known for its 'social parasitism' – that is, the female cuckoo does not build a nest, but leaves each of her eggs in a different nest every time while the male cuckoo stands by. The *cocu*, then, is the betrayed husband, who calmly accepts the fact that his wife lies and gives birth in the bed of other lovers. See Alinei (1982: 773–4).

2   The formulation of Leach is, of course, inspired by Lévi-Strauss (1966: 1–108; 1969b: 143–64).

3   See, for instance, Pitt-Rivers (1961: 116; 1965: 46), who sees in the horns of the cuckold the horns of the Devil and regards them as phallic symbols. Campbell (1964: 152), Brandes (1981: 227–30) and Barton (1993: 97, n. 68) have adopted this interpretation without question. These slips may have resulted from the conviction, also entertained by Lévi-Strauss himself, that complex civilizations, or so-called 'hot' societies, leave little room for the logic of the concrete and totemic classifications in general.

4 Cf. Zingarelli (1965); Pitt-Rivers (1965: 46); Cutileiro (1971: 142); and De Morais Silva (1950).
5 For a report of this experience, see Blok (1988).
6 *Vocabolario bolognese italiano* (1869–74), edited by Coronedi Berti. Quoted by Alinei (1982: 771).
7 *Vocabolario della lingua italiana* (1965). Compiled by Nicola Zingarelli. Bologna: Nicola Zanichelli Editore.
8 See Shore (1996: 172–3), who distinguishes between metaphorical and metonymic totemism. Metaphorical or 'logical' totemism is associated with the innovative work of Lévi-Strauss and stresses the intrinsic rationality and categorical nature of human thought: differences in natural categories are used to articulate differences in the cultural and social realms. Played down by Lévi-Strauss, metonymic totemism concerns a direct relationship between animals and humans, and can be best understood in terms of what Lévy-Bruhl called 'participation': the identifications between animals and humans reflect both a mystical bond and a practical interest in a species as a source of food or otherwise. As we shall see soon, the symbolism of horns and billy-goats is also part of the metaphorical or 'logical' form of Mediterranean totemic classifications.
9 Cf. Borgeaud (1979: 92–102).
10 In the ethnography of Mediterranean rural communities, information on the habits of domesticated animals is virtually absent and very little work is done on animal symbolism. Apart from my own work in western Sicily and Campbell's excellent study of the Sarakatsani in Greece (1964), I have drawn on Moyal's report (1956) on transhumant shepherds in southern France and Westermarck's volumes on Morocco (1926). I have also consulted the work of Brisebarre on the Cevennes (1978), Ravis-Giordani's study of Corsican shepherds (1983), and Mahdi's book on shepherds in the Atlas (1999). But these studies tell us more about the social and economic life of shepherds and their material culture than about the animals themselves and their representations. What could and has to be done is demonstrated by Caisson (1976) and suggested in a paper of Casanova (1997). For my purposes, I have also profited from the work of non-ethnographic authors, in particular Keller (1909), Zeuner (1963), Richter (1968), Clutton-Brock (1981), Alinei (1982), Whittaker (1988), Burkert (1990), and Ryder's treatise on the subject (1983).
11 See Keller (1909: 322) and Hodkinson (1988: 60).
12 See Keller (1909: 319–26) and Ryder (1983: 104–9).
13 Cf. *Klassiek Vademecum* (Fuchs), p. 15; Ryder (1983: 147–8).
14 See Westermarck (1926, I: 100–1); Germain (1948); Frankfurt (1948: 384–5 n. 46); Ryder (1983: 103–9); and *Encyclopédie des Symboles* (1996: 78). See also Frobenius on palaeolithic rock-engravings of the 'widderköpfige Sonnengott' in the Sahara-Atlas (1923: 36–41).
15 Artemis is called 'Mistress of the Animals' and as goddess of hunting and of hunters is associated with wild nature (Burkert 1985: 149). Burkert writes that Aphrodite's sphere of activity is the joyous consummation of sexuality, and also notes her close association with the goat, which animal belongs to

Aphrodite (Burkert 1985: 152, 155). See Aphrodite with billy-goat, a clay plaque found near Gela on the south coast of Sicily. Sixth century BC. Ashmolean Museum, Oxford. Reproduced in Pinsent (1982: 12–13). Pinsent notes that the figure is identified as Aphrodite by the billy-goat, 'one of her sacred animals'. Friedrich, who wrote a book about the meaning of Aphrodite (1978), discusses her liminality, her sexuality, her sensuousness, and the like, but there is not a single reference to her emblematic relationship with the goat. See also Jameson, who reports that female goats were especially Artemis' animals (1988: 104).

16 Louvre (Paris), G 185, *Lexicon Iconographicum Mythologiae Classicae*, III, 1, p. 461, no. 438 (Dionysos); and LMC, V, Z, no. 257 (Hermes) (Zurich/Munich, Artemis Verlag, 1986). The same stamnos (both sides) is also reproduced in Donna C. Kurtz, *The Berlin Painter*. Oxford 1983, pp. 25, 55, 55a and b. See also Hoffman (1982: 65, 70).

17 Two prominent classical scholars who have spent a lifetime on the study of early Greek thought and culture, Lloyd and Burkert, have only marginally touched upon animal symbolism, also in books in which one might expect them to address the issue, most notably Lloyd's *Polarity and Analogy* (1992). See, however, Hoffmann (1977; 1982) and note the anthropological impact on his work. See also the complaint of Garnsey (1988: 196–7) concerning the neglect of studying pastoral economies in early Greece and the importance of the study of contemporary mountain communities 'before they disappear'. See also note 10 of this chapter.

18 Cf. Rose (1964: 204) and Graves (1981: 65–6, 192–212).

19 *The Iliad*, Book IX.

20 *The Odyssey*, Book IV.

21 See Fellmann (1972: 87–8; fig. FL18). Cf. Hoffmann (1982: 65), who, for ancient Greece, stresses the role of the ram as 'heroic' sacrificial victim and points at his function as a vehicle of transport for deities and heroes.

22 *Oneirocritica*, Book 2.

23 In his account of the religion of the Egyptians, Herodotus (fifth century BC) discusses the cults of rams and billy-goats and traces the relationship with, respectively, Zeus (Ammon) and Dionysos (Book II: 42).

24 *The Economist* (3 September 1983) reports that in Mecca, 'in two weeks' time, Abraham's substitution of a ram for the sacrifice of his son Isaac was to be commemorated by the slaughter of 1,200,000 animals flown in from Australia, Bulgaria, Turkey, Argentina, and Uruguay and killed on behalf of 2 million Haj pilgrims'. Quoted in Jameson (1988: 87).

25 Cf. Ryder (1983: 1190) and Kanafadi-Zahar (1997).

26 On Abraham's sacrifice as depicted in western and Islamic art, see Delaney (1977; 1991, *passim*); and Schapiro (1980). The latter is primarily interested in the question how the ram came to this place of sacrifice; he takes it for granted that the animal is a ram. Discussing the pre-eminence of the ram as a sacrificial animal in the Maghreb, Hammoudi writes: 'Localement, on note la préférence donnée au bélier et l'on en connaît aussi la raison: n'est-il pas l'animal que Dieu lui-même substitua à Ismaël, sur le point d'être immolé? [La tradition musulmane veut que ce soit Ismaël. Mais il n'y a pas

unanimité sur ce point et certains soutiennent qu'il s'agit d'Isaac.]' (Locally, one notes the preference given to the ram and we also know the reason: is that not the animal that God himself substituted for Ishmael who was going to be sacrificed? [The Islamic tradition insists that it is Ishmael. But there is no unanimity on this point and some maintain that it concerns Isaac]) (1988: 170). It is obvious, however, that the local explanation is part of the problem and does not answer the question: why a ram?

27   See also the interview with Lévi-Strauss in Charbonnier (1969: 32–42). On bourgeois or modern totemism, in which manufactured objects have taken the place of totemic categories, see Sahlins (1976: 175ff).

28   See the constructive essay of Worsley (1967). For a more extensive and critical recent discussion, see Shore (1996: 165–204).

29   For the various terms denoting the pre-eminence of Aries/ram in the zodiacal belt, the animal realm and the social world (e.g. *Primus Aries*, *Signorum principes*, *astrorum dux*, *ductor gregis*, *signum regale*), see Bouché-Leclercq (1963: 131n.).

30   See Bouché-Leclercq (1963: 130–2, 144–6).

31   Barton (1994: 182, 71).

32   Gombrich (1978: 137, figs 144–5).

33   See Barton (1994: 9–31 and *passim*).

34   Benveniste demonstrates that the word *pecunia* produced *pecu*, not the other way around (1969: 47–61).

35   Cf. Worsley (1967: 156), and, in more detail, Shore (1996: 167–204).

36   Artemidorus, Book II, 12.

37   *The New Oxford Annotated Bible*. Revised Standard Edition, 1977.

38   For this description, I have drawn on Stützer (1989: 41), who also provides an illustration.

39   For Girard, the Lamb of God merges here with the scapegoat: 'The Gospels constantly reveal what the texts of historical persecutors, and especially mythological persecutors, hide from us: the knowledge that their victim is a scapegoat. . . . The expression scapegoat is not actually used, but the Gospels have a perfect substitute in *the lamb of God*. Like 'scapegoat', it implies the substitution of one victim for all the others but replaces all the distasteful and loathsome connotations of the goat with the positive associations of the lamb' (1986: 117).

40   See Lakoff and Johnson (1980) on conceptual metaphors. See Alinei (1982) on 'pastoral semantic', and the note by Ryder (1983: 119) on the multiple references to sheep in the Old Testament.

41   Cf. Ryder (1983: 93, 103–4, 117–22).

42   See also the perceptive and programmatic remarks on the symbolism of sheep and lambs in Casanova's paper (1997: 21–3).

43   See, for instance, Morris et al. (1979: 121–7).

44   Barker (1985: 42).

45   Clutton-Brock (1981: 57).

46   See Hodkinson (1988: 60).

47   Richter (1968: 55–6); see also Clutton-Brock (1981: 57–8); and Cherry (1988: 61).

48 Richter (1968: 53).
49 Ryder (1983: 86ff, 93–9, 122–3, 132–42). For a different dating of these innovations, see Cherry (1988: 6), who, on the basis of osteological evidence, argues that domesticated animals, including sheep and goats, reached the Aegean as early as the seventh millennium BC.
50 Richter (1968: 60). For example, 'ovicaprids': see Whittaker (1988: *passim*).
51 As Richter observes: 'dass bis in die neueste Zeit herab in den Hauptländern der homerischen Welt – Balkanhalbinsel, Ägäis, Kleinasien – das Schaf das quantitativ absolut dominierende Haustier geblieben ist . . .' (that until modern times in the main countries of Homer's world – the Balkan peninsula, the Aegean, Asia Minor – sheep have remained quantitatively the absolutely dominant domestic animal) (1968: 55–6). To illustrate his point, Richter gives figures for their distribution in 1924 in Yugoslavia, Greece and Bulgaria (1968: 56).
52 When one keeps in mind that the relationship between sheep and goats is considered analogous to that between men and women, and that they are both complementary, but asymmetrical and 'hierarchical', one is reminded of what Dumont, following his student Raymond Apthorpe, writes about 'the encompassing of the contrary': one category (the superior) includes the other (the inferior), which in turn excludes the first (1980: 239–45).
53 Ryder (1983: 100).
54 See Burkert (1990: 19).
55 Amiel (1987: 368–70, and *passim*). See also Alinei's observations regarding the *vecchio caprone* ('old goat') and the word *capra* (goat) for prostitute (1981: 774), to which we have already referred.
56 Ryder (1983: 7, 100–3, 377, 419–20, 429). 'The shepherd would feed the bell-wether, which would therefore follow him and lead the rest of the flock wherever desired' (Ryder 1983: 113).
57 Regarding the practice of castration, Moyal observes that 'unaltered rams would be too truculent to play the role of leaders of the flock. Removal of the sex glands made the *floucats* more docile and sedate, and also improved the quality and increased the weight of the clip' (1956: 110). Earlier in his account, Moyal mentions that the six *floucats* and six *menouns* had also been trained to lead the flock (1956: 16).
58 See Schippers (1986: 155n., 157, 163, 182, 257): 'Les caprins qui se trouvent dans le troupeau – leur nombre peut varier de 3 à 15' (The billy-goats in the flock – their number may vary between 3 and 15), and: 'Le menoun ou "grande bouc châtré", utilisé pour la conduite d'un troupeau transhumant' (The 'menoun', or 'big castrated billy-goat', used for leading the transhumant flock). One wonders about the implicit meaning of the practice of replacing testicles (back) by bells (front) when turning rams and billy-goats into leaders (of sheep). On the fabrication and use of *sonnailles* (bells) in the Cevennes, see Brisebarre (1978: 67–77). For Corsica, see Ravis-Giordani (1983: 249, 265–7).
59 Hodkinson (1988: 61).
60 Compare Ravis-Giordani (1983: 282–8) for details on the making of cheese and *ricotta* ('brocciu') in Niolu, Corsica.

61   Sicilian men are not alone in this. I have noticed the same attitude among males in other parts of the Mediterranean.

62   On the related oppositions between wine and milk in ancient Greece, see Cherry, who writes: 'From Homer to Ammianus Marcellinus, the pastoralist is defined simply via logical opposition to the essential criteria of civilisation: mobile and without established homes, non-urban, *polis*-less, without properly constituted rules or law-codes, lazy and parasitic (because he does not *work* the land and *harvest* the crops, like a farmer), an eater of meat (often *raw* flesh, and even raw *human* flesh) rather than grain, and a drinker of milk, not wine' (1988: 29). See also Shaw (1982/3).

63   'In seiner Wolle also liegt die Hauptbedeutung dieses Haustieres für die menschliche Wirtschaft' (In his wool, therefore, lies the principal importance of this domesticated animal for human economy) (Richter 1968: 57). Ryder (1983: 93) recalls that Babylonia is said to mean 'Land of Wool'.

64   On the use of goatskin in the Homeric world, see Richter's observation, '*Völlig normal*, noch in viel späterer Zeit gebräuchlich, ist die Verwendung der Ziegenhaut als bequem transportabler Behälter für Flüssigkeiten, insbesondere Wein' (Completely normal, still common in later times, is the use of the goat's skin as easily transportable containers for liquids, especially wine) (1968: 62).

65   See also the observation of Richter: 'Grossen, von Schafen getrennte, Ziegenherden mit eigenen Hirten gehörten sicher von altersher zum Besitz adeliger Grundherren. Melanthios, der Geisshirt des Odysseus, verwaltet nicht nur selbst eine reine Ziegenherde, sondern ist Vorgesetzter einer Vielzahl von Ziegenhirten, und neben den Herden des Königs gibt es noch andere auf Ithaka' (Substantial flocks of goats, separated from sheep, with their own herdsmen, certainly belonged since antiquity to the estate of noble landlords. Melanthios, the goatherd of Odysseus, does not only himself manage a genuine goat flock, but is also chief of several goatherds, and next to the flocks of the King there are others on Ithaca) (1968: 61).

66   The ruins of Entella have been recently explored by archaeologists of the University of Pisa. See Parra (1997).

67   Campbell (1964: 31).

68   Already Hammurabi's laws (about 1700 BC) mention the tensions and disputes between agriculturalists and pastoralists, 'foreshadowing the violent Hebrew story of Cain and Abel' (Ryder 1983: 94). For further details on the gradual displacement of pastoralists, see Jane Schneider's fine essay (1971). See also Freeman (1970: 177–84) and Braudel (1972: 94). On the stigmatization of shepherds in Central Europe, see Danckert (1963: 174–80) and Jacobeit (1961: 173–224). More recent scholarship emphasizes the low social status of herdsmen in classical antiquity (e.g. Whittaker 1988: 29–30 and *passim*).

69   On the decline of pastoralism in the Mediterranean, see McNeill (1992: 234–6). For urban people, the distinctions between rams and billy-goats may no longer be obvious. For example, in their interpretation of the *palio* of Siena, Dundes and Falassi follow urban (i.e. Sienese) views and translate the word *becco* as ram and cuckold (1975: 29–30). In a more recent account,

Gallant reports for a nineteenth-century Greek island community that rams' horns signified dishonour (1994: 703).

70 Clementine van Eck, personal communication.

71 The study *Gestures* (1979) is based on three years' research in forty localities in twenty-five European countries. The four authors were assisted by twenty-nine research workers and interpreters. Their research involved detailed interviews with 1,200 informants regarding twenty different gestures.

72 A very powerful man is sometimes described as *un uomo con i coglioni fino terra* ('a man with testicles reaching to the ground'). Both expressions evoke the image of the ram, whose testicles are large in proportion to the rest of his body.

73 The excellent monographs of Brisbarre, Schippers, Ott and Le Lannou on pastoral communities offer little information on animals and animal symbolism. These books deal primarily with people and their (transhumant) life as shepherds. Exceptions include Caisson's article on the spider and the oven (1976) and Fabre-Vassas's more recent study of pigs (1994). See also the remarks of Casanova (1997: 21–3).

74 Campbell (1964: 31–2); cf. Földes (1969).

75 Campbell (1964: 152); cf. Pitt-Rivers (1961: 116).

76 Antikenmuseum, Basle. Reproduced in Hoffmann (1982: 65, 70), who also refers to Boardman (1975: 140, fig. 304, 2).

77 See the critical comments of Worsley (1967); Schwartz (1981: 22–33, 111 and *passim*); and, especially, Shore (1996: 174–9).

78 Shore (1996: 175).

79 In her important essay on theory in anthropology, Ortner recognizes that the structuralism of Lévi-Strauss is the only genuinely original paradigm in the social sciences and the humanities to be developed in the twentieth century. Despite Lévi-Strauss' personal predilection, 'the theory has always had important implications for a much more historical anthropology than that practiced by the master' (1994: 379–81).

80 Pitt-Rivers (1961: 116; 1965: 46).

81 Cf. Lévi-Strauss (1969b: 160–1).

82 For the relations between honour and immunity, see Bourdieu (1979a), who writes: 'The man of honour, of whom people say that he "fulfils his role as a man" (*thirugza*), is always on his guard; and so he is immune from even the most unpredictable attack' (1979a: 115). Friedrich (1973) and J. Redfield (1975: 160–223) discuss Homeric honour in terms of integrity and purity. The meaning of the medieval concept of *honor* ranged between 'patrimony' and 'immunity' (cf. Niermeyer 1959). Of Sicilian *mafiosi*, men of honour of sorts, it is sometimes said that they are *intoccabili*, 'untouchable' in the sense of unapproachable and awe-inspiring, a quality which underscores the immunity of their person and patrimony (Blok 1988: 136–47). The close relationship between honour and sacredness (immunity) has only recently been fully recognized by anthropologists working in the Mediterranean (cf. Peristiany and Pitt-Rivers 1992). For earlier statements, see Goffman (1963; 1967), who, for his concept of the sacred character of the person and its territories, draws on Simmel's notion of the 'ideal sphere',

which lies around every human being: 'Although differing in size in varying directions and differing according to the person with whom one entertains relations, this sphere cannot be penetrated, unless the personality value of the individual is thereby destroyed. A sphere of this sort is placed around man by his "honor". Language very poignantly designates an insult to one's honor as "coming too close": the radius of this sphere marks, as it were, the distance whose trespassing by another person insults one's honor' (1950: 321). For more recent applications of these insights, see Barton's work on the gladiator (1994).

83   Cf. J. Schneider (1971); Gilmore (1987); Delaney (1991: 38–9); and Bourdieu (1979b).

84   This may also include, as Delaney puts it in her work on Turkish rural society, a man's ability to guarantee his paternity: 'The protection of women in Muslim societies is intimately and essentially related to the protection of seed. . . . A man's power and authority, in short his value as a man, derives from his power to generate life. His honor, however, depends on his ability to guarantee that a child is from his own seed' (1991: 39; cf. Delaney 1986).

85   Pitt-Rivers (1961: 89–91). The Spanish word *manso* is also used for bell-wethers, castrated rams, who, as we have seen before, are trained to lead flocks of sheep (Ryder 1983: 429).

86   See Schneider and Schneider (1976: 139–40) and Blok (1988: 225–9).

87   For a succinct description of the relations between power and gazing, which would perfectly describe the gaze of a *mafioso*, see Kafka's little sketch 'The Imperial Colonel': 'One is ashamed to say by what means the imperial colonel governs our little town in the mountains. . . . Ceremonial is something he does not care for and any form of play-acting far less, and so he does not go on writing, as he might, letting the visitor wait, but instantly interrupts his work and leans back, though he does keep his pen in his hand. And so, leaning back, his left hand in his trouser pocket, he gazes at the visitor. The petitioner has the impression that the colonel sees more than merely him, the unknown person who has emerged from the crowd for a little while, for why else should the colonel scrutinize him so closely, and long, and in silence? Nor is it a keen, probing, penetrating gaze . . . ; it is a nonchalant, roving, and yet steady gaze, a gaze with which one might, for instance, observe the movements of a crowd in the distance. And this long gaze is continuously accompanied by an indefinable smile, which seems to be now irony, now dreamy reminiscence' (Franz Kafka, *Parables and Paradoxes*. New York: Schocken Books, in German and English, 1961, pp. 107–9).

88   Significantly, like the term *manso*, the word *dayyuth* refers to both animals and humans: 'He broke or trained him, namely a camel, in some measure so as to subdue his refractoriness. He subdued him, or rendered him submissive, and gentle, namely a man' (Lane 1867: 941). I am grateful to Léon Buskens who provided me with this reference.

89   On duelling, cf. Frevert (1995); McAleer (1994); and Elias (1996).

90   Cf. Bourdieu (1979a: 99–103) and Jamous (1981: 67–71). Jamous writes: 'De toutes les différentes manifestations de l'honneur, le meurtre et la vio-

lence physique constituent les formes d'échange les plus redoutable. . . . c'est dans le meurtre et la violence physique que le sens de l'honneur s'affirme le plus totalement' (Of all different manifestations of honour, killing and physical violence constitute the most redoubtable forms of exchange. It is in killing and physical violence that the sense of honour asserts itself most completely) (1981: 69).

91   Cf. Pitt-Rivers (1965: 39; 1974: 7) and Berger (1970).
92   Cf. Steinmetz (1931); J. Schneider (1971); and Black-Michaud (1975).
93   J. Schneider (1971: 18); Black-Michaud (1975: 218).
94   In western Europe, the differentiation between moral and physical integrity is of recent origin. Until the early nineteenth century, the whole ritual of public torture and *post mortem* mutilation formed an integral part of punishment – adding infamy to death (cf. Foucault 1975: 36–72; Linebaugh 1975: 65–117; Ranum 1980; and Blok 1995a). The idea that honour can be more important than life itself has been known since antiquity – cf. Tacitus, who wrote in *Agricola* (ch. 33): 'an honourable death would be better than a disgraceful attempt to save our lives'; Snell (1975: 156); Walcot (1978: 15–16); the Arab proverb quoted in Farès (1932: 114); Ranum (1980: 66); and Elias (1969a: 145–6), who, writing on the French nobility under the *ancien régime*, also provides an explanation by stressing the relation between honour, personal identity and membership of the 'good society'.
95   Cf. Hampson (1973) and Pitt-Rivers (1974: 7).
96   Steinmetz has emphasized the dialectic relation between self-help and state control, when pointing out with a play of words (which is lost in translation) that self-help is the only device for people who are either abandoned (*im Stich gelassen*) or suffocated (*erstickt*) by central governments (1931: 522).
97   Cf. Elias (1969b).
98   Elias (1969a: 144–51); cf. Simmel (1983: 403–6). How slowly this process took place may be illustrated by the reception of the short story 'Leutnant Gustl' by Arthur Schnitzler. Its publication in 1900 caused a sensation, especially in military circles, and the author, who had been an officer in the Austro–Hungarian army, lost his military rank (see Scheible 1976: 84). For Germany, see Jones (1959), and Demeter (1964: 108–44, 260–86), who deals with the development of the jurisdiction concerning duelling. On the same issue, see the more recent studies of duelling in Wilhelminian Germany by Frevert (1995); McAleer (1994); and Elias (1996). The fate of honour in Britain has lately been dealt with by James (1978).

Chapter 11   Female Rulers and their Consorts

1   D. O'Brien (1977: 120–1).
2   Heisch (1980: 45).
3   D. O'Brien (1977: 119). See also Beattie (1968: 417). In Uganda (Kingdom Buganda), the male term of address *ssebo* was also used as a term of address

for princesses and wives of kings; in fact, all women in the royal family were addressed as men (J. Murphy 1972: 514).

4 For information on these three women I have drawn on the following news-papers: *NRC Handelsblad*, 22, 24, 31 July and 4 September 1989; *de Volk-skrant*, 25 July, 10 and 25 August 1989; *Time*, 7 August 1989 and 12 March 1990; and *New York Times*, 10, 19 September 1989 and 1 March 1990. For an interview with Intassir Al-Wazir, see *NRC Handelsblad*, 13 November 1993.

5 *Corriera della Sera*, 3 April 1990.

6 *New York Times*, 3 November 1989.

7 *New York Times*, 1 March 1991. A picture shows Mrs Khaleda Zia and several of her supporters laying wreaths on her husband's tomb in Dhaka, right after her victory. Her rival Sheik Hasina became Prime Minister in 1996 and let it be known she wished to be addressed as 'Sir'! (*Far Eastern Economic Review*, 5 September 1996). See also *NRC Handelsblad*, 9 December 1995; *Newsweek*, 15 January 1996; and *Time*, 11 August 1997.

8 *Parool*, 18 June 1993.

9 N. Thomas (1991: 308). Referring to Keesing (1989: 460), Thomas suggests that the discipline (of anthropology) 'is a discourse of alterity that magni-fies the distance between "others" and "ourselves" while suppressing mutual entanglement and the perspectival and political fracturing of the cultures of both observers and observed' (1991: 309).

10 Cf. Dundes (1989: 62–3).

11 Ortner (1974: 62–3); cf. Tambiah (1990: 63–4) and Thomas (1991: 309).

12 Cf. Geertz (1968: 4).

13 Terrill (1984: 313).

14 For some details about Lü's youth as a guerrilla organizer fighting at the side of the bandit Liu Bang (who later became Emperor and her husband) against the Confucianists, see Witke (1977: 464).

15 Cf. Yang (1960); Fitzgerald (1968); Terrill (1984: 308–16).

16 Fitzgerald (1968: 44).

17 Fitzgerald (1968: 129ff, 163–98).

18 M. Warner (1972: 260).

19 Cf. Heisch (1980).

20 Heisch (1980: 50–3).

21 Cf. Ranum (1980).

22 Troyat (1981: 181).

23 Cf. De Madariaga (1990: 217ff) for a careful assessment.

24 Alexander (1989: 9–10).

25 Quoted in Alexander (1989: 65); see also Troyat (1981: 71).

26 Quoted in Troyat (1981: 181); cf. De Madariaga (1990: 206) for a similar observation by the British ambassador, Sir James Harris.

27 Cf. Needham (1963: xxxix–xli); Babcock (1978).

28 Since there are few pastimes for women in patriarchal societies, it may be argued that pastimes have a masculine ring in that context.

29 Warner (1983: 139–58).

30 In its wider sense, patriarchy has been defined as the institutionalized system

of male dominance over women in society. See Lerner (1986: 212ff, 238–9); cf. Ortner (1974: 69) and N. Thomas (1991: 313–14). For the notion of 'hegemonic masculinity', see Connell (1987: 183–8).

31 On the informal forms of female power in peasant societies, see Rogers (1975).

32 Meir (1975: 112–16, 271).

33 See Mohan (1967: 144–6, 182–212); Bhatia (1974: 272–3); and Gupte (1992: 219–32), which does not contain one single picture of Indira's husband. It has been noted that India has a centuries-old tradition of accepting women as leaders and rulers, like Razia Sultana (1236–40), Chand Bibi (1547–99), Ahalyabai (1754–95) and Rani Lakshmibai of Jhansi, who died in 1857 during a revolt resisting British annexation (Kishwar and Vanita 1989: 135).

34 *Time*, 12 March 1990.

35 *Time*, 12 November 1984; *Newsweek*, 12 November 1984. See also the title of a recent biography, Gupte (1992).

36 Heisch (1980: 50).

37 Gavin Evans, 'The nasty case of Winnie Mandela', *New York Times*, 1 March 1991.

38 Cf. Warner (1983: 155); Heisch (1980); and Gorer (1966: 140–1). Shortly after Benazir Bhutto was elected Prime Minister in 1993 (for the second time), her brother Mir Murtaza returned to Pakistan. She had him arrested and he spent a year in prison on charges of terrorism before he was released on bail. In September 1996 he was gunned down at a police roadblock. Benazir Bhutto's husband Asif Zardari was jailed on charges of conspiring to murder his brother-in-law (*Time*, 11 August 1997).

39 Looking back on the period before her marriage, Benazir Bhutto remarked, 'If my name had been linked with a man, it would have destroyed my political career. Actually, I had reconciled myself to a life without marriage or children for the sake of my career.' Interview, *New York Times Magazine*, 15 May 1994, p. 39.

40 Tim McGirk, 'Feminine mystique', *Time*, 11 August 1997. From a comparative study of so-called warrior-queens (i.e. women who combine rule with martial leadership) it appears that most of them were widows (Fraser 1989). But the author does not recognize their autonomy, the significance of their independence from male control. On the contrary, in what she describes as the 'appendage syndrome', she emphasizes their dependence on male leaders: 'The appendage syndrome runs through the whole book: the stressed connection of so many warrior queens to the nearest masculine figure' (1989: 12; cf. 331–2). This view is far from exceptional. To my surprise, it seems to enjoy a certain popularity among feminists. In a forthcoming comparative essay on women politicians, the widows among them (of whom there are a considerable number) are condescendingly classified as 'political surrogates' – that is, women who inherit 'the mantle of power from an ill or deceased (usually martyred) male relative (father, husband, son)' (D'Amico n.d.: 40).

41 Contemporary female leaders who came to power after their husband or father was killed include Sirimavo Bandaranaike and her daughter Chan-

drika Kumaratunga, both from Sri Lanka; Khaleda Zia and Hasina Wazed, both from Bangladesh; Violeta Chamorro from Nicaragua; Cory Aquino from the Philippines; and Benazir Bhutto from Pakistan.

42   Buruma (1986: 22); and Steinberg (1986: 32–3).

43   Prince Henry, the German husband of Queen Wilhelmina of the Netherlands, once allegedly grumbled when walking behind his wife at a public ceremony as required by protocol, 'Ich bin nur das Gepäck' (I am only the luggage). Later, when Wilhelmina and members of her cabinet had taken refuge in London during the German occupation of their country, Winston Churchill, little impressed by the quality of the Dutch Government, allegedly said: 'The Queen is the only man in London.'

44   Cf. Crankshaw (1969: 25–6).

45   A biography of Denis Thatcher, written by his daughter Carol, recounts the switching of roles between Denis and his wife. As a reviewer of the book summarizes this turning point: 'After Margaret Thatcher became leader of the Conservative Party, her husband remembered that his father had told him as a boy, "whales don't get killed until they spout", and recognized that his only chance of survival was to keep absolutely quiet. Then, in 1979, after she became prime minister, the satirical magazine *Private Eye* began publishing a regular spoof letter from Denis. Boozy, slangy, racist, anti-intellectual, they depicted him as a gin-sodden buffoon haunting the bars of the *déclassé* Home Counties golf-clubs. . . . Initially he resented the caricature. . . . [Later] he adopted the image foisted on him, and exploited it' (Richard Davenport-Hines, 'The whale that didn't spout', *Times Literary Supplement*, 3 May 1996).

46   For this sketch I have drawn on Paul Hofmann's obituary, *New York Times*, 13 November 1989. See also Ibarruri (1966).

47   On the position of Dutch queens, see Braun (1992: 161–80), who describes the dilemmas and contradictions that faced the Dutch authorities in the late nineteenth century when Wilhelmina's marriage would inevitably involve the switching of gender roles.

48   These symbolic inversions can also be observed among single women working in other public domains, like scholars, artists, politicians, businesswomen and executives. See also Pitt-Rivers (1987) and Van Os (1997) on Spanish widows, Jansen (1987) on women without a father or husband in an Algerian town, and Robertson (1992) on Japanese actresses. The subversive leanings of gender inversions are obvious enough and underscore the ambiguity of these women, but they cannot be discussed here. Cf. Warner (1981: 147); Davis (1978); and the studies of cross-dressing by Dekker and Van de Pol (1989) and Wheelwright (1989). What holds for cross-dressing or transvestism may also be valid for the forms of gender-crossing discussed here. Wheelwright writes: 'Cross-dressing for women often remained a process of imitation rather than self-conscious claiming of the social privileges given exclusively to men for all women. Their exploits challenged existing categories of sexual difference but the terms of the debate usually remained the same. Was women's real oppression challenged by these heroines who felt only capable of grasping an individual liberation? The female

sailors who were discovered working on British naval and merchant ships were described as proving themselves "as good a man as any other" or even performing their duties so skilfully they "caused a degree of envy in the other lads". They were known to run up the mast with expertise, could hold their grog like any other tar and never shirked the most arduous of duties. They proved that women were equally capable of excelling in the masculine sphere but since the female soldiers and sailors remained such staunch individualists, they presented little threat to the established order' (1989: 11).

49   Cf. Dumont (1980: 116–18).

50   When husbands of female leaders fail to keep a low profile, as happened in the cases of Geraldine Ferraro and Benazir Bhutto, the results prove disastrous for their wives' political careers.

51   For a discussion of the notion of 'normal exceptions', see Muir (1991: xiv–xvi).

52   See *Time*, 25 September 1989. A similar case can be made for Hillary Rodham Clinton. Described as 'an icon of American womanhood', she is regarded as the most powerful first lady in the history of the United States, while women account for one-third of her husband's nominees to top Administration jobs. See *Time*, 10 May 1993. We should also consider what Ortner describes as the logic of hierarchy: 'It is in the nature of hierarchies that certain nongender-based principles of social organization take precedence over gender itself as a principle of social organization. . . . There is a sense, then, in which the logic of hierarchical systems inherently tends toward (even if it never reaches) gender equality' (1981: 396–7). One is reminded of the tendency to gender equality among European aristocracies, as exemplified in the eighteenth-century institutions of the literary salon and the *cicibeo* or *cavaliere servente*, the socially accepted male companion and friend of a married woman (Pitt-Rivers 1965: 66–71). Similar arrangements prevailed among the aristocratic and matrilineal Tuareg, where married women continued to see their male friends (R. Murphy 1964: 1262).

53   D. O'Brien (1977: 121–3).

54   Heisch (1980: 52–3). Isabel of Castile, who became Queen of Castile in 1474, never shared the crown with her husband (and cousin) Fernando of Aragon, but not without considerable efforts (cf. Liss 1992: 105–7). See also Fraser (1989: 210). O'Brien notes that 'king' has a more restricted meaning and pre-eminently refers to a ruler, while the husband of a ruling queen is called 'prince' or 'prince consort'. These distinctions are also found in other European languages and cultures (O'Brien 1977: 123n.). In everyday language (English, Dutch) the term 'prince consort' may be used (figuratively) to denote males who behave in a submissive way toward a female associate. The asymmetry between kings and queens is also rendered in an ancient, oral rhyme: 'Balls!' said the Queen./ 'If I had t(w)o, I'd be King.'/ The King laughed, because he had t(w)o./ The Queen cried, because she wanted t(w)o.

55   See Terrill (1984: 302–73).

56   This prompted an American observer to ask: 'Why do we need a First Lady, at all?' See R.W. Apple, Jr, 'Nancy Reagan's revenge is to tell her version of the stories', *New York Times*, 1 November 1989.

57 *Newsweek*, 21 August 1989.
58 *Newsweek*, 21 August 1989. For details on Imelda's ambition to succeed her husband, see Ellison (1988: 211–30). On the aspirations of Jiang Qing, see Terrill's chapter 'Bid to be empress' (1984: 302–73).
59 Cf. Laber (1993: 26) and *NRC Handelsblad*, 30 July 1997. Nexhmije Hoxha received an amnesty after five years in prison. Now in her late seventies, she lives in strict isolation in a few rooms of a decaying building. For many Albanians, she remains the symbol of concentration camps, exile, persecution and execution squads.
60 See *Time*, 16 December 1996 on Mirjana Markovic; and Prunier (1995: 86–7, 168ff and 350–1) on Aghate Habyarimana.
61 For further details, see Naipaul (1980) and Page (1983).
62 *New York Times*, 28 January, 1, 5, 12, 14, 17 February, 1, 7 and 8 March 1991; *Volkskrant*, 7 April 1992; and *NRC Handelsblad*, 14 April 1992.
63 The choice of an Attorney General in the United States in the beginning of 1993 also attests to the significance of singleness of female leaders. After two attempts to nominate a woman – attempts which failed since both candidates were mothers – the President settled for a single woman, the childless and unmarried Janet Reno. (*New York Times*, 12 February, 1 May 1993.) In the turmoil of embarrassment, resentment and moral outrage, this simple point went unnoticed. See, however, Claudia Wallis, 'The lessons of Nannygate', *Time*, 22 February 1993. A similar case can be made for several female governors in the United States, e.g. Ann Richards, who became Governor of Texas after her divorce, *New York Times Magazine*, 7 February 1993.
64 *New York Times*, 9 March and 21 April 1991.
65 On the humble origins of Empress Wu, see Witke (1977: 464).
66 See Taylor (1979: 34ff); Naipaul (1980: 112–13, 164); and Page (1983: 339–40).
67 See Terrill (1984: 29ff, 48–114). On the anomalous position of actresses in early twentieth-century China, see Witke (1977: 99), who observes that 'both [actresses and actors] were looked down on socially. Even in cosmopolitan Shanghai of the 1930's they were lumped together with butchers, criminals, vagrants, and prostitutes.' For similar attitudes in Tokugawa Japan, see Robertson (1992: 424, 317 n. 12). See also chapter 3 of this volume.
68 Cf. Ellison (1988: 1–48), and Rafael (1990), who has analysed the political implications of Imelda's (and Marcos's) theatrical capacities.
69 For the geographical distribution of the Cinderella folktale and the symbolism of shoes, see Dundes (1987: 30–2; 1988).
70 Compare what Wheelwright writes on transvestism: 'For the woman who so easily disguises herself makes transparent those fixed and immutable barriers between the sexes. She blurs distinctions and raises questions about how they are maintained' (1989: 28).
71 Cf. Robertson (1992: 426–7) on the 'new working woman' as the antithesis of the 'good wife, wise mother'.
72 See Lance Marrow, 'The shoes of Imelda Marcos', *Time*, 31 May 1986. For further details of Imelda's wealth, see Ellison (1988: 185ff).

73 Emphasis in original. See also B. Wilson (1975).
74 In a comparative essay Ortner reminds us that 'virginity downplays the uniquely feminine capacity to be penetrated and to give birth to children' (1981: 401).
75 Bhutto (1989: 63).
76 Bhutto (1989: 316).
77 M. Warner (1972: 258).
78 Terrill (1984: 311ff) and Witke (1977: 464–6).
79 Ellison (1988: 91, 155–9).
80 See note 37.
81 See note 64.

Chapter 12 Rediscovering *Ars Moriendi*

1 For detailed accounts of the Dutch situation, see Van der Wal and Van der Maas (1996); Hendin (1997); and Griffiths et al. (1998: 96ff and *passim*). The so-called *zorgvuldigheidseisen*, or requirements of careful practice, will be discussed later.
2 'Abstinence' refers both to ending (life-sustaining) treatment that has already been undertaken and to refraining from beginning such treatment. See Griffiths et al. (1998: 3 and *passim*).
3 On the changing terminology of euthanasia in the Netherlands, see Glossary in Griffiths et al. (1998: 3–6): *active euthanasia*: formerly contrasted with passive euthanasia but now referred to simply as 'euthanasia'; *direct euthanasia*: formerly contrasted with indirect euthanasia (i.e. death due to pain relief) but now referred to simply as 'euthanasia'; *indirect euthanasia*: term formerly used to refer to causing death as result of the use of pain-killers (usually morphine) in doses known to be likely to shorten life, no longer referred to as a form of euthanasia; *passive euthanasia*: term formerly used to refer to death caused by abstaining from life-sustaining treatment, no longer referred to as a form of euthanasia; *non-voluntary euthanasia*: termination of life without an explicit request (including coma patients, newborn babies, 'help in dying'), no longer referred to as euthanasia. These recent changes of the terminology prompted Hendin to remark that 'by narrowly defining euthanasia as referring only to "active voluntary euthanasia" rather than to all cases in which death is brought about on purpose as part of the medical care given to the patient, the Dutch minimize the frequency with which death is "intentionally accelerated by a doctor"' (1997: 108–9). In the United States, the Supreme Court ruled in June 1997 that states may continue to ban doctor-assisted suicide. This does not, writes Gina Kolata, affect passive euthanasia, which is the norm. According to the American Hospital Association, about 70 per cent of deaths in hospitals happen after a decision has been made to withhold treatment while others die when the medication they are taking to ease their pain depresses, then stops, their breathing (*International Herald Tribune*, 30 June 1997). See also Ronald Dworkin, 'Assisted suicide: what the court really said', *New York Review of Books*, 25 September 1997, pp. 40–4.

4   Figures from *NRC Handelsblad*, 27 November 1996 and *de Volkskrant*, 30 November 1996. See also Van der Wal and Van der Maas (1996).
5   Crump (1985: 182).
6   See Clark (1967); Glascock and Feinman (1980: 315); and Van der Geest (1996).
7   See Lindenbaum (1975); Scheper-Hughes (1984; 1987a; 1987b: 14; 1992: 375–6); Miller (1987); Mull and Mull (1987); and Harris (1993: 229–33, 349).
8   See Maxwell et al. (1982).
9   Adverse circumstances seem also to have been the most common reasons for the exposure or abandonment of children in pre-modern Europe. See Boswell (1988: 109, 256, 428 and *passim*).
10 Cf. Pool (1996: 222–9 and *passim*).
11 See note 3; and Griffiths et al. (1998: 6, 17 and *passim*).
12 See also Fabian (1972).
13 But see the pioneering work of Feifel (1959) and Kübler-Ross (1969) on dying in American hospitals, and the comments of Ariès (1981: 588–93). Yet the periodical *Mortality*, which promotes the interdisciplinary study of death and dying, was only founded in 1996.
14 For the concept of 'death-hastening behaviour', see Glascock (1982; 1983). See also below.
15 See Elias (1978b) and Blok (1995b). In his essay on dying, Elias notes that dying, 'however it is viewed', is an act of violence. Next to the technical perfection of the prolongation of life, the isolation of the dying in our day is the result of 'the greater internal pacification of developed industrial states and the marked advance of the embarrassment threshold in the face of violence. . . . Thus a higher level of internal pacification also contributes to the aversion towards death, or more precisely towards the dying. So does a higher level of civilizing restraint' (1985: 88–9).
16 See Ariès (1981: 570ff), and Gorer's (1965) innovative work.
17 See Sankar (1984: 274).
18 Sankar (1984: 274).
19 Myerhoff (1982: 111; 1984: 308). For further details, see Simmons (1970: 217–44) and Freuchen (1961: 140–54).
20 Quoted in Holmes and Holmes (1995: 153).
21 Rasing (1993; 1994: 157–9).
22 Rasing (1993: 96–101).
23 Hart (1988: 154).
24 Tonkinson (1978: 83); see also Venbrux (1995: 90–1).
25 See also Tonkinson (1978: 83).
26 See also Holmes and Holmes (1995: 216–17).
27 Chabot (1996: 27). Opponents of the law that made possible voluntary euthanasia on July 1996 in the northern territories of Australia carried posters with them with the text 'Euthan*azia* No Thanks. See *de Volkskrant*, 3 July 1996. About this law ('Rights of the Terminally Ill Act') and its application, see *NRC Handelsblad*, 29 June 1996; *Time*, 3 October 1996, p. 47; and *International Herald Tribune*, 28 October 1996, p. 2.

28 The Dutch word *stervensbekorting* is translated in a Dutch–English dictionary as 'reduction of the terminal phase' or 'euthanasia'. *Van Dale Groot Woordenboek Nederlands-Engels.* Utrecht/Antwerp: Van Dale Lexicografie, 1986. See also Griffiths et al. (1998: 92ff) on 'medical behavior that shortens life' (MBSL).

29 For an interview with Nitschke, see *International Herald Tribune,* 28 October 1996, p. 2.

30 Hilhorst (1983) quoted by Hendin (1997: 93), who throughout his book on Dutch euthanasia practices with the telling title *Seduced by Death* takes a strong position on this issue, and illustrates his thesis with harrowing examples of requests for euthanasia under pressure of family members and physicians (1997: 93, 114–20).

31 Chabot (1996: 29–30).

32 Pool (1996: 84–102, 205–9).

33 Pool (1996: 49–68).

34 For a discussion, see Griffiths et al. (1998: 65–73, 104–8 and *passim*).

35 Cf. Hendin (1997: 48–9); and Griffiths et al. (1998: 104–6).

36 See Hendin (1997: 48–9, 75–6, 88–90).

37 See interview with Van der Maas in *de Volkskrant,* 28 November 1996, p. 11.

38 On the monopoly of the medical profession over euthanasia, see Griffiths et al. (1998: 108).

39 On the polyinterpretable character of 'unbearable suffering', see the interview with the physician and member of parliament R. Oudkerk in *NRC Handelsblad,* 28 November 1996, p. 2. On medical paternalism, see Griffiths et al. (1998: 201 n. 13, 261 and *passim*). See also The (1997: 13–27).

40 Van Cleef (1996: 1).

41 See Griffiths et al. (1998: 135 and *passim*).

42 See also Griffiths et al. (1998: 137–8).

43 Griffiths et al. note that 'many cases of abstinence or of pain relief are in all practical, moral and legal respects essentially indistinguishable from euthanasia or termination of life without an explicit request' and that 'a doctor is usually in a position to "construct" a case either as one of euthanasia or termination of life without an explicit request, or as one of abstinence or pain relief' (1998: 269; cf. 107–8).

44 Cf. Pool (1996: 195–200).

45 Hendin (1997: 87–9), who is greatly concerned about these interpretations while Dutch law defines euthanasia as 'intentionally terminating or shortening a patient's life at his request or in his interests' (see also Griffiths et al. 1998: 68ff). For an evaluation of the actual reporting procedure, see Van der Wal and Van der Maas (1996). See also definitions in Glossary of Griffiths et al. (1998: 3–8).

46 See Van der Wal and Van der Maas (1996: 110–11, 225–6).

47 This society was officially founded on 25 October 1996. For further details see *NRC Handelsblad,* 5 November 1996, and *de Volkskrant,* 12 November 1996.

48 See the discussion in Griffiths et al. (1998: 189–90) on the opposition between the principle of autonomy and the principle of the sanctity of

human life. See also Griffiths's observations on medical paternalism: 'Medical paternalism can take the form both of putting a patient out of his misery without involving him fully in the decision-making, and of denying the patient euthanasia . . .' (1998: 26). See also Chabot's remarks on the growing autonomy of patients quoted in Griffiths et al. (1998: 201 n. 13).

49 See Hendin's observation: 'Euthanasia, advocated and instituted to foster patient autonomy and self-determination, has actually increased the paternalistic power of the medical profession. Doctors' organizations protect the interests of their members like guilds or unions everywhere. Doctors are especially unaccustomed to explaining their decisions to non-physicians' (1997: 94). Herbert Hendin is Director of the American Suicide Foundation and teaches at the New York Medical College. Over a period of four years he studied cases of euthanasia and assisted suicide in the Netherlands and the United States. The results are contained in his book *Seduced by Death* (1997). For an interview with Hendin, see *de Volkskrant*, 30 July 1996.

50 Hendin (1997: 90–2).

51 Ariès uses the expressions 'medicalization of death' and 'medicalization of society' interchangeably.

52 Cf. Hendin (1997). The Dutch Minister of Health acknowledged recently that palliative care of terminally ill patients leaves much to be desired. In the training of both medical doctors and nurses more attention should be paid to palliative care. She also emphasized that hospices should be integrated into 'ordinary' health care. *NRC Handelsblad*, 24 September 1998. More generally, the social skills of medical doctors in the Netherlands are poorly developed. The Academic Medical Centre in Amsterdam announced that, starting in September 1999, it will test medical students in their fifth year on two occasions during their apprenticeship on 'manners' and 'respect'. If they fail, they have to break off their study. *NRC Handelsblad*, 22 September 1998. Every year, an estimated number of 3,000 patients die in Dutch hospitals as the result of medical mistakes. In 1997 only 51 cases were reported. *NRC Handelsblad*, 21 September 1998.

53 On *artes moriendi*, see Ariès (1981: 105ff and *passim*).

54 When an earlier version of this essay was presented (at a conference of Medical Anthropology at the Department of Anthropology of the University of Amsterdam) in December 1996, the term *versterven* in this sense was hardly known and did not figure in Van Dale's *Groot Woordenboek der Nederlandse Taal* (Utrecht/Antwerp: Van Dale Lexicografie, 1984). The term '*versterven*', in the sense used in this essay, was only included in the 13th rev. edn of Van Dale (1999). The literature on *versterven* involved only a few references (Chabot 1996; Pikaar 1996). In the course of 1997 a handful of articles in Dutch newspapers addressed the issue. The most recent study on euthanasia contains the following cursory note: 'Because of the limited conditions under which euthanasia is legal and a variety of other difficulties that may stand in the way of a person who wishes to die, it has recently been noted by several observers in the Netherlands and elsewhere

that cancer patients and elderly people suffering from dementia can and do "let themselves die" (*versterven*) by starvation and dehydration (abstaining from food and drink)' (Griffiths et al. 1998: 93–4, 153–4, 216n).

55 The concept of 'self-help' was forged by Steinmetz, who distinguished twenty forms of *Selbsthilfe* and characterized it with a play on words as follows: 'Wo und wann der Einzelne aber von ihm [dem Staat] und seinen Organen entweder im Stich gelassen oder umgekehrt erstickt zu werden droht, tritt die Selbsthilfe als einzige Rettungsmöglichkeit wieder auf' (When and where the individual, however, threatens to be abandoned, or conversely, suffocated by the state and its institutions, self-help appears again as a saving device) (1931: 22).

56 Van Hooff (1990: 33–47).

57 Pikaar (1996); cf. Van Hooff (1990: 33).

58 Pikaar (1996: 61–77).

59 Elias described these institutions as 'deserts of loneliness' (1985: 74).

60 On the death of Vinoba Bhave, see *NRC Handelsblad*, 16 November 1982.

61 Personal communication, Peter van der Veer, 6 June 1996. The COD describes *samadhi* as 'a state of concentration induced by meditation'.

62 What in India is defined as a 'bad death' is a death that comes unexpectedly, not at the right time and the right place, a death for which one cannot prepare oneself (Parry 1994: 155–66 and *passim*). Discussing fifteenth-century representations of death, Ariès refers to the treatises on the techniques of dying well, the *artes moriendi*, and observes: 'The sudden death, the *mors improvisa*, was exceptional and greatly dreaded' (Ariès 1981: 107–8). Again we encounter an important contrast with beliefs and practices concerning dying and death in modern, western societies where people often say that they would 'sign up' for an unexpected death, for instance dying in their sleep. A recent obituary exemplifies this conception of a 'good death' in the following terms: 'My husband died from heart failure while he was rowing. He could not have wished for a more beautiful death' (*NRC Handelsblad*, 16 September 1998). Ariès writes: 'What today we call the good death, the beautiful death, corresponds exactly to what used to be the accursed death: the *mors repentina improvisa*, the death that gives no warning. "He died tonight in his sleep: He just didn't wake up. It was the best possible way to die"' (1981: 587).

63 Eastwell (1982).

64 R. Oudkerk, interview, *NRC Handelsblad*, 28 November 1996, p. 2. On the complexity of requests for euthanasia, see also Hendin (1997: 199–224).

65 Glascock (1982; 1983; 1990); cf. Maxwell et al. (1982).

66 Glascock (1983: 418); cf. Rasing (1993).

67 This point was earlier stressed by Harris (1971: 287).

68 Cf. Van Heek (1975: 37–40). One may think of people for whom suffering has not become utterly meaningless. On the subject of meaningful suffering in areas with a Roman Catholic tradition, see Zimdars-Swartz (1991: 266–7) and Scheper-Hughes (1992: 436). See also Hendin (1997: 94–5) and his observation that 'connectedness somewhat relieves our anxiety about death; it helps fulfill our need for [symbolic] immortality. . . . Pain, suffer-

ing, and death itself are easier to bear [when surrounded by loved ones]' (1997: 151–2).

69   Their numbers increase because people live longer and retire sooner.

70   *NRC Handelsblad*, 2 May 1996.

71   *International Herald Tribune*, 28 October 1996. See also Hendin (1997: 197).

72   See the perceptive notes on this tale in Ariès (1981: 21–2, 563–7, 573–5).

73   The large numbers of refugees and dying people in these areas, which is almost daily broadcasted, produced among western audiences a 'cultural anaesthesia' (Feldman 1994; Malkki 1996).

74   Bron (1980: 348), quoted in Klasen (1990: 10). For dying in the absence of a doctor in a Dutch hospital, see The (1998: 13–27), who based her research on participant observation in her role as a nurse. A possible exception is physicians who work in nursing homes. But in these institutions, as in hospitals, nurses routinely take care of the dying. The commonplace 'The doctor could only ascertain death' illustrates the distance between the physician and the dying, his absence from the dying process – both in reality and in the imaginary world. Hence Hendin's recommendations regarding the training of medical doctors, who 'should no longer be kept away from dying patients . . . they must be encouraged to learn that communicating with and caring for those who are dying is necessary to truly be a physician' (1997: 217–19).

75   Klasen (1990: 61–2).

76   See, for instance, Douglas (1982) and Myerhoff (1982). See also Ariès (1981: 579), who points out the disappearance of the codes for dying in western societies since the late nineteenth century.

77   Hendin (1997: 151–3) refers to the notions of symbolic and creative immortality which have lost much of their significance in the narcissistic orientation of modern culture.

78   See Marcus and Fischer (1986: 157ff).

79   Knight (1994: 3).

Bibliography

Abbink, J. 1987: A socio-structural analysis of the Beta Esra'el as an 'infamous group' in traditional Ethiopia. *Sociologus*, 37, 140–54.

Ahlmann, Hans W. 1925: Etudes de géographie humaine sur l'Italie subtropicale. La Sicile. *Geografiska Annaler*, 7, 257–322.

——1926: Etudes de géographie humaine sur l'Italie subtropicale. Calabre, Basilicate et Apulie. *Geografiska Annaler*, 8, 74–124.

Akenson, Donald H. 1988: *Small Differences: Irish Catholics and Irish Protestants, 1815–1922. An interpretational perspective.* Kingston/Montreal: McGill-Queen's University Press.

Alexander, John T. 1989: *Catherine the Great: life and legend.* New York: Oxford University Press.

Alinei, Mario 1980: Mariti traditi come 'becchi' e come 'cuculi'. In margine ad Anton Blok, 'Montoni e becchi'. *Quaderni di Semantica*, 1, 363–72.

——1982: Correspondence: Rams and billy-goats. *Man* (N.S.), 17, 771–5.

Alongi, Giuseppe 1891: *L'Abigeato in Sicilia.* Marsala: Tip. di Luigi Giliberto.

Amiel, Christiane 1987: Les caprices du mariage. *Ethnologie française*, 17, 367–80.

Angstmann, Else 1928: *Der Henker in der Volksmeinung. Seine Namen und sein Vorkommen in der mündlichen Volksüberlieferung.* Bonn: Fritz Klopp Verlag.

Antoun, Richard T. 1968a: On the significance of names in an Arab village. *Ethnology*, 7, 158–70.

——1968b: On the modesty of women in an Arab Muslim village: a study in the accommodation of tradition. *American Anthropologist*, 70, 671–97.

Appadurai, Arjun 1999: Dead certainty: ethnic violence in the era of globalization. In Birgit Meyer and Peter Geschiere (eds), *Globalization and Identity.* Oxford: Blackwell.

Ariès, Philippe 1981: *The Hour of our Death.* Harmondsworth: Penguin Books.

Arlacchi, Pino 1987: *Mafia Business.* London: Verso.

——1992: *Gli uomini del disonore. La mafia siciliana nella vita del grande pentito Antonino Calderone.* Milano: Mondadori.

—— 1994: *Addio Cosa Nostra. La vita di Tommaso Buscetta.* Milano: Rizzoli.

Artemidorus 1992: *The Interpretation of Dreams: Oneirocritica.* Tr. Robert J. White. Park Ridge, NJ: Noyes Classical Studies. Repr. Nelson St, Largs, Scotland: Banton Press.

Austin, J. L. 1980: *How to do Things with Words* [1962]. Oxford: Oxford University Press.

Aya, Rod 1990: *Rethinking Revolutions and Collective Violence: studies on concept, theory, and method.* Amsterdam: Het Spinhuis.

Babcock, Barbara A. 1975: A tolerated margin of mess: the trickster and his tales reconsidered. *Journal of the Folklore Institute*, 11, 145–86.

—— 1978: Introduction. In Babcock (ed.), *The Reversible World: symbolic inversion in art and society.* Ithaca: Cornell University Press, 13–36.

Bächtold-Stäubli, Hanns (ed.) 1929/30: Dieb, Diebstahl. In *Handwörterbuch des deutschen Aberglauben*, vol. II. Berlin/Leipzig: Walter de Gruyter Verlag.

Bakhtin, Mikhail 1968: *Rabelais and his World.* Tr. Helene Iswolsky. Cambridge, MA: Harvard University Press.

Balint, Käthe 1980: En nattmans öden under 1700-talet: ett exempel pa hur landskansliets diarier kan användes för personsökning. *Ale. Historisk Tidskrift för Skaneland*, 1, 1–8.

Banfield, Edward C. 1958: *The Moral Basis of a Backward Society.* Glencoe: The Free Press.

Barakat, R. A. 1973: Arabic gestures. *Journal of Popular Culture*, 6, 749–87.

Barker, Graeme 1985: *Prehistoric Farming in Europe.* Cambridge: Cambridge University Press.

Barnes, R. B. 1982: Personal names and social classification. In David Parkin (ed.), *Semantic Anthropology.* London: Academic Press, 211–26.

Barrett, Richard A. 1978: Village modernization and changing nicknaming practices in northern Spain. *Journal of Anthropological Research*, 34, 92–108.

Barth, Fredrik 1960: The system of social stratification in Swat, North Pakistan. In E. R. Leach (ed.), *Aspects of Caste in South India, Ceylon, and North-West Pakistan.* Cambridge: Cambridge University Press.

—— 1965: *Political Leadership among the Swat Pathans.* London: Athlone Press.

—— 1993: *Balinese Worlds.* Chicago: University of Chicago Press.

Barton, Carlin A. 1992: *The Sorrows of the Ancient Romans: the gladiator and the monster.* Princeton, NJ: Princeton University Press.

—— 1994: Savage miracles: the redemption of lost honor in Roman society and the sacrament of the gladiator and the martyr. *Representations*, 45, 41–71.

Barton, Tamsyn 1994: *Ancient Astrology.* London/New York: Routledge.

Bascom, William 1955: Urbanization among the Yoruba. *American Journal of Sociology*, 60, 446–54.

Beattie, John 1968: Aspects of Nyoro symbolism. *Africa*, 23, 413–42.

Becker, Jasper 1996: *Hungry ghosts: China's secret famine.* London: Murray.

Beneke, Otto 1863: *Von unehrlichen Leuten.* Hamburg: Perthes, Besser & Mauke Verlag.

Benveniste, Emile 1969: Livestock and money: *pecu* and *pecunia*. In Benveniste, *Indo-European Language and Society.* Tr. Elizabeth Palmer. London: Faber and Faber, 40–51.

——1973: The vocabulary of kinship. In Benveniste, *Indo-European Language and Society*. Tr. Elizabeth Palmer. London: Faber and Faber.

Berger, Peter 1970: On the obsolescence of the concept of honour. *European Journal of Sociology*, 11, 339–47.

Berland, Joseph C. 1982: *No Five Fingers are Alike: cognitive amplifiers in social context*. Cambridge, MA: Harvard University Press.

——1987a: Kanjar social organization. In Aparna Rao (ed.), *The Other Nomads: peripatetic minorities in cross-cultural perspective*. Cologne/Vienna: Bohlau Verlag.

——1987b: Territorial resiliency among peripatetic peoples in Pakistan. Paper presented at the 1987 Congress of the German Anthropological Association in Cologne, 4–9 October 1987.

Bernard, H. Russell 1969: Paratsoukli: Institutionalized nicknaming in rural Greece. *Ethnologia Europaea*, 2/3, 65–74.

Berndt, Ronald M. and Berndt, Catherine H. 1988: *The World of the First Australians* [1964]. Canberra: Aboriginal Studies Press.

Bhatia, Krishnan 1974: *Indira: a biography of Prime Minister Gandhi*. New York: Praeger.

Bhutto, Benazir 1989: *Daughter of the East: an autobiography*. London: Mandarin Press.

Bianconi, Giovanni 1980: *Valle Verzasca*. Locarno: Armando Dadò Editore.

Billacois, François 1986: *Le duel dans la société française des XVI e et XVIIe siècles*. Paris: Editions de l'Ecole des Hautes Etudes en Sciences Sociales.

Billingsley, Phil 1988: *Bandity in Republican China*. Stanford: Stanford University Press.

Biundi, Giuseppe 1851: *Vocabulario Siciliano–Italiano*. Palermo: Carini.

Black-Michaud, Jacob 1975: *Cohesive Force: feud in the Mediterranean and the Middle East*. Oxford: Blackwell.

——1986: *Sheep and Land: the economics of power in a tribal society*. Cambridge: Cambridge University Press; Paris: Editions de la Maison des Sciences de l'Homme.

Blincow, Malcolm 1986: Scavengers and recycling, a neglected domain of production. *Labour, Capital and Society*, 19, 94–115.

Bloch, Marc 1935: Avènements et conquêtes du moulin à eau. *Annales d'histoire économique et sociale*, 7, 538–63.

——1961: *Feudal Society* [1939]. Tr. L. A. Manyon. Chicago: University of Chicago Press.

——1973: *The Royal Touch: sacred monarchy and scrofula in England and France*. Tr. J. E. Anderson. London: Routledge.

——1983: *Les rois thaumaturges. Étude sur le caractère surnaturel attribué à la puissance royale particulièrement en France et en Angleterre* [1924]. Préface de Jacques Le Goff. Paris: Gallimard.

Bloch, Maurice and Parry, Jonathan (eds) 1982: *Death and the Regeneration of Life*. Cambridge: Cambridge University Press.

Blok, Anton 1966: Land reform in a west Sicilian latifondo village: the persistence of a feudal structure. *Anthropological Quarterly*, 39, 1–16.

——1974: Tijd en tragiek. De relatieve autonomie van klassieke romans and dramas. *De Gids*, 137, 701–8.

——1976: *Wittgenstein en Elias. Een methodische richtlijn voor de antropologie.* 2nd edn. Amsterdam: Athenaeum.

——1983: On negative reciprocity among Sicilian pastoralists. In Maria Pia di Bella (ed.), *Production pastorale et société. Bulletin de l'équipe écologie et anthropologie des sociétés pastorales*, 13, 43–6.

——1988: *The Mafia of a Sicilian Village, 1860–1960: a study of violent peasant entrepreneurs.* 2nd edn. Cambridge: Polity Press.

——1989: Charivari's als purificatie ritueel. *Volkskundig Bulletin*, 15, 266–80.

——1992: Reflections on 'making history'. In Kirsten Hastrup (ed.), *Other Histories*. London: Routledge.

——1995a: *De Bokkerijders. Roversbenden en geheime genootschappen in de Landen van Overmaas, 1730–1774.* Rev. edn. Amsterdam: Prometheus.

——1995b: Dieto le quinte. Compara la sfera del privato. In Maurice Aymard (ed.), *Storia d'Europa*, IV, *L'Età moderna*. Torrino: Einaudi.

——1999: Les ambiguités de l'amitié. A propos de quelques proverbes siciliens. In Georges Ravis-Giordani (ed.), *Amitiés. Anthropologie et l'histoire*. Aix-en-Provence: Publications de l'Université de Provence.

——and Driessen, Henk 1984: Mediterranean agro-towns as a form of cultural dominance. *Ethnologia Europaea*, 14, 111–24.

Blumer, Herbert 1969: *Symbolic Interactionism: perspective and method.* Englewood Cliffs, NJ: Prentice-Hall.

Boardman, J. 1975: *Athenian Red Figure Vases: the archaic period.* London: Thames and Hudson.

Bobek, Hans 1962: The main stages in socio-economic evolution from a geographical point of view. In Philip L. Wagner and Marvin W. Mikesell (eds), *Readings in Cultural Geography*. Chicago: University of Chicago Press.

Boehm, Christopher 1984: *Blood Revenge: the enactment and management of conflict in Montenegro and other tribal societies.* Philadelphia: University of Pennsylvania Press.

Boon, James A. 1984: Folly, Bali, and anthropology, or satire across cultures. In Edward M. Bruner (ed.), *Text, Play, and Story: the construction and reconstruction of self and society*. Washington, DC: American Ethnological Society.

Borgeaud, Philippe 1979: *Recherches sur le dieu Pan.* Bibliotheca Helvetica Romana XVII. Geneva: Institut Suisse de Rome.

Boswell, John 1988: *The Kindness of Strangers: the abandonment of children in western Europe from late antiquity to the Renaissance.* New York: Pantheon Books.

Bott, Elizabeth 1964: *Family and Social Network.* London: Tavistock.

Bouché-Leclercq, A. 1963: *L'astrologie grèque* [Paris 1899]. Repr. Brussels: Culture et Civilisation.

Boudon, Raymond 1982: *The Unintended Consequences of Social Action.* London: Macmillan.

Bourdieu, Pierre 1979a: The sense of honour. In Bourdieu, *Algeria 1960*. Cambridge: Cambridge University Press; Paris: Editions de la Maison des Sciences de l'Homme.

——1979b: The Kabyle house or the world reversed. In *Algeria 1960*. Cambridge: Cambridge University Press; Paris: Editions de la Maison des Sciences de l'Homme.

——1984: *Distinction: a social critique of the judgement of taste* [1979]. Tr. Richard Nice. London: Routledge.

——1998: Interview. *Libération*, 19 March, 43–4.

——(ed.) 1993: *La misère du monde*. Paris: Seuil.

Bourqia, Rahma 1991: Vol, pillage et banditisme dans le Maroc du XIXe siècle. *Hespéris-Tamuda*, 29, 191–226.

Bovenkerk, Frank 1991: Over selectiviteit gesproken!, *Tijdschrift voor Criminologie*, 33, 309–21.

——and Ruland, Loes 1984: De schoorsteenvegers. *Intermediair*, 20 (51), 23–39.

Brand, John 1877: *Observations on Popular Antiquities*. London: Chatto & Windus.

Brandes, Stanley 1975: The structural and demographic implications of nicknames in Navanogal, Spain. *American Ethnologist*, 2, 139–48.

——1981: Like wounded stags: male sexual ideology in an Andalusian town. In Sherry B. Ortner and Harriet Whitehead (eds), *Sexual Meanings: the cultural construction of gender and sexuality*. Cambridge: Cambridge University Press.

Braudel, Fernand 1972/3: *The Mediterranean and the Mediterranean World in the Age of Philip II* [1949]. 2 vols. Tr. S. Reynolds. New York: Harper & Row.

Braun, Marianne 1992: Het huwelijk der koningin of: de omgekeerde wereld. In Braun, *De prijs van de liefde. De eerste feministische golf, het huwelijksrecht en de vaderlandse geschiedenis*. Amsterdam: Het Spinhuis.

Breen, Richard 1982: Naming practices in western Ireland. *Man* (N.S.), 17, 701–13.

Bregenhoj, Carsten 1978: Rodfluesvamp, skorstensfeger og mariehone pa jule-og nytarskort. In *Folk og Kultur. Arbog for Dansk Etnologi og Folkemindevidenskab*. Copenhagen: Udgivet af Foreningen Danmarks Folkeminder.

Brenan, Gerald 1962: *The Spanish Labyrinth: an account of the social and political background of the Spanish Civil War*. Cambridge: Cambridge University Press.

Breteau, Claude H. and Zagnoli, Nello 1980: Le système de gestion de la violence dans deux communautés rurales méditerranéennes. La Calabre méridionale et le N.E. Constantinois. In Raymond Verdier (ed.), *La vengeance*. 4 vols. Paris: Editions Cujas/CNRS, I.

Brigaglia, Manlio 1971: *Sardegna perchè banditi*. Milan: Edizioni Leader.

Brightman, Robert 1995: Forget culture: replacement, transcendence, relexification. *Cultural Anthropology*, 10, 509–46.

Brinkgreve, Christien and Van Daalen, Rineke 1991: Huiselijk geweld. In Herman Franke et al. (eds), *Alledaags en ongewoon geweld*. Groningen: Wolters/Noordhoff.

Brisebarre, Anne-Marie 1978: *Bergers des Cévennes*. Nancy: Berger-Levrault.

Brögger, Jan 1971: *Montevarese: a study of peasant society and culture in southern Italy*. Oslo: Universitetsforlaget.

Bromberger, Christian 1982: Pour une analyse anthropologique des noms de personnes. *Langages*, 16 (66), 103–24.

——and Lenclud, G. (eds) 1982: La chasse et la cueillette aujourd'hui. *Études rurales*, 87/8, 1–421.

——et al. 1995: *Le match de football. Ethnologie d'une passion partisane à Marseille, Naples et Turin*. Paris: Editions de la Maison des Sciences de l'Homme.

Bron, Bernard 1980: Der Psychiater und der sterbende Patient. In U. P. Peters (ed.), *Die Psychologie des 20. Jahrhunderts*. Zurich: Kindler.

Brown, Philip 1960: Black luck. *Folklore*, 71, 188–92.

Brownmiller, Susan 1975: *Against our Will: men, women, and rape*. New York: Simon & Schuster.

Brundage, W. Fitzhugh 1993: *Lynching in the New South: Georgia and Virginia*. Urbana: University of Illinois Press.

Brunschvig, R. 1962: Métiers vils en Islam. *Studia Islamica*, 16, 4–61.

Buckley, Thomas and Gottlieb, Alma (eds) 1988: *Blood Magic: the anthropology of menstruation*. Berkeley: University of California Press.

Bühler, Linus 1984: Die Bündner Schwabengänger und die Tessiner Kaminfegerkinder. *Schweizerisches Archiv für Volkskunde*, 80 (3/4), 165–82.

Buijtenhuijs, Robert 1971: *Le mouvement 'Mau Mau'. Une révolte paysanne et anti-coloniale en Afrique noire*. The Hague/Paris: Mouton.

Bulmer, Ralph 1967: Why is the cassowary not a bird? A problem of zoological taxonomy among the Karam of the New Guinea Highlands. *Man* (N.S.), 2, 5–25.

Buñuel, Luis 1971: *Tristana: a film by Luis Buñuel*. Modern Film Scripts. Tr. Nicholas Fry. New York: Simon & Schuster.

——1982: *My Last Breath*. Tr. Abigail Israel. London: Fontana.

——1984: *Viridiana. Scénario et dialogues. Variantes. Dossier historique et critique*. Paris: Filméditions Pierre Lherminier Editeur.

Burch, E. S., Jr 1975: *Eskimo Kinsmen*. AES monograph. St Paul, MN: West.

Burke, Peter 1978: *Popular Culture in Early Modern Europe*. New York: Harper & Row.

Burkert, Walter 1983: *Homo Necans: the anthropology of ancient Greek sacrificial ritual and myth*. Tr. Peter Bing. Berkeley: University of California Press.

——1985: *Greek Religion*. Tr. John Raffan. Cambridge, MA: Harvard University Press.

——1990: *Wilder Ursprung. Opferritual und Mythos bei den Griechen*. Berlin: Wagenbach.

——1996: *Creation of the Sacred: tracks of biology in early religions*. Cambridge, MA: Harvard University Press.

Buruma, Ian 1986: Saint Cory and the Yellow Revolution. *New York Review of Books*, 33 (17), 13–24.

——1987: St Cory and the Evil Rose. *New York Review of Books*, 34 (10), 10–14.

Busse, Thomas V. 1983: Nickname usage in an American high school. *Names*, 31, 300–6.

Cagnetta, Franco 1963: *Bandits d'Orgosolo* [1954]. Tr. Michel Thurlotte. Paris: Buchet/Chastel.

Caisson, Max 1976: Le four et l'araignée. *Ethnologie française*, 6, 365–80.

Campbell, J. K. 1964: *Honour, Family and Patronage: a study of institutions and moral values in a Greek mountain community*. Oxford: Clarendon Press.

Camporesi, Piero 1984: *Il sugo della vita. Simbolismo e magia del sangue*. Milano: Edizioni di Comunità.

Carlyle, Margaret 1962: *The Awakening of Southern Italy*. London: Oxford University Press.

Caro Baroja, Julio 1963: The city and the country: reflexions on some ancient common places. In J. A. Pitt-Rivers (ed.), *Mediterranean Countrymen*. Paris/The Hague: Mouton.

Carpenter, T. H. 1991: *Art and Myth in Ancient Greece*. London: Thames and Hudson.

Casagrande, Carla and Vecchio, Silvana 1979: Clercs et jongleurs dans la société médiévale. *Annales – Economies Sociétés Civilisations*, 34, 913–28.

Casanova, Antoine 1997: Permanence et mouvement dans les outillages et les structures sociales des campagnes en Méditerranée. Paper presented at the conference 'Anthropology and the Mediterranean: unity, diversity, and prospects', Aix-en-Provence, 14–17 May 1997.

Cazenave, Michel (ed.) 1996: *Encyclopédie des symboles*. Tr. Françoise Périgaut et al. Paris: La Pochothèque.

Chabot, B. E. 1996: *Sterven op drift*. Nijmegen: SUN.

Chandler, Billy J. 1979: *The Bandit King: Lampião of Brazil*. College Station, TX: A&M Press.

Chapman, Charlotte Gower 1971: *Milocca: a Sicilian village*. New York: Schenkman.

Charbonnier, G. 1969: *Conversations with Claude Lévi-Strauss*. Tr. John and Doreen Weightman. London: Jonathan Cape.

Cherry, John F. 1988: Pastoralism and the role of animals in the pre- and protohistoric economies of the Aegean. In C. R. Whittaker (ed.), *Pastoral Economies in Classical Antiquity*. Cambridge: Cambridge University Press.

Childs, John 1982: *Armies and Warfare in Europe, 1648–1789*. Manchester: Manchester University Press.

Chirot, Daniel 1976: *Social Change in a Peripheral Society: the creation of a Balkan colony*. New York: Academic Press.

Christian, William. A., Jr 1972: *Person and God in a Spanish Valley*. New York: Academic Press.

Clark, Margaret 1967: The anthropology of aging: a new area for studies in culture and personality. *Gerontologist*, 7, 55–66.

Clutton-Brock, Juliet 1981: *Domesticated Animals from Early Times*. London: British Museum.

Cobb, Richard 1972: La bande d'Orgères, 1790–1799. In Cobb, *Reactions to the French Revolution*. London: Oxford University Press.

——1975: *Paris and its Provinces, 1792–1802*. London: Oxford University Press.

Cocchiara, Giuseppe 1977: *Il linguaggio del gesto* [1932. Torino: Fratelli Bocca.] Rep. Palermo: Sellerio.

Cohen, Eugene N. 1977: Nicknames, social boundaries, and community in an Italian village. *International Journal of Contemporary Sociology*, 14, 102–13.

Cole, John W. and Wolf, Eric R. 1974: *The Hidden Frontier: ecology and ethnicity in an Alpine valley*. New York: Academic Press.

Collier, George A. and Bricker, Victoria R. 1970: Nicknames and social structure in Zinacantan. *American Anthropologist*, 72, 289–302.

Comaroff, Jean 1985: *Body of Power, Spirit of Resistance: the culture and history of a South African people*. Chicago: University of Chicago Press.

Compagna, Francesco 1963: *La questione meridionale*. Milano: Garzanti.

Connell, R. W. 1987: *Gender and Power*. Stanford: Stanford University Press.

Corbin, Alain 1986a: Commercial sexuality in nineteenth-century France: a system of images and regulations. *Representations*, 14, 209–19.

——1986b: *The Foul and the Fragrant: odor and the French social imagination*. Cambridge, MA: Harvard University Press.

Crankshaw, Edward 1969: *Maria Theresa*. New York: Longmans.

Crump, Thomas 1985: Death. In Adam and Jessica Kuper (eds), *The Social Science Encyclopedia*. London: Routledge.

Cutileiro, José 1971: *A Portuguese Rural Society*. Oxford: Clarendon Press.

D'Alessandro, Enzo 1959: *Brigantaggio e mafia in Sicilia*. Messina / Firenze: Casa Editrice G. D'Anna.

D'Amico, Francine n.d.: Women as shapers of world politics. In D'Amico et al. (eds), *Women and World Politics*.

Dahles, Heidi 1990: *Mannen in het groen. De wereld van de jacht in Nederland*. Nijmegen: SUN.

Daley, Martin and Wilson, Margo 1988: *Homicide*. New York: Aldine.

Danckert, Werner 1963: *Unehrliche Leute. Die verfehmten Berufe*. Berne/Munich: Francke Verlag.

Danner, Mark 1998: The killing fields of Bosnia. *New York Review of Books* (24 September), 45 (14), 63–77.

Davis, Natalie Zemon 1975: *Society and Culture in Early Modern France*. Stanford: Stanford University Press.

——1978: Women on top: symbolic sexual inversion and political disorder in early modern Europe. In Barbara A. Babcock (ed.), *The Reversible World*. Ithaca/London: Cornell University Press.

——1983: *The Return of Martin Guerre*. Cambridge, MA: Harvard University Press.

De Heusch, Luc 1985: *Sacrifice in Africa: a structuralist approach*. Manchester: Manchester University Press.

——1997: The symbolic mechanisms of sacred kingship: rediscovering Frazer. *Journal of the Royal Anthropological Society*, 3, 213–32.

De Jongh, E. 1995: *Kwesties van betekenis. Thema en motief in de Nederlandse schilderkunst van de zeventiende eeuw*. Leiden: Primavera Pers.

De Jorio, Andrea 1832: *La mimica degli Antichi. Investigata dal gestire Napoletano*. Napoli: Fibreno.

De Madariaga, Isabel 1990: *Catherine the Great: a short history*. New Haven, CT: Yale University Press.

De Morais Silva, Antonio 1950: *Grande dicionário da língua portuguesa*. Lisboa: Confluência.

De Seta, Vittorio 1962: *Banditi ad Orgosolo*. Film. Scenario: Vittorio de Seta.

De Vos, George and Wagatsuma, Hiroshi (eds) 1972: *Japan's Invisible Race: caste in culture and personality*. 2nd edn. Berkeley/Los Angeles: University of California Press.

Dekker, Rudolf 1982: *Holland in beroering. Oproeren in de 17e en 18e eeuw*. Baarn: Ambo.

——and Van de Pol, Lotte 1989: *The Tradition of Female Transvestism in Early Modern Europe*. London: Macmillan Press.

Del Treppo, Mario and Leone, Alfonso 1977: *Amalfi medioevale*. Naples: Giannini Editore.

Delaney, Carol 1977: The legacy of Abraham. In Rita M. Gross (ed.), *Beyond Androcentrism*. Missoula, MT: Scholars Press.

——1986: The meaning of paternity. *Man* (N.S.), 21, 494–513.

——1991: *The Seed and the Soil: gender and cosmology in Turkish village society*. Berkeley: University of California Press.

Dell, William 1987: St Dominic's: an ethnographic note on a Cambridge college. *Actes de la Recherche en Sciences Sociales*, 70, 74–90.

Demangeon, A. 1927: La géographie de l'habitat rural. *Annales de Géographie*, 36, 1–24 and 97–115.

Demeter, Karl 1964: *Das deutsche Offizierkorps in Gesellschaft und Staat, 1650–1945*. Frankfurt am Main: Bernard & Graefe.

Den Hollander, A. N. J. 1960/61: The Great Hungarian Plain: a European frontier area. *Comparative Studies in Society and History*, 3, 74–88 and 155–69.

Denich, Bette 1994: Dismembering Yugoslavia: nationalist ideologies and the symbolic revival of genocide. *American Ethnologist*, 21, 367–90.

Di Bella, Maria Pia 1992: Name, blood and miracles: the claims to renown in traditional Sicily. In J. G. Peristiany and J. Pitt-Rivers, *Honor and Grace in Anthropology*. Cambridge: Cambridge University Press.

Dickinson, Robert A. 1955: *The Population Problem of Southern Italy: an essay in social geography*. Syracuse: Syracuse University Press.

Djilas, Milovan 1958: *Land without Justice*. New York: Harcourt Brace.

Dolci, Danilo 1963: *Waste: an eye-witness report on some aspects of waste in western Sicily*. London: Macgibbon & Kee.

Dollard, John 1988: *Caste and Class in a Southern Town* [1937]. Madison: University of Wisconsin Press.

Donoghue, J. D. 1957: An Eta community in Japan: the social persistence of outcaste groups. *American Anthropologist*, 59, 1000–17.

Dorian, N. C. 1970: A substitute name system in the Scottish Highlands. *American Anthropologist*, 72, 303–19.

Dossier Andreotti 1993: *Il testo completo delle accuse dei giudici di Palermo*. Milan: Mondadori.

Douglas, Mary 1966: *Purity and Danger*. London: Routledge & Kegan Paul.

——1970: *Natural Symbols: explorations in cosmology*. New York: Pantheon.

—— 1975: Jokes. In Douglas, *Implicit Meanings: essays in anthropology.* London: Routledge & Kegan Paul, 90–114.

—— 1982: Away from ritual. In Douglas, *Natural Symbols* [1970]. New York: Pantheon Books.

Douglass, William A. and Zulaika, Joseba 1990: On the interpretation of terrorist violence: ETA and the Basque political process. *Comparative Studies in Society and History,* 32, 238–57.

Dovring, Folke 1965: *Land and Labor in Europe in the Twentieth Century.* 3rd edn. The Hague: Martinus Nijhoff.

Dreyfus, Hubert L. and Rabinow, Paul 1982: *Michel Foucault: beyond structuralism and hermeneutics.* Chicago: University of Chicago Press.

Driessen, Henk 1981: *Agro-town and Urban Ethos in Andalusia.* Ph.D thesis, Catholic University of Nijmegen.

Duerr, Hans Peter 1988: *Nacktheit und Scham. Der Mythos vom Zivilisationsprozess.* Vol. I. Frankfurt am Main: Suhrkamp Verlag.

—— 1990: *Intimität. Der Mythos vom Zivilisationsprozess.* Vol. II. Frankfurt am Main: Suhrkamp Verlag.

Dumont, Louis 1980: *Homo Hierarchicus: the caste system and its implications.* Completely rev. edn. Tr. Mark Sainsbury. Chicago: University of Chicago Press.

Dundes, Alan 1987: *Parsing through Customs: essays by a Freudian folklorist.* Madison: University of Wisconsin Press.

—— 1988: *Cinderella: a folklore casebook.* Madison: University of Wisconsin Press.

—— 1989: The anthropologist and the comparative method in folklore. In Dundes (ed.), *Folklore Matters.* Knoxville: University of Tennessee Press, 57–82.

—— and Falassi, Alessandro, 1975: *La terra in piazza: an interpretation of the palio of Siena.* Berkeley: University of California Press.

Dunning, Eric et al. 1986: 'Casuals', 'terrace crews' and 'fighting firms': towards a sociological explanation of football hooligan behaviour. In D. Riches (ed.), *The Anthropology of Violence.* Oxford: Blackwell.

Durham, Mary Edith 1928: *Some Tribal Origins, Laws, and Customs of the Balkans.* London: Allen & Unwin.

Durkheim, Emile and Mauss, Marcel 1963: *Primitive Classification* [1903]. Tr. Rodney Needham. Chicago: University of Chicago Press.

Eastwell, Harry D. 1982: Voodoo death and the mechanism for dispatch of the dying in East Arnhem, Australia. *American Anthropologist,* 84, 5–18.

Eberhard, Wolfram 1965: *Conquerors and Rulers: Social forces in medieval China.* Leiden: Brill.

—— 1970: *Studies in Chinese Folklore and Related Essays.* Indiana University Folklore Monograph Series, vol. XXIII. The Hague: Mouton.

Eco, Umberto 1988: Horns, hooves, insteps: some hypotheses on three types of abduction. In Eco and Sebeok, *The Sign of Three: Dupin, Holmes, Peirce* [1983]. Bloomington: Indiana University Press.

—— and Thomas A. Sebeok (eds) 1988: *The Sign of Three: Dupin, Holmes, Peirce* [1983]. Bloomington: Indiana University Press.

Egardt, Brita 1962: *Hästslakt och rackarskam. (Pferdeschlachtung und Abdeck-*

ersschande. Eine ethnologische Untersuchung volkstümlicher Vorurteile.)
Stockholm: Nordiske Museet.
Egmond, Florike 1986: *Banditisme in de Franse Tijd. Profiel van de Grote
Nederlandse Bende, 1790–1799.* Zutphen: De Bataafsche Leew.
——1993: *Underworlds: organized crime in the Netherlands, 1650–1800.*
Cambridge: Polity Press.
Eidelberg, Philip G. 1974: *The Great Rumanian Peasant Revolt of 1907: origins
of a modern jacquerie.* Leiden: Brill.
Eliade, Mircea 1978: *The Forge and the Crucible* [1956]. 2nd edn. Tr. Stephen
Corrin. Chicago: University of Chicago Press.
Elias, Norbert 1969a: *Die höfische Gesellschaft.* Berlin: Luchterhand.
——1969b: *Über den Prozess der Zivilisation* [1939]. 2 vols. Berne/Munich:
Francke Verlag.
——1969c: Sociology and psychiatry. In S. H. Foulkes and Stewart Prince (eds),
Psychiatry in a Changing Society. London.
——1978a: *What is Sociology?* Tr. Stephen Mennell and Grace Morrissey.
London: Hutchinson.
——1978b: *The History of Manners: the civilizing process* [1939]. Vol. I. Tr. E.
Jephcott. New York: Pantheon Books.
——1983: *The Court Society.* Tr. Edmund Jephcott. Oxford: Blackwell.
——1985: *The Loneliness of the Dying.* Oxford: Blackwell.
——1986: An essay on sport and violence. In Norbert Elias and Eric Dunning,
Quest for Excitement: sport and leisure in the civilizing process. Oxford:
Blackwell.
——1996: *The Germans: power struggles and the development of habitus in the
nineteenth and twentieth centuries.* Ed. Michael Schröter. Tr. Eric Dunning and
Stephen Mennell. Cambridge: Polity Press.
——and Scotson, John L. 1965: *The Established and the Outsiders.* London:
Frank Cass.
Ellison, Katherine 1988: *Imelda: steel butterfly of the Philippines.* New York:
McGraw-Hill.
Eloy, Arnold 1983: *De schoorsteenveger. Een terreinverkenning.* Ghent:
Koninklijke Bond der Oostvlaamse Volkskundigen.
Elworthy, F. T. 1958: *The Evil Eye: the origins and practices of superstitions*
[1895]. New York: Julian Press.
Ensel, Remco 1999: *Saints and Servants in Southern Morocco.* Leiden: Brill.
Estrich, Susan 1987: *Real Rape.* Cambridge, MA: Harvard University Press.
Evans-Pritchard, E. E. 1940: *The Nuer.* Oxford: Oxford University Press.
——1956: *Nuer Religion.* Oxford: Clarendon Press.
——1976: *Witchcraft, Oracles, and Magic among the Azande.* Abbr. edn.
Oxford: Clarendon Press.
Fabian, Johannes 1972: How others die – reflections on the anthropology of
death. *Social Research*, 39, 543–67.
Fabre-Vassas, Claudine 1983: Le charme de la syrinx. *L'Homme*, 23 (3), 5–39.
——1994: *La bête singulière: Les juifs, les chrétiens et le cochon.* Paris:
Gallimard.
Faral, Edmond 1910: *Les jongleurs en France au moyen âge.* Paris: Champion
Editeur.

Farès, Bichr 1932: *L'honneur chez les Arabes avant l'Islam*. Paris: Adrien-Maisonneuve.

Feifel, H. 1959: *The Meaning of Death*. New York: McGraw-Hill.

Feldman, Allen 1991: *Formation of Violence: the narrative of the body and political terror in Northern Ireland*. Chicago: University of Chicago Press.

—— 1994: On cultural anaesthesia. *American Ethnologist*, 21, 404–18.

Fellman, B. 1972: Die antiken Darstellungen des Polyphemabenteuers. Munich: W. Fink Verlag.

Ferrand, Renaud 1989: Le vol dans les églises en Lyonnais et en Beaujolais (1679–1789): le sacrilège des exclus. *Bulletin du centre d'histoire économique et sociale de la region lyonnaise*, 2, 43–76.

Firth, Raymond 1966: Twins, birds and vegetables: Problems of identification in primitive religious thought. *Man* (N.S.), 1, 1–17.

—— 1973: *Symbols Public and Private*. London: Allen & Unwin.

Fitzgerald, C. P. 1968: *Empress Wu*. London: Cresset Press.

Fiume, Giovanna 1984: *Le bande armate in Sicilia (1819–1849). Violenza e organizzazione del potere*. Palermo: Annali della Facoltà di Lettere e Filosofia dell'Università di Palermo.

Földes, László (ed.) 1969: *Viehwirtschaft und Hirtenkultur. Ethnographische Studien*. Budapest: Akadémiai Kiadó.

Follain, John 1995: *A Dishonoured Society*. London: Warner Books.

Fontaine, Laurence 1996: *History of Pedlars in Europe*. Tr. Vicki Whittaker. Cambridge: Polity Press.

Forge, Anthony 1972: The Golden Fleece. *Man* (N.S.), 7, 527–40.

Foucault, Michel 1973: *The Birth of the Clinic: an archaeology of medical perception*. Tr. A. M. Sheridan Smith. New York: Pantheon Books.

—— 1975: *Surveiller et punir. Naissance de la prison*. Paris: Gallimard.

—— 1977: *Discipline and Punish: the birth of the prison*. Tr. Alan Sheridan. New York: Pantheon Books.

Fox, Robin 1978: *The Tory Islanders: a people of the Celtic fringe*. Cambridge: Cambridge University Press.

Frankfurt, Henri 1948: *Kinship and the Gods: a study of ancient Near Eastern religion as the integration of society and nature*. Chicago: University of Chicago Press.

Fraser, Antonia 1989: *The Warrior Queens*. New York: Knopf.

Frazer, J. G. 1957: *The Golden Bough* [1922]. 2 vols. London: Macmillan, Vol. I.

Freeman, Susan Tax 1970: *Neighbors: the social contract in a Castilian hamlet*. Chicago: University of Chicago Press.

—— 1979: *The Pasiegos: Spaniards in no man's land*. Chicago: University of Chicago Press.

Freuchen, P. 1961: *Book of the Eskimos*. Greenwich, CN: Fawcett Crest.

Freud, Sigmund 1960: *Jokes and their Relation to the Unconscious* [1905]. Standard edn. Tr. James Strachey. New York: Norton.

—— 1990: Moses and monotheism [1939]. The Penguin Freud Library. Albert Dickson (ed.). Tr. and ed. by James Strachey. *The Origins of Religion*, vol. XIII. Harmondsworth: Penguin Books.

——1991a: The taboo of virginity [1917]. The Penguin Freud Library. Angela Richards (ed.). Tr. and ed. by James Strachey. *On Sexuality*, vol. VII. Harmondsworth: Penguin Books.

——1991b: Group psychology and the analysis of the ego [1921]. The Penguin Freud Library. Albert Dickson (ed.). Tr. and ed. by James Strachey. *Civilization, Society and Religion*, vol. XII, 91–178. Harmondsworth: Penguin Books.

——1991c: Civilization and its discontents [1930]. The Penguin Freud Library. Albert Dickson (ed.). Tr. and ed. by James Strachey. *Civilization, Society and Religion*, vol. XII, 243–340. Harmondsworth: Penguin Books.

——1991d: *Introductory Lectures on Psychoanalysis* [1917]. Vol. I. Tr. James Strachey. London: Penguin Books.

Frevert, Ute 1995: *Ehrenmänner. Das Duell in der bürgerlichen Gesellschaft.* Munich: Deutscher Taschenbücher Verlag.

Frey, Albert R. 1887: *Sobriquets and Nicknames*. London: Whittaker.

Friedrich, Paul 1962: Assumptions underlying Tarascan political homicide. *Psychiatry*, 25 (2), 315–27.

——1965: A Mexican cacicazgo. *Ethnology*, 4 (2), 190–209.

——1973: Defilement and honor in the Iliad. *Journal of Indo-European Studies*, 1, 119–26.

——1977: Sanity and the myth of honor: the problem of Achilles. *Ethos*, 5, 281–305.

——1978: *The Meaning of Aphrodite*. Chicago: University of Chicago Press.

——1979: Proto-Indo-European kinship. In Friedrich, *Language, Context, and the Imagination*. Stanford: Stanford University Press.

Frijhoff, Willem 1983: Non satis dignitatis . . . Over de maatschappelijke status van geneeskundigen tijdens de Republiek. *Tijdschrift voor Geschiedenis*, 96: 379–406.

Frobenius, Leo 1923: *Das unbekannte Afrika. Aufhellung der Schicksale eines Erdteiles.* Munich: Oskar Beck.

Frykman, Jonas 1977: *Horan i bonde samhället.* Lund: Liber Läromedel.

——and Löfgren, Orvar 1987: *Culture Builders: a historical anthropology of middle-class life.* Tr. Alan Crozier. New Brunswick, NJ: Rutgers University Press.

Fuchs, J. W. n. d: *Klassick Vademecum.* The Hague: Van Goor.

Gaja, Filippo 1962: *L'esercito della lupara. Baroni e banditi siciliani contro Italia.* Milan: Area Editore.

Gallant, Thomas W. 1994: Turning the horns: cultural metaphors, material conditions, and the peasant language of resistance in Ionian Islands (Greece) during the nineteenth century. *Comparative Studies in Society and History*, 36, 702–19.

Gambetta, Diego 1993: *The Sicilian Mafia: the business of private protection.* Cambridge, MA: Harvard University Press.

Garnsey, Peter 1988: Mountain economies in southern Europe: thoughts on the early history, continuity and individuality of Mediterranean upland communities. In C. R. Whittaker (ed.), *Pastoral Economies in Classical Antiquity.* Cambridge: Cambridge University Press.

Garufi, C. A. 1946: Patti agrari e comuni feodali di nuova fondazione in Sicilia. *Archivio Storico Siciliano*, 3 (2), 7–131.

Gay, Peter 1978: *Freud, Jews and Other Germans: masters and victims in modernist culture*. New York: Oxford University Press.

——1988: *Freud: a life for our time*. New York: Norton.

Geertz, Clifford 1968: *Islam Observed: religious development in Morocco and Indonesia*. Chicago: University of Chicago Press.

——1973a: Thick description. In Geertz, *The Interpretation of Cultures*. New York: Basic Books.

——1973b: The impact of the concept of culture on the concept of man. In Geertz, *The Interpretation of Cultures*. New York: Basic Books.

——1973c: Deep play: notes on the Balinese cockfight. In Geertz, *The Interpretation of Cultures*. New York: Basic Books.

——1973d: Person, time and conduct in Bali. In Geertz, *The Interpretation of Cultures*, New York: Basic Books.

——1980: *Negara: the theatre state in nineteenth-century Bali*. Princeton: Princeton University Press.

——1995: *After the Fact: two countries, four decades, one anthropologist*. Cambridge, MA: Harvard University Press.

Geertz, Hildred 1975: An anthropology of religion and magic. *Journal of Interdisciplinary History*, 6, 71–89.

Gelfand, Toby 1980: *Professionalizing Modern Medicine: Paris surgeons and medical science and institutions in the eighteenth century*. London: Greenwood Press.

George, M. Dorothy 1966: *London Life in the Eighteenth Century* [1925]. Harmondsworth: Penguin Books.

Geremek, Bronislaw 1987: *The Margins of Society in Late Medieval Paris*. Cambridge: Cambridge University Press.

Gerholm, Tomas 1980: Knives and sheaths: notes on the sexual idiom of social inequality. *Ethnos*, 45, 82–91.

Germain, Gabriel 1948: Le culte du bélier en Afrique du Nord. *Hespéris*, 35, 93–124.

Gernet, Louis 1981: Capital punishment. In Gernet, *The Anthropology of Ancient Greece*. Tr. John Hamilton. Baltimore: Johns Hopkins University Press.

Gerth, H. H. and Mills, C. Wright 1958: *From Max Weber: sociological essays*. New York: Oxford University Press.

Gilmore, David D. 1982: Some notes on community nicknaming in Spain. *Man* (N.S.), 17, 686–700.

——(ed.) 1987: *Honor and Shame and the Unity of the Mediterranean*. Washington, DC: American Anthropological Association.

Ginzburg, Carlo 1980: *The Cheese and the Worms: the cosmos of a sixteenth-century miller*. Tr. John and Anne Tedeschi. London: Routledge & Kegan Paul.

——1987: Saccheggi rituali. *Quaderni Storici*, 22, 615–36.

——1989: Clues: roots of an evidential paradigm [1980]. In Ginzburg, *Clues, Myths, and the Historical Method*. Tr. John and Anne C. Tedeschi. Baltimore: Johns Hopkins University Press.

——1992: *Ecstasies: deciphering the witches' sabbath*. Tr. Raymond Rosenthal. New York: Penguin Books.

Girard, René 1979: *Violence and the Sacred*. Tr. Patrick Gregory. Baltimore: Johns Hopkins University Press.

——1986: *The Scapegoat*. Tr. Yvonne Freccero. Baltimore: Johns Hopkins University Press.

Glascock, Anthony P. 1982: Decrepitude and death-hastening: the nature of old age in Third World countries. In Jay Sokolovsky (ed.), *Aging and the Aged in the Third World*. Part I. *Studies in Third World Societies*, 22, 43–66.

——1983: Death-hastening behavior: an expansion of Eastwell's thesis. *American Anthropologist*, 85, 417–21.

——1990: By any other name it is still killing: a comparison of the treatment of the elderly in America and other societies. In Jay Sokolovsky (ed.), *The Cultural Context of Aging: worldwide perspectives*. New York/London: Bergin & Garvey Publishers, 43–56.

——and Feinman, Susan L. 1980: A holocultural analysis of old age. *Comparative Social Research*, 3, 311–32.

——1981: Social asset or social burden: treatment of the aged in non-industrial societies. In C. L. Fry (ed.), *Aging, Culture, and Health: comparative viewpoints and strategies*. Brooklyn: J. F. Bergin.

Glenny, Misha 1992: *The Fall of Yugoslavia: the Third Balkan War*. Harmondsworth: Penguin Books.

Goffman, Erving 1959: *The Presentation of Self in Everyday Life*. New York: Anchor Books.

——1967: The nature of deference and demeanor [1956]. In Goffman, *Interaction Ritual*. New York: Pantheon Books.

——1968: *Stigma: notes on the management of spoiled identity*. Harmondsworth: Penguin Books.

——1971: Territories of the self. In Goffman, *Relations in Public*. New York: Harper & Row.

——1972: *Interactional Ritual: essays on face-to-face behaviour*. Harmondsworth: Penguin Books.

Goldhagen, Daniel J. 1996: *Hitler's Willing Executioners: ordinary Germans and the Holocaust*. New York: Knopf.

Gombrich, E. H. 1978: *Symbolic Images: studies in the art of the Renaissance II*. Oxford: Phaidon Press.

Goodenough, William H. 1965: Personal names and modes of address in two Oceanic societies. In M. E. Spiro (ed.), *Context and Meaning in Cultural Anthropology*. New York: The Free Press: 265–76.

Goody, Jack 1983: *The Development of the Family and Marriage in Europe*. Cambridge: Cambridge University Press.

Gorer, Geoffrey 1965: *Death, Grief, and Mourning in Contemporary Britain*. Garden City, NJ: Doubleday.

——1966: Woman's place. In Gorer, *The Danger of Equality and Other Essays*. New York: Weybright and Talley.

Goudsblom, Johan 1974: *Balans van de sociologie*. Utrecht: Aula.

——1977: *Sociology in the Balance*. Oxford: Blackwell.

Gould, Stephen Jay 1991a: *Wonderful Life: the Burgess Shale and the nature of history.* London: Penguin Books.

——1991b: *Ever since Darwin* [1978]. London: Penguin Books.

——1992: Not necessarily a wing. In Gould, *Bully for Brontosaurus.* London: Penguin Books.

——1994: *Eight Little Piggies: reflections on natural history.* London: Penguin Books.

Gouldner, Alvin 1960: The norm of reciprocity. *American Sociological Review*, 25, 161–78.

Graburn, N. H. H. 1969: *Eskimos without Igloos.* Boston: Little, Brown.

Graus, Frantisek 1981: Randgruppen der städtischen Gesellschaft im Spätmittel-alter. *Zeitschrift für historische Forschung*, 8 (4), 385–437.

Gravel, Pierre Bettez 1968: *Remera: a community in eastern Ruanda.* The Hague/Paris: Mouton.

Graves, Robert 1981: *Greek Myths.* Illustrated edn. London: Penguin Books.

Griffiths, John, Bood, Alex and Weyers, Helen 1998: *Euthanasia and Law in the Netherlands.* Amsterdam: Amsterdam University Press.

Guemple, D. Lee 1969: Human resource management: the dilemma of the aging Eskimo. *Sociological Symposium*, 2, 59–74.

Guidi, P. 1912: *Regesto del capitolo di Lucca.* Vol. II. Istituto Storico Italiano. Rome: Ermanno Loescher & Co.

Gupte, Pranay 1992: *Mother India: a political biography of Indira Gandhi.* New York: Macmillan Press.

Gutmann, Myron P. 1980: *War and Rural Life in the Early Modern Low Countries.* Princeton: Princeton University Press.

Haas, J. A. K. 1978: *De verdeling van de Landen van Overmaas, 1644–1662.* Assen: Van Gorcum.

Hamerton-Kelly, R. G. (ed.) 1987: *Violent Origins: Walter Burkert, René Girard and Jonathan Z. Smith on ritual killing and cultural formation.* Stanford: Stanford University Press.

Hammel, Eugene A. 1993: Demography and the origins of the Yugoslav Civil War. *Anthropology Today*, 9 (1), 4–9.

Hammoudi, Abdellah 1988: *La victime et ses masques.* Paris: Editions du Seuil.

Hampson, Norman 1973: The French Revolution and the nationalisation of honour. In M. R. D. Foot (ed.), *War and Society.* London: Elek.

Hand, W. D. 1984: Onomastic magic in the health, sickness, and death of man. *Names*, 32, 1–13.

Harris, Marvin 1956: *Town and Country in Brazil.* New York: Columbia University Press.

——1971: *Culture, Man, and Nature: an introduction to general anthropology.* New York: Thomas Y. Crowell.

——1993: *Culture, Man and Nature: an introduction to general anthropology.* 6th edn. New York: HarperCollins.

Hart, C. W. M., Pilling, Arnold R. and Goodale, Jane C. 1988: *The Tiwi of North Australia.* 3rd edn. New York: Holt, Rinehart & Winston.

Hart, David M. 1987: *Banditry in Islam: case studies from Morocco, Algeria and the Pakistan North West Frontier.* Menas Studies in continuity and change. Wisbech, Cambridgeshire: Middle East and North Africa Studies Press.

Hastrup, Kirsten 1978: The semantics of biology: virginity. In Shirley Ardener (ed.), *Defining Females*. London: Croom Helm.

Haudricourt, André-Georges 1987: *La technologie science humaine. Recherches d'histoire et d'ethnologie des techniques*. Paris: Editions de la Maison des Sciences de l'Homme.

Hayden, Robert M. 1996: Imagined communities and real victims: self-determination and ethnic cleansing in Yugoslavia. *American Ethnologist*, 23, 783–801.

Heering, Aart 1985: *Van schoorsteenvegers en pizzabakkers. Vier eeuwen Italianen in Groningen*. Stad en Lande Historische Reeks. Utrecht: Stichting Matrijs.

Heisch, Allison 1980: Queen Elizabeth I and the persistence of patriarchy. *Feminist Review*, 4, 45–56.

Hemingway, E. 1977: *Death in the Afternoon* [1932]. London: Triad/Panther Books.

Hendin, Herbert 1997: *Seduced by Death: doctors, patients, and the Dutch cure*. New York/London: W. W. Norton.

Henry, Jules 1973: *Pathways to Madness* [1965]. New York: Random House, Vintage Books.

Herbert, Eugenia W. 1993: *Iron, Gender, and Power: rituals of transformation in African societies*. Bloomington: Indiana University Press.

Herodotus 1972: *The Histories*. Tr. Aubrey de Sélincourt and A. R. Burn. Harmondsworth: Penguin Books.

Hertz, Robert 1960: A contribution to the study of the collective representation of death [1906]. Tr. Rodney and Claudia Needham. In Hertz, *Death and the Right Hand*. Glencoe: The Free Press.

Herzfeld, Michael 1992: *The Social Production of Indifference: exploring the symbolic roots of western bureaucracy*. Chicago: University of Chicago Press.

Hilhorst, H. W. 1983: *Euthanasie in het ziekenhuis*. Lochem: De Tijdstroom.

Hobsbawm, E. J. 1959: *Primitive Rebels: studies in archaic forms of social movement in the nineteenth and twentieth centuries*. Manchester: Manchester University Press.

——1969: *Bandits*. London: Weidenfeld & Nicolson.

——1972: Social bandits: Reply. *Comparative Studies in Society and History*, 14 (4), 503–5.

——1974: Social banditry. In Henry A. Landsberger (ed.), *Rural Protest: peasant movements and social change*. London: Macmillan.

——1981: *Bandits*. Rev. edn. New York: Pantheon.

——1983: Introduction: inventing traditions. In Hobsbawm and Terence Ranger (eds), *The Invention of Tradition*. Cambridge: Cambridge University Press.

——and Scott, Joan Wallach 1980: Political shoemakers. *Past & Present*, 89, 86–114.

Hodkinson, Stephen 1988: Animal husbandry in the Greek polis. In C. R. Whittaker (ed.), *Pastoral Economies in Classical Antiquity*. Cambridge: Cambridge University Press.

Hoffmann, Herbert 1977: Sexual and asexual pursuit: a structuralist approach to Greek vase painting. *Royal Anthropological Institute*, Occasional Paper no. 34.

——1982: Υβριν ορθίαν κνωδάλων. *Antidoron. Festschrift für J. Thimme.* Karlsruhe: C. F. Müller.

Hoffmann-Krayer, E. and Bächtold-Staubli, Hanns (eds) 1932: *Handwörterbuch des deutschen Aberglaubens.* Berlin: Walter de Gruyter & Co.

Holmes, Ellen Rhoads and Holmes, Lowell D. 1995: *Other Cultures, Elder Years.* 2nd edn. London: Sage.

Homer 1949: *The Odyssey.* Tr. W. H. D. Rouse. New York: Mentor Books.

——1950: *The Iliad.* Tr. W. H. D. Rouse. New York: Mentor Books.

Honigmann, John J. 1964: Survival of a cultural focus. In Ward H. Goodenough (ed.), *Explorations in Cultural Anthropology.* New York: McGraw-Hill.

Houston, J. M. 1964: *The Western Mediterranean World: an introduction to its regional landscapes.* London: Longman.

Howe, James 1981: Fox hunting as ritual. *American Ethnologist*, 8, 278–300.

Hughes, John 1967: *Indonesian Upheaval.* New York: David McKay.

Huisman, Frank 1989: Itinerant medical practitioners in the Dutch Republic: the case of Groningen. *Tractrix: yearbook for the history of science, medicine, technology, and mathematics*, 1, 63–83.

Huizinga, Johan 1955: *Homo Ludens: a study of the play-element in culture* [1938]. Boston: Beacon Press.

Huntington, Richard and Metcalf, Peter 1980: *Celebration of Death.* Cambridge: Cambridge University Press.

Huntington, Samuel P. 1996: *The Clash of Civilizations and the Remaking of World Order.* New York: Simon & Schuster.

Ibarruri, Dolores 1966: *They Shall not Pass: the autobiography of 'La Pasionaria'.* New York: International Publishers.

Isaevich, Abraham 1980: Household renown: the traditional naming system in Catalonia. *Ethnology*, 19, 315–25.

Itzkowitz, David C. 1977: *Peculiar Privilege: a social history of English foxhunting, 1753–1885.* Hassocks: Harvester Press.

Jackson, Bruce 1978: Deviance as success: the double inversion of stigmatized roles. In Barbara A. Babcock (ed.), *The Reversible World.* Ithaca/London: Cornell University Press.

Jackson, Harold 1972: *The Two Irelands: the double minority – a study of intergroup tensions.* Report no. 2, new edn. London: Minority Rights Group.

Jacobeit, Wolfgang 1961: *Schafhaltung und Schäfer in Zentraleuropa bis zum Beginn des 20. Jahrhunderts.* Berlin: Akademie der Wissenschaften.

Jacquemet, Marco 1992: Namechasers. *American Ethnologist*, 19, 733–48.

James, Mervyn 1978: English politics and the concept of honour, 1485–1642. *Past & Present*, Supplement 3.

Jameson, Michael H. 1988: Sacrifice and animal husbandry in classical Greece. In C. R. Whittaker (ed.), *Pastoral Economies in Classical Antiquity.* Cambridge: Cambridge University Press.

Jamous, Raymond 1981: *Honneur et Baraka. Les structures sociales traditionelles dans le Rif*. Cambridge: Cambridge University Press; Paris: Editions de la Maison des Sciences de l'Homme.

Janes, Regina 1991: Beheadings. *Representations*, 35, 21–51.

Jansen, Willy 1987: *Women without Men: gender and marginality in an Algerian town*. Leiden: Brill.

Janssen de Limpens, K. J. Th. 1982: Genealogische en biografische geschiedenis van het geslacht De Limpens. *Publications*, 11, 9–53.

Jemma, D. 1971: *Les tanneurs de Marrakech*. Paris: CNRS.

Jones, George Fenwick 1955: Chaucer and the medieval miller. *Modern Language Quarterly*, 16, 3–15.

——1959: *Honor in German Literature*. Chapel Hill: University of North Carolina Press.

Joseph, Gilbert M. 1990: On the trail of Latin American bandits: a reexamination of peasant resistance. *Latin American Research Review*, 25 (3), 7–53.

Judge, Roy 1979: *The Jack-in-the-Green: a May-Day custom*. Cambridge: D. S. Brewer Ltd and Rowman and Littlefield for the Folklore Society.

Just, Roger 1988: A shortage of names: Greek proper names and their use. *Journal of the Anthropological Society of Oxford*, 19, 140–50.

Kanafadi-Zahar, Aïda 1997: Le religieux sublimé dans le sacrifice du mouton. Un exemple de coexistence communautaire au Liban. *L'Homme*, 141, 83–100.

Keeley, Lawrence H. 1996: *War before Civilization: the myth of the peaceful savage*. New York/Oxford: Oxford University Press.

Keesing, R. M. 1989: Exotic readings of cultural texts. *Current Anthropology*, 30, 459–79.

Keller, Otto 1909: *Die antike Tierwelt*. Vol. I. Leipzig: Engelman.

Kelly, Rita Mae and Boutilier, Mary 1978: *The Making of Political Women*. Chicago: Nelson-Hall.

Kenny, Michael 1966: *A Spanish Tapestry: town and country in Castile*. New York: Harper & Row.

Kertzer, David and Keith, Jennie (eds) 1984: *Age and Anthropological Theory*. Ithaca/London: Cornell University Press.

Khare, R. S. 1984: *The Untouchable as Himself: ideology, identity and pragmatism among the Lecknow Chamars*. Cambridge: Cambridge University Press.

Kiernan, V. G. 1988: *The Duel in European History: honour and the reign of aristocracy*. New York: Oxford University Press.

Kish, George 1953: The *marine* of Calabria. *The Geographical Review*, 43, 495–505.

Kishwar, Madhu and Vanita, Ruth 1989: Indian women. In Marshall M. Bouton and Philip Oldenburg (eds), *India Briefing*. San Francisco: Westview Press.

Klasen, Henrikje 1990: *Die alten Niha und ihre Einstellung zu Krankheit und Tod. Ergebnisse einer ethnomedizinischen Feldstudie von der Insel Nias, Indonesien*. Papenburg (Ems): Verlag Eissing.

Kluckhohn, Clyde 1968: Recurrent themes in myth and mythmaking. In Henry A. Murray (ed.), *Myth and Mythmaking*. Boston: Beacon Press.

Knauft, Bruce M. 1985: *Good Company and Violence: sorcery and social action in a lowland New Guinea society*. Berkeley/Los Angeles: University of California Press.

——1987: Reconsidering violence in simple societies. *Current Anthropology*, 28, 457–500.

Knight, John 1994: 'The Mountain People' as a tribal people. *Anthropology Today*, 10 (6), 1–3. *Highland New Guinea*. Cambridge, MA: Harvard University Press.

Koch, Klaus-Friedrich 1974: *War and Peace in Jalémó: the management of conflict in Highland New Guinea*. Cambridge, MA: Harvard University Press.

Koestler, Arthur 1964: *The Sleepwalkers: a history of man's changing vision of the universe*. Harmondsworth: Penguin Books.

Kolenda, Pauline 1978: *Caste in Contemporary India: beyond organic solidarity*. Menlo Park, CA: Benjamin/Cummings Publishing Company.

Koliopoulos, John S. 1987: *Brigands with a Cause: brigandage and irredentism in modern Greece, 1821–1912*. Oxford: Clarendon Press.

König, René 1958: *Grundformen der Gesellschaft. Die Gemeinde*. Hamburg: Rowohlt.

Kramer, K. S. 1971: Ehrliche/unehrliche Gewerbe. In Adalbert Erler and Ekkehard Kaufmann (eds), *Handwörterbuch zur deutschen Rechtsgeschichte*. Berlin: Erich Schmidt Verlag.

Krickeberg, Dieter 1983: On the social status of the *Spielmann* ('folk musician') in 17th- and 18th-century Germany, particularly in the Northwest. In Walter Salmen (ed.), *The Social Status of the Professional Musician from the Middle Ages to the 19th Century*. Tr. Herbert Kaufmann and Barbara Reisner. New York: Pendragon Press.

Kris, Ernst 1975: *Selected Papers of Ernst Kris*. New Haven, CT: Yale University Press.

Kübler-Ross, Elisabeth 1969: *On Death and Dying*. New York: Macmillan.

Kuhn, Thomas S. 1970: *The Structure of Scientific Revolutions*. Rev. edn. Chicago: University of Chicago Press.

Küther, Carsten 1983: *Menschen auf der Strasse. Vagierende Unterschichten in Bayern, Franken, und Schwaben in der zweiten Hälfte des 18. Jahrhunderts*. Göttingen: Vandenhoeck & Ruprecht.

Kyrova, Magda 1994: *Music in Seventeenth-century Dutch Painting: the Hoogsteder exhibition of music and painting in the Golden Age*. Zwolle: Waanders.

La Fontaine, Jean 1985: *Initiation: ritual drama and secret knowledge across the world*. Harmondsworth: Penguin Books.

La Mantia, G. 1904: *I capitoli delle colonie Greco-Albanesi di Sicilia dei secoli XV e XVI*. Palermo: Giannitrapani.

La Rochefoucauld, François 1844: *Réflexions ou sentences et maximes morales*. Paris: Lefèvre.

Laber, Jeri 1993: Slouching toward democracy: miserable Albania. *The New York Review of Books*, 40 (1–2), 24–7.

Laermann, Klaus 1976: Raumerfahrungen und Erfahrungsraum. Einige Überlegungen zu Reiseberichten aus Deutschland vom Ende des 18. Jahrhunderts.

In Hans Joachim Piechotta (ed.), *Reise und Utopie. Zur Literatur der Spätaufklarung*. Frankfurt am Main: Suhrkamp.

Lafranchi-Branca, Lucia 1981: *L'emigrazione degli spazzacamini ticinesi 1850–1920*. Bellinzona: Centro Didattico Cantonale.

Lakoff, George and Johnson, Mark 1980: *Metaphors We Live By*. Chicago: University of Chicago Press.

Lambek, Michael 1992: Taboo as cultural practice among Malagasy speakers. *Man* (N.S.), 27, 245–66.

Landsberger, Henry A. 1969: *Latin American Peasant Movements*. Ithaca/London: Cornell University Press.

Lane, Edward William 1867: *Arabic – English Lexicon*. Vol. I. London: Williams and Norgate, part 3.

Langbein, John H. 1974: *Prosecuting Crime in the Renaissance: England, Germany, France*. Cambridge, MA: Harvard University Press.

——1977: *Torture and the Law of Proof: Europe and England in the Ancient Régime*. Chicago: University of Chicago Press.

Lapidus, Ira M. 1984: *Muslim Cities in the Later Middle Ages* [1967]. Cambridge: Cambridge University Press.

Lawson, Edwin D. 1987: *Personal Names and Naming: an annotated bibliography*. New York: Greenwood Press.

Le Goff, Jacques 1972: The town as an agent of civilization, *c*. 1200–1500. In Carlo Cipolla (ed.), *The Middle Ages*. London/Glasgow: Fontana Books.

——1977: Métiers licites et métiers illicites dans l'Occident médiéval. In Le Goff, *Pour un autre moyen âge*. Paris: Gallimard.

——1980a: Licit and illicit trades in the medieval West. In Le Goff, *Time, Work and Culture in the Middle Ages*. Tr. Arthur Goldhammer. Chicago: University of Chicago Press.

——1980b: Towards a historical anthropology. In Le Goff, *Time, Work and Culture in the Middle Ages*. Tr. Arthur Goldhammer. Chicago: University of Chicago Press.

——1988: *Your Money or your Life: Economy and religion in the Middle Ages*. Tr. Patricia Ranum. New York: Zone Books.

——and Schmitt, J. C. (eds) 1981: *Le charivari*. Paris/The Hague: Mouton.

Le Lannou, Maurice 1936: Le role géographique de la malaria. *Annales de Géographie*, 45, 113–36.

——1938: Les nuraghes de Sardaigne. Contribution de la préhistoire à l'étude du peuplement rural de l'île. *Comptes rendus du congrès international de géographie* (Amsterdam), 2, 101–6. Leyden: Brill.

Le Roi Ladurie, Emmanuel 1979a: *Le carnaval de romans*. Paris: Gallimard.

——1979b: Interview. *Newsweek*, 30 April.

Leach, E. R. 1961: Two essays concerning the symbolic representation of time. In Leach, *Rethinking Anthropology*. New York: Humanities Press.

——1964a: Anthropological aspects of language: animal categories and verbal abuse. In E. H. Lenneberg (ed.), *New Directions in the Study of Language*. Cambridge, MA: M.I.T. Press.

——1964b: *Political Systems of Highland Burma*. 2nd edn. London: Bell.

——1966: Ritualization in man in relation to conceptual and social development. In J. Huxley (ed.), *A Discussion on Ritualization of Behaviour in Animals and Men. Philosophical Transactions of the Royal Society of London*, Series B.

——1973a: Levels of communication and problems of taboo in the appreciation of primitive art. In Anthony Forge (ed.), *Primitive Art and Society*. London: Oxford University Press.

——1973b: Structuralism in social anthropology. In David Robey (ed.), *Structuralism: An introduction*. Oxford: Clarendon Press.

——1976: *Culture and Communication*. Cambridge: Cambridge University Press.

——1982: *Social Anthropology*. Glasgow: Fontane.

——(ed.) 1967: *The Structural Study of Myth and Totemism*. London: Tavistock.

——and Aycock, D. Alan 1983: *Structuralist Interpretations of Biblical Myth*. Cambridge: Cambridge University Press.

Leal, João 1999: Saudade, la construction d'un symbole 'charactère national' et identité nationale. *Ethnologie française*, 29, 177–89.

Lerner, Gerda 1986: *The Creation of Patriarchy*. New York/Oxford: Oxford University Press.

Levack, Brian P. 1987: *The Witch-hunt in Early Modern Europe*. London/New York: Longman.

Levi, Carlo 1963: *Christ Stopped at Eboli*. Tr. Frances Frenaye. New York: Farrar, Strauss and Company.

Lévi-Strauss, Claude 1958: La structure des mythes. In Lévi-Strauss, *Anthropologie structurale*. Paris: Plon.

——1963: *Totemism*. Tr. Rodney Needham. Boston: Beacon Press.

——1966: *The Savage Mind* [1962]. Chicago: University of Chicago Press.

——1967: Introduction: history and anthropology. In Lévi-Strauss, *Structural Anthropology*. Tr. Claire Jacobson and Brooke Grundfest Schoepf. New York: Doubleday Anchor Books.

——1969a: *The Raw and the Cooked* [1964]. Tr. John and Doreen Weightmann. New York: Harper & Row.

——1969b: *Totemism* [1962]. Tr. Rodney Needham. With an Introduction by Roger C. Poole. Harmondsworth: Penguin Books.

Lewis, B., Pellat, C. and Schacht, J. (eds) 1977: *Encyclopédie de l'Islam*. Leiden: Brill.

Liebeschütz, Hans 1926: *Fulgentius Metaforalis. Ein Beitrag zur Geschichte der antiken Mythologie im Mittelalter*. Leipzig: Teubner.

Lincoln, Bruce 1985: Revolutionary exhumations in Spain, July 1936. *Comparative Studies in Society and History*, 27, 241–60.

——1991: *Death, War, and Sacrifice: studies in ideology and practice*. Chicago: University of Chicago Press.

Lindenbaum, Shirley 1975: The last course: nutrition and anthropology in Asia. In Thomas Fitzgerald (ed.), *Nutrition and Anthropology in Action*. Atlantic Highlands, NJ: Humanities Press.

Linebaugh, Peter 1975: The Tyburn Riot against the surgeons. In Douglas Hay et al., *Albion's Fatal Tree: crime and society in eighteenth-century England* New York: Pantheon Books, 65–117.

Linke, Uli 1985: Blood as metaphor in Proto-Indo-European. *Journal of Indo-European Studies*, 13, 333–76.

Liss, Peggy K. 1992: *Isabel the Queen: life and times*. New York/Oxford: Oxford University Press.

Lloyd, G. E. R. 1983: *Science, Folklore and Ideology: studies in the life sciences in ancient Greece*. Cambridge: Cambridge University Press.

——1992: *Polarity and Analogy: two types of argumentation in early Greek thought*. Bristol: Bristol Classical Press.

Lurati, Ottavio and Pinana, Isidoro 1983: *Le parole di una valle. Dialetto, gergo e tiponimia della Val Verzasca*. Lugano: Fondazione di Arturo e Margherita Lang.

Luria, Keith and Gandolfo, Romulo 1986: Carlo Ginzburg: An interview. *Radical History Review*, 35, 89–111.

Mack, Burton 1987: Introduction. In Robert G. Hamerton-Kelly (ed.), *Violent Origins: Walter Burkert, René Girard, and Jonathan Z. Smith on ritual killing and cultural formation*. Stanford: Stanford University Press.

Mack Smith, Denis 1950: The Peasants' Revolt in Sicily in 1860. In *Studi in onore di Gino Luzzatto*. Milano: Giuffrè, vol. III, 210–40.

——1968: *A History of Sicily*. 2 vols. London: Chatto & Windus.

MacKenzie, Norman (ed.) 1967: *Secret Societies*. London: Aldus Books.

Mackerras, Colin 1990: *Chinese Drama: a historical survey*. Beijing: New World Press.

Mahdi, Mohamed 1999: *Pasteurs de l'Atlas. Production pastorale, droit et rituel*. Casablanca: Fondation Konrad Adenauer.

Malkki, Liisa H. 1995: *Purity and Exile: violence, memory and national cosmology among Hutu refugees in Tanzania*. Chicago: University of Chicago Press.

——1996: Speechless emissaries: refugees, humanitarianism and dehistoricization. *Cultural Anthropology*, 11, 377–404.

Manning, Frank E. 1974: Nicknames and number plates in the British West Indies. *Journal of American Folklore*, 87, 123–32.

Maquet, Jacques J. 1957: *Ruanda. Essai photographique sur une société africaine en transition*. Avec la collaboration de Denyse Hierneux-L'Hoest. Brussels: Elsevier.

——1961: *The Premise of Inequality in Rwanda: a study of political relations in a Central African kingdom*, Oxford: Oxford University Press.

Maranelli, Carlo 1946: *Considerazioni geografiche sulla questione meridionale*. Bari: Laterza.

Marcus, George E. and Fischer, Michael M. J. 1986: *Anthropology as Cultural Critique: an experimental moment in the human sciences*. Chicago: University of Chicago Press.

Martin, Georges 1981: *Les ramoneurs de la Vallée de Rhêmes*. Aosta: Musumeci Editeur.

Marvin, Garry 1986: Honour, integrity and the problem of violence in the Spanish bullfight. In David Riches (ed.), *The Anthropology of Violence*. Oxford: Blackwell.

Marx, Karl 1951: Der 18. Brumaire des Louis Bonaparte [1852]. In Marx and Engels, *Ausgewählte Schriften*. 2 vols. Berlin: Dietz Verlag.

——1973: The Eighteenth Brumaire of Louis Bonaparte. In Marx, *Surveys from Exile: political writings*. Vol. II. ed. David Fernbach. Harmondsworth: Penguin Books.

Massolo, M. L. 1987: Nicknames: an annotated bibliography. Department of Anthropology, University of California, Berkeley: Mimeo.

Mauss, Marcel 1975: *A General Theory of Magic* [1903]. Tr. Robert Brain. New York: Norton.

Maxwell, Gavin 1957: *God Protect Me from my Friends*. London: Longmans.

Maxwell, Robert J. and Maxwell, Eleanor K. 1980: Contempt for the elderly: a cross-cultural analysis. *Current Anthropology*, 21, 569–70.

——Silverman, Philip and Maxwell, Eleanor K. 1982: The motive for gerontocide. In Jay Sokolovsky (ed.), *Aging and the Aged in the Third World*. Part I. *Studies in Third World Societies*. Williamsburg, VA: College of William and Mary.

Maybury-Lewis, David 1984: Name, person, and ideology in Central Brazil. In Elisabeth Tooker (ed.), *Naming Systems: 1980 Proceedings of the American Ethnological Society*. Washington, DC: American Ethnological Society, 1–10.

Mayhew, Henry 1968: *London Labour and the London Poor* [1862]. 4 vols. New York: Dover Publications.

McAleer, Kevin 1994: *Dueling: the cult of honor in fin-de-siècle Germany*. Princeton: Princeton University Press.

McDonald, J. S. 1956: Italy's rural social structure and emigration. *Occidente*, 12, 432–57.

McDowell, John H. 1981: Toward a semiotics of nicknaming: the Kamsá example. *Journal of American Folklore*, 94, 1–18.

McFarlane, Graham 1986: Violence in Northern Ireland. In D. Riches (ed.), *The Anthropology of Violence*. Oxford: Blackwell.

McNaughton, Patrick R. 1988: *The Mande Blacksmiths: knowledge, power and art in West Africa*. Bloomington: Indiana University Press.

McNeill, J. R. 1992: *The Mountains of the Mediterranean World*. Cambridge: Cambridge University Press.

McNeill, William H. 1982: *The Pursuit of Power: technology, armed force, and society since AD 1000*. Chicago: University of Chicago Press.

Meeker, Michael E. 1976: Meaning and society in the Near East: examples from the Black Sea Turks and the Levantine Arabs. *International Journal of Middle Eastern Studies*, 7, 243–70, 383–422.

Meggitt, Mervyn 1977: *Blood is their Argument: warfare among the Mae Enga tribesmen of the New Guinea Highlands*. Palo Alto: Mayfield.

Meir, Golda 1975: *My Life*. New York: Weidenfeld & Nicolson.

Mengels, Winand 1887: Memorie of Kronyckboek [1773]. *Publications*, 24, 167–297.

Meredith, Martin 1997: *Nelson Mandela: a biography*. London: Hamish Hamilton.

Merriman, John M. 1991: *The Margins of City Life: explorations on the French urban frontier, 1815–1851*. New York: Oxford University Press.

Merton, Robert K. 1968: Manifest and latent functions. In Merton, *Social Theory and Social Structure*. Enlarged edn. New York: Free Press.

——1976: The unanticipated consequences of social action [1936]. In Merton, *Sociological Ambivalence and Other Essays*. New York: Free Press.

Mesina, Graziano 1993: *Io, Mesina. Dal Supramonte ad Asti. Un ergastolano, nove evasioni, una prigione*. Raccontati a Gabriella Banda e Gabriele Moroni. Cosenza: Edizioni Periferia.

Meuli, Karl 1975a: Über einige alte Rechtsbräuche/Charivari. In Meuli, *Gesammelte Schriften*, I. Basle: Schwabe & Co. Verlag.

——1975b: Griechische Opferbräuche. In Meuli, *Gesammelte Schriften*, II. Basle: Schwabe & Co. Verlag.

Mewett, Peter C. 1982: Exiles, nicknames, social identities and the construction of local consciousness in a Lewis crofting community. In Anthony P. Cohen (ed.), *Belonging: identity and social organisation in British rural culture*. Manchester: Manchester University Press.

Michels-Gebler, Ruth 1984: *Schmied und Musik. Über die traditionelle Verknüpfung von Schmiedehandwerk und Musik in Afrika, Asien und Europa*. Bonn: Verlag für systematische Musikwissenschaft GmbH.

Miller, Barbara D. 1987: Female infanticide and child neglect in rural North India. In Nancy Scheper-Hughes (ed.), *Child Survival: anthropological perspectives on the treatment and maltreatment of children*. Dordrecht: Reidel.

Mills, C. Wright 1959: *The Sociological Imagination*. New York: Oxford University Press.

Mohan, Anand 1967: *Indira Gandhi*. New York: Meredith Press.

Monheim, Rolf 1969: *Die Agrostadt im Siedlungsgefüge Mittelsiziliens*. Bonn: Bonner Geografische Abhandlungen.

Montaigne, Michel de 1958: *Essais*. 3 vols. Paris: Garnier.

——1991: *The Essays of Michel de Montaigne*. Tr. and ed. with an Introduction and notes by M. A. Screech. London: Allen Lane.

Moore, Barrington, Jr 1968: *Social Origins of Dictatorship and Democracy: lord and peasant in the making of the modern world*. Boston: Beacon Press.

Mooyman, Ellen 1986: The ladybird in the Germanic dialects: a contribution to the study of motivations of naming of the *coccinella septempunctata*. Unpublished manuscript. Department of Dialectology, Catholic University of Nijmegen.

Mori, Cesare 1933: *The Last Struggle with the Mafia*. London: Putnam.

Morris, Desmond et al. 1979: *Gestures: their origins and distribution*. London: Jonathan Cape.

Moss, Leonard W. and Cappannari, Stephen C. 1962: Estate and class in a south Italian hill village. *American Anthropologist*, 64, 287–300.

——and Thompson, Walter H. 1959: The south Italian family: literature and observation. *Human Organization*, 18, 35–41.

Moyal, Maurice 1956: *On the Road to Pastures New*. London: Phoenix House.

Muir, E. 1991: Introduction: observing trifles. In Muir and Ruggiero (eds), *Microhistory and the Lost People of Europe*. Baltimore: Johns Hopkins University Press.

Mull, Dorothy S. & Mull, J. Dennis 1987: Infanticide among the Tarahumara of the Mexican Sierra Madre. In Nancy Scheper-Hughes (ed.), *Child Survival: anthropological perspectives on the treatment and maltreatment of children*. Dordrecht: Reidel.

Murphy, J. D. (ed.) 1972: *Ugandan–English Dictionary*. Washington, DC: Catholic University of America Press.

Murphy, R. F. 1964: Social distance and the veil. *American Anthropologist*, 66, 1257–74.

——1990: The dialectics of deeds and words. *Cultural Anthropology*, 5, 331–7.

Myerhoff, Barbara 1982: Rites of passage: process and paradox. In Victor Turner (ed.), *Celebration: Studies in festivity and ritual*. Washington, DC: Smithsonian Institution Press.

——1984: Rites and signs of ripening: the intertwining of ritual, time, and growing older. In David Kertzer and Jenny Keith (eds), *Age and Anthropological Theory*. Ithaca / London: Cornell University Press.

Nabokov, Vladimir 1975: *Commentary to Aleksander Pushkin, Eugen Onegin: a novel in verse*. 2 vols. Tr. Nabokov. Princeton: Princeton University Press.

Nahoume-Grappa, Véronique 1996: L'usage politique de la cruauté. L'épuration ethnique (ex-Yougoslavie, 1991–1995). In Françoise Héritier (ed.), *De la violence*. Paris: Editions Odile Jacob.

Naipaul, V. S. 1980: *The Return of Eva Perón*. New York: Penguin Books.

——1989: *A Turn in the South*. Harmondsworth: Penguin Books.

Needham, Rodney 1963: Introduction. In Emile Durkheim and Marcel Mauss, *Primitive Classification*. Tr. R. Needham. Chicago: University of Chicago Press.

Nieboer, H. J. 1910: *Slavery as an Industrial System: ethnological researches*. The Hague: Martinus Nijhoff.

Niederer, Arnold 1980: Economie et formes de vie traditionelles dans les Alpes. In Paul Guichonnet (ed.), *Histoire et civilisation des Alpes*, vol. II. Toulouse: Privat; Lausanne: Payot.

Niermeyer, J. F. 1959: De semantiek van *honor* en de oorsprong van het heerlijk gezag. In *Dancwerc*. Groningen: J. B. Wolters.

Nieuwenhuis, Tom 1994: *Vroedmeesters, vroedvrouwen en verloskunde in Amsterdam 1746–1805*. Amsterdam: Het Spinhuis.

Ninomiya, Shigeaki 1933: An inquiry concerning the origin, development, and present situation of the Eta in relation to the history of social classes in Japan. *Transactions of the Asiatic Society of Japan*, Series II, 10, 47–154.

Nye, R. A. 1991: Honor codes in modern France. *Ethnologia Europaea*, 21, 5–17.

O'Brien, Conor Cruise 1986: *The Siege: the saga of Israel and Zionism*. London: Weidenfeld & Nicolson.

O'Brien, Denise 1977: Female husbands in southern Bantu societies. In Alice Schlegel (ed.), *Sexual Stratification: a cross-cultural view*. New York: Columbia University Press.

Ohnuki-Tierney, Emiko 1981: *Illness and Healing among the Sakhalin Ainu: a symbolic interpretation*. Cambridge: Cambridge University Press.

——1984: Monkey performances: a multiple structure of meaning and reflexivity in Japanese culture. In Edward M. Bruner (ed.), *Text, Play, and Story: the construction and reconstruction of self and society. 1983 Proceedings of the American Ethnological Society*. Washington, DC: American Ethnological Society.

——1987: *The Monkey as Mirror: symbolic transformations in Japanese history and ritual*. Princeton: Princeton University Press.

Onians, R. B. 1951: *The Origins of European Thought*. Cambridge: Cambridge University Press.

Ortner, Sherry B. 1973: On key symbols. *American Anthropologist*, 75, 1338–46.

——1974: Is female to male as nature is to culture? In Michelle Rosaldo and Louise Lamphere (eds), *Woman, Culture and Society*. Stanford: Stanford University Press.

——1978: The virgin and the state. *Feminist Studies*, 4 (3), 19–35.

——1981: Gender and sexuality in hierarchical societies. In Ortner and Whitehead (eds), *Sexual Meanings: the cultural construction of gender and sexuality*. Cambridge: Cambridge University Press.

——1994: Theory in anthropology since the sixties [1984]. In Nicholas B. Dirks et al. (eds), *Culture/Power/History*. Princeton: Princeton University Press.

——1998: Generation X: anthropology in a media-saturated world. *Cultural Anthropology*, 13, 414–40.

Ott, Sandra 1981: *The Circle of Mountains: A Basque Shepherding Community*. Oxford: Clarendon Press.

Page, Joseph A. 1983: *Perón: a biography*. New York: Random House.

Palgi, Phillis and Abramovich, Henry 1984: Death: a cross-cultural perspective. *Annual Review of Anthropology*, 13, 385–417.

Palmer, Susan and Palmer, Samuel 1980: *The Hurdy-Gurdy*. Oxford: Alden Press.

Pantaleone, Michele 1966: *Mafia and Politics*. London: Chatto & Windus.

Parker, Alexander A. 1967: *Literature and the Delinquent: the picaresque novel in Spain and Europe, 1599–1753*. Edinburgh: University of Edinburgh Press.

Parra, M. Cecilia (ed.) 1997: *Antiquarium di Entella*. Museum Guide. Contessa Entellina.

Parry, Jonathan 1982: Sacrificial death and the necrophagous ascetic. In Maurice Bloch and Jonathan Parry (eds), *Death and the Regeneration of Life*. Cambridge: Cambridge University Press.

——1985: Taboo. In Adam Kuper and Jessica Kuper (eds), *The Social Science Encyclopaedia*. London: Routledge.

——1994: *Death in Banaras*. Cambridge: Cambridge University Press.

Passin, Herbert 1955: Untouchability in the Far East. *Monumenta Nipponica*, 11, 247–67.

Peirce, Charles Sanders 1992/8: *The Essential Peirce: selected philosophical writings*. 2 vols. Ed. Nathan Houser, Christian Kloesel and the Peirce Edition Project. Bloomington: Indiana University Press.

Pereira de Queiros, Maria Isaura 1968: *Os Cangaceiros. Les bandits d'honneur brésiliens*. Paris: Julliard.

Pérez Turrent, Tomás and De la Colina, José 1993: *Conversations avec Luis Buñuel. Il est dangereux de se pencher au-dedans*. Paris: Cahiers du Cinéma.

Peristiani, J. G. and Pitt-Rivers, Julian 1992: *Honour and Grace in Anthropology*. Cambridge: Cambridge University Press.

Peters, Edward 1990: Wounded names: the medieval doctrine of infamy. In Edward B. King and Susan J. Ridyard (eds), *Law in Mediaeval Life and Thought*. Sewanee Mediaeval Studies, 5. Sewanee, TN: The Press of the University of the South.

Peters, Emrys L. 1990: Aspects of the feud [1967]. In Peters, *The Bedouin of Cyrenaica: studies in personal and corporate power*. Ed. Jack Goody and Emanuel Marx. Cambridge: Cambridge University Press.

Phillips, George L. 1949: May-Day is sweeps' day. *Folklore*, 60, 217–27.

——1962: Chimney sweepers' signboards and symbols of the nineteenth century. *Folklore*, 73, 113–19.

——1963: Six saints of sweepdom. *Folklore*, 74, 377–85.

Phythian-Adams, Charles 1983: Milk and soot: the changing vocabulary of a popular ritual in Stuart and Hanoverian England. In Derek Fraser (ed.), *The Pursuit of Urban History*. London: Arnold.

Pigliaru, Antonio 1975: *Il banditismo in Sardenga. La vendetta barbaricina come ordinamento giuridico* [1959]. Varese: Giuffrè.

Pikaar, S. A. 1996: *Endura. Jeune ou suicide. Voedselweigering of zelfmoord?* Ph.D thesis, University of Utrecht.

Pilcher, William W. 1972: *The Portland longshoremen: a dispersed urban community*. New York: Holt, Rinehart & Winston.

Pina-Cabral, João de 1984: Nicknames and the experience of community. *Man* (N.S.), 19, 148–50.

Pinsent, John 1982: *Greek Mythology*. London: Hamlyn.

Pirenne, Henri 1936: *Economic and Social History of Medieval Europe*. Tr. I. E. Clegge. London: Routledge & Kegan Paul.

Pitkin, Donald S. 1959: Land tenure and family organization in an Italian village. *Human Organization*, 18, 169–73.

——1963: Mediterranean Europe. *Anthropological Quarterly*, 36, 120–30.

Pitrè, Giuseppe 1978a: *Proverbi siciliani* [1880]. 4 vols. Palermo: Il Vespro.

——1978b: *Proverbi, motti e scongiuri del popolo siciliano* [1910]. Palermo: Il Vespro.

——1978c: *Usi e costumi credenze e pregiudizi del popolo siciliano* [1887–8]. Vol. II. Palermo: Il Vespro.

Pitsch, Marguerite 1949: *La vie populaire à Paris au XVIIIe siècle*. 2 vols. Paris: Editions Picard.

——1952: *Essai de catalogue sur l'iconographie de la vie populaire à Paris au XVIIIe siècle*. Paris: Editions Picard.

Pitt-Rivers, J. A. 1961: *The People of the Sierra* [1954]. Chicago: University of Chicago Press.

——1965: Honour and social status. In J. G. Peristiany (ed.), *Honour and Shame: The values of Mediterranean Society*. London: Weidenfeld & Nicolson.

——1968: Honor. *Encyclopedia of the Social Sciences*, 6, 503–11. New York: Macmillan.

——1974: *Mana: an inaugural lecture*. London: London School of Economics and Political Science.

——1977: *The Fate of Shechem or the Politics of Sex*. Cambridge: Cambridge University Press.

——1983: Le sacrifice du taureau. *Le Temps de la Réflexion*, 4, 281–98.

——1987: La veuve andalouse. In G. Ravis-Giordani (ed.), *Femmes et patrimoines dans les sociétes rurales de l'Europe méditerranéenne*. Paris: Editions CNRS.

Pool, Robert 1996: *Vragen om te sterven. Euthanasie in een Nederlands ziekenhuis*. Rotterdam: WYT Uitgeefgroep.

Pourcher, Yves 1989: *La trémie et le rouet. Moulins, industrie textile et manufactures de Lozere à travers leur histoire*. Montpellier: Les Presses de Languedoc.

Price, John 1972: A history of the outcast: untouchability in Japan. In George de Vos and Hiroshi Wagatsuma (eds), *Japan's Invisible Race*. Berkeley/Los Angeles: University of California Press.

Price, Richard and Price, Sally 1972: Saramaka onomastics: an Afro-American naming system. *Ethnology*, 11, 341–67.

Propp, Vladimir 1968: *Morphology of the Folk Tale*. 2nd edn. Tr. Laurence Scott. Austin: University of Texas Press.

Prunier, Gérard 1995: *The Rwanda Crisis, 1959–1994: history of a genocide*. London: Hurst.

Radbruch, Gustav (ed.) 1960: *Die peinliche Gerichtsordnung Karls V. von 1532 (Carolina)*. Stuttgart: Reclam.

Radcliffe-Brown, A. R. 1952a: *Structure and Function in Primitive Society*. London: Cohen & West.

——1952b: Taboo. In Racliffe-Brown, *Structure and Function in Primitive Society*. London: Cohen & West.

Rafael, Vicente L. 1990: Patronage and pornography: ideology and spectatorship in the early Marcos years. *Comparative Studies in Society and History*, 32, 282–304.

Raggio, Osvaldo 1990: *Faide e parentele. Lo stato Genovese visto dalla Fontanabuona*. Torino: Einaudi (Microstorie 18).

Ramsey, M. 1988: *Professional and Popular Medicine in France, 1770–1830*. Cambridge: Cambridge University Press.

Ranum, Orest 1980: The French ritual of tyrannicide in the late sixteenth century. *Sixteenth Century Journal*, 11, 63–82.

Rao, Aparna (ed.) 1987: *The Other Nomads: peripatetic minorities in cross-cultural perspective*. Cologne/Vienna: Bohlau Verlag.

Rappaport, Roy A. 1979: The obvious aspects of ritual. In Rappaport, *Ecology, Meaning, and Religion*. Richmond, CA: North Atlantic Press.

Rasing, Willem C. 1993: The case of Kolitalik: on the encounter of Iglulingmiut culture and Canadian justice. In Cunera Buijs (ed.), *Continuity and Discontinuity in Arctic Cultures*. Leiden: Centre of Non-Western Studies, 91–107.

——1994: *Too Many People: order and nonconformity in Iglulingmiut social process*. Ph.D thesis, Nijmegen: Catholic University.

Rasmussen, K. 1908: *The People of the Polar North*. Philadelphia: Lippincot.

Ravis-Giordani, Georges 1983: *Bergers corses. Les communautés villageoises du Niolu*. Aix-en-Provence: Edisud.

Raymond, André 1985: *Grandes villes arabes à l'époque ottomane*. Paris: Sindbad.

Redfield, James M. 1975: *Nature and Culture in the Iliad: the tragedy of Hector*. Chicago: University of Chicago Press.

Redfield, Robert 1955: *The Little Community*. Chicago: University of Chicago Press.

——1960: *Peasant Society and Culture* [1956]. Chicago: University of Chicago Press.

Reketzki, Else 1952: *Das Rauchfangkehrergewerbe in Wien. Seine Entwicklung vom Ende des 16. Jahrhunderts bis ins 19. Jahrhundert, unter Berücksichtigung der übrigen österreichischen Länder*. Dissertation, Faculty of Philosophy, University of Vienna.

Richlin, Amy 1983: *The Garden of Priapus: sexuality and aggression in Roman culture*. New Haven, CT: Yale University Press.

Richter, Will 1968: *Die Landwirtschaft im Homerischen Zeitalter*. Archaeologica Homerica. Göttingen: Vandenhoeck & Ruprecht.

Robertson, J. 1992: The politics of androgyny in Japan: sexuality and subversion in the theater and beyond. *American Ethnologist*, 19, 419–42.

Robinson, Geoffrey 1995: *The Dark Side of Paradise: political violence in Bali*. Ithaca, NY: Cornell University Press.

Rochefort, Renée 1961: *Le travail en Sicile*. Paris: Presses Universitaires de France.

Rockwell, Joan 1974: The Danish peasant village. *Journal of Peasant Studies*, 1, 409–61.

Rogers, Susan Carol 1975: Female forms of power and the myth of male dominance. *American Ethnologist*, 2, 727–56.

Rohde, David 1997: *Endgame. The betrayal and fall of Srebrenica: Europe's worst massacre since World War II*. New York: Farrar, Straus & Giroux.

Romano, S. F. 1952: Sul brigantaggio e sulla mafia. In Romano, *Momenti del Risorgimento in Sicilia*. Messina/Firenze: Casa Editrice G. D'Anna.

——1966: *Storia della Mafia*. Milan: Feltrinelli.

Rooijakkers, Gerard 1994: *Rituele repertoires*. Nijmegen: SUN.

Rosaldo, Renato 1980: *Ilongot Headhunting, 1883–1974*. Stanford: Stanford University Press.

——1984: Ilongot naming: the play of associations. In Elisabeth Tooker (ed.), *Naming Systems. 1980 Proceedings of the American Ethnological Society.* Washington, DC: American Ethnological Society.

Rose, H. J. 1964: *A Handbook of Greek Mythology.* London: Routledge.

Rowen, H. H. 1978: *John de Witt, Grand Pensionary of Holland, 1625–72.* Princeton: Princeton University Press.

Ruffini, Julio L. 1978: Disputing over livestock in Sardinia. In Laura Nader and Harry F. Todd, Jr (eds), *The Disputing Process: law in ten societies.* New York: Columbia University Press.

Rupp, Jan C. C. 1992: Michel Foucault, body politics and the rise and expansion of modern anatomy. *Journal of Historical Sociology*, 5, 31–60.

Ryder, M. L. 1983: *Sheep and Man.* London: Duckworth.

Sahlins, Marshall 1974a: The original affluent society. In Sahlins, *Stone Age Economics.* London: Tavistock.

——1974b: On the sociology of primitive exchange. In Sahlins, *Stone Age Economics.* London: Tavistock.

——1976: *Culture and Practical Reason.* Chicago: University of Chicago Press.

Sakata, Hiromi Lorraine 1983: *Music in the Mind: the concepts of music and musician in Afghanistan* [1976]. Kent, OH: Kent State University Press.

Salmen, Walter 1960: *Der fahrende Musiker im europäischen Mittelalter.* Kassel: Johann Philipp Hinnenthal Verlag.

——1983: The social status of the musician in the Middle Ages. In Salmen (ed.), *The Social Status of the Professional Musician from the Middle Ages to the 19th Century.* Tr. Herbert Kaufmann and Barbara Reisner. New York: Pendragon Press.

Sankar, Andrea 1984: 'It's just old age': old age as a diagnosis in American and Chinese medicine. In David Kertzer and Jennie Keith, *Age and Anthropological Theory.* Ithaca/London: Cornell University Press.

Sansone, V. and Ingrasci, I. G. 1950: *Sei anni di banditismo in Sicilia.* Milano: Le Edizioni Sociali.

Sartono, Kartodirdjo 1966: *The Peasants' Revolt of Banten in 1888: its conditions, course, and sequel.* Ph.D thesis, University of Amsterdam.

Sartorius von Walershausen, A. 1913: *Die sizilianische Agrarverfassung und ihre Wandlungen, 1780–1912.* Leipzig: Deichert.

Schapiro, Meyer 1980: The angel with the ram in Abraham's sacrifice: a parallel in Western and Islamic art [1943]. In Schapiro, *Late Antique, Early Christian and Mediaeval Art: selected papers.* London: Chatto & Windus.

Scheible, Hartmut 1976: *Arthur Schnitzler in Selbstzeugnissen und Bilddokumenten.* Hamburg: Rowohlt.

Scheper-Hughes, Nancy 1984: Infant mortality and infant care: cultural and economic constraints on nurturing in north-eastern Brazil. *Social Science & Medicine*, 19, 535–46.

——1987a: Introduction: The cultural politics of child survival. In Scheper-Hughes (ed.): *Child Survival: anthropological perspectives on the treatment and maltreatment of children.* Dordrecht: Reidel.

——1987b: *Child Survival: anthropological perspectives on the treatment and maltreatment of children.* Dordrecht: Reidel.

—— 1992: *Death without Weeping: the violence of everyday life in Brazil*. Berkeley/Los Angeles: University of California Press.

Schild, Wolfgang 1980: *Alte Gerichtsbarkeit. Vom Gottesurteil bis zum Beginn der modernen Rechtsprechung*. Munich: Verlag Georg D. W. Callwey.

Schippers, Thomas K. 1986: *Temps vécus, temps perçus. Au fil des saisons en Provence intérieure*. Paris: CNRS.

Schneider, David M. 1968: *American Kinship: a cultural account*. Englewood Cliffs, NJ: Prentice-Hall.

—— 1977: Kinship, nationality, and religion in American culture: toward a definition of kinship. In Janet L. Dolgin et al. (eds), *Symbolic Anthropology*. New York: Columbia University Press.

—— 1984: *A Critique of the Study of Kinship*. Ann Arbor, MI: University of Michigan Press.

Schneider, Jane 1971: Of vigilance and virgins: honor, shame and access to resources in Mediterranean societies. *Ethnology*, 10 (1), 1–24.

—— and Schneider, Peter 1976: *Culture and Political Economy in Western Sicily*. New York: Academic Press.

Schoonen, Marije 1998: Voortdurend verleden. Een verkenning van het repertoire van de Portugese saudade. MA thesis, Department of Anthropology, University of Amsterdam.

Schwartz, Barry 1981: *Vertical Classification: a study in structuralism and the sociology of knowledge*. Chicago: University of Chicago Press.

Sciacchitano, G. 1982: *Requisitoria del PM Sciacchitano nel processo contro Rosario Spatola più 119*. Palermo: Public Prosecutor's Office.

Sciascia, Leonardo 1982: *La sentenza memorabile*. Palermo: Sellerio.

—— 1990: *Occhio di capra*. Torino: Adelphi.

Scott, James C. 1985: *Weapons of the Weak: everyday forms of peasant resistance*. New Haven, CT: Yale University Press.

—— 1990: *Domination and the Arts of Resistance: hidden transcripts*. New Haven, CT: Yale University Press.

Sebeok, Thomas A. and Umiker-Sebeok, Jean 1988: You know my method: a juxtaposition of Charles S. Peirce and Sherlock Holmes. In Eco and Sebeok, *The Sign of Three: Dupin, Holmes, Peirce*. Bloomington: Indiana University Press.

Seeman, Mary V. 1983: The unconscious meaning of personal names. *Names*, 31, 237–44.

Semple, Ellen Churchill 1932: *The Geography of the Mediterranean Region: its relation to ancient history*. London: Constable & Co.

Sen, Mala 1995: *India's Bandit Queen*. New York: HarperCollins.

Shaw, B. D. 1982/83: 'Eaters of flesh, drinkers of milk': The ancient Mediterranean ideology of the pastoral nomad. *Ancient Society*, 13 (14), 5–31.

Shawcross, Tim and Young, Martin, 1987: *Men of Honour: the confessions of Tommaso Buscetta*. London: Collins.

Shore, Bradd 1996: *Culture in Mind: cognition, culture, and the problem of meaning*. New York: Oxford University Press.

Siebenmorgen, Harald and Brümmer, Johannes (eds) 1995: *Schurke oder Held? Historische Räuber und Räuberbanden*. Sigmaringen: Jan Thorbecke Verlag.

Siebert, Renate 1997: *Le donne, la mafia*. 2nd edn. Milano: EST.

Silverman, Sydel 1968: Agricultural organization, social structure, and values in Italy: amoral familism reconsidered. *American Anthropologist*, 70, 1–20.

——1975: *Three Bells of Civilization: the life of an Italian hill town*. New York: Columbia University Press.

Simmel, Georg 1950a: The secret society [1908]. In *The Sociology of Georg Simmel*. Tr. Kurt H. Wolff. Glencoe, IL: The Free Press.

——1950b: The stranger. In *The Sociology of Georg Simmel*. Tr. Kurt H. Wolff. Glencoe, IL: The Free Press.

——1983: Das Geheimnis und die geheime Gesellschaft. In Simmel, *Soziologie. Untersuchungen über die Formen der Vergesellschaftung. Gesammelte Werke* [1908]. Berlin: Duncker & Humblot.

Simmons, Leo W. 1970: *The Role of the Aged in Primitive Society* [1945]. New Haven CT: Archon Books.

——1960: Aging in pre-industrial societies. In C. Tibbits (ed.), *Handbook of Social Gerontology*. Chicago: University of Chicago Press.

Singal, Daniel J. 1997: *William Faulkner: the making of a modernist*. Chapel Hill: University of North Carolina Press.

Sittl, Carl 1890: *Die Gebärden der Griecher und Römer*. Leipzig: Tenbner.

Sjoberg, Gideon 1960: *The Preindustrial City: past and present*. Glencoe, IL: The Free Press.

Skipper, James K. 1986: Nicknames, coal miners and group solidarity. *Names*, 34, 134–45.

Slatta, Richard W. 1987: Conclusion: banditry in Latin America. In Slatta (ed.) *Bandidos: the varieties of Latin American banditry*. New York: Greenwood Press.

——1991: Bandits and rural social history: a comment on Joseph. *Latin American Research Review*, 26 (1), 145–51.

——(ed.) 1987: *Bandidos: the varieties of Latin American banditry*. New York: Greenwood.

Sleinada, S. J. P. 1972: *Oorsprong, oorzaeke, bewys en ondekkinge van een godlooze bezwoorne bende nachtdieven en knevelaers binnen de Landen van Overmaeze en aenpaelende landtstreeken ontdekt, etc.* [1779]. Repr. Maastricht: Schrijan.

Snell, Bruno 1975: *Die Entdeckung des Geistes. Studien zur Entstehung des europäischen Denkens bei den Griechen*. Göttingen: Vandenhoeck & Ruprecht.

Sorre, Max 1952: *Les fondemants de la géographie humaine. L'Habitat*. Vol. III. Paris: Armand Colin.

Spierenburg, Pieter 1984: *The Spectacle of Suffering. Executions and the evolution of repression: from a preindustrial metropolis to the European experience*. Cambridge: Cambridge University Press.

Spiesberger, Else 1974: *Die 'Schwarze Zunft' im Wandel der Zeiten. Die Geschichte des Rauchfangkehrergewerbe in Niederösterreich*. Vienna: Handelskammer Niederösterreich. (Based on the author's dissertation; see under Reketzki.)

Spruit, J. E. 1966: *De juridische en social positie van Romeinse acteurs*. Assen: Van Gorcum.

——1969: *Van vedelaars, trommers en pijpers*. Utrecht: A. Oosthoek's Uitgeversmaatschappij.

Stajano, Corrado (ed.) 1986: *Mafia. L'atto d'accusa dei giudici dei Palermo*. Rome: Editori Riuniti.

Steinberg, David 1986: Tradition and response. In John Bresnan (ed.), *Crisis in the Philippines: the Marcos era and beyond*. Princeton: Princeton University Press, 30–55.

Steinmetz, S. R. 1931: Selbsthilfe. In Alfred Vierkandt (ed.), *Handwörterbuch der Soziologie*. Stuttgart: Ferdinand Enke Verlag.

Sterling, Claire 1990: *Octopus: the long reach of the international Sicilian Mafia*. New York: Simon & Schuster.

Stewart, Frank Henderson 1994: *Honor*. Chicago: University of Chicago Press.

Stille, Alexander 1995: *Excellent Cadavers: the Mafia and the death of the First Italian Republic*. London: Jonathan Cape.

Stoett, F. A. 1935: Schoorsteenveger zonder leer. *De Nieuwe Taalgids*, 29, 119–21.

Stokvis, Ruud 1991: Voetbalvandalisme in Nederland. In Herman Franke et al. (eds), *Alledaags en ongewoon geweld*. Groningen: Wolters/Noordhoff.

Stützer, Herbert Alexander 1989: *Ravenna und seine Mosaiken*. Cologne: DuMont Buchverlag.

Sudetic, Chuck 1998: *Blood and Vengeance: one family's story of the war in Bosnia*. New York/London: W. W. Norton.

Sulloway, Frank J. 1996: *Born to Rebel: birth order, family dynamics, and creative lives*. New York: Vintage Books.

Tacitus 1970: *The Agricola and the Germania*. Tr. H. Mattingly and S. A. Handford. Harmondsworth: Penguin Books.

Tak, Herman 1988: Changing campanilismo: localism and the use of nicknames in a Tuscan mountain village. *Ethnologia Europaea*, 18, 149–60.

Tambiah, S. J. 1985a: Animals are good to think and good to prohibit [1969]. In Tambiah, *Culture, Thought, and Social Action: an anthropological perspective*. Cambridge, MA: Harvard University Press.

——1985b: Form and meaning of magical acts. In Tambiah, *Culture, Thought, and Social Action: an anthropological perspective*. Cambridge, MA: Harvard University Press.

——1990: *Magic, Science, Religion, and the Scope of Rationality*. Cambridge: Cambridge University Press.

——1991: *Sri Lanka: ethnic fratricide and the dismantling of democracy*. Chicago: University of Chicago Press.

Taylor, Julie M. 1979: *Eva Perón: the myths of a woman*. Chicago: University of Chicago Press.

Terrill, Ross 1984: *The White-Boned Demon: a biography of Madam Mao Zedong*. New York: Bantam Books.

The, Anne-Mei 1997: '*Vanavond om 8 uur . . .*'. *Verpleegkundige dilemma's bij euthanasie en andere beslissingen rond het levenseinde*. Houten/Diegem: Bohn Stafleu Van Loghum.

Thoden van Velzen, H. U. E. and Van Wetering, W. 1960: Residence, power and intrasocietal aggression. *International Archives of Ethnography*, 49, 169–200.

Thomas, Keith 1983: *Man and the Natural World: a history of the modern sensibility*. New York: Pantheon Books.

Thomas, Nicholas 1991: Against ethnography. *Cultural Anthropology*, 6, 306–22.

Thompson, E. P. 1974: Patrician society, plebeian culture. *Journal of Social History*, 7, 382–405.

—— 1972: 'Rough music': le charivari anglais. *Annales – Economies, Sociétés, Civilisations*, 27, 285–312.

—— 1978: Folklore, anthropology, and social history. *Indian Historical Review*, 3, 247–66.

—— 1981: 'Rough music' et charivari. Quelques réflexions complementaires. In Jacques Le Goff and Jean-Claude Schmitt (eds), *Le charivari*. Paris/La Haye: Mouton.

Thurlings, Th. J. M. and van Drunen, A. A. P. 1960: *Sociaal-economische geschiedenis. Limburgs Verleden*. Part 1.

Tilly, Charles 1978: Anthropology, history, and the *Annales*. *Review*, 1 (3/4), 207–13.

—— 1990: *Coercion, Capital and European States*, AD *900–1990*. Cambridge: Cambridge University Press.

Tolstoy, Leo 1960: *The Death of Ivan Ilyich and Other Stories*. Tr. Rosemary Edmonds. Harmondsworth: Penguin Books.

Tonkinson, Robert 1978: *The Maradudjara Aborigines: living the dream in Australia's desert*. New York: Holt, Rinehart & Winston.

Tooker, Elisabeth (ed.) 1984: *Naming Systems*. Washington, DC: American Ethnological Society.

Troyat, Henri 1981: *Catherine the Great*. Tr. Joan Pinkman. New York: Berkeley Books.

Turner, Victor 1967: *The Forest of Symbols*. Ithaca: Cornell University Press.

—— 1969: *The Ritual Process*. Ithaca: Cornell University Press.

—— 1974: *Dramas, Fields, and Metaphors*. Ithaca: Cornell University Press.

Uglow, Jennifer (ed.) 1989: *The Continuum Dictionary of Women's Biography*. New York: Continuum.

Unger, Leonard 1953: Rural settlements in the Campania. *The Geographical Review*, 43, 506–25.

Valeri, Valerio 1985: *Kinship and Sacrifice: ritual and society in ancient Hawaii*. Tr. Paula Wissing. Chicago: University of Chicago Press.

Van Beek, Walter 1992: The dirty smith: smell as a social frontier among the Kapsiki/Higi of north Cameroon and north-eastern Nigeria. *Africa*, 62, 38–58.

Van Cleef, Alfred 1996: De koninklijke weg. Portret van de Nederlandse vereniging voor vrijwillige euthanasie. *NRC Handelsblad*, Z, 27 July 1996.

Van de Brink, Gabriël 1991: Van gevecht tot gerecht. In Herman Franke et al. (eds), *Alledaags en ongewoon geweld*. Groningen: Wolters/Noordhoff.

Van den Muyzenberg, Otto D. 1971: Politieke mobilisering en geweld in Centraal Luzon (Philippijnen). *Sociologische Gids*, 18 (2), 148–60.

Van der Borg, Els 1992: *Vroedvrouwen: beeld en beroep. Ontwikkelingen in het vroedvrouwschap in Leiden, Arnhem, 's-Hertogenbosch en Leeuwarden, 1650–1865*. Wageningen: Academic Press.

Van der Geest, Sjaak 1996: Ouderen en welzijn. *Medische Antropologie*, 8, 185–96.

Van der Wal, G. and Van der Maas, P. J. 1996: *Euthanasie en andere medische beslissingen rond het levenseinde. De praktijk en de meldingsprocedure*. The Hague: Sdu Uitgevers.

Van Gennep, Arnold 1960: *The Rites of Passage* [1909]. Tr. M. B. Vizedom and G. L. Caffee. Chicago: University of Chicago Press.

Van Heek, F. 1975: *Actieve euthanasie als sociologisch probleem*. Meppel: Boom.

Van Hooff, Anton J. L. 1990: *From Autothanasia to Suicide: self-killing in classical antiquity*. London: Routledge.

Van Nieuwkerk, Karin 1995: *'A trade like any other': female singers and dancers in Egypt*. Austin: University of Texas Press.

Van Os, G. 1997: *De vrouwen van de doden. Betekenis en beleving van het weduwschap in Extremadura*. Ph.D thesis, University of Amsterdam.

Venbrux, Eric 1995: *A Death in the Tiwi Islands: conflict, ritual, and social life in an Australian aboriginal community*. Cambridge: Cambridge University Press.

Verdier, Y. 1979: *Façons de dire, façons de faire. La laveuse, la couturière, la cuisinière*. Paris: Gallimard.

Verga, G. 1983: *The House by the Medlar Tree [I Malavoglia]*. Tr. R. Rosenthal. Berkeley: University of California Press.

Vialles, Noëlie 1994: *Animal to Edible*. Tr. J. A. Underwood. Cambridge: Cambridge University Press.

Vidal. Claudine 1996: Le génocide des Rwandais tutsi. Cruauté délibérée et logiques de haine. In Françoise Héritier (ed.), *De la violence*. Paris: Editions Odile Jacob.

Vigarello, Georges 1988: *Concepts of Cleanliness: changing attitudes in France since the Middle Ages*. Tr. Jean Birrell. Cambridge: Cambridge University Press.

Vincent, Bernard (ed.) 1979: Les marginaux et les exclus dans l'histoire. *Cahiers Jussieu*, 5, 1–439. [Paris: Union Générale d'Editions.]

Vöchting, Friedrich 1951: *Die italienische Südfrage. Entstehung und Problematik eines wirtschaftlichen Notstandsgebietes*. Berlin: Duncker & Humblot.

Voltaire 1961: Zadig or destiny: an oriental tale [1747]. In Voltaire, *Candide, Zadig, and Selected Stories*. Tr. D. M. Frame. New York: New American Library, 102–72.

Von Amira, Karl 1922: Die germanische Todesstrafen. *Abhandlungen der Bayerischen Akademie der Wissenschaften, philosophisch-historische Klasse*, 31, 1–415.

Von Dülmen, Richard 1984: Das Schauspiel des Todes. In von Dülmen and Schindler (eds), *Volkskultur. Zur Wiederentdeckung des vergessenen Alltags (16.–20. Jahrhundert)*. Frankfurt am Main: Suhrkamp Verlag.

Von Hentig, Hans 1958: *Vom Ursprung der Henkersmahlzeit*. Tübingen: J. C. B. Mohr.

Walcot, Peter 1978: *Envy and the Greeks*. Warminster: Aris & Phillips.

Walker, Mack 1971: *German Home Towns: community, state and general estate, 1648–1871*. Ithaca/London: Cornell University Press.

Wallerstein, Immanuel 1974: *The Modern World-System*. New York: Academic Press.

Walter, Eugene Victor 1969: *Terror and Resistance: a study of political violence with case studies of some primitive African communities*. New York: Oxford University Press.

Warner, Marina 1972: *The Dragon Empress: the life and times of Tz'u-Hsi [Ci Xi], Empress Dowager of China 1835–1908*. New York: Macmillan Press.

——1983: *Joan of Arc: the image of female heroism*. Harmondsworth: Penguin Books.

Warner, W. Lloyd 1958: *A Black Civilization: a social study of an Australian tribe* [1937]. New York: Harper & Row.

Watson, R. S. 1986: The named and the nameless: gender and person in Chinese society. *American Ethnologist*, 13, 619–31.

Watson, William 1958: *Tribal Cohesion in a Money Economy: a study of the Mambwe people of Northern Rhodesia*. Manchester: Manchester University Press.

Weber, Eugen 1977: *Peasants into Frenchmen: the modernization of rural France, 1870–1914*. Stanford: Stanford University Press.

Weber, Max 1958a: The social psychology of the world religions. In H. H. Gerth and C. Wright Mills (eds), *From Max Weber: essays in sociology*. New York: Oxford University Press.

——1958b: *The Protestant Ethic and the Spirit of Capitalism* [1904]. Tr. Talcott Parsons. New York: Scribner.

——1962: *The City*. New York: Collier Books.

Weiss, Richard 1946: *Volkskunde der Schweiz. Grundriss*. Erlenbach–Zurich: Eugen Rentsch Verlag.

Wellman, Kathleen 1992: *La Mettrie. Medicine, philosophy, and Enlightenment*. Durham/London: Duke University Press.

Wertheim, W. F. 1964: Society as a composite of conflicting value systems. In Wertheim, *East–West Parallels: sociological approaches to modern Asia*. The Hague: Van Hoeve.

West, Richard 1994: *Tito and the Rise and Fall of Yugoslavia*. London: Sinclair-Stevenson.

Westermarck, Edward 1926: *Ritual and Belief in Morocco*. 2 vols. London: Macmillan.

Weulersse, Jacques 1946: *Paysans de Syrie et du Proche-Orient*. Paris: Gallimard.

Wheelwright, Julie 1989: *Amazons and Military Maids: women who dressed as men in the pursuit of life, liberty, and happiness*. London: Pandora.

Whittaker, C. R. (ed.) 1988: *Pastoral Economies in Classical Antiquity*. Cambridge: Cambridge University Press.

Wichers, A. J. 1965: *De oude plattelandsbeschaving. Een sociologische bewustwording van de 'overherigheid'*. Assen: Van Gorcum.

Wiedemann, Thomas 1992: *Emperors and Gladiators*. London/New York: Routledge.

Wilbertz, Gisela 1979: *Scharfrichter und Abdecker im Hochstift Osnabrück. Untersuchungen zur Sozialgeschichte zweier 'unehrlicher' Berufe im nordwestdeutschen Raum vom 16. bis zum 19. Jahrhundert*. Osnabrück: Kommissionsverlag H. Th. Wenner.

Willems, Emilio 1970: Peasants and city: cultural persistence and change in historical perspective, a European case. *American Anthropologist*, 72, 528–44.

Wilson, Bryan 1975: *The Noble Savages: the primitive origin of charisma and its contemporary survival*. Berkeley/Los Angeles: University of California Press.

Wilson, Stephen 1988: *Feuding, Conflict and Banditry in Nineteenth-Century Corsica*. Cambridge: Cambridge University Press.

Wissell, Rudolf 1971: *Des alten Handwerks Recht und Gewohnheit*. Vol. I. Berlin: Colloquium Verlag.

Witke, Roxane 1977: *Comrade Chiang Ch'ing* [Jiang Qing]. Boston: Little, Brown and Company.

Wittgenstein, Ludwig 1967: *Philosophical Investigations*. Oxford: Blackwell.

Woeikof, A. 1909: Le groupement de la population rurale en Russie. *Annales de Géographie*, 18, 13–24.

Wolf, D. R. 1991: *The Rebels: a brotherhood of outlaw bikers*. Toronto: University of Toronto Press.

Wolf, Eric R. 1964: *Anthropology*. Englewood Cliffs, NJ: Prentice-Hall.

—— 1966a: Kinship, friendship, and patron–client relationships in complex societies. In Michael Banton (ed.), *The Social Anthropology of Complex Societies*. London: Tavistock.

—— 1966b: *Peasants*. Englewood Cliffs, NJ: Prentice-Hall.

—— 1969: *Peasant Wars of the Twentieth Century*. New York: Harper & Row.

Worsley, Peter 1967: Groote Eylandt totemism and *Le Totémisme aujourd'hui*. In Edmund Leach (ed.), *The Structural Study of Myth and Totemism*. London: Tavistock.

Wouters, H. H. E. 1970: *Grensland en bruggehoofd. Historische studies met betrekking tot het Limburgse Maasdal en, meer in het bijzonder, de stad Maastricht*. Assen: Van Gorcum.

Yalman, Nur 1969: De Tocqueville in India: an essay on the caste system. *Man* (N.S.), 4, 123–31.

Yang, Lien-Sheng 1960: Female rulers in Imperial China. *Harvard Journal of East Asian Studies*, 23, 47–61.

Zetterberg, Hans 1965: *On Theory and Verification in Sociology*. 3rd enlarged edn. Totowa, NJ: Bedminster Press.

Zeuner, Frederick E. 1963: *A History of Domesticated Animals*. London: Hutchinson.

Zimdars-Swartz, Sandra L. 1992: *Encountering Mary: from La Salette to Medjugorje*. Princeton: Princeton University Press.

Zingarelli, Nicola 1965: *Vocabolaria della lingua italiano*. Bologna: Zanichelli.

Zizek, Slavoj 1989: *The Sublime Object of Ideology*. London: Verso.

Zonabend, Françoise 1977: Pourquoi nommer? In Claude Lévi-Strauss (ed.), *L'Identité*. Paris: Grasset, 257–79.

——1980: Le nom de personne. *L'Homme*, 20 (4), 7–23.

Zulaika, Joseba 1988: *Basque Violence: metaphor and sacrament*. Reno/Las Vegas: University of Nevada Press.

Index